Pro Drupal 7 for Windows Develo"plers

Brian Travis

Apress®

Pro Drupal 7 for Windows Developers

ISBN-13 (pbk): 978-1-4302-3153-0

ISBN-13 (electronic): 978-1-4302-3154-7

Printed and bound in the United States of America (POD)

President and Publisher: Paul Manning
Lead Editors: Frank Pohlmann and Michelle Lowman
Technical Reviewer: Seth Cohn
Editorial Board: Steve Anglin, Mark Beckner, Ewan Buckingham, Gary Cornell, Jonathan Gennick, Jonathan Hassell, Michelle Lowman, Matthew Moodie, Jeff Olson, Jeffrey Pepper, Frank Pohlmann, Douglas Pundick, Ben Renow-Clarke, Dominic Shakeshaft, Matt Wade, Tom Welsh
Coordinating Editor: Mary Tobin
Copy Editor: Sharon Terdeman
Compositor: MacPS, LLC
Indexer: BIM Indexing & Proofreading Services
Artist: April Milne
Cover Designer: Anna Ishchenko

Distributed to the book trade worldwide by Springer Science+Business Media, LLC., 233 Spring Street, 6th Floor, New York, NY 10013. Phone 1-800-SPRINGER, fax 201-348-4505, e-mail orders-ny@springer-sbm.com, or visit www.springeronline.com.

For information on translations, please e-mail rights@apress.com, or visit www.apress.com.

Apress and friends of ED books may be purchased in bulk for academic, corporate, or promotional use. eBook versions and licenses are also available for most titles. For more information, reference our Special Bulk Sales–eBook Licensing web page at www.apress.com/info/bulksales.

The source code for this book is available to readers at www.apress.com. You will need to answer questions pertaining to this book in order to successfully download the code.

For Cynthia and Malena. And pie.

Contents at a Glance

Contents

About the Author

 **Brian Travis** has been disassembling technology since shortly after birth. Before computers came along, he was content to focus his attention on household appliances. An advocate of the "learn by making mistakes" school, Brian has never been afraid of doing exactly that. As a member of the original SGML committee and involved in the creation of various XML-based standards, he is an expert in information interchange. In addition to working as a consultant to large enterprises, Brian has shared his experience as an author, lecturer, and teacher to audiences all over the world. He lives in beautiful New Hampshire.

About the Technical Reviewer

 **Seth Cohn** has been an "alpha geek" all his life. He has been using computers for over 25 years, and has been involved with various Open Source causes for most of that time. He has been building sites with Drupal for over six years, and founded the New Hampshire Drupal User Group. Seth has spoken on a number of Drupal-related topics across the country, and loves that moment when someone comes back to him proclaiming, "I took that tidbit idea you spoke about and wrote more code using it." He is known as "the wiki" among his friends, for the breadth and depth of his knowledge. Seth works as a partner in a web development company, GnuHampshire, as well as serving as a State Representative in the New Hampshire House, where he is attempting to bring the principles of Open Source to government. He lives in the wilds of New Hampshire on a dirt road with wild turkeys and deer, minutes away from the State House.

Acknowledgments

This book could not have happened without the support and encouragement of Seth Cohn. When I was bitching about the lack of helpful content for the Windows user new to Drupal, Seth said, "You've written books before. Why don't you write a Drupal book for the Windows user?" Write a book that I need to read? That was such a ridiculous idea that I had to try it.

Seth was just a phone call or e-mail away from any questions I had (which were legion), even though he was building top-notch Drupal sites for his day job and running for the New Hampshire State House of Representatives at the same time. By the way, he won his race and promptly introduced bills to bring more open source usage and values (i.e., transparency and accessibility) to state government.

Seth has been involved in Drupal for quite a while and understands a lot more than just the technical aspects of the system. He follows the development community discussions and often knows the details about why any particular feature came about. That was very helpful for me to understand the plexus of Drupal. Without Seth, this book would just be some guy writing his observations about code. Seth helped me give it depth and direction.

Jake Strawn helped me understand the relationship between the theming layer and the business logic of Drupal modules. Jake is one of those rare types who is as talented in the design half of the web as he is in the back-end programming side.

Jake wrote the Omega theme and has been tireless in pitching its features and benefits to the community. Jake is committed to getting his theme into the Drupal 8 core and I believe he can pull it off. He has created a lot of innovations that will pull Drupal forward in the larger market of web-based content management systems.

Seth and Jake are both members of the New Hampshire Drupal Users' Group, which meets once a month in Manchester. At least three of the members of our group are writing books on various aspects of Drupal. This is a testament to the great sharing of ideas in that group.

Preface

This is the book I needed when I was learning Drupal. There are a lot of great books out there on Drupal, but none was written for someone with my perspective.

You see, I'm a Windows guy. I cut my teeth on DOS 1.0 in 1982. Edlin and batch files were my friends. I remember the happy day when I got my copy of DOS 2.0. Hierarchical directories! From there it was boxy windows and then overlapping windows, and then, before you knew it, Visual Studio and C#. Along the way, I've programmed in pretty much every OS out there, from CP/M on an 8-bit S-100 machine to VMS on a VAX, to z/OS on an IBM mainframe, not to mention pretty much every flavor of *nix that came along. But I keep coming back to Windows.

I've spent most of my career programming in the realm of the infrastructure, working a certain magic by getting machines to talk to each other in an enterprise setting. I've written books on SGML, XML, BizTalk, and web services, all of which are very comfortable with their roles as the invisible glue that holds an enterprise together. I've felt the pain of a web developer trying to expose enterprise information to customers only to be thwarted by IT security goons.

I've also written plenty of web sites the hard way, by hand or with some help from programming tools. So, when I was looking for a toolkit for a site that I didn't want to spend time hand-coding, some friends mentioned Drupal.

Drupal is most comfortable running under the LAMP stack, with Linux as the operating system, Apache as the web server, MySQL as the database, and PHP as the programming language. As a guy familiar with enterprises, I prefer Windows Server as the operating system, IIS as the web server, SQL Server as the database, and C# as the programming language. Still, PHP looked like it could be worth learning.

So I checked out Drupal. I looked at the features, went to some users' group meetings, and talked to people about programming the Drupal way. It, too, looked like something worth learning.

I spent some time investigating a development environment. People were using Eclipse and NetBeans. So I tried both and, frankly, just couldn't get into it. Eclipse seemed like a tool with so much power you had to have a BSEE degree (Bachelor of Science, Eclipse Engineering) to make it work. NetBeans was a bit easier, but, when I ran into a problem, I just didn't have the chops to fix it and really didn't feel like spending the time to track it down.

Part of the problem was the OS. I picked Ubuntu, running as a VM on my Windows 7 laptop. The performance was fine but my Linux shell skills were rusty—I kept using the backslash as a directory separator. And why should I have to create an alias just to do a "dir"?

So I tried the Eclipse version compiled for Windows and threw it out right away—just too many options and add-ins to learn. Add to that the evangelistic zealots manning the forums and it all became just too much to bear.

I was about to quit my Drupal quest when I stumbled on VS.Php, an add-in for Visual Studio. Finally, I found a way to learn PHP and Drupal without leaving my beloved Visual Studio! And then, at about the same time, a group announced it was partnering with Microsoft to create a Drupal environment that ran on IIS and used SQL Server as the database, using a new database-agnostic data access layer. My quest was back in gear, and it didn't take long until I was stepping through PHP code on my Windows 7 box running Visual Studio.

VS.Php, with its integration with Visual Studio, meant I could still use the familiar F5/F10/F11 step-debugging trifecta and have a site that could be deployed on the Windows/IIS/SQL/PHP (WISP) stack or any LAMP stack. Time to learn this stuff and write a book!

So here it is. At the same time I was learning the whole environment, the newest version, Drupal 7, was in the final stages of development but still full of bugs. I decided to write for that version instead of the more mature and entrenched version 6. It was painful to learn a new language and a new framework while that framework was in flux, but it really forced me to understand what was happening since all of the gears were in motion at the same time.

As I write this introduction, Drupal version 7 was just released, and it is looking pretty darn stable. So if you see any differences between the code in the book and the bits that you download from the Drupal community site, it's because of the evolving nature of community-supported software.

I created `http://drupalforwindows.com` as a place to store the sample code in this book so you don't have to key in everything from scratch. The site is running on WordPress.

Just kidding.

■ ■ ■

## PART I

Drupal Basics

■ ■ ■

Wherefore Drupal?

Drupal started as a content management system, and that's what its core is all about. Since its inception in 2001, the Drupal environment has attracted thousands of users and developers who have improved all aspects of the environment.

There are many industrial-strength Drupal installations built on shared and custom code. This chapter discusses the Drupal core and modules that are commonly used.

If you are reading this book, you probably have some experience with Windows programming and perhaps are familiar with content management systems that run in a Windows environment. I'll mention a couple of these in this chapter and take you though the path that led me to Drupal. Perhaps you've had a similar journey.

Version 7 of Drupal marks an important direction for the framework. It is probably the most significant major release because it propels Drupal into the enterprise by abstracting the database layer and providing richer role-based administrative functionality. The user interface has also been streamlined to keep up with the other products in the marketplace.

What is a CMS?

We've had content management systems for decades. If you have information, you probably have some kind of system to manage it. At one time, systems that manage textual information were called "document management systems." At one end of the complexity scale are file-directory-document-naming systems. How many times have you seen a directory with document names like "Chapter1.doc", "Chapter1–v2.doc", and "Chapter1–v2-reviewcopy.doc"?

While such systems can work in a small office with limited participants, they get unwieldy when more authors or reviewers are involved.

Moreover, documents increasingly began to have rich content added to them, which gave rise to a new issue—how to manage this rich content apart from the words of the document. That's when vendors began calling these systems "content management systems."

At the complex end of the market are systems designed to store rich content types and allow authors to collaborate on content across the enterprise, with the final intent of publishing the content externally or using it internally to run the enterprise. These systems make use of technologies such as SGML, XML, scanning, and OCR, as well as translation bridges to move data between different electronic formats.

These content management systems are widely used in large enterprises. Microsoft is putting a lot of effort into establishing its SharePoint Server as the content management tool to use in large enterprises.

In the realm of the World Wide Web, however, content management has entered a new era with new challenges. The person in an enterprise who likes to dictate content guidelines and formatting tools will be very frustrated with the relative anarchy of the Web. In this environment, tools that help manage the chaos will be the winners. That's where the new generation of content management systems comes in.

Content Management on the Web

I like to think of the new generation of content management systems as third-generation web-site building tools.

First, there was HTML. In the beginning of the World Wide Web, programmers created most sites by hand-coding files using HTML markup. But it didn't take long for the people who built these pages to tire of the verbose markup that HTML requires. Plus, those static pages were…static. For information that changes often, or sites that have lots of similar information, such as catalogs or personnel information, creating a static page for each item is exceedingly tedious.

The second generation of web-site building involved attaching a custom database. This type of site used a server-side scripting language, such as Microsoft's Active Server Pages (ASP), that allowed developers to programmatically connect to a database or other resources and build a page on the fly. Sites using this type of technology were flexible and could be built in a robust way depending on the skill of the programmer.

The downside to such an approach is that this type of technology creates "one-off" solutions. That is, a programmer would create a site according to some requirements, and then move to the next project and build a site from scratch using new requirements. If he was lucky, the programmer could reuse some components from previous sites.

I've built plenty of sites using both of these approaches. They're great if you're being paid by the hour, but not so good if you need to create sites cheaply or if you have a backlog of sites to build with limited budget resources.

Many programmers started to see the problems with these approaches, engendering a rash of projects where programmers would take the code they developed for a particular site and make it available to some community of programmers, who would, hopefully, take it from there, fix the problems, and extend it. This would propel the original designer into the programmer equivalent of "rock star" and it would be easy street from that point on.

That gets us to what I consider the third generation of web site development: community-supported content management systems. These are development frameworks that usually start as someone's personal project, and then are expanded into something more stable as others work with it.

In the .NET world, the most popular such system is DotNetNuke (see Figure 1–1), which has evolved into a framework for building content-rich sites in a Microsoft .NET environment.

Figure 1–1. DotNetNuke is a community-supported content management system based on ASP.NET.

There are other content management systems for Windows. The grandfather is Microsoft's SharePoint, which is mainly used by large enterprises to manage content behind their firewall. It has great support for integrating with other back-end systems such as SQL Server and BizTalk, but it is very expensive. And, while it has an extensive API, it is not very friendly for programmers building customer-facing web sites.

Another content management framework that intrigued me is Sitefinity (see Figure 1–2), which, unlike tools written by volunteers and available for free, is a commercial product and comes with a price tag and support. Sitefinity was written by Telerik, a Bulgarian-based company that makes a great toolkit for .NET programming. I'm a fan of Telerik's toolkits as they have saved me a lot of programming time over the years. But Sitefinity's $900/year license fee and relatively closed environment were a problem. Moreover, the fact that they've been promising version 4 for more than a year lowered my trust of this framework.

Figure 1–2. Sitefinity is a commercial content management system for the .NET platform.

Some friends had been using Drupal and liked it a lot. They talked about how easy the platform was for creating sites and yet how it was also programmer-friendly, allowing customization to any level of granularity. They also pointed out the size and quality of the community and the sheer number of add-on packages available. This sounded exactly like what I was looking for, so I embarked on a research mission.

Open Source Content Management Tools

In the open source content management space, three systems seem to come up in research: WordPress, Joomla, and Drupal (see Figure 1–3). WordPress seems to have the largest market share because it is easy to configure and get a site up and running quickly. But it is designed mainly for end-users, who generally use it to write and maintain blogs; the programmability is just not there at this point. Joomla looks slick out of the box and can be customized to some extent, but doesn't seem to have been designed as a foundation for large-scale customization and integration. Also, it doesn't have the sizeable community that Drupal has, particularly in my geographical area. Your results may vary.

Figure 1–3. WordPress, Joomla, and Drupal compete for various types of content management solutions.

But my main problem with all of these systems is that they don't use the .NET Framework. And, with Drupal in particular, that it's written in a language I've never used, PHP. Instead of .NET, Drupal runs on a LAMP stack. Still, it seems to have all of the functionality you'd expect from a third-generation web-site building environment and a large, active support community. Perhaps I could look to this community for support as I learned these new technologies.

The LAMP Stack

Drupal, like many open source web tools, runs under a set of tools known as the "LAMP Stack" (see Figure 1–4). LAMP stands for Linux/Apache/MySQL/PHP. The server is where the stack is, and a browser accesses the site through a call to the web server, Apache. Let's look at the individual pieces.

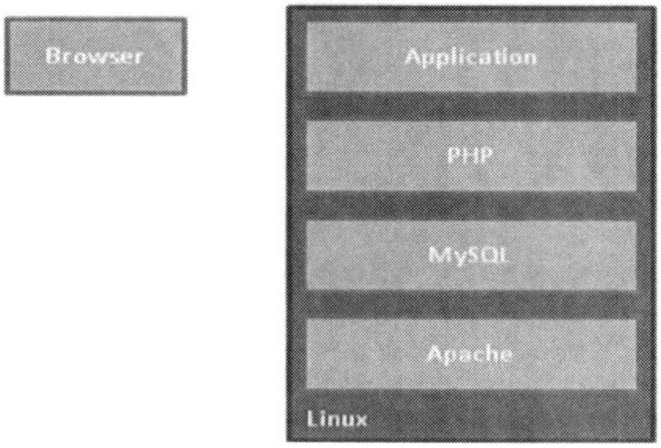

Figure 1–4. Drupal is built on the LAMP stack.

Linux: The operating system on which all of this goodness runs. Depending on where you're running the stack, this could be a server-oriented flavor of Linux for production sites, or a development-oriented flavor of Linux with a GUI for development work.

Apache: The web server that runs on the operating system and fields calls from web browsers in order to build pages and send them back. Apache invokes various engines to build parts of the page as required by the request. This is the functional equivalent of Internet Information Services (IIS) in the Windows environment.

MySQL: A SQL database that stores all data and configuration information for the web site. MySQL started as a basic open source SQL database and has evolved into an industrial strength platform for relational data storage. I don't think it is as evolved as Microsoft SQL Server or Oracle, but you can't beat the price. Oracle recently acquired MySQL when it bought Sun Microsystems, so there is some concern in the open source community about the fate of MySQL.

PHP: A language for creating web pages. Actually, PHP is a general-purpose language for doing almost any kind of programming, but it is used mainly to build web pages. It is similar in functionality to Active Server Pages in the Microsoft world. Unlike Visual Basic or C#, PHP is interpreted as the page is being created, and so suffers from performance issues. I'll talk more about that, and how to get around such problems later in the book.

All of these pieces are free and community supported. They are open source and are quite robust and secure. All are almost infinitely configurable, which is good, though it can also make tuning seem daunting. Fortunately, you'll find a lot of people who have been there and done that to help with any aspect of configuration.

Since this book is for Windows developers, the first thing we are going to do is to replace the "L" in LAMP with "W" for Windows. It is possible to replace the "A" with "I" for Microsoft's Internet Information Server, but I refuse to work on a system called "WIMP."

So we'll stick with Apache for now. In Appendix A, I'll show you how you can install Drupal to run on IIS and use Microsoft SQL Server as the database. At that point, I guess you'd have a WISP stack.

The Drupal Core

Drupal is centered on a set of functions that handle basic bootstrapping, database access, error reporting, and other essential services. These programs are called *modules* and form the system known as the *Drupal core*.

Core modules provide a significant amount of functionality out of the box:

- **IP Address Blocking:** Access to the site can be managed by restricting IP addresses (see Figure 1–5).

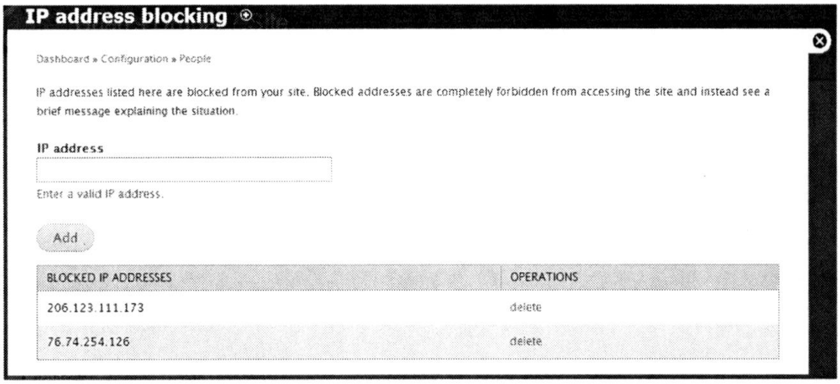

Figure 1–5. Rule-based security provides access control.

- **Access statistics and logging:** You get information about page accesses so you can determine the popular areas of your site. Logging reports various levels of activity, including unauthorized access attempts and database errors (see Figure 1–6).

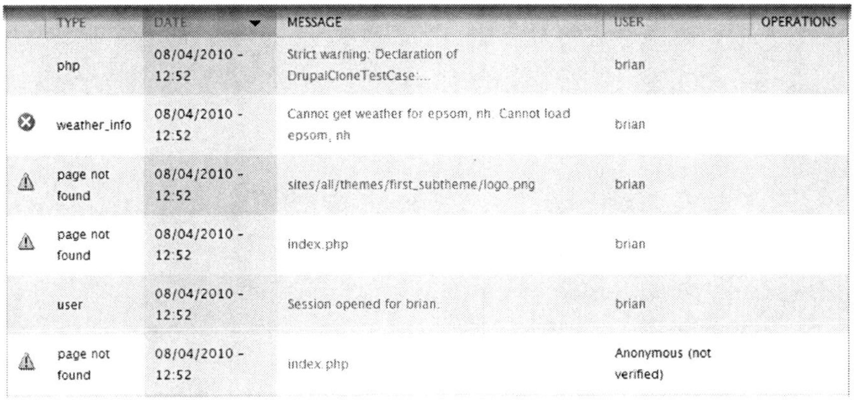

Figure 1–6. Rich logging support informs administrators of potential problems.

- **Node Access:** Any content can be restricted by various parameters, such as the type of user.

- **Site Status Report:** You get a single overview of any problems detected for your installation, as Figure 1–7 shows.

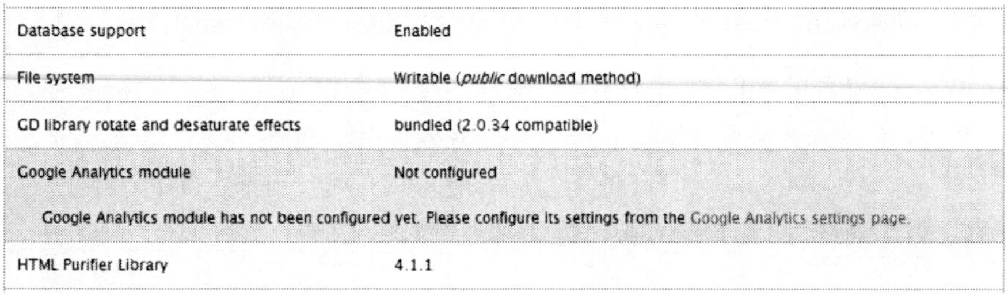

Database support	Enabled
File system	Writable (*public* download method)
GD library rotate and desaturate effects	bundled (2.0.34 compatible)
Google Analytics module	Not configured
Google Analytics module has not been configured yet. Please configure its settings from the Google Analytics settings page.	
HTML Purifier Library	4.1.1

Figure 1–7. The status report provides a single place to view information about installation problems.

- **Advanced search functionality:** Every piece of every page can be indexed, and searching can be configured to allow your site visitors to find the information they need (see Figure 1–8).

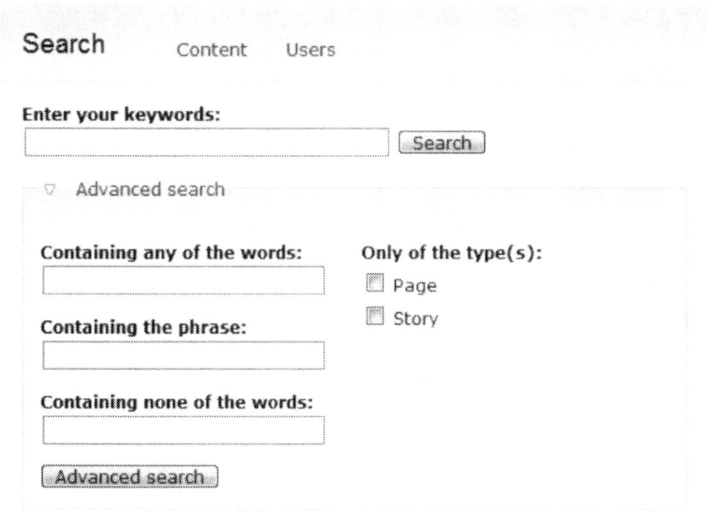

Search   Content   Users

Enter your keywords:

[   ] [Search]

▽ Advanced search

Containing any of the words: **Only of the type(s):**

[   ]   ☐ Page

Containing the phrase: ☐ Story

[   ]

Containing none of the words:

[   ]

[Advanced search]

Figure 1–8. All content can be indexed for fast, advanced searching.

- **Blogs, books, comments, forums, and polls:** The most popular page types are included by default (see Figure 1–9).

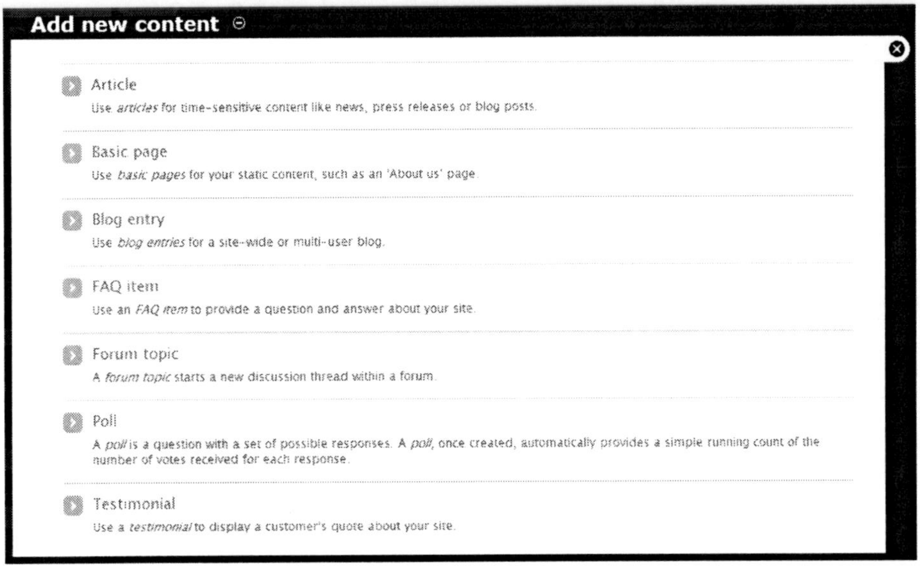

Add new content ⊖

 ⊠ Article
   Use *articles* for time-sensitive content like news, press releases or blog posts.

 ⊠ Basic page
   Use *basic pages* for your static content, such as an 'About us' page.

 ⊠ Blog entry
   Use *blog entries* for a site-wide or multi-user blog.

 ⊠ FAQ item
   Use an *FAQ item* to provide a question and answer about your site.

 ⊠ Forum topic
   A *forum topic* starts a new discussion thread within a forum.

 ⊠ Poll
   A *poll* is a question with a set of possible responses. A *poll*, once created, automatically provides a simple running count of the number of votes received for each response.

 ⊠ Testimonial
   Use a *testimonial* to display a customer's quote about your site.

Figure 1–9. Drupal comes with a number of content types built in. Additional content types can be loaded or created.

- **Caching:** A lot goes into building a page in Drupal. The cache is an important feature for improved performance under load (see Figure 1–10).

Figure 1–10. *Intelligent page caching provides impressive performance gains, especially for pages that don't change often.*

- **Descriptive URLs:** Normally, a page in Drupal is numbered based on its identity in the database. Any page can also be given a custom URL for easy access and sharing (see Figure 1–11).

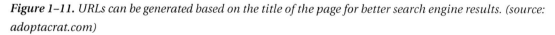

Figure 1–11. *URLs can be generated based on the title of the page for better search engine results. (source: adoptacrat.com)*

- **Multi-level menu system:** You'll find several menu buckets that can be used to help users navigate the system. Menus can also be customized and access-restricted by user role (see Figure 1–12).

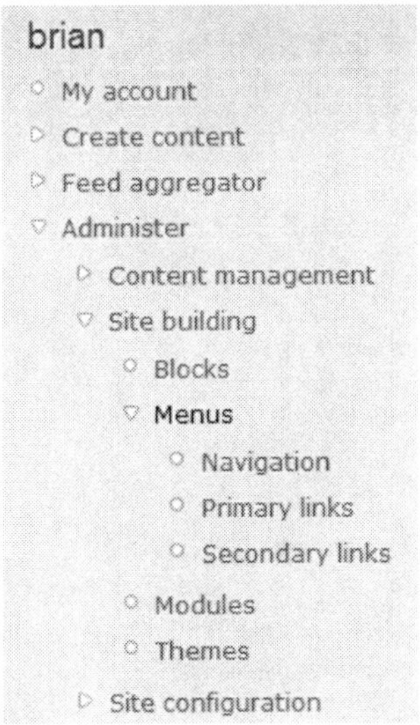

brian

○ My account
▷ Create content
▷ Feed aggregator
▽ Administer
   ▷ Content management
   ▽ Site building
      ○ Blocks
      ▽ **Menus**
         ○ Navigation
         ○ Primary links
         ○ Secondary links
      ○ Modules
      ○ Themes
   ▷ Site configuration

Figure 1–12. Context-sensitive hierarchical menus provide navigation help for all users.

- **Multi-site support:** A single Drupal installation can host many different sites. This makes the process of creating new sites relatively straightforward.

- **New release update notification:** All Drupal modules are updated by their maintainers for bug fixes and security patches. A core module interrogates each module's project page on drupal.org for updates and notifies the administrator when a module has been updated (see Figure 1–13).

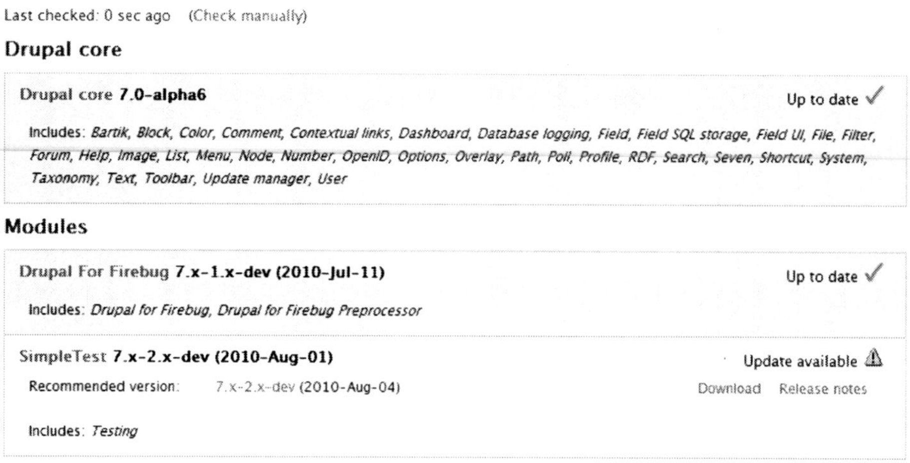

Last checked: 0 sec ago (Check manually)

Drupal core

Drupal core **7.0-alpha6**	Up to date ✓

Includes: *Bartik, Block, Color, Comment, Contextual links, Dashboard, Database logging, Field, Field SQL storage, Field UI, File, Filter, Forum, Help, Image, List, Menu, Node, Number, OpenID, Options, Overlay, Path, Poll, Profile, RDF, Search, Seven, Shortcut, System, Taxonomy, Text, Toolbar, Update manager, User*

Modules

Drupal For Firebug **7.x-1.x-dev (2010-Jul-11)**	Up to date ✓

Includes: *Drupal for Firebug, Drupal for Firebug Preprocessor*

SimpleTest **7.x-2.x-dev (2010-Aug-01)**	Update available ⚠
Recommended version: 7.x-2.x-dev (2010-Aug-04)	Download Release notes

Includes: *Testing*

Figure 1-13. The Drupal core checks to see if new versions of installed modules are available.

- **Multi-user content creation and editing:** Users are assigned one or more roles, which can be configured to allow access to certain content types (see Figure 1–14).

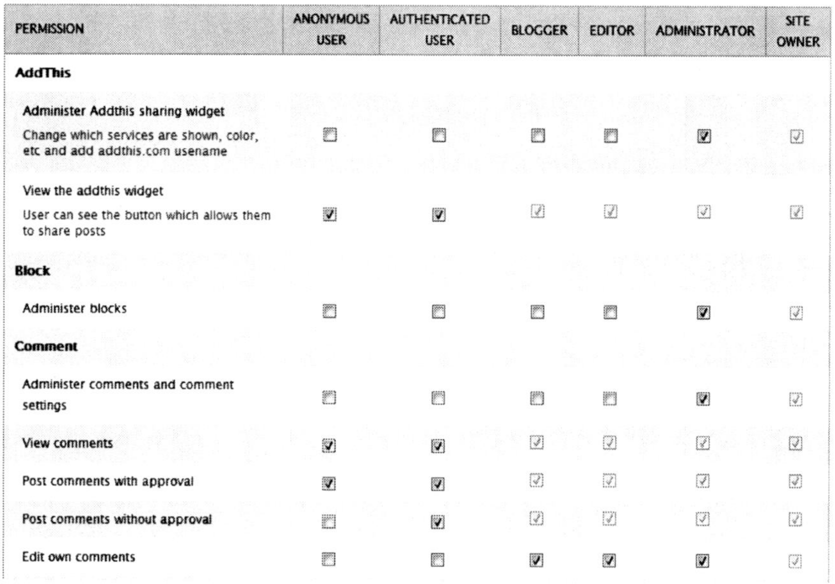

PERMISSION	ANONYMOUS USER	AUTHENTICATED USER	BLOGGER	EDITOR	ADMINISTRATOR	SITE OWNER
AddThis						
Administer Addthis sharing widget Change which services are shown, color, etc and add addthis.com usename	☐	☐	☐	☐	☑	☑
View the addthis widget User can see the button which allows them to share posts	☑	☑	☑	☑	☑	☑
Block						
Administer blocks	☐	☐	☐	☐	☑	☑
Comment						
Administer comments and comment settings	☐	☐	☐	☐	☑	☑
View comments	☑	☑	☑	☑	☑	☑
Post comments with approval	☑	☑	☑	☑	☑	☑
Post comments without approval	☐	☑	☑	☑	☑	☑
Edit own comments	☐	☐	☑	☑	☑	☑

Figure 1-14. Role-based security provides granular control over user access.

- **OpenID support:** Drupal has its own user logon system but also supports OpenID for users who already have an OpenID account elsewhere (see Figure 1–15).

Figure 1–15. You can turn OpenID on so users can get to your site more easily.

RSS Feed and Feed Aggregator: The Drupal core has a module that allows RSS feeds from other sites to be used as a content type (see Figure 1–16).

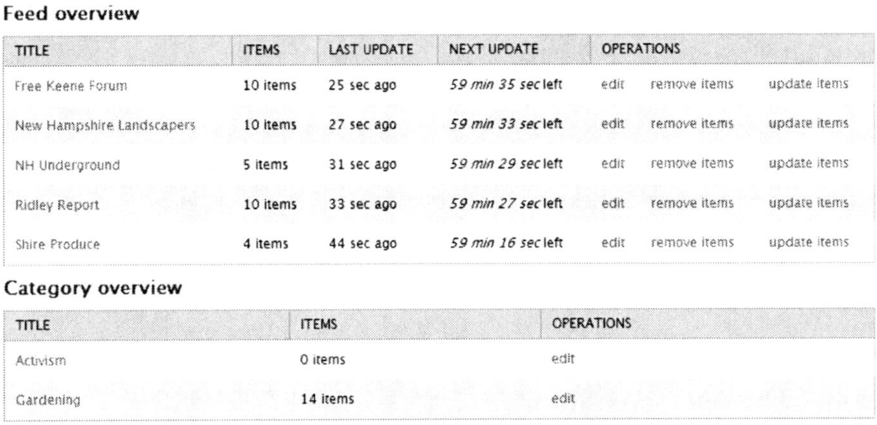

Feed overview

TITLE	ITEMS	LAST UPDATE	NEXT UPDATE	OPERATIONS		
Free Keene Forum	10 items	25 sec ago	*59 min 35 sec* left	edit	remove items	update items
New Hampshire Landscapers	10 items	27 sec ago	*59 min 33 sec* left	edit	remove items	update items
NH Underground	5 items	31 sec ago	*59 min 29 sec* left	edit	remove items	update items
Ridley Report	10 items	33 sec ago	*59 min 27 sec* left	edit	remove items	update items
Shire Produce	4 items	44 sec ago	*59 min 16 sec* left	edit	remove items	update items

Category overview

TITLE	ITEMS	OPERATIONS
Activism	0 items	edit
Gardening	14 items	edit

Figure 1–16. RSS feeds can be integrated into your site, or used as content, processed by custom modules.

- **User profiles:** Drupal has a rich user-management framework that lets administrators assign roles and permissions to users. This framework is available to programmers so they can integrate user management into their code. See Figure 1–17.

	Username	Status	Roles	Member for	Last access	Operations
☐	cynthia	active	• Donor	12 weeks 1 day	1 sec ago	edit
☐	molly	active		12 weeks 3 days	4 hours 26 min ago	edit
☐	Samlam	active	• Blogger	12 weeks 3 days	12 weeks 2 days ago	edit
☐	Brian	active	• Blogger • Forum Moderator	12 weeks 5 days	1 sec ago	edit

Figure 1–17. Out of the box, Drupal supports users and roles, but this can be extended to provide rich profile information as well.

- **Workflow tools:** Certain actions taken by users can trigger events in unrelated modules. For example, creating a blog entry can trigger an e-mail that notifies the administrator of the addition (see Figure 1–18).

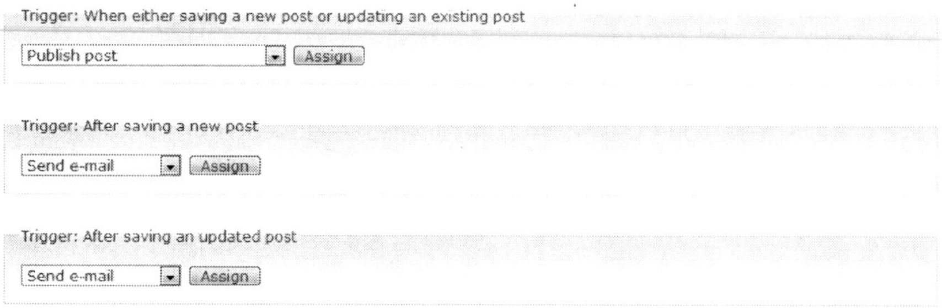

Trigger: When either saving a new post or updating an existing post

Publish post   Assign

Trigger: After saving a new post

Send e-mail   Assign

Trigger: After saving an updated post

Send e-mail   Assign

Figure 1–18. *Users who have the ability to create content can be given access to workflow functionality.*

Security

Drupal has security built in at the lowest levels of the core code, and the team that maintains the core takes security very seriously. There is also a security team that provides assistance to programmers writing core modules and contributed modules as well.

The security team pays attention to current threats and hacking attempts. It maintains http://drupal.org/security, which reports security advisories for core and contributed modules. In this way, breaches are communicated to module developers so they can issue a patch, in many cases on the same day.

The security team provides information for various purposes:

- Site administrators running Drupal sites can find out how to harden their servers against attacks.

- Module programmers learn the importance of sanitizing text inputs and formatting outputs safely.

The Drupal core has many security features built in that makes writing secure code relatively painless. Of course, it is up to the module developer to use these features.

Content Types

Since Drupal is all about content, it's not surprising that it comes with several useful content types. Each piece of content in Drupal is considered a "node" and so all are treated pretty much the same by the database. Understanding the Drupal node is crucial to understanding Drupal itself. Regardless of the content type, the fact that every piece of content has certain things in common with every other piece makes it possible to leverage content in ways that are useful for building a site. For example, the indexing subsystem will create the index database for all content types, and provide that to the search engine, which will return all content. Of course, by now you probably realize that this is also totally customizable—by the administrator in most cases, and the programmer in all cases.

It is in the modules and theming that different contents types might be treated differently.

Out of the box, Drupal makes available the following content types:

- **Blog Entry:** A journal or diary that is kept by a user. The Drupal Blog module lets your site's registered users create their own blogs, which usually consist of a number of blog entry nodes (see Figure 1-19).

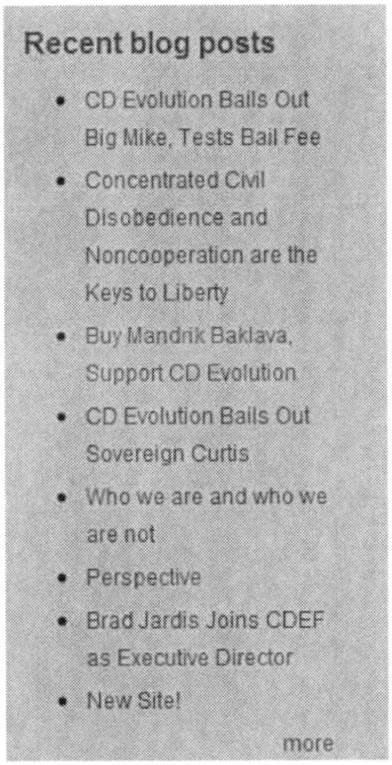

Recent blog posts

- CD Evolution Bails Out Big Mike, Tests Bail Fee
- Concentrated Civil Disobedience and Noncooperation are the Keys to Liberty
- Buy Mandrik Baklava, Support CD Evolution
- CD Evolution Bails Out Sovereign Curtis
- Who we are and who we are not
- Perspective
- Brad Jardis Joins CDEF as Executive Director
- New Site!

more

Figure 1-19. Blog entries from multiple authors can be aggregated to a single list. (source: cdevolution.org)

- **Book Page:** A content type that's designed to be part of a collaborative book. It is enabled by Drupal's Book module. A collaborative book might be documentation for a programming project or some other ongoing endeavor that has multiple participants. See Figure 1-20.

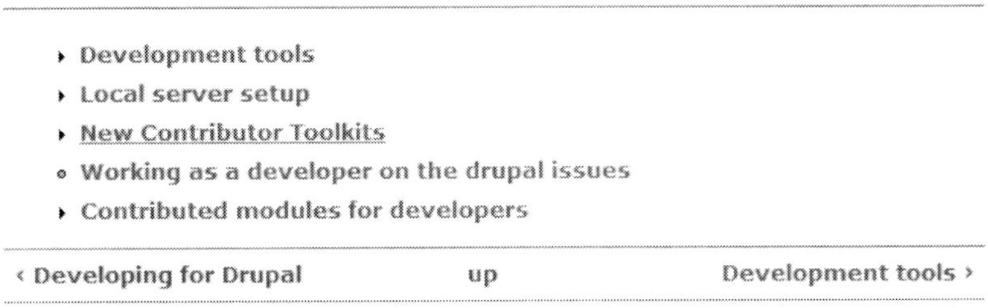

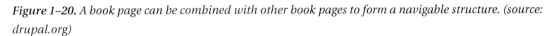

- ▸ Development tools
- ▸ Local server setup
- ▸ New Contributor Toolkits
- ◦ Working as a developer on the drupal issues
- ▸ Contributed modules for developers

| ‹ Developing for Drupal | up | Development tools › |

Figure 1-20. A book page can be combined with other book pages to form a navigable structure. (source: drupal.org)

- **Comment:** Virtually any piece of content can have comments, which are added by users in reaction to a published piece of content. Comments aren't actually nodes, so they aren't technically a "content type" (see Figure 1–21).

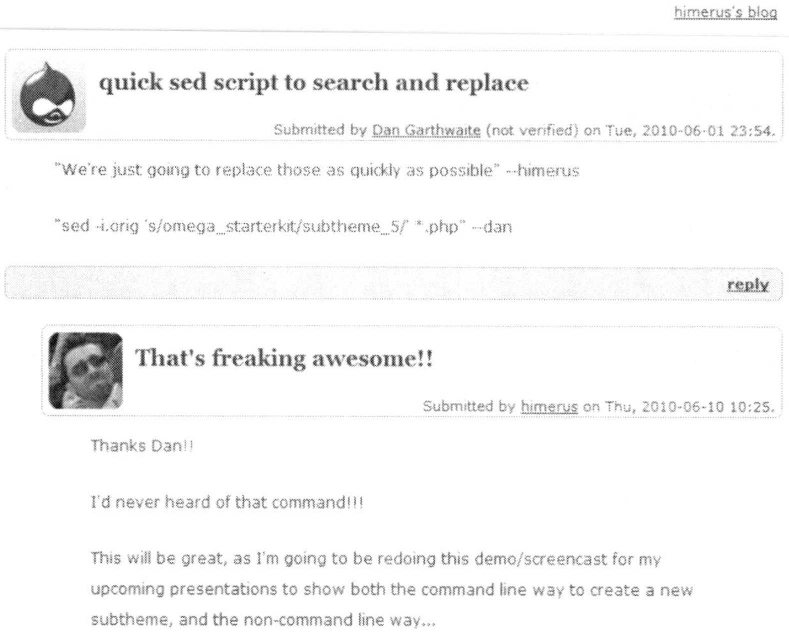

himerus's blog

quick sed script to search and replace

Submitted by Dan Garthwaite (not verified) on Tue, 2010-06-01 23:54.

"We're just going to replace those as quickly as possible" --himerus

"sed -i.orig 's/omega_starterkit/subtheme_5/' *.php" --dan

reply

That's freaking awesome!!

Submitted by himerus on Thu, 2010-06-10 10:25.

Thanks Dan!!

I'd never heard of that command!!!

This will be great, as I'm going to be redoing this demo/screencast for my upcoming presentations to show both the command line way to create a new subtheme, and the non-command line way...

Figure 1–21. Comments can be enabled for virtually any content type. (source: himerus.com)

- **Forum:** Drupal's Forum module defines a topic for a forum discussion. Users can reply to the forum topic by using comments. Figure 1–22 shows an example.

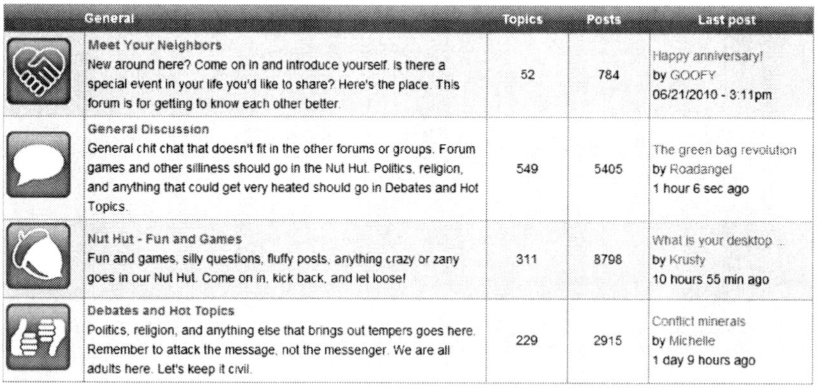

		Topics	Posts	Last post
	Meet Your Neighbors New around here? Come on in and introduce yourself. Is there a special event in your life you'd like to share? Here's the place. This forum is for getting to know each other better.	52	784	Happy anniversary! by GOOFY 06/21/2010 - 3:11pm
	General Discussion General chit chat that doesn't fit in the other forums or groups. Forum games and other silliness should go in the Nut Hut. Politics, religion, and anything that could get very heated should go in Debates and Hot Topics.	549	5405	The green bag revolution by Roadangel 1 hour 6 sec ago
	Nut Hut - Fun and Games Fun and games, silly questions, fluffy posts, anything crazy or zany goes in our Nut Hut. Come on in, kick back, and let loose!	311	8798	What is your desktop ... by Krusty 10 hours 55 min ago
	Debates and Hot Topics Politics, religion, and anything else that brings out tempers goes here. Remember to attack the message, not the messenger. We are all adults here. Let's keep it civil.	229	2915	Conflict minerals by Michelle 1 day 9 hours ago

Figure 1–22. Forum provides a hierarchical topic/response thread. (source: couleeregiononline.com)

- **Page:** Typically, the Page content type is used for static content that can (but is not required to) be linked into the main navigation bar (see Figure 1–23).

NH Trading Marketplace for Surplus Produce

Do you have a garden... small, medium or large? Are you raising livestock... chickens, goats, rabbits? Wouldn't it be great if you could *trade* your surplus(rather than just give it away) for produce you weren't able to grow?

ShireProduce.com is a place where food producers can gently collide to trade, and balance their alimentary pallets.

Wouldn't it be great to meet together somewhere local, at your own convenience to trade those tomatoes (more than you'll ever eat) for some fresh eggs (aren't you glad someone has put up with those chicks?!). Are you a brave one with nanny-goats and have more milk than you know what to do with, but have no fresh spinach or carrots? (those darlings beasts would eat them up before your eyes anyways!)

Figure 1–23. You can use the page content type to create pages that provide certain, usually static, information to your users. (source: shireproduce.com)

- **Poll:** Polls provide a way to ask a multiple-choice question of the site's visitors, and let users vote. Users can answer and see other people's answers to questions. (See Figure 1–24.)

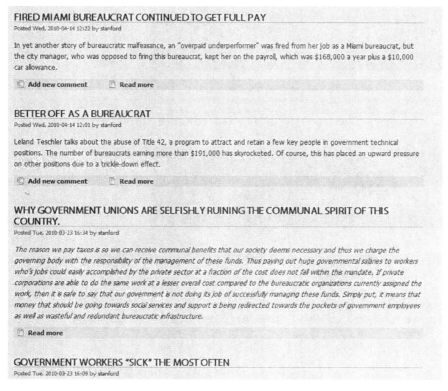

Figure 1–24. *Drupal's built-in poll content type lets you place a single-choice poll on a page.*

- **Story:** A story is generally used for information whose relevance decreases as time passes (such as a news item). By default, newer stories are typically placed higher on the page than older stories. (See Figure 1–25.)

FIRED MIAMI BUREAUCRAT CONTINUED TO GET FULL PAY
Posted Wed, 2010-04-14 12:22 by stanford

In yet another story of bureaucratic malfeasance, an "overpaid underperformer" was fired from her job as a Miami bureaucrat, but the city manager, who was opposed to firing this bureaucrat, kept her on the payroll, which was $168,000 a year plus a $10,000 car allowance.

Add new comment   Read more

BETTER OFF AS A BUREAUCRAT
Posted Wed, 2010-04-14 12:01 by stanford

Leland Teschler talks about the abuse of Title 42, a program to attract and retain a few key people in government technical positions. The number of bureaucrats earning more than $191,000 has skyrocketed. Of course, this has placed an upward pressure on other positions due to a trickle-down effect.

Add new comment   Read more

WHY GOVERNMENT UNIONS ARE SELFISHLY RUINING THE COMMUNAL SPIRIT OF THIS COUNTRY.
Posted Tue, 2010-03-23 16:34 by stanford

The reason we pay taxes is so we can receive communal benefits that our society deems necessary and thus we charge the governing body with the responsibility of the management of these funds. Thus paying out huge governmental salaries to workers who's jobs could easily accomplished by the private sector at a fraction of the cost does not fall within this mandate. If private corporations are able to do the same work at a lesser overall cost compared to the bureaucratic organizations currently assigned the work, then it is safe to say that our government is not doing its job of successfully managing these funds. Simply put, it means that money that should be going towards social services and support is being redirected towards the pockets of government employees as well as wasteful and redundant bureaucratic infrastructure.

Read more

GOVERNMENT WORKERS "SICK" THE MOST OFTEN
Posted Tue, 2010-03-23 16:09 by stanford

Figure 1–25. *A story is similar to a blog, in that the teaser can be promoted to the front page. (source: adopt-a-bureaucrat.com)*

- **Field UI:** You can also create your own content types with your own fields. This is a very powerful feature as it allows administrators to create data structures and capture information without any programming. (See Figure 1–26.)

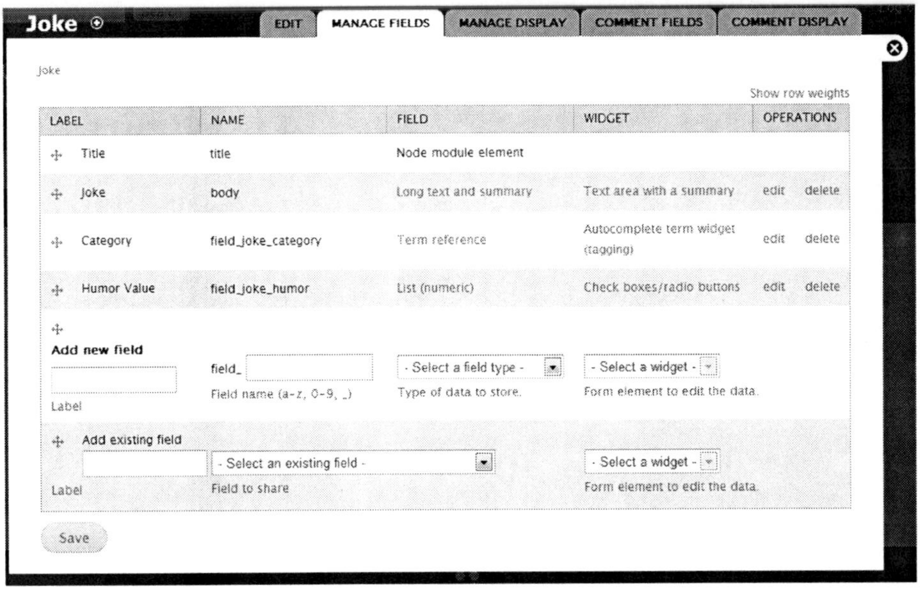

Figure 1–26. New content types can be created and managed by Drupal's powerful content management infrastructure.

Contributed Modules

In addition to the core modules, an administrator of a Drupal site can add any number of modules contributed by members of the community. These modules supply a dizzying array of functionality and features. In Drupal parlance, these are called *contributed modules*. There are a certain contributed modules that administrators of most systems install by default because they are so useful. I use a number of these modules in virtually every Drupal site I create. Here are some of the most valuable.

- **Views:** So you have all of this information in your database, how do you expose just what is needed to your users? The Views module is basically a graphical interface for creating SQL SELECT statements to access data. It provides a way to access your data by establishing relationships between records (think JOIN), filtering by content (WHERE), and sorting the results (ORDER BY). Views also provides various presentation hooks you can use later when you are theming the page. (See Figure 1–27.)

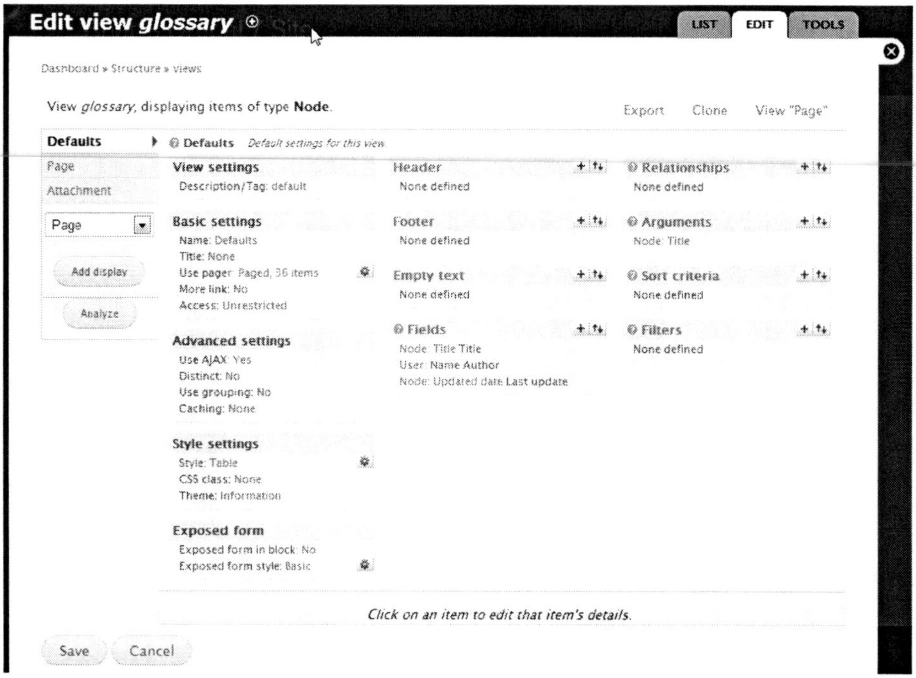

Figure 1–27. Views provides an interface for creating queries into your content.

- **Commerce:** Drupal was originally designed as a content management system but, given its popularity and extensibility, it was only a matter of time before people started demanding some sort of e-commerce capability. Drupal Commerce is a fork of the popular Ubercart module that has everything you need in a shopping cart system. It provides a cart, payment gateways, inventory tracking, reporting, and other goodies to manage your e-commerce site. Plus, there's a rich API for integrating it into the rest of your site. (See Figure 1–28.)

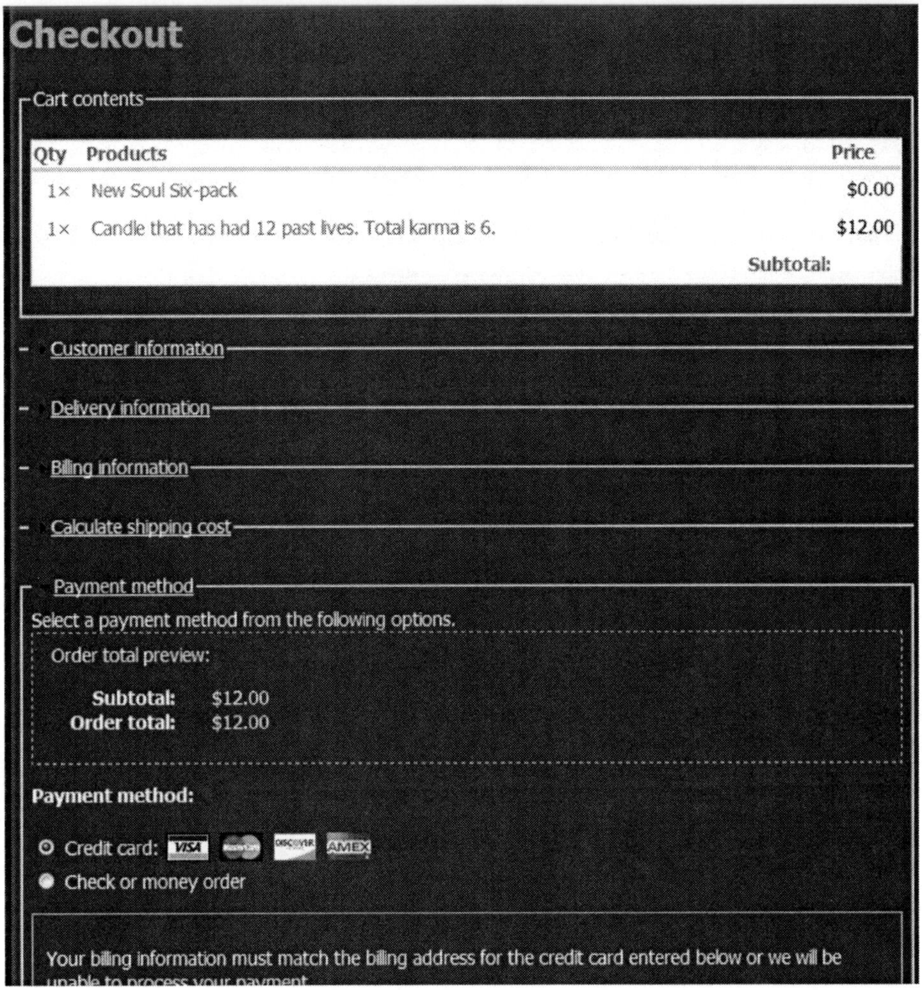

Figure 1–28. *Drupal Commerce is a full-featured e-commerce solution with its own API for great extensibility. (source: karmakandles.com)*

- **WYSIWYG:** By default, you enter content into Drupal using simple HTML text boxes. The user can be limited to certain HTML tags to do specific things, or the administrator can allow full HTML in this text box. Either way, it's a pain. Isn't this what we did two generations ago? Luckily, the WYSIWYG module allows the installation of a number of different editors that let users edit rich text in a way that's more like modern word processors. I'll pass you the Geritol if you remember watching Flip Wilson's drag persona, Geraldine, on *Rowan and Martin's Laugh-In* in the late 1960s. For the rest of you, it was Geraldine who popularized the phrase, "What you see is what you get, honey!" (See Figure 1–29.)

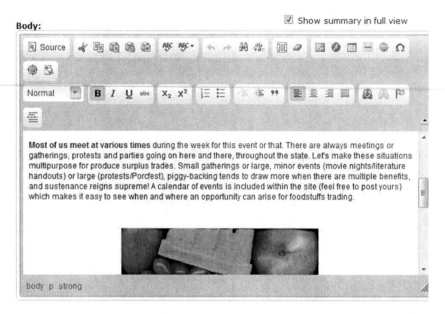

Figure 1–29. The WYSIWYG module allows third-party editors to be plugged into Drupal.

- **Drupal for Firebug:** A lot goes into creating a page in Drupal. As a developer, you might want to get a snapshot of certain events as they happen. There's a debugging module for developers that tracks things as they happen and makes them available to the browser. A browser add-on, Firebug was originally developed for Firefox but is now available for Chrome as well. (See Figure 1–30.)

```
/index.php?XDEBUG_SESSION_START=10

  Information   Forms   Sql   User   Node   View   Php

  $form->search_block_form
  $form = stdClass Object (
    [search_block_form] => array (
      [#type] => [textfield]
      [#size] => [15]
      [#default_value] => []
      [#attributes] => array (
        [title] => [Enter the terms you wish to search for.]
      )
    )
    [actions] => array (
      [#type] => [actions]
      [submit] => array (
        [#type] => [submit]
        [#value] => [Search]
      )
    )
    [#submit] => array (
      [0] => [search_box_form_submit]
    )
    [#form_id] => [search_block_form]
    [#build_id] => [form-
_tF19wAoDlbo1hl9AmAGNsGxioHSH5qygpZwDqidPlE]
    [#type] => [form]
    [form_build_id] => array (
      [#type] => [hidden]
      [#value] => [form-
```

Figure 1–30. Drupal for Firebug works with Firebug to display internal information as it is created by Drupal's page engine.

There are hundreds of modules that users have shared with the community to do many different things. These range in quality from excellent in functionality, updating, and support, to fairly useless for most applications. If you are looking for a particular functionality, it's helpful to ask a more experienced person, though some people like to just start downloading the modules and checking them out for their purposes.

Since all of the modules are delivered in PHP source code, you can see exactly how they work and make any changes you need. Changing them is discouraged because you are essentially creating a branch from the main development effort, but if you don't expect to update your customized module, it's not really a problem.

One nice thing about the contributed modules is that they range in price from free to free. Note, however, that some ventures might charge for a particular service. For example, Mollom is a service you can set up on your site to blocks spam from certain forms. The module for doing this is free, and there is a free service that is limited in its protection. However, for more protection and high availability, Mollom offers a monthly subscription. This service is quite popular, which shows that there are people making money by giving away Drupal software.

Themes

Once a page is created using Drupal's module engine, it must be formatted and delivered to the user. That is the job of the theming engine. You can do some processing work in your theme, but the main purpose is to get a page to your user. (See Figure 1–31.)

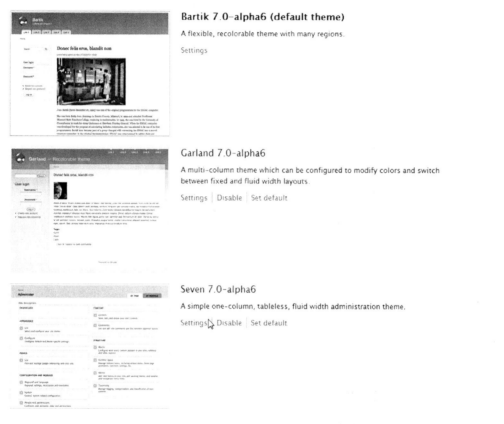

Figure 1–31. *Themes give your site a look and feel, as well as additional functionality.*

The theming engine receives all of the artifacts of a page that have already been processed. This includes snippets of content (nodes), images and other non-text objects (as file pointers), and other information that might be handy, such as the current user and permissions settings.

You can think of the modules as doing the data portion of the page, and the theme doing the visual part. You can use themes to change the graphical and typographical look and feel of the site, but you can also use them to provide some client-side processing, like AJAX/AHAH server communication and jQuery display automation.

A theme can have a few or many regions where content can be placed. Such pieces of content are called "blocks," and they form one of the basic Drupal object types. (See Figure 1–32.) The block subsystem provides a graphical way to place content in various regions on the page.

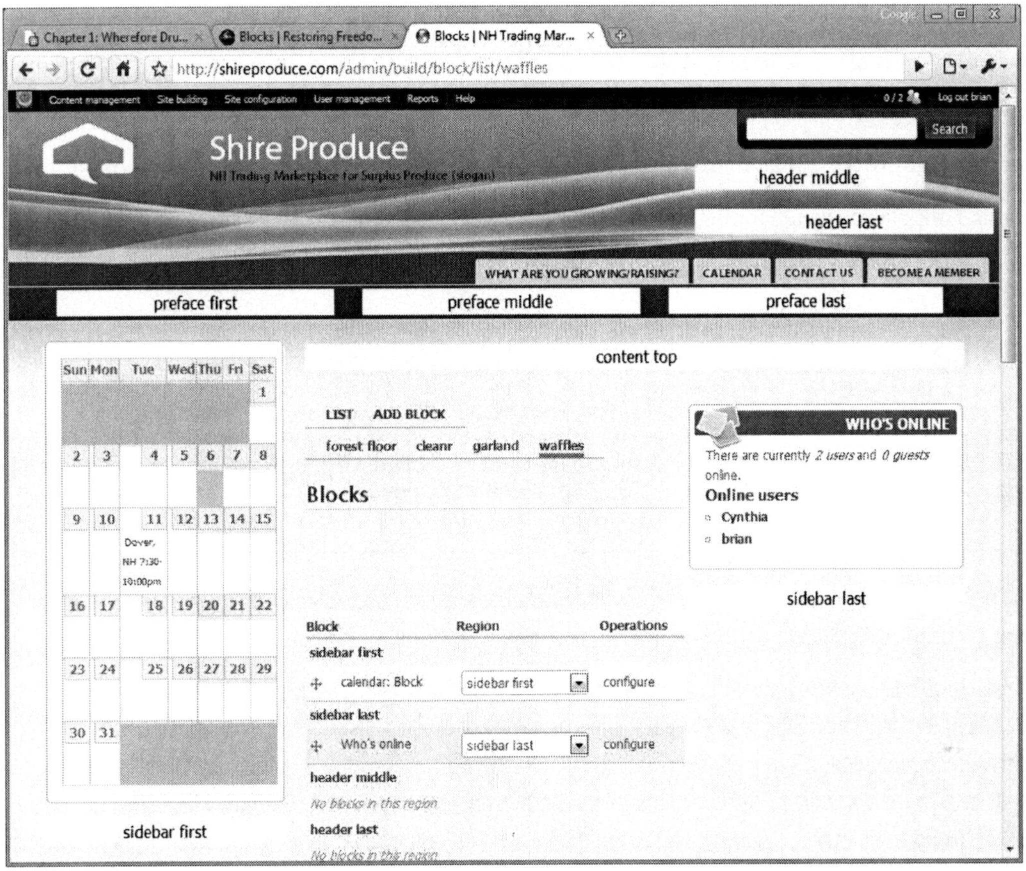

Figure 1–32. Themes can use predefined regions for placing blocks of content. (source: shireproduce.com)

Using a theme can be anywhere from zero-effort simple to very complex, depending on what you want to do. Drupal 6 comes with several different themes, and literally hundreds more are available on the Drupal site. We'll discuss themes in Chapter 7.

The Drupal Design Philosophy

The Drupal engine is based on a series of hooks. I've heard this referred to as "sorta like object-oriented." Don't believe it. If you fall into the Drupal-is-sorta-like-OO camp, you'll miss the point and end up thinking of Drupal as something it isn't.

Rather, every call to a Drupal site starts at index.php. The PHP code creates a list of modules that have been registered using calls to the database. It then opens each of those modules' PHP source code files and looks for carefully crafted function names. If it finds a function that matches the particular hook the system is looking for, it will execute that function.

That hooked function can, in turn, call other functions that have asked to be hooked to it.

As a .NET programmer, I thought at first that this method was wasteful and redundant. I mean, opening source code files on a production site and scanning for strings? How primitive! How insecure!

But as I started using Drupal, I found that the hook model is quite elegant and is not burdened with the overhead of the huge, albeit pretty well-tuned, .NET framework. Performance is acceptable right out of the box, though it tends to slow down significantly as you add modules because each page is looking for hooks on every page in all registered modules.

Fortunately, you can take advantage of a lot of experience in optimizing the speed. Drupal has an excellent caching subsystem that bypasses the entire hook-searching process for static pages or parts of pages. Plus, there are things you can do to streamline your system once it is ready for production. To be assured that Drupal is designed for high performance, all you need to do is look at some of the high-profile, high-traffic sites that use Drupal.

The Drupal page lifecycle is discussed in Chapter 2.

Database

All data is stored in a central repository. As I mentioned earlier, this repository is MySQL by default. But Drupal 7 comes with a database abstraction layer that decouples the dependency on MySQL, and opens the door to using other databases. And a group at Microsoft has created a SQL Server driver that takes advantage of PHP's data object interface (PDO). I cover this in Appendix A.

■ **Caution** Before you get too excited about cross-database support, you should know that Drupal's support for SQL Server is not so straightforward.

Drupal's core development team is committed to writing to the PDO layer, and the Drupal core is compatible. However, one of the great advantages of Drupal is its community of module contributors. While database abstraction is recommended, it is not possible to force all module authors to adhere to the new standard. The committed users in the community will put pressure on module authors to adhere to the new standards, but until this threat of ostracism is in place, you should realize that you might miss out on a module or two, or be prepared to upgrade your modules to use the database abstraction layer.

Having said that, I am heartened to see that the most popular modules are being written to support the new data abstraction framework.

You'll find core functions that do much of the database access, including the node_load() and node_save() functions that will retrieve a node by its node identifier and store nodes with all of the necessary data.

In addition to specific data access functions, there's also a more generalized data abstraction layer that provides a safe interface to the database and allows for efficient processing of record sets returned. The data abstraction layer is described as being engine-agnostic, but as long as people write SQL code directly in their modules, the database engine is tightly bound.

The data abstraction layer is good for parsing SQL query strings to help guard against SQL injection attacks and other techniques that might lead to an insecure system.

Forms

Whenever you need to get some information from a user, you typically use the HTML `<form>` element. This element contains all of the text fields, check boxes, pull-down lists, and other components that web users are familiar with. And, of course, it has the necessary "Submit" button to post the information back to the web site. (See Figure 1–33.)

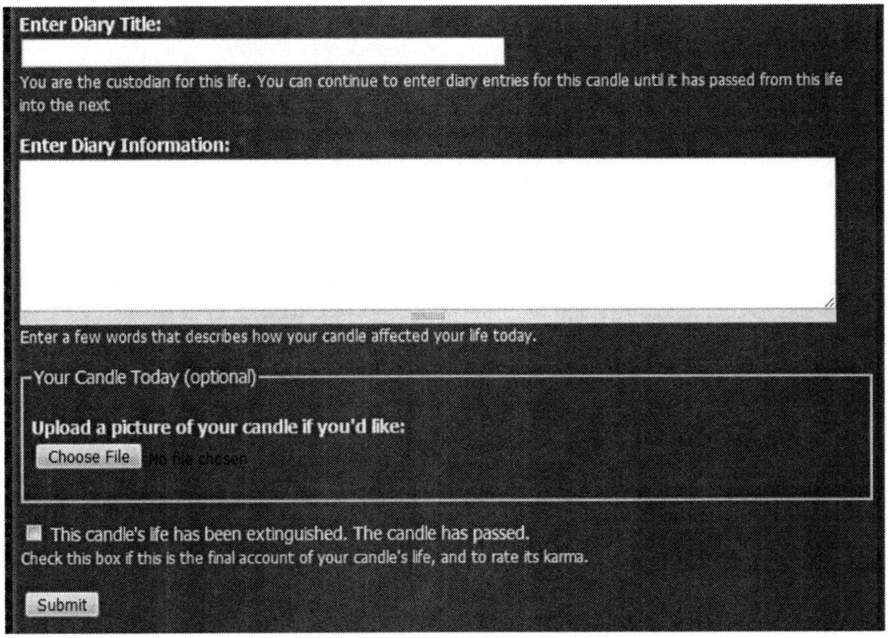

Figure 1–33. Forms are an integral part of Drupal. (source: karmakandles.com)

Drupal abstracts the form with an engine that can be extended with hooks. The Drupal form engine will take arrays of fields that you pass to it and build the form along with hooks that allow theming of the form. Then you create a couple of callback functions that first validate the information from the form, and then do something useful with it.

Security

A significant amount of thought has been put into making the core secure. There are also guidelines for module developers to assure that they create modules that can't be easily hacked. For example, scanners for SQL code can help prevent SQL insertion attacks. (See Figure 1–34.)

Figure 1-34. Drupal has protection against SQL insertion attacks. (source: xkcd.com)

Since Drupal sits (usually) on top of the Apache web server, it can take advantage of Apache's security layers, including file access permissions, compartmentalized execution space, and SSL access.

In addition to best practices for securing code, the Drupal core has built-in safeguards, like user password protection and role-based permissions for all users, e-mail confirmation for new user registration, and stateful session tracking. And that's just in the core.

There are myriad contributed modules that address various security aspects:

- Various CAPTCHA techniques using images, math problems, even grammar challenges ("Knives can ____ butter." reflect? heat? play poker with?). I'm not sure I'd pass this one. (See Figure 1-35.)

Figure 1-35. Installing CAPTCHA helps avoid spam on a site.

- User access techniques, like ACL (access control lists), LDAP integration, login using OpenID, and modules to blacklist by IP. (See Figure 1-36.) There are also modules for managing the complexity, age, and expiration of passwords.

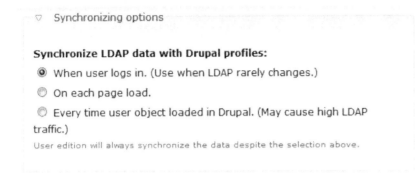

Figure 1-36. LDAP is one of the uesr authentication integration techniques available

- Legal issues like terms of use, privacy policies, and age validation.

You'll also find modules to check that you're adhering to security policies in your code, and that pages that should be accessed with SSL are redirected to HTTPS.

Menus and Paths

When we talk about menus in Drupal, we mean more than just a set of clickable links that load pages. There are three such standard menus in Drupal, two of which, Main menu and Secondary menu, are created by an administrator. I usually set the Main menu to standard pages like "About Us," "Contact," or "Home," and the Secondary menu to various interesting pages that may be on the site or may point to external partner sites. (See Figure 1-37.)

Figure 1-37. Two special administrator-created menus are included in Drupal, but you can create any
number of specialized menu structures .(source: cdevolution.org)

A third menu, Navigation, is built by the system based on who you are, the role you play on the site, and other, possibly personal, options. All of these menus can be placed in blocks on the page and rendered by the theming engine.

The path of a page is really just an abstraction and does not point to an actual "page" that sits on a server. As I mentioned earlier, all processing starts at `index.php`. The path is passed to the page processing engine, which interrogates the database to figure out what to display to the user.

For example, `http://adoptacrat.com/cratomatic/details` will pass "cratomatic/details" to the engine, which will parse it and pass it along to any modules that have registered an interest in dealing with the page. At some point, someone in the chain of hooks will recognize the path and start to build the page. Once it's built, the content is passed to the theme engine, which might also do something with the path string before sending the completed page back to the browser.

▓ **Note** You might notice I said that everything starts at `index.php`, but then I showed a URL that doesn't include index.php. Which is the lie?

Neither, actually. Drupal takes advantage of the "rewrite url" functionality of the web server (both Apache and IIS support this through external modules). The rule for rewrites will turn the example URL above into `http://adoptacrat.com/index.php?q=cratomatic/details` by the time it gets to the Drupal engine.

Users, Roles, and Permissions

What good is a site that doesn't have users? This reminds me of something I overheard at Sears. Two tired sales clerks were talking behind the cash register and said, "This would be a great job if it weren't for the customers!"

When you create your site, the setup subsystem asks for the site administrator. This is a special user who has access to absolutely every aspect of the system. If you like, you can set up other users who have almost as much control as the super user.

Every user has one or more roles. When a person first accesses your site, she is considered "anonymous" and given a role of "anonymous user". Drupal has a rich, extensible permissions framework that gives the administrator the flexibility to grant virtually any permission to any role. And as a programmer, you can plug into the permissions subsystem and provide whatever granularity of access for your module you feel appropriate.

Summary

Drupal is a third-generation web development engine that provides content management, forms management, and a rich platform for custom development. The Drupal community of users and developers is vast, and seasoned developers are eager to help new users get started.

The amount of contributed code is so extensive that there's a good chance that whatever you need to do, a "module for that" probably already exists. And if a contributed module doesn't do exactly what you need, you can rest assured you can get help to create your own module or customize an existing one. In the next chapter, I'll walk you through the lifecycle of a page as it is rendered through Drupal's engine and point out how it differs from the ASP.NET page lifecycle.

■ ■ ■

## CHAPTER 2

The Page Lifecycle

Getting a page to your browser using Drupal is quite a roundabout process. The final content is a mashup of data retrieved from a database, modified by modules, and finally formed for presentation by a theming layer. Understanding the steps a page goes through is critical to being able to develop custom modules for Drupal. This chapter covers the page lifecycle, and shows where you can attach your own code to do something an existing module can't do. If you are a developer who has created web sites using ASP.NET, you are probably well aware of the concept of the .NET page lifecycle—the stages a page goes through before being sent to the browser.

Directly comparing the Drupal model to the ASP.NET page lifecycle isn't really possible since the basic architecture of the two frameworks is just different. However, I've found it easier to understand Drupal by comparing it, at least at a high level, to something else I'm familiar with.

I'm assuming you're at least somewhat familiar with the ASP.NET page lifecycle of events and processing, and so you probably know the order of events that are fired during the page-building process. As a review, I'd like to first cover the Drupal 7 page lifecycle, and then show where the ASP.NET page building process is similar.

This way, you can hook into something that is already familiar to you (pun intended).

The Drupal Page Lifecycle

Every call to a Drupal-powered site begins with a trip through `index.php`. Every single page call. It would make sense, then, that this particular page is pretty efficient. And, in fact, it is, as Listing 2–1 shows. The efficiency comes in as it calls the bootstrap routines, which fail as quickly as possible if there is a problem, and use cached data if available.

■ **Note** If you are reading this, you may be new to PHP. In this section, you'll see a lot of PHP code pulled from the version of the Drupal core that was current when I wrote the book. As patches are applied, the code here might not be the same as the code in your version of Drupal. However, I want to include the code is so you can get a feeling for PHP syntax and start to feel comfortable with "The Drupal Way" of coding.

Listing 2–1. The `index.php` Page Efficiently Calls Procedures to Build a Page

```
define('DRUPAL_ROOT', getcwd());

require_once DRUPAL_ROOT . '/includes/bootstrap.inc';
drupal_bootstrap(DRUPAL_BOOTSTRAP_FULL);
```

```
menu_execute_active_handler();
```

Take a look at Figure 2–1. The basic steps are:

- Get started with the bootstrapper (`drupal_bootstrap`).

- Figure out what information is needed (`menu_execute_active_handler`).

- Fail if there is a known error.

- Theme the page (`theme`).

- Close everything and finalize the page (`drupal_page_footer`).

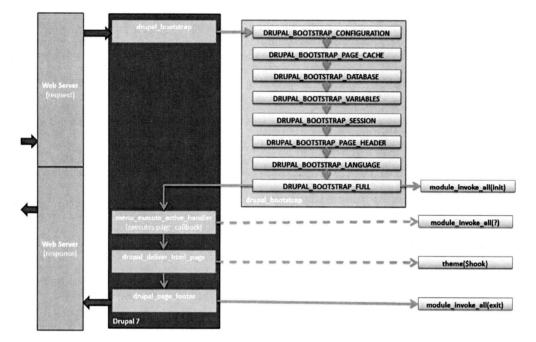

Figure 2–1. *The Drupal bootstrapping process.*

The bootstrapper goes through a number of stages, as described in the sections below.

Configuration Bootstrap

The configuration routine is shown in Listing 2–2.

Listing 2–2. *Bootstrap Configuration Routine*

```
/**
 * Bootstrap configuration: Setup script environment and load settings.php.
 */
function _drupal_bootstrap_configuration() {
  // Set the Drupal custom error handler.
```

```
set_error_handler('_drupal_error_handler');
set_exception_handler('_drupal_exception_handler');

drupal_environment_initialize();
// Start a page timer:
timer_start('page');
// Initialize the configuration, including variables from settings.php.
drupal_settings_initialize();
}
```

First, the configuration routine sets up the error handlers so that if any errors happen from this point on, they are dealt with. Drupal creates an entire error-handling infrastructure that takes care of logging errors to a central database table through the watchdog() function. Since the watchdog process is integrated with Drupal, you can set up your own hooks to grab the error after it is generated, before it is logged to the database.

Setting the error and exception handlers is done through the PHP functions set_error_handler() and set_exception_handler(), which define callback handlers for that functionality. In PHP, an exception is generated when a system event occurs that is not trapped inside a try...catch block. Exceptions are always considered fatal and Drupal will write the exception to the error log and then exit with a screen full of information.

Errors, on the other hand, can be recovered from, or at least reported in a way that allows the process to continue, with a note provided to the user. For example, if your module tries to update a table in the database and the table doesn't exist, Drupal will trap the error, write to the error log, and display a nastygram to the user, but the system will attempt to process the page and recover.

Next the routine calls the drupal_environment_initialize() function, which initializes various parts of the PHP environment, such as HTTP settings, error reporting, and session information. It then starts a page timer that can be used for performance metrics and then calls drupal_settings_initialize().

The drupal_settings_initialize() function loads the PHP settings file (settings.php) for the site. This phase also parses the URL to find which page is needed and sets up the session and cookie information.

The Drupal settings file, which you'll find in the sites/default directory, is an important part of your installation. It is where much of the site-specific information is. The settings file, settings.php, after it has been modified by the installation routine is shown in Listing 2–3.

Listing 2–3. A Typical Drupal Settings File

```php
<?php
// $Id: default.settings.php,v 1.50 2010/08/08 19:35:49 dries Exp $

$databases = array (
  'default' =>
  array (
    'default' =>
    array (
      'driver' => 'mysql',
      'database' => 'drupal7',
      'username' => 'brian',
      'password' => 'super-secret-password',
      'host' => 'localhost',
      'port' => '',
      'prefix' => '',
    ),
  ),
);

$update_free_access = FALSE;
$drupal_hash_salt = 'V7lO82TATKeB2rlow-xK8ZNABIa6yoNuRb3gt4wrCEm';
# $base_url = 'http://www.example.com';  // NO trailing slash!
```

```
ini_set('session.gc_probability', 1);
ini_set('session.gc_divisor', 100);
ini_set('session.gc_maxlifetime', 200000);
ini_set('session.cookie_lifetime', 2000000);
# ini_set('pcre.backtrack_limit', 200000);
# ini_set('pcre.recursion_limit', 200000);
# $cookie_domain = 'example.com';
# $conf['site_name'] = 'My Drupal site';
# $conf['theme_default'] = 'garland';
# $conf['anonymous'] = 'Visitor';
# $conf['maintenance_theme'] = 'bartik';
# $conf['reverse_proxy'] = TRUE;
# $conf['reverse_proxy_header'] = 'HTTP_X_CLUSTER_CLIENT_IP';
# $conf['reverse_proxy_addresses'] = array('a.b.c.d', ...);
# $conf['omit_vary_cookie'] = TRUE;
# $conf['locale_custom_strings_en'][''] = array(
#   'forum'       => 'Discussion board',
#   '@count min' => '@count minutes',
# );
# $conf['blocked_ips'] = array(
#   'a.b.c.d',
# );
# $conf['allow_authorize_operations'] = FALSE;
```

The settings file gives Drupal enough information about *your* site to get started. This includes information about the all-important database it will be using, as well as information on how to access the database.

A nice feature of the settings file is that it will allow you to access the system without a password. Setting the $update_free_access variable to TRUE will cause Drupal to skip the access checking. I probably don't have to tell you how important it is to keep this value at FALSE for a live site, but it's a nice option if you should forget your password or for some other reason can't get in.

The salted hash is generated randomly at install time as a key to do form tokens, one-time password links, and for other areas where one-way encryption is needed. If you have a multiple-server farm, this value needs to be the same on all servers servicing the site.

The rest of the settings (commented lines begin with a hash) are important, but if you need to know more about them you can refer to the comments in the settings file or the links that are included therein.

Note that the settings file should not be in a path that can be served by your web server, and it should be write-protected. The Drupal installation routine takes care of write-protecting the file when it is finished modifying it, but if you replicate the site to other servers, you should make sure to take the same precaution.

Page Cache Bootstrap

This phase calls the _drupal_bootstrap_page_cache() function, which sets up the environment for caching if that's necessary. The function is shown in Listing 2–4.

Listing 2–4. The Page Cache Bootstrapping Function (edited for clarity)

```
function _drupal_bootstrap_page_cache() {
  global $user;

  // Check for a cache mode force from settings.php.
  if (variable_get('page_cache_without_database')) {
    $cache_enabled = TRUE;
  }
  else {
    drupal_bootstrap(DRUPAL_BOOTSTRAP_VARIABLES, FALSE);
```

```
    $cache_enabled = variable_get('cache');
  }
  drupal_block_denied(ip_address());
  // If there is no session cookie and cache is enabled (or forced), try
  // to serve a cached page.
  if (!isset($_COOKIE[session_name()]) && $cache_enabled) {
    // Get the page from the cache.
    $cache = drupal_page_get_cache();
    // If there is a cached page, display it.
    if (is_object($cache)) {
      header('X-Drupal-Cache: HIT');
      // Restore the metadata cached with the page.
      $_GET['q'] = $cache->data['path'];
      drupal_set_title($cache->data['title'], PASS_THROUGH);
      drupal_serve_page_from_cache($cache);
      exit;
    }
    else {
      header('X-Drupal-Cache: MISS');
    }
  }
}
```

Drupal has a pretty intelligent caching mechanism that saves pages that don't change for anonymous users. For example, though your front page might change throughout the day as things happen, it will probably look much the same to visitors. Thus there's no need for the system to rebuild the same information for every person who hits your site, so Drupal's page cache infrastructure kicks in.

▓ **Note** The caching mechanism in Drupal normally works only for anonymous users, since authenticated users will most likely have custom content generated individually for each user.

The caching mechanism is well-designed, so if you are building low-volume sites you probably will never need to worry about how it works or how to optimize it. However, if you expect to get heavy traffic, you'll want to take advantage of the many ways to tweak the cache system to optimize page-loading time. And there are things you can do as a designer or a programmer to get maximum benefit out of the cache.

The cache bootstrap routine checks to see if caching is turned on and available for this page. This stage also checks to see if the requesting IP address has been banned by the administrator. If a cache is available and the address hasn't been banned, the cached page is retrieved from the database and sent to the requestor. An HTTP header is written to tell the client that it is receiving a cached page.

Database Bootstrap

The _drupal_bootstrap_database() function sets up the database handling routines using the database settings that were specified in settings.php and included in DRUPAL_BOOTSTRAP_CONFIGURATION. The code in Listing 2–5 shows the database bootstrapping logic.

Listing 2–5. The Database Bootstrapping Sequence (edited for clarity)

```
function _drupal_bootstrap_database() {
  // Initialize the database system. Note that the connection
  // won't be initialized until it is actually requested.
  require_once DRUPAL_ROOT . '/includes/database/database.inc';
  // Register autoload functions so that we can access classes and interfaces.
  // The database autoload routine comes first so that we can load the database
  // system without hitting the database. That is especially important during
  // the install or upgrade process.
  spl_autoload_register('drupal_autoload_class');
  spl_autoload_register('drupal_autoload_interface');
}
```

The system does not open the database yet. If an external database is required, this is where it is called, and it invokes database.inc, which defines the database abstraction layer.

One of the important performance-enhancing features of Drupal is that it maintains an internal registry of all functions or classes in the system, allowing it to lazy-load code files as needed. This, in turn, reduces the amount of code that must be parsed for each request. The spl_autoload_register() functions set up the registry and check the cache to make sure they have integrity before moving on.

Variable Bootstrap

Drupal has a table, variable, where any module can create its own named variables that are persisted between page calls and even between calls from different users. Think of them as persistent global variables. The variable bootstrapper routine, _drupal_bootstrap_variables(), is shown in Listing 2–6.

Listing 2–6. The Variable Bootstrapping Function

```
function _drupal_bootstrap_variables() {
  global $conf;

  // Initialize the lock system.
  require_once DRUPAL_ROOT . '/' . variable_get('lock_inc', 'includes/lock.inc');
  lock_initialize();

  // Load variables from the database, but do not overwrite variables set in settings.php.
  $conf = variable_initialize(isset($conf) ? $conf : array());
  // Load bootstrap modules.
  require_once DRUPAL_ROOT . '/includes/module.inc';
  module_load_all(TRUE);
}
```

Before getting the variables, the _drupal_bootstrap_variables() function sets up Drupal's locking mechanism, which coordinates long-running operations across requests. The locking mechanism is necessary because multiple Drupal page requests may execute in parallel, potentially leading to conflicts or race conditions when two requests execute the same code at the same time. The lock system built into Drupal is cooperative and advisory and is not managed by a higher process. For this reason, you should play nice with other processes that might need a lock. Any long-running operation that could potentially be attempted in parallel by multiple requests should try to acquire a lock before proceeding. By obtaining a lock, one request notifies any other requests that a specific operation is in progress that must not be executed in parallel.

This routine initializes the lock mechanism so it can be used later in the bootstrapping process and while building the page.

After initializing the lock system, all variables are retrieved from the variable table, as well as any variables declared in the settings file. The routine then loads all variable values into the cache for fast retrieval. Plus, all modules in the system table are loaded, making them available to the rest of the bootstrapping process.

Finally, the dblog module is loaded into memory. The dblog module manages the database logging engine. The module_load_all() function will load all enabled modules, but for the bootstrapper, only a small subset of modules are loaded. We will load all of the other modules a bit later.

Session Bootstrap

The session initialization function, drupal_session_initialize(), is shown in Listing 2–7.

Listing 2–7. The Session Initialization Function

```
function drupal_session_initialize() {
  global $user, $is_https;

  session_set_save_handler('_drupal_session_open',
    '_drupal_session_close', '_drupal_session_read',
    '_drupal_session_write', '_drupal_session_destroy',
    '_drupal_session_garbage_collection');

  if (!empty($_COOKIE[session_name()])
      || ($is_https && variable_get('https', FALSE)
      && !empty($_COOKIE[substr(session_name(), 1)]))) {
    drupal_session_start();
    if (!empty($user->uid) || !empty($_SESSION)) {
      drupal_page_is_cacheable(FALSE);
    }
  }
  else {
    $user = drupal_anonymous_user();
    session_id(drupal_hash_base64(uniqid(mt_rand(), TRUE)));
  }
  date_default_timezone_set(drupal_get_user_timezone());
}
```

Because Drupal deals with session information instead of relying on PHP, we need to register the Drupal functions that do the work so PHP can offload them. We do this by telling PHP, through the session_set_save_handler() function, which Drupal functions we will use. This function registers the user-level session storage functions that are used for storing and retrieving data associated with a session.

Next, the function checks to see if there is a current session based on the user's credentials. Like sessions in .NET, a Drupal session is used because HTTP is a stateless protocol. This allows us to provide stateful access from page to page.

Page Header Bootstrap

The header bootstrapping function, _drupal_bootstrap_page_header(), is shown in Listing 2–8.

Listing 2–8. The Page Header Bootstrapper

```
function _drupal_bootstrap_page_header() {
  bootstrap_invoke_all('boot');

  if (!drupal_is_cli()) {
    ob_start();
    drupal_page_header();
  }
}
```

This phase collects a list of all modules that have registered an interest in the bootstrap process. For all modules so registered, this function will load and invoke them. So, if you create a module that you want to have a say in the bootstrapping process, you just need to write a function that hooks into the boot process and your module will be loaded here. This will make more sense to you as we get into the hook mechanism.

Finally, this function turns on output buffering and writes the default HTML header records.

Language Bootstrap

Drupal is designed, at its core, to be language-agnostic. There are Drupal sites in virtually any language you can imagine. This phase checks for the language that should be used, and sets some variables for future use. It is shown in Listing 2–9.

Listing 2–9. The Language Bootstrap Function

```
function drupal_language_initialize() {
  $types = language_types();

  // Ensure the language is correctly returned, even without multilanguage
  // support. Also make sure we have a $language fallback, in case a language
  // negotiation callback needs to do a full bootstrap.
  // Useful for eg. XML/HTML 'lang' attributes.
  $default = language_default();
  foreach ($types as $type) {
    $GLOBALS[$type] = $default;
  }
  if (drupal_multilingual()) {
    include_once DRUPAL_ROOT . '/includes/language.inc';
    foreach ($types as $type) {
      $GLOBALS[$type] = language_initialize($type);
    }
    // Allow modules to react on language system initialization in multilingual
    // environments.
    bootstrap_invoke_all('language_init');
  }
}
```

The default language is extracted from the database. The language object contains all necessary information about the language to be used, including its international standard name, the common name, writing direction, and other characteristics.

Finally, the language_init hook invokes all modules that would like to have a say in a multilingual site.

Full Bootstrap

Once the bootstrapper has the information it needs, the work of building the page continues here. The function, _drupal_bootstrap_full() is shown in Listing 2–10.

Listing 2–10. The Full Bootstrap Function

```
function _drupal_bootstrap_full() {
  $called = &drupal_static(__FUNCTION__);

  if ($called) {
    return;
  }
  $called = 1;
  // ...core include files included here
  // Detect string handling method
  unicode_check();
  // Undo magic quotes
  fix_gpc_magic();
  // Load all enabled modules
  module_load_all();
  // Make sure all stream wrappers are registered.
  file_get_stream_wrappers();

  $test_info = &$GLOBALS['drupal_test_info'];
  if (!empty($test_info['in_child_site'])) {
    // Running inside the simpletest child site, log fatal errors to test
    // specific file directory.
    ini_set('log_errors', 1);
    ini_set('error_log', 'public://error.log');
  }

  // Initialize $_GET['q'] prior to invoking hook_init().
  drupal_path_initialize();

  // Let all modules take action before the menu system handles the request.
  // We do not want this while running update.php.
  if (!defined('MAINTENANCE_MODE') || MAINTENANCE_MODE != 'update') {
    // Prior to invoking hook_init(), initialize the theme (potentially a custom
    // one for this page), so that:
    // - Modules with hook_init() implementations that call theme() or
    //   theme_get_registry() don't initialize the incorrect theme.
    // - The theme can have hook_*_alter() implementations affect page building
    //   (e.g., hook_form_alter(), hook_node_view_alter(), hook_page_alter()),
    //   ahead of when rendering starts.
    menu_set_custom_theme();
    drupal_theme_initialize();
    module_invoke_all('init');
  }
}
```

After assuring that this module has not been called yet, some initialization is done to set up the PHP environment for character and quoting standards, and then all modules are loaded.

When you deploy your Drupal site, the installer program makes a note of all modules that are present for enabling and then gives you an opportunity to enable them. I cover the installation process in Chapter 4 and the deployment process in Chapter 10.

When a module is enabled and installed, the initializing subsystem walks through all code looking for certain specially named functions called "hooks" that may be present. If Drupal finds what it is looking for, it makes note of the function and the module in a registry. This registry is then interrogated whenever a program needs to use one of these special functions.

This, in brief, is how Drupal's hook mechanism works. In .NET, you can use the event manager to indicate that a particular method is to be invoked when a certain event is generated. The Drupal hook mechanism performs pretty much the same functionality, and it does so by using some optimized functions, the first of which we see here, module_load_all(),shown in Listing 2–11.

Listing 2–11. The Module-Loading Function

```
function module_load_all($bootstrap = FALSE) {
  static $has_run = FALSE;

  if (isset($bootstrap)) {
    foreach (module_list(TRUE, $bootstrap) as $module) {
      drupal_load('module', $module);
    }
    // $has_run will be TRUE if $bootstrap is FALSE.
    $has_run = !$bootstrap;
  }
  return $has_run;
}
```

The module-loading function first gets a list of all modules that are in the registry and are enabled. As I write this and watch the process in the debugger, I see 26 modules that are ready. The function loads each module, which simply means that it does a PHP include_once call to put them in memory. By putting all the modules in memory, it becomes possible to invoke functions that have been registered for certain events.

And that's exactly this function does. The module_invoke_all() function is shown in Listing 2–12.

Listing 2–12. The module_invoke_all()Function

```
function module_invoke_all() {
  $args = func_get_args();
  $hook = $args[0];
  unset($args[0]);
  $return = array();
  foreach (module_implements($hook) as $module) {
    $function = $module . '_' . $hook;
    if (function_exists($function)) {
      $result = call_user_func_array($function, $args);
      if (isset($result) && is_array($result)) {
        $return = array_merge_recursive($return, $result);
      }
      elseif (isset($result)) {
        $return[] = $result;
      }
    }
  }

  return $return;
}
```

This function is the core of Drupal's hook system. The module_implements() function interrogates the registry for a list of all modules that contain a function that implements a particular hook. In this case, we are looking only for modules that implement the init hook. I will cover how hooks are written a little later, but for now you can see that it is appending the name of the hook (in this case, init), to the name of the module and seeing if that exists.

Let's take a look at one of these modules as an example. The tablesort module is one of the modules included in the Drupal core. Its job is to aid in the creation of sortable tables. The author of the module felt certain things should be done during the initialization of the page so he wrote an init hook, which is shown in Listing 2–13.

Listing 2–13. A Typical init Hook

```
function tablesort_init($header) {
  $ts = tablesort_get_order($header);
  $ts['sort'] = tablesort_get_sort($header);
  $ts['query'] = tablesort_get_query_parameters();
  return $ts;
}
```

This function simply needs to get certain information from the query string that indicates the current sort parameters, if any. As part of the page bootstrapping process, the tablesort_init() function is eventually found and executed.

And that's it for the bootstrapping process. At this point, the system is primed for dealing with the particular page that needs to be delivered. The database has been opened, the variables loaded, the modules are ready for duty, and all who needed to weigh in on the initialization process have had their say. Now it's time to deliver the page requested.

Menu Handler

After bootstrapping, the menu_execute_active_handler() function, shown in Listing 2–14, is called.

Listing 2–14. The Menu Handler Determines the Page to Be Delivered

```
function menu_execute_active_handler($path = NULL, $deliver = TRUE) {
  // Check if site is offline.
  $page_callback_result = _menu_site_is_offline() ? MENU_SITE_OFFLINE : MENU_SITE_ONLINE;

  // Allow other modules to change the site status
  $read_only_path = !empty($path) ? $path : $_GET['q'];
  drupal_alter('menu_site_status', $page_callback_result, $read_only_path);

  // Only continue if the site status is not set.
  if ($page_callback_result == MENU_SITE_ONLINE) {
    // Rebuild if we know it's needed
    if (variable_get('menu_rebuild_needed', FALSE)
        || !variable_get('menu_masks', array())) {
      menu_rebuild();
    }
    if ($router_item = menu_get_item($path)) {
      if ($router_item['access']) {
        if ($router_item['include_file']) {
          require_once DRUPAL_ROOT . '/' . $router_item['include_file'];
        }
        $page_callback_result =
          call_user_func_array($router_item['page_callback'],
            $router_item['page_arguments']);
      }
      else {
        $page_callback_result = MENU_ACCESS_DENIED;
      }
    }
    else {
      $page_callback_result = MENU_NOT_FOUND;
    }
  }

  // Deliver the result of the page callback to the browser, or if requested,
  // return it raw, so calling code can do more processing.
```

```
    if ($deliver) {
      $default_delivery_callback = (isset($router_item) && $router_item) ?
        $router_item['delivery_callback'] : NULL;
      drupal_deliver_page($page_callback_result, $default_delivery_callback);
    }
    else {
      return $page_callback_result;
    }
}
```

The function first calls all modules that might need to report that the site should be offline. This is necessary because it is conceivable that a single module could be in such need of attention that the site would be compromised if it is allowed to load.

If no one objects ($page_callback_result == MENU_SITE_ONLINE), the function can start looking for the page content that was requested in the URL. This takes the form of something called a "router item." You can think of a router item as a page, though there is really no physical concept of a page until the Drupal engine cooks the page from lots of ingredients. The router item is the recipe for cooking the page. Router information is stored in the menu_router table and executed by the next few lines of this function. The magic is done by two calls. First, the line:

```
$router_item = menu_get_item($path)
```

loads the content from the database depending on the $path string. This is the primary key of the menu_router table that comprises the router item. Once the raw data is gathered, the lines:

```
$page_callback_result =
    call_user_func_array($router_item['page_callback'],
    $router_item['page_arguments']);
```

call the function with the name of the 'page_callback' key in the router item. For a page that displays a single story, the value of the 'page_callback' key is node_page_view, and the arguments indicate the number of the node in the database and other information the function needs to build its content. The function that is called in that case is shown in Listing 2–15.

Listing 2–15. The Menu Calls Back the node_page_view Function

```
function node_page_view($node) {
    // If there is a menu link to this node, the link becomes the last part
    // of the active trail, and the link name becomes the page title.
    // Thus, we must explicitly set the page title to be the node title.
    drupal_set_title($node->title);
    $uri = entity_uri('node', $node);
    // Set the node path as the canonical URL to prevent duplicate content.
    drupal_add_html_head_link(array(
        'rel' => 'canonical',
        'href' => url($uri['path'], $uri['options'])), TRUE);
    // Set the non-aliased path as a default shortlink.
    drupal_add_html_head_link(array(
        'rel' => 'shortlink',
        'href' => url($uri['path'], array_merge($uri['options'],
        array('alias' => TRUE)))
    ), TRUE);
    return node_show($node);
}
```

The function returns a nice little package with all the information we need to pass off to the theming layer so it can be made into HTML and delivered.

Finally, once Drupal has all of the pieces needed for the page, the menu_execute_active_handler() function calls the drupal_deliver_page() function, which calls the drupal_deliver_html_page() function. The job of this function is to return an HTML string that will form the basis of the page. Each module is given a chance to create HTML by calling the theme() function with its own set of data. This separation of data content and output rendering gives Drupal a lot of power and provides a way to separate tasks between developers and designers.

Theming is such a large topic that I'll cover it in its own chapter, Chapter 7, and then show how to go from a Photoshop mockup to a themed site in Appendix B.

▓ **Caution** The theming layer allows programmers to hook into the page building and perform all kinds of processing. But—the theming layer is meant for theming. That is, the theming layer gives you the power to do whatever kind of processing you want, but with that power comes responsibility, Peter Parker. You should never add content in the theming layer.

Almost done. At this point, drupal_page_footer() is called. The function finalizes the cache by storing the rendered page in the database so that the next time the page is called the caching logic will have it available (if it hasn't changed).

Finally, the module_invoke_all('exit') is called, which gives all modules a chance to react to the finalizing of the page.

At this point, the content is ready, and the HTML has been generated and modified by the theming engine. All that's left is to send the HTML out to the browser. Since the script we've been running is index.php, simply falling out of the code will cause the web server to stream its value out to the calling browser.

Drupal vs. the .NET Page Lifecycle

If you are familiar with the .NET page lifecycle, you can probably see some similarities in how Drupal builds a page. The main difference is that .NET is built around an event model (see Figure 2–2), while Drupal calls hooks looking for something to do. I'll talk in much more depth about the hook model in Chapter 5.

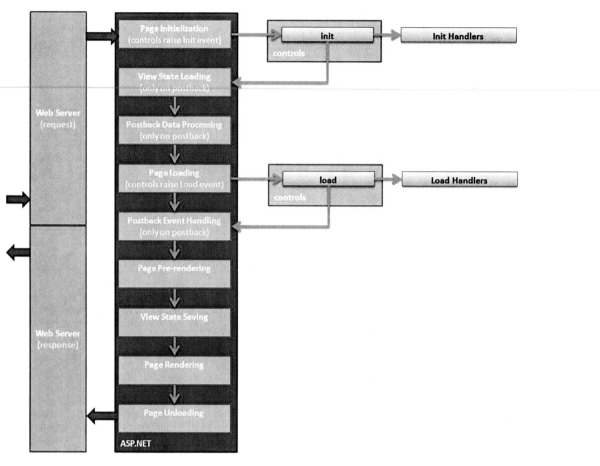

Figure 2–2. The ASP.NET page lifecycle

Let's take a look at the .NET model and see how Drupal compares. The ASP.NET page lifecycle goes through the following stages:

- **Page request:** This stage technically starts before the page lifecycle. One of the main tasks of this stage is to determine if the page needs to be created or if there is a cached version available. In Drupal, these tasks are performed in the DRUPAL_BOOTSTRAP_CONFIGURATION and DRUPAL_BOOTSTRAP_PAGE_CACHE stages.

- **Start:** In the start stage, the Request and Response objects are set. At this stage, the system determines whether the request is a postback from a form or a new request, and sets the IsPostBack property appropriately. It also sets the UICulture property so applications can build the page in the appropriate language. Drupal's DRUPAL_BOOTSTRAP_LANGUAGE stage performs a similar task.

    The following events are raised during this stage:

- **PreInit:** This is the first event you might encounter for your page, but only if you need to set values dynamically from code or if you need to set values such as a master page or theme. You also use this event when you are working with controls that are dynamically created in code. You want to create the controls inside this event. In Drupal, such controls are usually built using the form subsystem.

- **Init:** After each control has been initialized, the init event is fired. You can use this event to change initialization values for controls. The Drupal form_alter() hook provides a way to modify form structures that are created elsewhere.

- **InitComplete:** This event is raised once all initializations of the page and its controls have been completed. At this stage of the page's lifecycle, all declared controls on the page are initialized, but the state of the page is not yet populated. You can access server controls but they will not yet contain information returned from the user. There really isn't a Drupal corollary for this event as it would be somewhat redundant.

- **Initialization:** During page initialization, controls on the page are available and each control's unique ID property is set. If there is a master page, it is applied at this point, and themes are also applied if applicable. If the current request is a postback, the postback data has not yet been loaded and control property values have not been restored to the values from view state.

  In Drupal, the template files, including html.tpl.php and page.tpl.php, perform similar functions as ASP.NET's master page. In Drupal, theming is done after the entire page has been built.

- **Load:** During load, if the current request is a postback, control properties are loaded with information recovered from view state and control state.

  The following events are raised during this stage:

  - **PreLoad:** This event fires before view state has been loaded for the page and its controls and before postback processing. Because of the difference in architecture, there is really no equivalent to this event in Drupal.

  - **Load:** By the time the load event fires, the page is stable, it has been initialized, and its state has been reconstructed. Code inside this event will usually check to see if the request is a postback and set control properties appropriately. The page's load event is called first. Then, the load event for each child control is called in turn (and their child controls, if any).

    In Drupal, the invoke_all() function is used for this purpose

- **Postback event handling:** If the request is a postback, control event handlers are called. After that, the Validate method of all validator controls is called, which sets the IsValid property of individual validator controls and of the page. ASP.NET then calls any events on the page or its controls that caused the postback to occur, such as a button's click event.

  When a form is submitted in Drupal, the validate hook is first called. This provides an opportunity to assure that all information is within program boundaries before continuing. The code in this hook is analogous to the code inside of an ASP.NET Validate event.

  If validation is successful, the submit hook is called. The code in this hook is analogous to the code inside of any ASP.NET control that registered with the Postback event.

- **Rendering:** Before rendering, view state is saved for the page and all controls. During the rendering stage, the page calls the Render method for each control, providing a text writer that writes its output to the OutputStream object of the page's Response property.

  In Drupal, the rendering is much more straightforward. The $output variable is concatenated by any party that wants to send something to the page. This would be equivalent to the ASP.NET OutputStream.Response property.

  In ASP.NET, theming is done by the master pages and, optionally, by skins that can be attached thereto. In Drupal, the theming engine uses templates, including page, block, and node, to drive the styling of the output.

■ **Note** In Drupal, you can create a template for just about any object type or for a specific object itself. In Chapter 7, I discuss these templates, as well as the specific processing Drupal employs to pick one if more than one template is vying for attention in a particular case.

The following events are raised during this stage:

- **LoadComplete, PreRender, and SaveStateComplete:** At this point, all controls are loaded, the ViewState is set, and the page is ready to render. There really isn't a Drupal equivalent to these individual phases.

- **Render:** ASP.NET calls the Render method on each of the page's controls to get its output. The Render method is responsible for generating the client-side HTML and browser scripts that are necessary to display page contents in the browser.

- In Drupal, this task is performed by the appropriately named drupal_deliver_html_page() function, which eventually calls the theme() function to apply the page theme. The theme() function asks every interested party to add its theming information to the stream that is eventually sent to the browser.

- **Unload:** The Unload event is raised after the page has been fully rendered and sent to the client and is ready to be discarded. At this point, page properties such as Response and Request are unloaded and cleanup is performed.

  The following event is raised during this stage:

- **UnLoad:** This event is used for cleanup code. It can be used to release any managed resources from the page.

- In Drupal, The drupal_page_footer() function does pretty much the same thing. There is a global variable, $page_bottom, that collects all of the code needed at the end of the page.

> ■ **Tip** It is important that you print the $page_bottom variable after page processing is complete. There are numerous functions that depend on code that is placed at the bottom of the page.
>
> While we're at it, you also need to put the $page_top variable before page processing is done. If you use the standard HTML template (`html.tpl.php`) this is done for you with these three lines:
>
> ```php
> <?php print $page_top; ?>
> <?php print $page; ?>
> <?php print $page_bottom; ?>
> ```

This is a general overview of the two page models and how they differ, but there's no way that a simple comparison will enable you to transition seamlessly from one model to the other. Rather, it should give you a general idea of how the two systems compare. To understand Drupal, you must understand the hook model and how it is called.

So when you hear "hooks are like events," you'll be able to understand the difference.

Menus

In Drupal, content is tracked by a hierarchical system of menus. The easiest way to think of this is as a tree consisting of elements that the system can represent as pages. For example, there are nodes that are rendered as content, administrative functions that are rendered as lists or forms, and user profiles that can be accessed as content

Out of the box, Drupal provides three methods of accessing the menu tree. First, there's the Navigation menu, which provides a way of getting around the site. The Navigation menu changes itself according to where you are, who you are, and what roles you have been assigned. This menu is highly customizable by Drupal modules and can provide pretty much any level of detailed access to the system for your users.

The User menu contains information that is pertinent to the currently logged-on user (or anonymous user). For example, if the current user is registered on the site as a blogger, the User menu might have a link that would let her create a blog post. Authenticated users would find the logout link in this menu as well.

The Management menu provides links for many administrative tasks and is usually seen only by site administrators.

And then there are two less-dynamic menus: Main and Secondary. These two menus are pretty much the same conceptually. They both provide a way for you to assign common links that make sense for your site. The Main menu and Secondary menu can also, like the Navigation menu, be placed anywhere a Drupal block can be placed. I'll talk more about blocks in Chapter 5.

The difference between the Main and Secondary menus is really more philosophical. I usually use the Main menu to provide navigation to common pages on the site, such as the "About Us" or "Contact" pages, or to things I want the user to be able to see right away, such as major features or popular pages. (See Figure 2–3.)

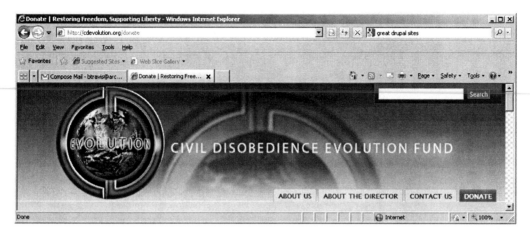

Figure 2–3. Many themes automatically place the Main menu at the top of the page. (source: cdevolution.org)

I usually use the Secondary menu for a list of links to other sites that my visitors might be interested in. It is usually lower on the page or only accessible from some other pages. You can use the two menus any way you see fit or neither one at all. (See Figure 2–4.)

Figure 2–4. You can use the Secondary menu to provide a list of external resources. (source: freestateproject.org)

You can also set the Secondary menu to point to the Main menu's children. This gives you a submenu, so when you are looking at a section of the site (Section A) in the Main menu, the submenu of section A appears as links on the Secondary menu: A1, A2, A3. Some of this is based on the theme, but most core themes support this usage.

Having said all of that, I'll now point out that all of the three menus I just mentioned can really just be thought of as windows into the menu tree mechanism. You can create new menus pretty easily, but you should first become comfortable with the menu tree before you start creating your own menus.

The Menu Tree

As I mentioned, there's really only one actual page in any Drupal site. That page is /index.php. All requests to your site are routed through the bootstrapping functions mentioned above. Following the bootstrapping stages is a function called menu_execute_active_handler(). This is the function that tries to figure out, using the URL, what content the user wants to display, or what processing the site must perform.

Sometimes, the URL indicates that a page is to be shown to the user:

http://drupalforwindows.com/index.php?q=node/42.

This will display the contents of a node that has a "node identifier" of 42. The URL could also indicate that some type of form should be displayed:

http://drupalforwindows.com/index.php?q=node/42/edit.

In this case, the contents of node 42 will be displayed in a form where the title, body, and whatever other fields it contains can be modified. This assumes, of course, that the logged-in user has been granted access to modify the node.

In addition to the URL, you might see a query string:

http://drupalforwindows.com/index.php?q=node/42/edit&destination=admin/content/node.

The query string is the part of the URL that appears after the question mark. In this particular case, the node will be displayed to the user and (assuming the user has been granted access to modify the node) made available for modification. The query string is then used to indicate a destination that Drupal should display after the changes are successfully submitted.

■ **Note** The URLs shown in the previous couple of paragraphs are examples of raw queries processed through Drupal's default index page. From this syntax, it's easy to see that all pages indeed go through index.php. Fortunately, Drupal incorporates the concept of "Clean URLs," which, with the help of your web server's rewrite logic, can transform these queries into more readable strings. This makes your site friendlier to search engines.

So how do you know, by looking at the URL, what Drupal will do? It's up to the various stages of the page-building process that such things are made evident and that the appropriate processing takes place.

In order to start understanding what Drupal will do, you can take a look at the table called menu_router in your site's database. This is the master table where all content is tracked. This table keeps track of menu items and how they are accessed. It also provides hints so the page-building mechanism can determine if the current user has the authority to access the page generated by the current request.

The menu_router table returns a router item array, which is used to invoke the appropriate callback function. At this point, it is up to the callback function to build the page according to the task at hand. The return from this function will either be an integer, which indicates some kind of problem with the page, or a string that contains the HTML that will be passed to the next step, theming.

Theming

Once the page-creation logic has generated the content for the page, it's time to render it for viewing in the browser. This process involves invoking the theming engine, which will perform a series of tasks. First, it figures out what needs to be themed. Since it is the page, everything that is on the page will be themed, one object at a time.

The actual theming process is quite complex as it involves several different technologies, including PHP, HTML, CSS, and, sometimes, JavaScript. It also uses different program source files and styling files for processing different parts of the page.

But don't let that discourage you. Although the theming process is complex, Drupal's designers have made the process pretty simple for the programmer and, ultimately, for the site designer. As a programmer, all you really need to know is that pretty much everything is accomplished with the theme() function. Your designers will need to understand the way your modules use CSS classes and ids.

I've found that, when learning to develop in Drupal, you definitely need to understand the hook model because that's how you tie into the underlying functionality of the whole system. But for theming, lots of themes have already been written. You can just plop one of those into your site and then learn a little bit more each time you need to make a change to the look and feel of the site. In other words, the learning curve is much more drawn out and you can get great results by learning just a little at a time.

You'll find literally hundreds of themes available online for free. The Drupal site has pointers to most of them. There are also aggregator sites, like Theme Garden, that give you a real example of what each theme looks like with content. (See Figure 2–5.)

Figure 2–5. *There are hundreds of themes available for the Drupal administrator. (source: themegarden.org)*

I will cover the theming process in Chapter 7, and we will go from Photoshop to final site with a theme in Appendix B.

Summary

In this chapter, I discussed the general lifecycle of a Drupal page and contrasted it with the .NET page lifecycle. As you might guess, there is a lot more going on under the covers, but I hope you now have a general feeling about how pages are created, from URL invocation through database access, and then to theming, and then back to the browser.

When you write Drupal code, you will create carefully named PHP files in a carefully named folder in a certain area of the site's file directory structure. And then you will create functions that are carefully named. The reason for taking all this care is so the Drupal engine can find your code. Unlike .NET or other compiled object-oriented programming environments, Drupal uses the concept of hooks to discover what needs to be executed and when.

Having the properly named function in the properly named file placed in the properly named directory will make your function available to the Drupal engine, but there's one last step before the code can be invoked. You need to enable the module in the admin section of your site.

When we get into the modules in a more in-depth fashion, I'll show you some best practices and ways to make sure you build modules that don't break the page and provide opportunities for maintenance going forward.

In the next chapter, I will cover the two technologies that are critical to understand when building a Drupal site: the PHP programming language and MySQL database engine.

## CHAPTER 3

PHP and MySQL

Drupal is written purely in PHP, an open source, interpreted scripting language. PHP relies on multidimensional arrays for a lot of its processing, and Drupal continues this methodology. PHP has evolved into a serious object-oriented programming language that powers many of the hottest sites on the Internet today.

MySQL is an open source relational database engine that runs pretty efficiently on Linux platforms. Since its humble beginnings, MySQL has evolved into a scalable, robust database platform that's supported in many different operating environments.

This chapter will familiarize you with the basic syntax of PHP and introduce MySQL, with an emphasis on how Drupal uses both technologies, and is aimed at the programmer who already knows one or more computer languages. I will make references to C#, since most Windows programmers have had exposure to C# or some related language at some point in their career.

PHP

PHP is a server-side scripting language for generating HTML. Actually, PHP can also be used as a stand-alone scripting language, but for Drupal, PHP is used as a powerful scripting language to extract information from databases, apply business rules and theming instructions, and eventually create HTML that is sent to a browser.

No one really knows what PHP actually stands for any more. When it was first created, the initials stood for "personal home page." At some point, the name behind the letters was changed to reflect its use beyond web pages. By that time, the term "PHP" had a life of its own, so the developers kept the acronym and made up a recursive definition. So now, if you insist, PHP stands for "PHP: Hypertext Processor." But I guess it's probably safer to just say that PHP stands for PHP.

For the Windows developer familiar with Microsoft tools, it is probably best to think of PHP as an analogue to classic Active Server Pages (ASP). As with ASP, you can mix PHP code with HTML to create your output page.

I suppose you could also think of PHP as similar to ASP.NET except there's no concept of "code behind." That is, all PHP code is clear text, and is normally interpreted on the fly, though there are some pre-compilers that will shorten execution time.

PHP is pretty easy to learn, particularly if you have experience with any language that has a C-like syntax, such as Java or C#. In learning PHP, you'll notice two things pretty quickly:

- PHP is very rich in built-in functions. You'll find a built-in function to do pretty much anything you want.

- PHP in general—and Drupal in particular—make heavy use of arrays. Learn to love them.

I must say I thought I was all finished with interpreted languages, but I've come to enjoy coding in PHP. If you are a C# programmer like me, you may be frustrated at first, but give it a few days and you might end up finding the same comfort.

Just Enough PHP Syntax

This section is not intended for the new programmer. It is also not my intent to make you fluent in all aspects of PHP. It is a very rich language, and even I haven't been all of the way through it. Rather, this section is meant to get you up to speed pretty quickly, to acquaint you with some of the unique features of PHP and show how the syntax might differ from what you already know. The emphasis is on how PHP is used in Drupal.

To learn more about PHP syntax, I recommend downloading one of the syntax manuals from the PHP site, `http://php.net/download-docs.php`. I like the CHM version because it is self-contained and works well on Windows development machines. The web version of the manual at `http://php.net/manual` has the same material, but also includes a lot of user comments, recommendations, examples, and, of course, the predictable rantings. The online version is worth reading if you have a fast connection, if only for the occasional gold nugget you'll get in the comments sections.

Here are the basics of PHP.

Scripting Blocks

PHP scripting blocks are specified using starting and ending tags with the form:

```
<?php
?>
```

Much like ASP, these blocks can be placed anywhere in the file that is executing. Anything that is not inside of a PHP block will be send directly to the browser. This allows you to insert HTML directly, along with PHP scripting blocks that get something from the server:

```
<html>
    <body>
        <p>The current time is: <?php print date("g:i a"); ?></p>
    </body>
</html>
```

■ **Tip** The PHP start block indicator, `<?php`, is required. The end marker, `?>`, is necessary only when you are placing an inline code snippet. If you have a page that contains PHP code, you don't need to insert the end marker. In fact, the end marker is deprecated, particularly in Drupal, because an accidental space after the end marker can cause unpredictable results.

Comments

Inside of a scripting block, comments follow the C/Java conventions:

```php
<?php
/*
Block comments use this form.
*/

// everything to the right of double slashes on a line is considered a comment
```

In Drupal, like in .NET, there are some conventions for generating documentation for your code. Visual Studio's IntelliSense processor makes use of some of these, so you should use them as well.

Drupal uses the Doxygen documentation framework. We'll get to that in a bit.

Types

PHP is a loosely typed language. Variables need not be declared before they are used; a variable that is assigned a value is declared then and there. So,

```php
$bee_count = 10000;
```

is the simplest form of a variable declaration/assignment.

Table 3–1 shows the types available in PHP.

Table 3–1. PHP Types

Type	Description	Values	Notes
Boolean	Indicates a truth value.	TRUE or FALSE	0 is considered FALSE, while any non-zero number (including -1) is TRUE.
Integer	Signed whole number.	32- or 64-bit depending on your OS	PHP will convert overflowed integers to float.
Float	Decimal number.	Depends on platform, but typically ~1.8e308	Can be represented in several different ways, such as 1.234, 1.2e3, 7E-10.
String	A series of characters typically consisting of bytes.	The size of a string is limited only by the available memory.	Double-quoted and single-quoted strings act differently, as I'll discuss later.
Array	A loosely typed collection of related data.	The size of an array is limited only by the available memory.	Array members can be accessed by index or key. You'll find more information about arrays below.

Type	Description	Values	Notes
Object	A fundamental part of PHP's object-oriented programming functionality.	The characteristics of an object are defined by the object itself.	With PHP 5, objects were added to make PHP more competitive with other OOPs like Java and C++.
Resource	A special variable that holds a reference to some external resource.	Can be virtually any resource, such as a database, a Java program, an LDAP table, or an XML document.	Once freed, a resource is removed by the garbage collector.
NULL	A special variable that represents no value.	The only value this object can contain is NULL.	Casting a variable to NULL will remove the variable and unset its value. It is important to note that NULL is different from FALSE, which is a value.

Type conversion is done automatically by the PHP engine when a conversion is required. For example, a number can usually be accessed as a string without a lot of trouble. And a string can be treated as a number if it looks like a number.

There are some simple rules for variable names:

- A variable name must start with a letter or an underscore "_".

- A variable name can only contain alphanumeric characters and underscores (a-z, A-Z, 0-9, and _).

- A variable name can't contain spaces. If a variable name is more than one word, Drupal conventions dictate that it should be separated with an underscore ($my_string).

The scope of a variable is generally within the context in which it is defined. So it is possible that the same variable name will point to two different variables.

The global keyword provides a way to access globally defined variables that would otherwise not be visible. For example:

```php
<?php
$g = 42;

function return_g() {
  // undefined variable $g
  return $g;
}
?>
<p>The value of $g is: <?php print return_g();?></p>
```

The function return_g() will not produce any output because $g is not defined within the context of the function. If we define $g with the global keyword, however, it does pull the variable into the function:

```php
<?php
$g = 42;

function return_g() {
  global $g;
  return $g;
}
?>
<p>The value of $g is: <?php print return_g();?></p>
```

The second way to access global variables is by using the $GLOBALS array.

```php
<?php
$g = 42;

function return_g() {
  return $GLOBALS['g'];
}
?>
<p>The value of $g is: <?php print return_g();?></p>
```

The reason the $GLOBALS variable is significant is that it lets you access any of the myriad global variables that are available at a given time. Drupal makes extensive use of this, for example, to access global variables having to do with the state of the current page-request conditions:

```php
return $GLOBALS['base_url'] .'/'.
       file_directory_path() .'/'.
       str_replace('\\', '/', $path);
$variables['language']->dir      = $GLOBALS['language']->direction ? 'rtl' : 'ltr';
$account = $GLOBALS['user'];
```

And then there are the "superglobal" variables, which mostly have to do with the state of the parser or web server. Superglobals don't need the global keyword:

```php
$base_url = $base_root .= '://'. $_SERVER['HTTP_HOST'];
$query = drupal_query_string_encode($_GET, array('q'));
$form_state = $_SESSION['batch_form_state'];
```

The superglobals are:

- $GLOBALS: An associative array containing references to all variables that are currently defined in the global scope of the script. The variable names are the keys of the array.

- $_SERVER: An array containing information such as headers, paths, and script locations. The entries in this array are created by the web server. There is no guarantee that every web server will provide any of these; servers may omit some, or provide others not listed here.

- $_GET: An associative array of variables passed to the current script via the URL parameters.

- $_POST: An associative array of variables passed to the current script via the HTTP POST method.

- $_FILES: An associative array of items uploaded to the current script via the HTTP POST method.

- $_REQUEST: An associative array that by default contains the contents of $_GET, $_POST, and $_COOKIE.

- $_SESSION: An associative array containing session variables available to the current script.

- $_ENV: An associative array of variables passed to the current script via the environment method. These variables are imported into PHP's global namespace from the environment in which the PHP parser is running. Many are provided by the shell in which PHP is running, and as different systems are likely running different kinds of shells, a definitive list is impossible.

- $_COOKIE: An associative array of variables passed to the current script via HTTP cookies.

- $php_errormsg: A variable containing the text of the most recent error message generated by PHP. This variable is available only within the scope in which the error occurred, and only if the track_errors configuration option is turned on (it defaults to off).

- $HTTP_RAW_POST_DATA: Raw POST data.

- $http_response_header: HTTP response headers.

- $argc: The number of arguments passed to a script. Contains the number of arguments passed to the current script when run from the command line. Note that the script's filename is always passed as an argument to the script, so the minimum value of $argc is 1. Since Drupal is a web-based system, this variable is not used.

- $argv: An array of arguments passed to script. Contains an array of all the arguments passed to the script when run from the command line. Note that the first argument is always the current script's filename, so $argv[0] is the script's name. Since Drupal is a web-based system, this variable is not used.

■ **Note** A Drupal global variable can often provide the information you're looking for. It is always better to use the Drupal-managed global variable than the PHP-supplied variable. For example, using the Drupal-managed variable allows other modules to modify it before you get it, which may keep you from doing a lot of work. Plus, it's the polite thing to do. Drupal's global variables can be found in global.inc, and are documented at http://api.drupal.org/api/drupal/developer--globals.php/7, and explained in Appendix C.

Strings

Strings in PHP are straightforward. Like any other variable, a string can be declared and assigned at the same time:

```
$winning_name = 'Spaceship One';
```

PHP has a string concatenation operator, which is a period:

```
$full_name = $first_name . ' ' . $last_name;
```

You can use single quotes or double quotes to delimit strings. If you want to use a literal quote inside of your string, it must be escaped with a backslash:

```
$warning = 'If you kids don\'t stop yelling, I\'m coming back there!';
```

By single-quoting a string ('), everything in the string (except escaped characters) is a literal. But if you use double quotes ("), the PHP engine will parse the string looking for variables:

```
$address = '123 Elm St';
print "I live at $address.";
```

You can also put the variable in curly braces if the string requires close concatenation:

```
$insect_type = 'bee';
$insect_qty = 25;
print "I caught $insect_qty {$insect_type}s yesterday!";
```

If you use the curly-brace method, your string must be delimited in double quotes. Another form of string variable in PHP is called "heredoc." It is usually used for multiple-line string values. I use it a lot when creating complex SQL query strings. A heredoc-formatted string is in the form:

```
$str = <<<EOS
Haikus are easy.
But sometimes they don't make sense.
Refrigerator.
EOS;
```

The text following the three angle brackets is the delimiter. As soon as the PHP string parser sees the same text, the string ends. Heredoc strings act like double-quoted strings, and so variable substitution is done:

```
$which_name = 'Reginald';
$query = <<<Query
SELECT title
    FROM report
    WHERE name = '$which_name'
    ORDER BY title
Query;
```

Drupal does not make very extensive use of heredoc-formatted strings, but they are available if you need them. The SQL query example shown here is an acceptable way to create queries in Drupal, but is becoming more and more deprecated as the Drupal core and contributed modules move towards the data abstraction layer. I cover this extensively in Chapter 9.

PHP has a wide range of string processing functions, such as strlen(), and strpos(), as well as functions for doing Perl-style regular expression processing.

■ **Tip** PHP is not Unicode-aware. There are, however, plenty of Unicode-friendly string-processing functions in Drupal. They are defined in unicode.inc and documented at http://api.drupal.org/api/drupal/includes--unicode.inc/7.

Operators

PHP has a pretty standard set of operators, which are similar to those in C or Java. One thing you might find new, however, is the concatenation assignment operator. It works just like any other assignment operator, however, so the following are equivalent:

```
$string = $string . ', and that\'s what she said';
$string .= ', and that\'s what she said';
```

PHP provides bitwise operators that can also assign. Many of these are used in the Drupal core (see Table 3–2).

Table 3–2. Bitwise Operators

Assignment Operator	Example
Bitwise And	$a &= $b
Bitwise Or	$a |= $b
Bitwise Xor	$a ^= $b
Left shift	$a <<= $b
Right shift	$a >>= $b

In addition to comparison operators (==, !=, etc.), PHP also has an "identical" operator that indicates that two objects have the same type. Therefore, $a === $b is true if $a and $b are equal, and of the same object type. This is used in Drupal to test if something is really TRUE or FALSE, instead of the integers 1 or 0. For example, the destination member of the file object contains either the path to the file or a FALSE, indicating that it was not set. The test, if ($file->destination == FALSE), would pass if the destination was set and its value was a literal string '0'. Instead, use the type test to differentiate between '0' and FALSE: if ($file->destination === FALSE).

Conditional Statements

PHP has the expected set of conditional statements, namely if and switch. The syntax is similar to many other languages:

```
if (knock_at_door()) {
  answer_door();
}
else {
  sit_on_couch();
}
```

Drupal conventions suggest that braces always be used, even if they are not necessary. In the example above, braces are not required because there is only one statement in each block. But braces make the code more robust because someone might add statements without remembering to also add braces.

The switch statement is also similar to those in other languages:

```
switch ($number) {
  case 0:
    print 'You typed zero.';
    break;
  case 1:
  case 9:
    print 'number is a perfect square.';
    break;
  case 2:
    print 'number is an even number.';
  case 3:
  case 5:
  case 7:
    print 'number is a prime number.';
    break;
  case 4:
    print 'number is a perfect square.';
  case 6:
  case 8:
    print 'number is an even number.';
    break;
  default:
    print 'Only single-digit numbers are allowed.';
    break;
}
```

The label following the case statement must be a static value, not a variable or a function. However, you can do some evaluation based on the variable in the switch statement. Consider the following:

```
switch ($month) {
  case 'Jan':
  case 'Feb':
  case 'Mar':
    $quarter = "Q1";
    break;
  case 'Apr':
  case 'May':
  case 'Jun':
    $quarter = "Q2";
    break;
  case 'Jul':
  case 'Aug':
  case 'Sep':
    $quarter = "Q3";
    break;
  case 'Oct':
  case 'Nov':
  case 'Dec':
    $quarter = "Q4";
    break;
}
```

Changing the way the cases are evaluated actually runs more efficiently:

```
switch ($month) {
  case ($month=='Jan' || $month=='Feb' || $month=='Mar'):
    $quarter = "Q1";
    break;
  case ($month=='Apr' || $month=='May' || $month=='Jun'):
    $quarter = "Q2";
```

```
      break;
    case ($month=='Jul' || $month=='Aug' || $month=='Sep'):
      $quarter = "Q3";
      break;
    case ($month=='Oct' || $month=='Nov' || $month=='Dec'):
      $quarter = "Q4";
       break;
}
```

This feature allows you do to things that aren't as enumerated:

```
switch ($hour) {
  case ($hour < 12):
    print: 'am';
    break;
  case ($hour < 24):
    print: 'pm';
    break;
  default:
    print: 'fail';
    break;
}
```

■ **Note** If you are accustomed to the way C# handles case statement fall-through, you should be aware that PHP handles this condition the same way C and C++ do, which is different from the way C# handles things.

In C#, the code will only fall through from one case to the next when there is no code between the cases. If you have code in a case, you need either a break or a goto or the compiler will issue an error.

In PHP, if you don't put a break in each case, you'll fall through to the next case statement and your compiler will not complain. While I prefer this old-style method (I never got used to the C# way of doing things), you could set yourself up for some unintended consequences.

Objects

Version 5 of PHP brought a rewritten and pretty nearly full implementation of an object model. PHP objects should be familiar to anyone who has worked in other object-based languages, like Java or C#.
     Classes are declared using the class keyword. Inside, methods and properties are declared as functions and variables, as shown in Listing 3–1.

Listing 3–1. PHP Classes Are Declared Using the class Keyword

```php
<?php

class NewClass
{
  // property declaration
  public $var = 'some default value';

  // method declaration
  public function showProperty() {
    return $this->var;
  }
}
```

Properties are accessed using the -> accessor. This is analogous to the "dot" accessor used by C#.

```
$myClass = new NewClass();
print 'property: ' . $myClass->var;
$myClass->var = 'changed value';
print '<br>method: ' . $myClass->showProperty();
```

This will print:

```
property: some default value
method: changed value
```

PHP classes also have the usual characteristics of modern object-oriented languages:

- Public, private, and protected visibility of methods and properties

- Static methods and properties

- Class constants

- Constructors and destructors

- Inheritance

- Class abstraction

- Object interfaces

And there are other features that make PHP objects pretty powerful. But PHP also has something odd—what it calls "overloading" is not what overloading means in most other object-oriented languages.

There's nothing to keep you, the module developer, from using classes in this way. PHP classes provide a handy, powerful way to deal with the logic of your application. You should know, though, that using classes in this way might make your module less than maintainable by members of the Drupal community.

The Drupal core, and many contributed modules, use classes, but not in this formal, declarative way. Rather, classes are created on the fly using the stdClass object.

Take, for example, the $user variable. This object contains information about the currently logged-in user. If there's no one logged in, then it contains default, anonymous, properties. See Listing 3–2.

Listing 3–2. Classes Are Created on the Fly and Properties Set and Returned to the Caller

```
function drupal_anonymous_user($session = '') {
  $user = new stdClass();
  $user->uid = 0;
  $user->hostname = ip_address();
  $user->roles = array();
  $user->roles[DRUPAL_ANONYMOUS_RID] = 'anonymous user';
  $user->session = $session;
  $user->cache = 0;
  return $user;
}
```

You can then access these properties from your module:

```
$user = drupal_anonymous_user();
print $user->hostname;
```

Drupal 7 is the first version that uses classes extensively in the core. The main driver here is the new Simpletest module. Prior to version 7of Drupal, Simpletest was a contributed module. With the desire to be more test-centered, the head Drupal developers decided to include Simpletest in the core. I talk about test-driven development in Chapter 8.

To create tests, you must create a class that extends the `DrupalWebTestCase` class. Since tests are required for core modules and expected for contributed modules, I expect to see more use of classes in contributed modules as more are developed for Drupal 7.

Arrays

As I mentioned earlier, there is a heavy emphasis on arrays in Drupal. You will either learn to love arrays, or you will learn to hate Drupal. Arrays are very powerful, so once you understand how they are used, you will probably learn to love them.

PHP has three different types of arrays:

- *Numeric:* An array with a numeric index.

- *Associative:* An array where each ID key is associated with a value. This is sort of like a `Hashtable` or `Dictionary` object in .NET.

- *Multidimensional:* An array containing one or more arrays.

You can declare a numeric array by simply listing the values in an assignment:

```
$beers = array ('ale', 'lager', 'stout', 'wheat');
```

Or you can assign the values to specific indexes:

```
$beers[0] = 'ale';
$beers[1] = 'lager';
$beers[2] = 'stout';
$beers[] = 'wheat';
```

In this example, both types of assignments result in the same array. Notice that the fourth line omits the number in the brackets. This results in a new item being added to the array with the index being the next available integer, which is 3. In fact, this example could have omitted the numbers in all four lines.

An associative array is an array in which each item has a key associated with the value:

```
$beer_color['ale'] = 'pale';
$beer_color['lager'] = 'extra pale';
$beer_color['stout'] = 'dark';
$beer_color['wheat'] = 'pale';
```

Each key in a given array must be unique, but the values need not be. If you attempt to add an array member with a key that already exists, you will not generate an error. Rather, you will overwrite the value that is already set in that member.

You can use the key association operator, =>, as a syntactical shortcut to create array members and assign them a value at the same time. In the previous example, I could have written the assignments like this:

```
$beer_color = array(
    'ale' => 'pale',
    'lager' => 'extra pale',
    'stout' => 'dark',
    'wheat' => 'pale',
);
```

Each of the examples I've shown so far contain a one-dimensional array. If the value of an array is another array, you've got yourself a multidimensional array. The => key association operator is used, in this case, to create sub-arrays and assign values to them:

```
$beers = array (
  'ale' => array (
    'English Bitter',
    'Pale Ale',
    'Scottish Ale',
  ),
  'lager' => array (
    'American Lager',
    'Pilsner',
    'Marzen',
  ),
  'stout' => array (
    'Sweet Stout',
    'Cream Stout',
  ),
  'wheat' => array (
    'Weizen' => array (
      'Dunkelweizen',
      'Weizenbock',
    ),
    'Berliner Weisse',
    'Wit',
  )
);
```

Notice that multidimensional arrays can be symmetrical or asymmetrical. The values in this array can be accessed by walking down the array tree:

```
print "I believe I'll have a {$beers['ale'][1]}";
```

Prints out, "I believe I'll have a Pale Ale".

Notice that the 'wheat' item has an array that includes 'Weizen'. Notice, also, that 'Weizen' itself is an array. So $beers['wheat']['Weizen'][0] resolves to 'Dunkelweizen'

■ **Note** If an array member is itself an array, you must specify the array accessor of the internal array in order for it to evaluate. For example, printing $beers['wheat']['Weizen'] in the previous example will result in a reference to an object, not the value of the first array member.

PHP has dozens of functions that act on arrays, making it convenient and easy to use this type of variable structure. You'll find functions for sorting, printing, copying, searching, splitting, combining, and for doing other helpful tasks.

If you want to see the structure of an array, use the recursive-print function, print_r. So, print_r ($beers); yields:

```
Array
(
    [ale] => Array
        (
            [0] => English Bitter
            [1] => Pale Ale
            [2] => Scottish Ale
        )

    [lager] => Array
        (
            [0] => American Lager
```

```
            [1] => Pilsner
            [2] => Marzen
        )

    [stout] => Array
        (
            [0] => Sweet Stout
            [1] => Cream Stout
        )

    [wheat] => Array
        (
            [Weizen] => Array
                (
                    [0] => Dunkelweizen
                    [1] => Weizenbock
                )

            [0] => Berliner Weisse
            [1] => Wit
        )
)
```

In Drupal, you'll often see arrays of objects. To access an object in PHP, you use the -> accessor:

```
if ($files[$filename]->status == 0)
$result = isset($variables['node']->tid) ? $variables['node']->tid : 0;
```

It gets more fun when objects inside the array are arrays themselves:

```
$regions = $theme_data[$theme]->info['regions'];
```

This example looks into the $theme_data array and finds the key that matches $theme. It then takes the result and gets the info property (which is an array). Finally, the value of the array member that has a key of 'regions' is returned.

As you can see, PHP arrays provide a lot of flexibility, but you need to be careful that you are using the indexes correctly.

Loops

PHP has four looping constructs:

- while: loops through a block of code while a specified condition is true.

- do...while: loops through a block of code once, and then repeats the loop as long as a specified condition is true.

- for: loops through a block of code a specified number of times.

- foreach: loops through a block of code for each element in an array.

The while and do...while loops iterate through a block of code waiting for a condition to become true. The while loop will first evaluate the condition and then execute the block if it is true:

```
$temperature = 65;
while ($temperature < 71) {
  $temperature = adjust_thermostat(1);
}
```

The do...while loop is guaranteed to execute the block at least once because the condition is evaluated after the block has been executed.

```
$i=1;
do {
  $i++;
  echo "The number is " . $i . "<br />";
}
while ($i <= 5);
```

The for loop will iterate through a block a certain number of times depending upon a condition, which is evaluated each time the structure loops.

```
for ($i = 1; $i < 100; $i += 2) {
  print $i;
}
```

This code will print every odd number between 0 and 100.

The foreach loop is helpful in that it efficiently iterates through an array. This control structure is used extensively in Drupal.

The foreach loop uses the "as" token to assign the value of an item in the array to a new variable. In this case, $beer will contain a different value each time the loop executes.

```
foreach ($beers as $beer) {
  print ("{$beer[0]}\n");
}
```

This will print

```
English Bitter
American Lager
Sweet Stout
Berliner Weisse
```

for the $beer array declared earlier in this chapter.

In C#, the values are reversed and the keyword "in" is used:

```
foreach (int beer in beers)
```

Drupal makes heavy use of a slightly different foreach structure when it comes to keyed arrays. The expanded use takes this form:

```
foreach ($beers as $beerkey => $beervalue) {
  print ("key: {$beerkey}, value: {$beervalue[0]}<br>");
}
```

This will print out both the key and value:

```
key: ale, value: English Bitter
key: lager, value: American Lager
key: stout, value: Sweet Stout
key: wheat, value: Berliner Weisse
```

Functions

A function provides a way of executing common code from other places. This example shows the basic syntax for a function:

```
function get_something () {
  $query = 'SELECT something FROM {somewhere}';
  $result = db_query($query);
  return $result;
}
```

A function is called by name:

```
$record_set = get_something();
```

Like variables, functions are loosely typed. The type of the return value is interpreted when the function is called.

As you might expect, functions can have parameters—or not. PHP functions can even have a variable number of parameters. Parameters are declared in the function declaration:

```
function get_something_else ($search_term) {
  $query = "SELECT something FROM {somewhere} WHERE $search_term";
  $result = db_query($query);
  return $result;
}
```

This function is called by name, passing parameters:

```
$record_set = get_something_else("this = 'that'");
```

To set a default value for an argument, you can assign it in the function declaration:

```
function get_beer($quantity = 6) {
  print "I'll get $quantity beers.";
}
```

You can pass arguments by value, as we have so far, or you can pass by reference, which sends a pointer to the value. This is handy if you want to affect the values of many variables, or if you have a large value and you don't want to pass the whole thing to the function.

```
function twss(&$string) {
  $string .= ' That\'s what she said.';
}
$str = 'There are a lot of crabs on that rock.';
twss($str);
print $str; // now contains the extra sentence.
```

A PHP function can be called with a variable number of arguments. This is used a lot in Drupal and works using the function argument functions:

```
function food_list() {
  $numargs = func_num_args();
  print "Number of foods: $numargs<br>\n";
  if ($numargs >= 2) {
    print 'The second food is: ' . func_get_arg(1) . "<br>\n";
  }
  $arg_list = func_get_args();
  for ($i = 0; $i < $numargs; $i++) {
    print "Food $i is: {$arg_list[$i]}<br>\n";
  }
}

food_list('tomato', 'egg', 'rutabaga', 'pie');
```

Exceptions

PHP has a try...catch block for handling exceptions. Earlier versions of Drupal don't make much use of try...catch, but the maintainers of the core are using it more and more in version 7, and so are the authors of contributed modules. The syntax is the same as in Java or C#:

```
function inverse($x) {
  if (!$x) {
      throw new Exception('Division by zero.', 4321);
  }
  else return 1/$x;
}

try {
  print inverse(5) . "\n ";
  print inverse(0) . "\n ";
} catch (Exception $e) {
  print "Caught exception ({$e->getCode()}): {$e->getMessage()}\n";
}

// Continue execution
print 'Hello World\n';
```

This will output:

```
0.2
Caught exception (4321): Division by zero.
Hello World
```

One thing to note is that PHP does not have a finally block like C# does. As with C#, however, you can create your own exception classes in PHP.

This should get you started with PHP syntax. PHP is a very rich language with plenty of handy features. There's a relatively new object model with PHP 5. Drupal doesn't make very much use of this, but you certainly can in your own modules.

I encourage you to go to the PHP site and check out the language reference if you want to learn more about the details of PHP syntax. Or, you can just dive in to your Drupal site and start to figure things out.

Drupal Coding Conventions

The Drupal developer community provides a set of style conventions for PHP programmers, which is intended to make your code maintainable by others should you want to give it to the community.

The Drupal Coding Standards cover everything from the use of white space and indenting to a suggested use of database calls and source control specifics.

Before starting your programming project, it's a good idea review those standards and develop good habits early. At first, I had trouble with the standards concerning braces. It's different from how Visual Studio handles C# braces by default. Also, the Drupal standards insist on indenting with 2 spaces at a time instead of tabs. I found that by adopting these new standards early, they became second nature pretty quickly.

To get you started, here are the basics:

- Use an indent of two spaces, with no tabs.

- Lines should have no trailing whitespace at the end.

- Files should be formatted with \n as the line ending (the Unix line ending), not \r\n (the Windows line ending).

- All text files should end in a single newline (\n).

- All binary operators (+, -, =, !=, ==, etc.) should have a space before and after the operator, for readability. For example, an assignment should be formatted as $foo = $bar; rather than $foo=$bar;.Unary operators, such as ++, should not have a space between the operator and the variable or number they are operating on.

- Put a space between the (type) and the $variable in a cast: (int) $mynumber.

This keeps the code tight and readable.

I had a bit of trouble with this formatting style, as I was accustomed to Visual Studio's C# defaults. Fortunately, you can customize Visual Studio to deal with the different guidelines. Plus, there are PHP code beautifiers with Drupal's conventions built-in if you insist on sticking with your style.

Control Structures

Control structures use the old Pascal-style braces and indenting.

Control statements should have one space between the control keyword and opening parenthesis, to distinguish them from function calls.

```
if (my_hair == 'on fire') {
  douse_with(water);
}
elseif (is_cold && !windy()) {
  zip_jacket();
}
else {
  print 'keep walking';
}
```

You should always use curly braces, even in situations where they are technically optional.

Function Calls

Here are some simple rules for function calls:

- Functions should be called with no spaces between the function name, the opening parenthesis, and the first parameter.

- Put spaces between commas and each parameter.

- No space between the last parameter, the closing parenthesis, and the semicolon, like so:

```
$var = foo($bar, $baz, $quux);
```

Use one space on either side of an equals sign used to assign the return value of a function to a variable.

In the case of a block of related assignments, more spaces may be inserted to promote readability:

```
$short        = foo($bar);
$long_variable = foo($baz);
```

Function Declarations

Functions should be declared using the following tight form:

```
function funstuff_system($field) {
  $system['description'] = t('This module does random things.');
  return $system[$field];
}
```

Arguments with default values usually go at the end of the argument list.

Always attempt to return a meaningful value from a function if one is appropriate.

Arrays

Arrays should be formatted with a space separating each element (after the comma), and spaces around the => key association operator, if applicable:

```
$some_array = array('hello', 'world', 'foo' => 'bar');
```

Note that if the line declaring an array spans longer than 80 characters (often the case with form and menu declarations), each element should be broken into its own line, and indented one level:

```
$form['title'] = array(
  '#type' => 'textfield',
  '#title' => t('Title'),
  '#size' => 60,
  '#maxlength' => 128,
  '#description' => t('The title of your node.'),
);
```

Note the comma at the end of the last array element. Fortunately, PHP does not flag this as an error like some programming languages do. While it is optional, it helps prevent parsing errors if another element is later placed at the end of the list.

Naming Conventions

- Classes and interfaces should use UpperCamel naming.

- Methods and class properties should use lowerCamel naming.

- Classes should not use underscores in class names unless absolutely necessary to derive inherited class names dynamically.

- Interfaces should always have the suffix "Interface".

- Protected or private properties and methods should not use an underscore prefix.

In addition to these style conventions, there are a number of conventions regarding the use of certain preferred PHP constructs and higher-level calls, such as database access and communication with other Drupal hooks.

- Use try…catch exception handling wherever possible.

- Put a CVS header at the top of each code file.

- Don't use reserved words for database column or table names

- Avoid "`SELECT * FROM ...`". In fact, avoid embedding SQL in your code at all. Instead, use the data abstraction layer. See Chapter 9.

- Use Unicode functions for strings so your code is translatable.

For more information, see the Drupal Coding Standards at `http://drupal.org/coding-standards`.

Doxygen

If you are a .NET programmer, you are probably familiar with Visual Studio's XML Documentation facility. With the careful placement of properly formatted comments, you can create a base document that you can later expand to document your system.

In the Drupal world, this facility is called Doxygen. In order for Doxygen to read comments as documentation directives, you need to observe the careful placement of properly formatted comments.

To document a block of code, the syntax is:

```
/**
 * Documentation here.
 */
```

Doxygen will parse any comments located in such a block. You should use as few Doxygen-specific commands as possible, to keep the source legible.

Any mentions of functions or file names within the documentation will automatically link to the referenced code, so typically no markup need be introduced to produce links.

To document a block of code, you should use the block comments, but add an extra asterisk on the first line as shown in Listing 3–3.

***Listing 3–3.** Block Comments Can Be Used to Generate Documentation Using Doxygen*

```
/**
 * Summary here; one sentence on one line should not exceed 80 chars).
 *
 * A more detailed description goes here.
 *
 * A blank line forms a paragraph. There should be no trailing white-space
 * anywhere.
 *
 * @param $first
 *   "@param" is a Doxygen directive to describe a function parameter. Like some
 *   other directives, it takes a term/summary on the same line and a
 *   description (this text) indented by 2 spaces on the next line. All
 *   descriptive text should wrap at 80 chars, without going over.
 *   Newlines are NOT supported within directives; if a newline would be before
 *   this text, it would be appended to the general description above.
 * @param $second
 *   There should be no newline between multiple directives (of the same type).
 * @param $third
 *   (optional) Boolean whether to do Third. Defaults to FALSE.
 *   Only optional parameters are explicitly stated as such. The description
 *   should clarify the default value if omitted.
 *
 * @return
 *   "@return" is a different Doxygen directive to describe the return value of
 *   a function, if there is any.
 */
function mymodule_foo($first, $second, $third = FALSE) {
}
```

There are many other conventions for adding documentation to your code using comments. See http://drupal.org/node/1354 for more information.

All documentation and comments always form proper sentences and use proper grammar and punctuation.

The full documentation for Doxygen is in the Drupal Coding Standards area.

MySQL

Drupal has a legacy of using MySQL as its database. In Drupal 7, one of the most important innovations is the new data abstraction layer. This more loosely coupled database layer allows for the use of other database engines. I'd prefer to use Microsoft SQL Server but, for now, MySQL is the norm. In Appendix A, I show you how to create a Drupal development environment based on IIS and SQL Server.

MySQL has the ability to store and execute stored procedures, but Drupal, by and large, does not make use of this capability. There's nothing stopping you, as a developer, from using stored procs but, since one of the goals of Drupal development is code sharing, using stored procs will make your code less maintainable by others simply because there is not an ethos of stored procedure use in the Drupal development community.

MySQL vs. SQL Server

If you are a Windows programmer, you probably have experience with Microsoft's SQL Server. If so, you are probably familiar with SQL Server's support for enterprise-level data storage, access, security, and integration. And you've probably heard of this little high school science project called MySQL. It even has a childlike name.

I hope you're sensing my sarcasm, because that's what I originally thought about MySQL: a science fair project created by a bunch of kids that accidentally made it into the mainstream. If so, you're like me, because that's what I thought when I first heard of MySQL. I was confident that Microsoft SQL Server was the best database out there, bar none. It has a long history of enterprise-level applications and, with the exception of that little "Slammer Worm" (http://en.wikipedia.org/wiki/SQL_Slammer) a few years ago that brought down the Internet, it's pretty secure. Well, I guess that was kind or a big problem, but Microsoft says they've fixed it. Actually, I was on the Microsoft campus during the months they were reeling from that bug, and I must say, they did a great job of stopping everything and going over every line of code in SQL Server to tighten things up. And they established guidelines for all programmers to prevent such things from happening in other Microsoft products in the future. Some of those guidelines have now been adopted by many projects, including Drupal.

Back to MySQL.

The more I work with MySQL, particularly the current version 5, the more impressed I am with its features and performance. It is certainly more than enough database for a content management system such as Drupal.

Before version 5, MySQL was criticized for its lack of stored procedures, triggers, and views. None of that mattered in a Drupal environment, though, since Drupal doesn't use those things. Stored procedures, triggers, views, cursors, and a few more things were added in version 5, but SQL Server still has the edge as it's had those features for many versions and they are rock-solid.

SQL Server definitely has the edge in enterprise features such as replication and advanced security; MySQL provides one-way replication and is pretty robust because it persists change data in a binary table. This allows replication even if the server goes down, as long as slave machines have been set up.

SQL Server uses clustering to provide high availability and it has a publish-subscribe replication model to provide two- or multi-way replication. SQL Server also provides a more robust recovery model because of its checkpoint logic. MySQL databases, when using the default MyISAM data structure, are prone to corruption in the event of a sudden power outage. MySQL supports alternative table structures for performance and stability reasons. INNODB is a popular structure for this.

Security is another area where Microsoft has quite an edge. MySQL provides basic security at the table level, but SQL Server has full column-level security. SQL Server has also passed C2 security certification from the NSA (No Such Agency), which means it can be used to spy on people. MySQL hasn't yet been certified and probably won't be until it gets a few more features, like column-level security.

But that's not really a problem in the context of a Drupal installation. Most of the database access in Drupal has to do with with managing content and configuration information on the site, not with enterprise-level secrets.

As for performance related to content management, SQL Server running on a Windows server and MySQL running on a Unix server are probably equivalent. MySQL may have a slight edge, just because it's quite a bit smaller and doesn't have to worry about all of the enterprise-level features I mentioned. When it comes to terabyte-sized databases, SQL Server wins hands down. But that's not usually what we have in a content management environment.

So SQL Server is a better database and we should still look down our noses at MySQL, right? Not really. I'm not ready to rewrite my enterprise applications to use MySQL, but for Drupal, I see little reason not to use MySQL unless you need to run in a SQL Server environment.

Oh, and I saved the best part for last. MySQL is free.

Enterprise Data

If you are a Windows programmer, you've probably worked on systems that access your enterprise data store. There's a good chance that the data is stored in some version of SQL Server. And since it's in an enterprise environment, you probably take advantage of clustering, mirroring, job scheduling, and perhaps analysis and integration services.

It's tempting, then, to think of using your enterprise SQL Servers as the data store for your Drupal system, especially if you're running your Drupal site on your Windows servers.

This might not be a good idea. Your enterprise data is probably sitting behind a DMZ where it is relatively safe from the outside world, while your web servers are probably in a less-secure environment and have less-sensitive information stored in them. Getting data from one side of the DMZ to the other requires some sort of service to communicate across the walls.

Since you will need a separate database for your customer-facing web sites anyway, MySQL makes sense because of its price and efficiency.

But if you want to use SQL Server for your Drupal installations, I'll show you how you can get started in Appendix A.

Summary

PHP and MySQL are critical technologies for understanding Drupal. PHP should feel pretty familiar to anyone who has used most any modern programming language as the syntax is identical or similar in most areas.

MySQL is a surprisingly powerful database, especially considering its genesis and open source status.

Later, in Chapter 9, I will discuss the database layer, which provides an API for accessing data in your deployed system, regardless of the database engine used.

First, though, in Chapter 4, we will go over the specifics of installing and configuring Drupal on your local machine.

CHAPTER 4

■ ■ ■

Drupal Installation and Configuration

All Drupal source code is in standard text format, so you *could* use any text editor to create and edit code. For those with more macho flash than deadlines, this is certainly an option. For the rest of us, there are visual development environments. In this chapter, I cover the steps required to install the Drupal core and the tools you need to add modules and start your own development process.

To get Drupal up and running, you must first pick a hosting environment. This can be either your own server or a shared server environment. Many internet service providers (ISPs) offer Drupal as a standard application, and usually provide a Linux account with FTP and shell access.

If you have your own servers or want to put a Drupal development environment on your workstation or laptop, you'll need to install the Drupal bits yourself.

Drupal consists of a set of modules called "the Drupal Core." The core contains a number of required modules, which are automatically enabled when the service is installed. Plus, there are a number of optional modules that are handy to have, but not needed in all circumstances.

■ **Note** The Drupal maintainers are constantly balancing the goals of making Drupal useful while keeping it simple. There are always discussions about what functionality and which modules should be included in the core distribution. This discussion became somewhat heated as the architecture of the Drupal 7 upgrade was in the works, and it will probably heat up again as the authors of contributed modules try to get their code into the Drupal 8 core.

Some modules included in the Drupal core are not enabled by default, such as the Blog module. Though blogging is common on many sites, it is certainly not universal. For this reason, Blog is included in the core, but not enabled. On the other hand, every site has pages and most have articles, so these are included in the core distribution and they are enabled. You can disable them later if you'd like.

Drupal as a Standard Service

If your service provider offers Drupal as a standard service, it probably also offers to keep the core and common modules updated according to the available releases. That's just one less thing you have to worry about.

On the down side, using an ISP's standard Drupal application usually means you are running Drupal on a machine shared with dozens or hundreds of other users and sites—which could significantly slow response time. Plus, by having your application hosted, it is difficult or impossible to carry out certain performance-tuning tasks.

Drupal Gardens, by Acquia, is an example of an easy-to-use hosted environment. It was probably the first site to use Drupal 7. Acquia has added special modules to make starting a site very easy. It is definitely designed for those who have little or even no experience with Drupal. You can get a site up and running quickly without knowing anything about programming.

On the other hand, Drupal Gardens does not allow you to upload your own modules. This model focuses on users rather than programmers.

If you want to be able to upload your own modules, you'll need to find a hosting service that allows that capability. For an exhaustive list of ISPs that host Drupal, visit http://drupal.org/hosting.

For a hosted application, most of the installation steps are already done. The provider probably has a multi-site Drupal installation running, and the provisioning of your site is just a matter of them running a script to add your domain name to their multi-site installation and adding some directories to your shell account directory structure.

If an ISP offers Drupal as an application, it probably also offers MySQL as a database. A pretty common setup is a single instance of Drupal plus 25 MySQL database instances.

■ **Tip** You can host a number of individual sites with this single instance, each of which can use a single database or a shared database. For simplicity, it is probably best to use one database per site.

There are as many techniques for installing Drupal as there are service providers offering that service. It's best to check with your chosen provider for details.

Installing Drupal for Yourself

If you are doing development, you'll probably want to set up the Drupal core code on your local machine.

The big advantages of doing your own installation are:

- You have complete control over the application.

- Depending on your user authorities, you can tune your setup to optimize performance and response time.

- You can add custom debugging tools, particularly those that interact with the core modules.

Installing your own Drupal application is pretty straightforward. Note, though, that in taking the initiative to install your own you also are responsible for keeping the core and contributed modules up to date. A module that is invoked by your server's scheduling system (usually cron) will tell you when modules need to be updated.

First, you should have the required services installed and ready. This includes:

- **Operating System.** You're probably using Windows. I've tested the entire stack on Windows XP and Windows 7. Otherwise, you can use Macintosh or most Unix or Linux versions.

- **HTTP Server.** This is sometimes called a web server. You could use IIS, but it's easier, at least to get started, to use Apache, an open source HTTP service.

- **Database.** MySQL is the best choice for new users because of its support by the community and in the code itself. In Chapter 9 we will learn about the data abstraction layer, which isolates the programmer from a particular database engine.

- **PHP.** For Drupal 7, you can use PHP version 5.2 or 5.3. Even though PHP 5.3 is a more advanced version with more features, PHP 5.2 remains supported by Drupal 7 because many service providers have not upgraded yet.

Fortunately, you don't need to choose all of these for yourself. I've worked with two different pre-packaged collections of tools, XAMPP and WAMPServer. They both use the same components but have different wrappers to make it easy to install and use. I prefer WampServer simply because it allows an easy change between PHP versions 5.2 and 5.3.

For information about installing WampServer and integrating everything with Visual Studio, see Appendix A.

Next, download the Drupal core bits. A tarball is available from the drupal.org site. For Windows developers, a tarball is basically a compressed library, similar to a ZIP file. In fact, your favorite unzipping tool— 7Zip (a free archiver), WinZip, WinRAR, etc.—will probably recognize the .tar.gz extension and do the right thing. I use Total Commander because of its familiarity and awesome set of features.

Unpack the files wherever you like. I use the WAMP directory structure just to make things easier— C:\wamp\www\drupal7\. It doesn't matter where you put them, as long as you tell Apache where they are.

Apache Configuration

By default, Apache is configured to use C:\wamp\www as its root. If you put your Drupal installation under that directory, you will be able to access it but you'll always have to enter an extra path, i.e., http://localhost/drupal7. Just like in IIS, you can specify your root directory to be anywhere you want.

To do this in Apache, you need to edit the HTTP daemon configuration file, httpd.conf. The easiest way to do this is through the WampServer control panel, as shown in Figure 4–1.

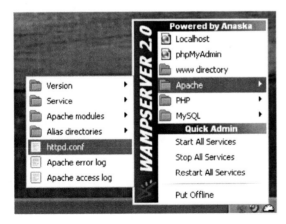

Figure 4–1. WampServer control panel

This will bring up the configuration file in the text editor shown in Figure 4–2. Search for the line that contains DocumentRoot and change it to the directory where Drupal's index.php file is.

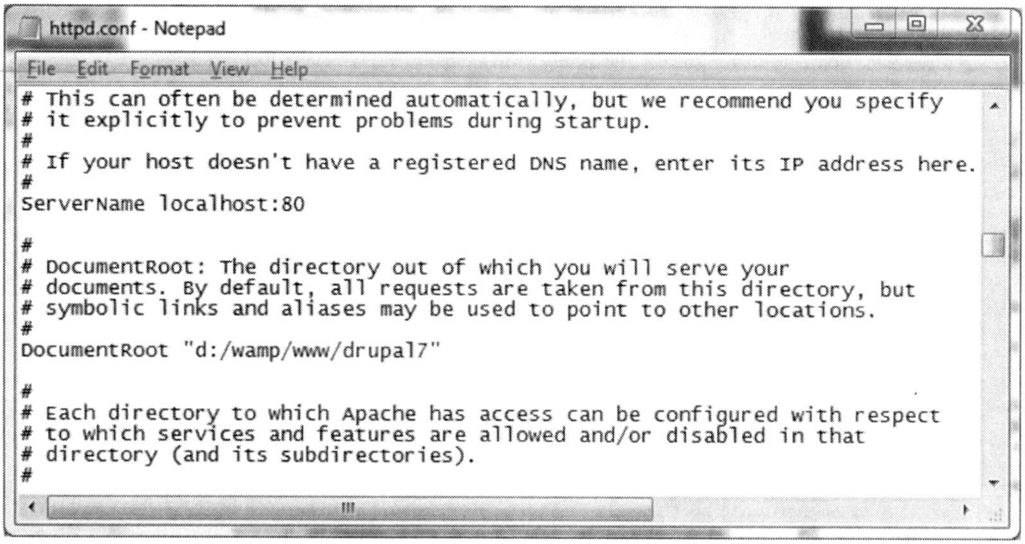

Figure 4–2. Setting the document root

Notice that the configuration file uses forward slashes instead of the standard Windows backslashes. You could probably use either, but I've gotten into the habit of using forward slashes for any piece of software that has a Unix lineage.

Whenever you make a change to Apache's configuration file, you need to restart the service as Apache only reads the configuration file when it starts (see Figure 4–3).

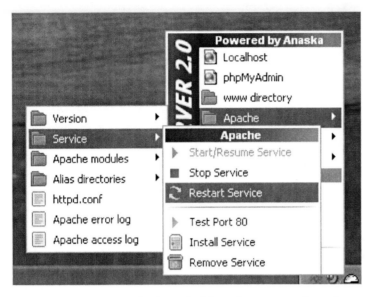

Figure 4–3. Restart Apache from the WampServer control panel.

Make sure the WampServer indicator is white and the needle is pegged to the right. If it isn't, there's a chance that there's something wrong with your path or that you accidentally changed something in the configuration file.

If there's a problem with Apache starting up, you can take a look at the logs. There are actually two logs, the error log, which shows any errors that Apache discovered, and the access log, which indicates the access activity of the server. Both are accessible from the WampServer control panel.

Good luck with these. They are quite voluminous.

■ **Tip** A utility that shows only the last part of a text file (like the `tail` command in Linux) can be helpful in analyzing these logs, especially during debugging.

Database

Before starting Drupal, you'll need to create a MySQL database instance to hold all of the tables. MySQL has a command-line interface you can use to create the database instance, but there's also a web-based interface, which I prefer because I just bought a new mouse. Once you're familiar with the workings of MySQL, you may want to switch to the command-line version so you can script new sites.

From the WampServer icon, select phpMyAdmin from the menu shown in Figure 4–4. That's the web-based interface to MySQL.

Figure 4–4. phpMyAdmin is available from the WampServer control panel.

This will load the application in your default browser. You'll want to create a new database. Give it any name that feels good to you. (See Figure 4–5.)

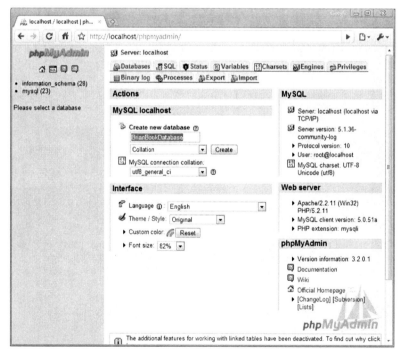

Figure 4–5. Creating a database using phpMyAdmin

You'll see a confirmation screen like the one in Figure 4–6.

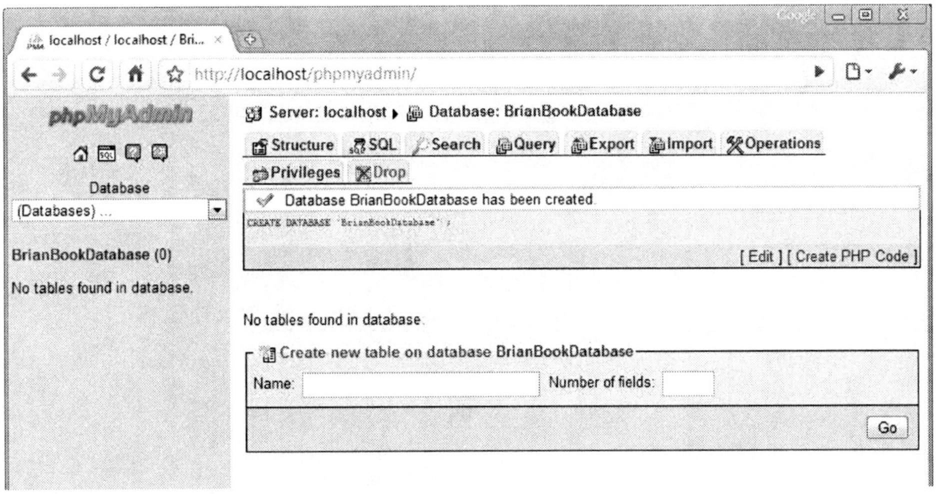

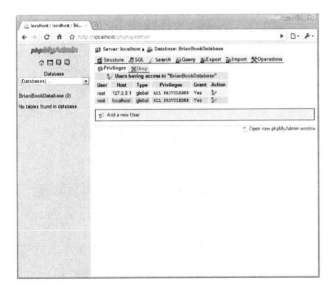

Figure 4–6. Database creation confirmation screen

Now we need to create a user and set some privileges for the new database. Since you are the administrator of this machine, you have root access. Click on "Privileges", and then "Add a new User", as shown in Figure 4–7.

Figure 4–7. New database screen showing user privileges

Create a user name and password. This is the account that will be used by Drupal to access all portions of the database, so we need to grant it all privileges. (See Figure 4–8.)

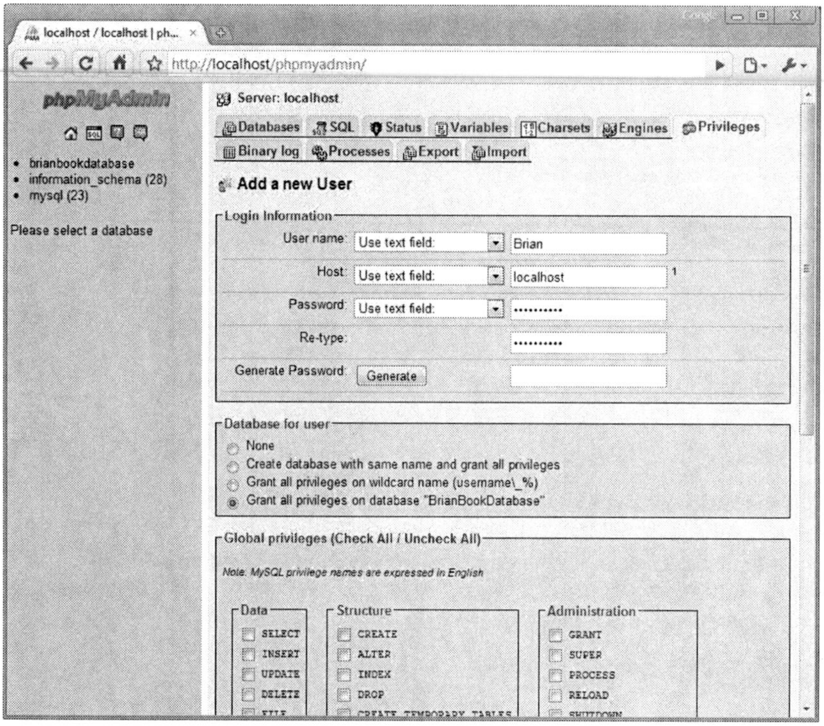

Figure 4–8. Adding a new user to a MySQL database .

You'll see the confirmation shown in Figure 4–9.

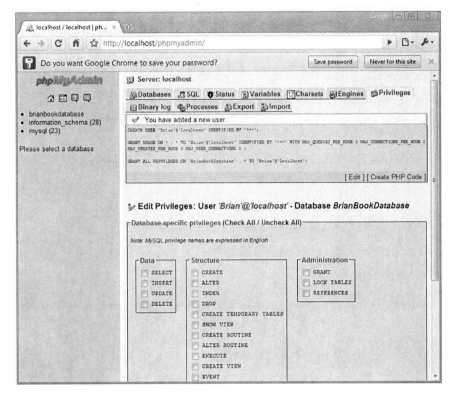

Figure 4–9. New user confirmation screen

That's it for the database. The Drupal installation process will create the tables and populate them with the necessary information for bootstrapping your site.

The last preinstallation step is to create a writeable settings file that the install program will use. When you installed the Drupal core bits, it included a default settings file, default.settings.php. You'll need to make a copy of this. The file is in the directory where you installed Drupal, under sites/default. Copy default.settings.php and give the copy the name settings.php. (See Figure 4–10.)

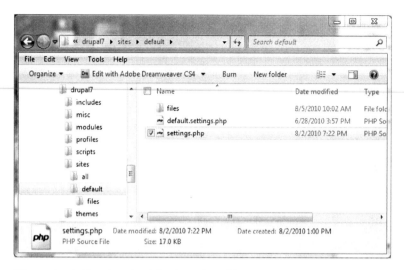

Figure 4–10. Copying the default settings file

Make sure the file is writeable by SYSTEM. Right-click on settings.php and select the Security tab, as shown in Figure 4–11.

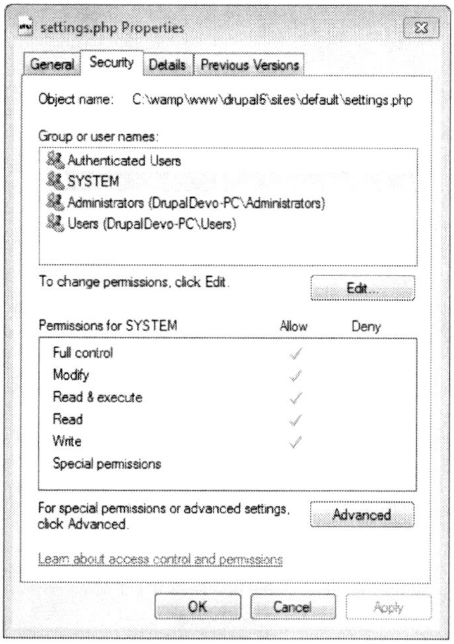

Figure 4–11. Setting permissions on the settings.php file

The next step is to configure the site.

Site Configuration

Once you've created the database and settings.php file, you can open the site using a web browser and have Drupal go through its configuration process.

Load your favorite web browser. I used Google Chrome for this because of its light weight and minimal features.

Make sure the WampServer services are running and then enter http://localhost in the browser address bar. Assuming you have Apache listening on port 80 (the default), this will invoke Apache and load index.php in the server's document directory.

The Drupal core will check the new settings.php file to see if there's a database specified. Since this is a fresh install, that test will fail and you'll be directed to the site configuration page, install.php, shown in Figure 4–12. You can choose whether to load a standard set of features or a minimal set.

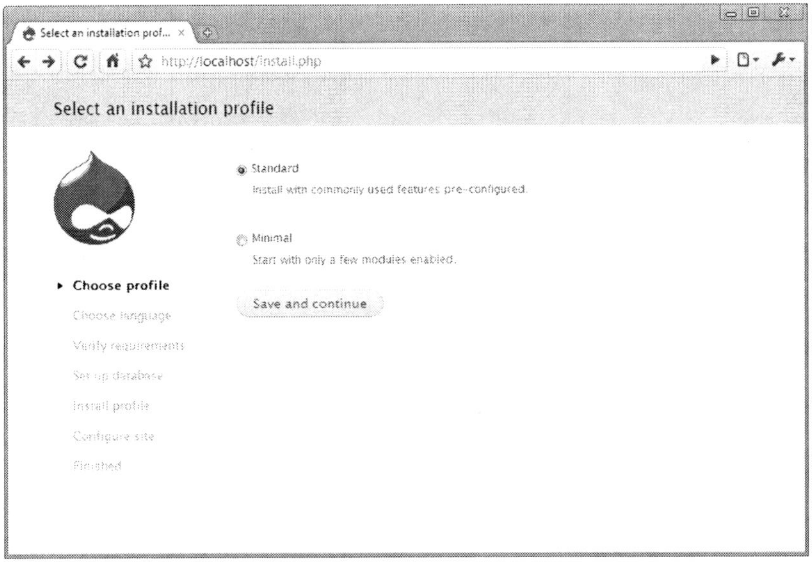

Figure 4–12. Two installation profiles are available with the default Drupal distribution.

The Minimal installation profile enables only the help subsystem, user management, and vital system functions. Standard loads all of the core modules and enables the most common ones.

After clicking "Save and continue", you have the opportunity to install your language of choice (see Figure 4–13).

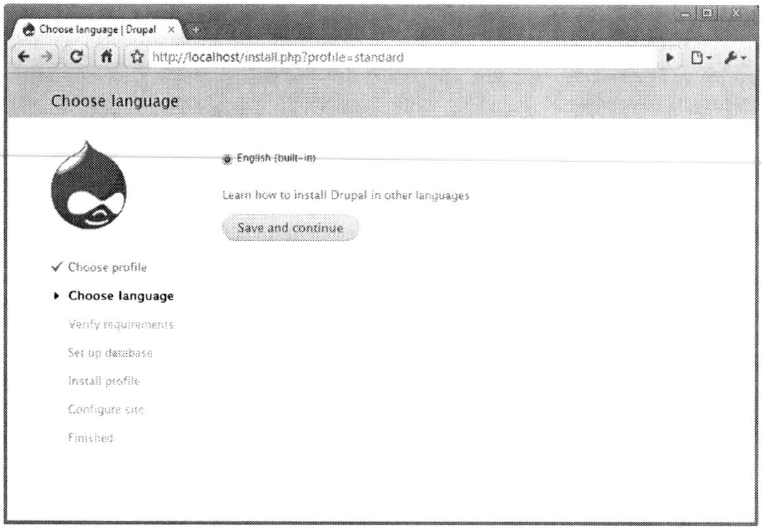

Figure 4–13. *Drupal has been translated into many languages.*

If you want to install Drupal in other languages, *via con dios, amigo*; you're on your own. I've only done this in English. If you need other language support, though, you'll find a great network of people devoted to localizing Drupal. The localization efforts for Drupal are centered on the community site, `http://localize.drupal.org`.

Now it's time to tell Drupal about your database (see Figure 4–14). Here, you insert the name of the database you created earlier, along with the username and password.

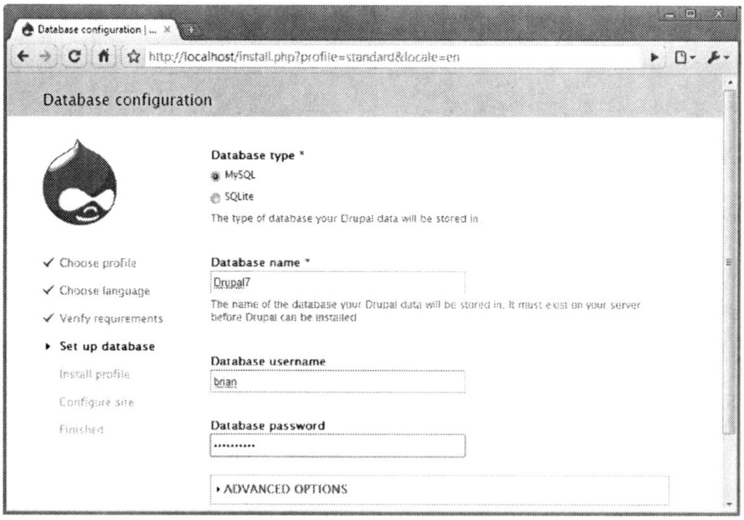

Figure 4–14. *Database name and credentials are specified to bootstrap the database loading.*

You can also specify some options here, including the name of the host if it's not localhost, and a nonstandard port for communicating with the database. There's also a setting that lets you prefix all tables. Ideally, you'll have an entire database instance to yourself for your site. But if you find yourself in a situation where you must share your database instance with other instances of Drupal, you can cause each table to be prefixed with a string so that all sites can live together. Not an optimal situation, but it's nice to know that such a capability exists.

Once the installation program has this information, it will start its work (see Figure 4–15).

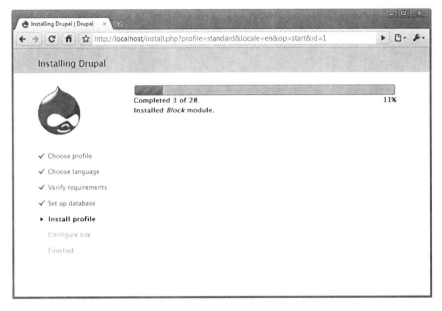

Figure 4–15. The installer will load modules and upate the database.

This process will take a few minutes as the modules are loaded into the database tables and enabled.

When this step finishes, you'll see a screen asking you to enter information about your site (see Figure 4–16).

Figure 4–16. *Adding information about your site, as well as the name and password of the super administrator*

Now you can enter information about your site. The name and password you enter here are for the administrator. There is only one administrator, and that account has access to all aspects of the system. Later, you can create a role called "administrator" or "admin" or "site god," but that will be for just normal users that the real administrator can grant or revoke access to.

Because of the super-administrator access this user has, it's important to remember the name and password and keep it secure. There is a technique for resetting the super-administrator's password, but it requires access to the database root user if you haven't given a valid e-mail address or don't have a mail server wired up to your site.

■ **Tip** If you forget the super administrator's password, you can have the system e-mail you the password—assuming you've set up a proper e-mail address and your SMTP server is running. As a last resort, it is possible to log on to the database and change the password for user 1. This will require salting the password and inserting it into the database. Best not to lose the password.

Once this information is set, click "Save and continue". You'll hear gears grinding and see puffs of smoke coming from the exhaust manifold as Drupal creates the tables. And then you'll see the lovely completion screen, as shown in Figure 4–17.

Figure 4–17. The happy completion screen indicates that the installation was successful.

From here, clicking on "Visit your new site." will take you to your site's default page, which is now quite lonely. (See Figure 4–18.)

Figure 4–18. The front page of a completely empty default site.

Clean URLs

The first thing you'll want to do before we get into debugging is to set up Clean URLs.

By default, Drupal uses general-purpose URLs to display content. All content, regardless of its type, is stored and accessed as a thing called a "node." Each node has a number, which Drupal assigns when the node is created. This is an integer and it increments with each new node of any type.

Because of this architecture, Drupal content is accessed using URLs that contain the node identifier (nid) as part of the query: http://drupalforwindows.com/index.php?q=node/6. This isn't a very friendly way of accessing nodes, especially if you want to publish a URL for a particular page, say http://drupalforwindows.com/catalog or something like that.

Fortunately, Drupal has a way to work with your web server to rewrite friendly URLs like this into Drupal's internal format.

If you are in a hosted environment, your service provider probably already has this feature turned on, but if you loaded WampServer, it is turned off by default.

Open the httpd.conf file from the WampServer control panel as you did earlier. The configuration file will show up in your default text editor, probably Notepad. (See Figure 4–19.)

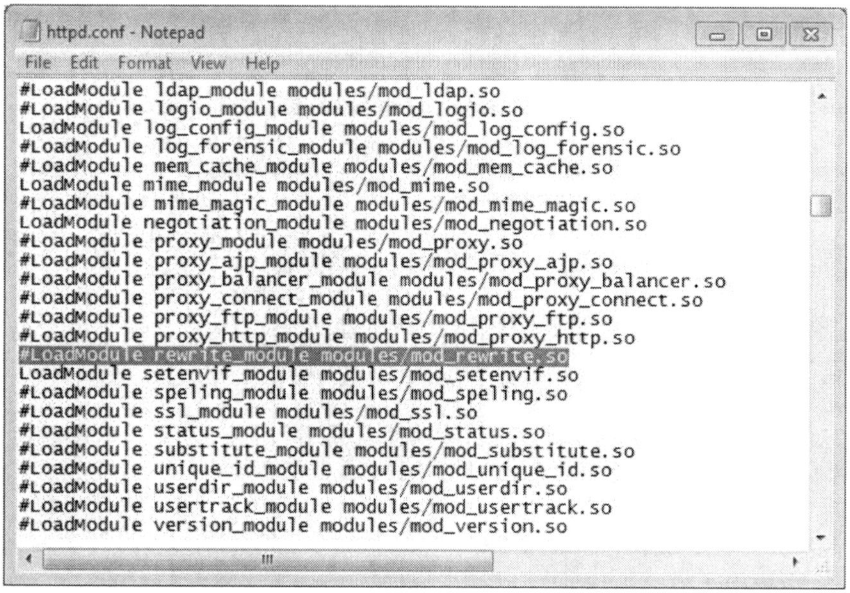

Figure 4–19. Updating the Apache configuration file to enable the rewrite module

Look for the line that loads the rewrite_module. It will probably have a hash in front indicating that it is commented out. Remove the hash, save the file, and restart Apache so it can read the new settings.

Now, go back to your new site and click "administration section," which will take you to the main administration page. Find Clean URLs under "Configuration" and click it. (See Figure 4–20.)

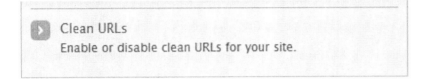

Figure 4–20. Clean URLs are accessed from the Configuration menu

If you have enabled the rewrite module successfully, the "Enable clean URLs" box will be checkable. Check the box and click "Save configuration". You will see the success screen shown in Figure 4–21.

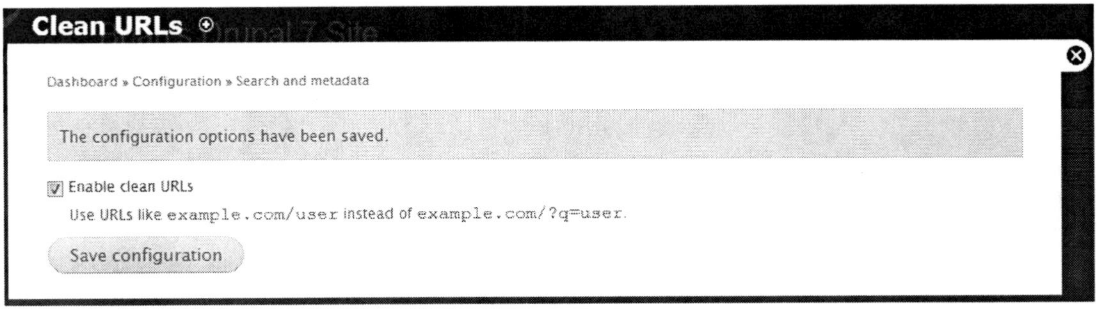

Clean URLs ⊙

Dashboard » Configuration » Search and metadata

The configuration options have been saved.

☑ Enable clean URLs

Use URLs like example.com/user instead of example.com/?q=user.

(Save configuration)

Figure 4–21. Voila! Clean URLs!

Drupal will check to see if the server has been set up to allow clean URLs. If it has, you'll get a green band of goodness and the "Enabled" radio button will be selected. There are some stubborn scenarios in which clean URLs just won't work. For a thread on various places to look, see http://drupal.org/node/128068.

Visual Studio

Now that we've gotten all of the prerequisites, it's time to load the project into our development environment and get to work!

I'm assuming you've loaded Visual Studio and VS.Php. You'll find guidelines for this in Appendix A. For the screenshots that follow, I use Visual Studio 2010 Ultimate and VS.Php 2.9 as described in Appendix A. If you use a different combination of versions, you'll see something slightly different, but it should be similar enough to deal with.

Drupal Project

First, let's load the Drupal core into Visual Studio with a new project. From Visual Studio, select File➤New➤Php Project from Existing Source. You'll see the new project wizard, as shown in Figure 4–22.

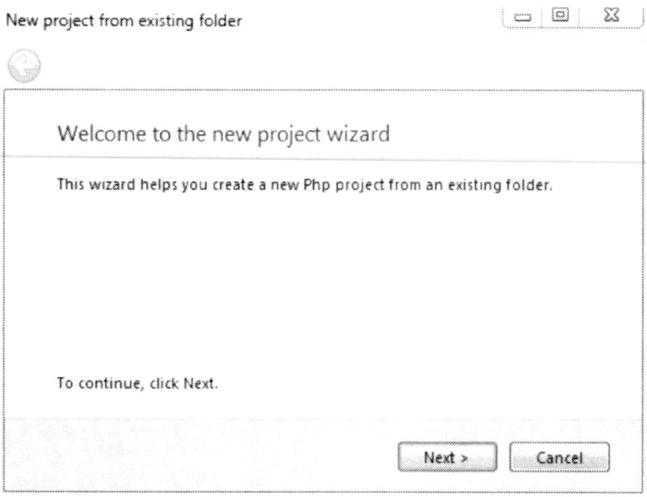

Figure 4–22. VS.Php's New Project Wizard

Clicking "Next" takes you to the screen asking for the location of the existing code. (See Figure 4–23.)

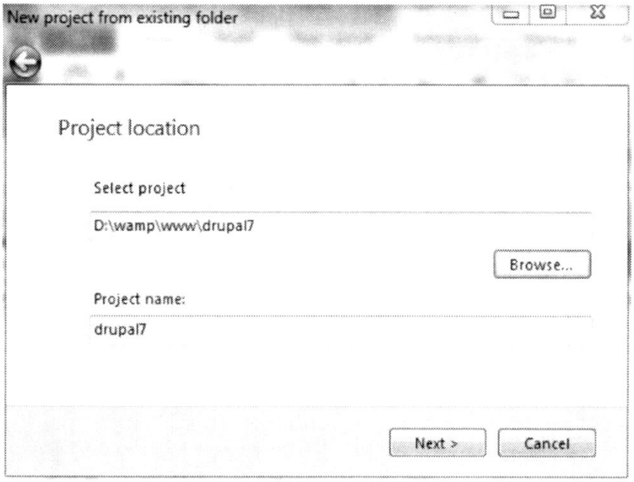

Figure 4–23. Project location screen

This is the directory where you installed the Drupal bits. Notice that this is the same as Apache's DocumentRoot setting. Give the project a name you like and press "Next >". This takes you to the project type screen shown in Figure 4–24.

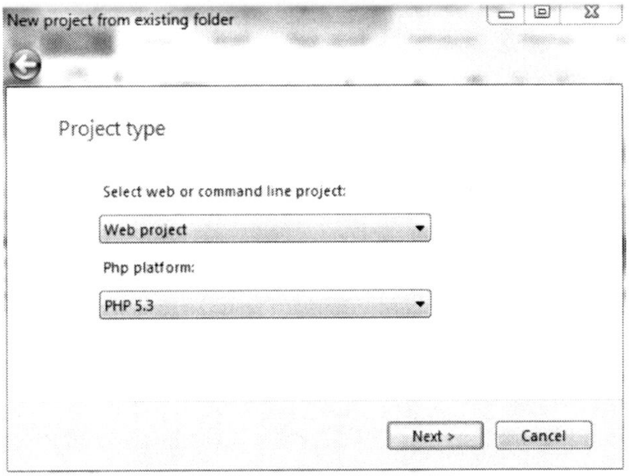

Figure 4–24. VS.Php's Project type screen

Be sure to select Web project so the appropriate tools are incorporated into the development environment. You can select either PHP version 5.2 or 5.3.

The wizard will scan the directory and ask which subdirectories to include in the solution. Since you're in the process of learning Drupal, it's probably best just to include everything for now. This will allow you to step-debug the entire core so you can see how things work. (See Figure 4–25.)

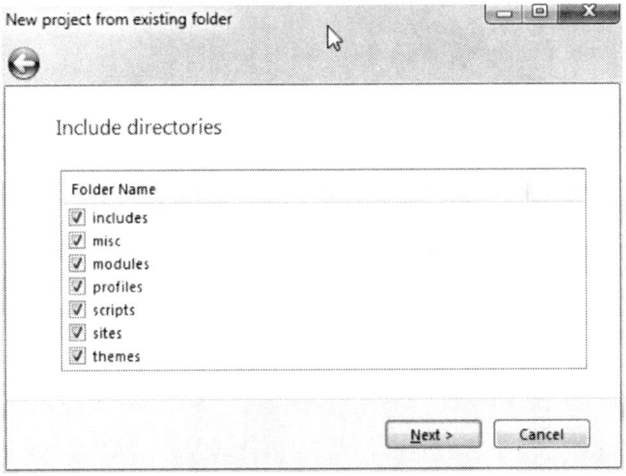

Figure 4–25. Include whatever directories you want to be part of the project.

That's the last step; press "Next >" and then "Finish".

The project will load and you'll see the familiar Visual Studio environment. You are only a couple steps away from starting a debugging session! (See Figure 4–26.)

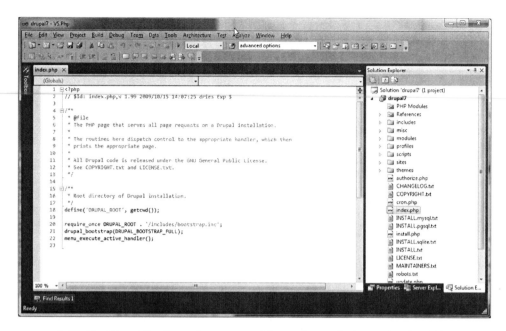

Figure 4-26. *The Visual Studio project screen with your Drupal PHP project loaded*

By default, Visual Studio will use Internet Explorer as the browser for the debugging session. If you'd rather use a different browser, you need to install it and set it as your default browser. Then, in Visual Studio, select Project➤drupal7 Properties and get to the Debug area. (See Figure 4–27.)

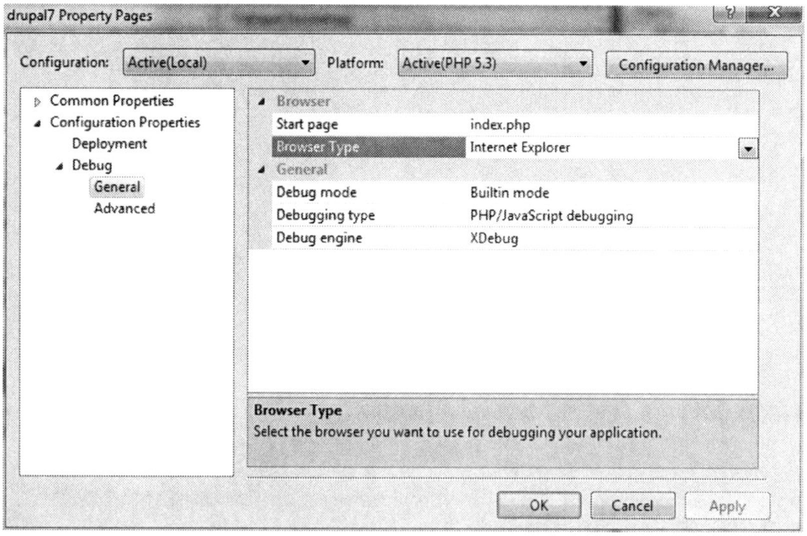

Figure 4-27. *The Visual Studio property pages allow you to set various parameters*

As you might expect, Internet Explorer is slightly more integrated with Visual Studio, but I've used both Google Chrome and Firefox as the default browser and debugging works well.

Debugging

All Drupal calls route through index.php in the document root. This is the jump-off point for all page building. The best way to start learning how the Drupal core works is to put a breakpoint in that file just where the bootstrapping occurs.

So find the line that has the drupal_bootstrap() function call and set a breakpoint using F9. (See Figure 4–28.)

```
20    require_once DRUPAL_ROOT . '/includes/bootstrap.inc';
21    drupal_bootstrap(DRUPAL_BOOTSTRAP_FULL);
22    menu_execute_active_handler();
23
```

Figure 4–28. Setting a breakpoint on Drupal's main page

Now just press F5 to start debugging. Depending on your firewall settings, you might see a notice that VS.Php is trying to access the network, as shown in Figure 4–29.

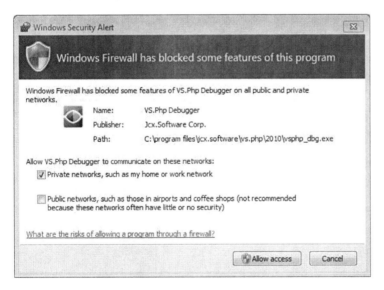

Figure 4–29. Windows firewall alert

Select the options that make you feel comfortable and click "Allow access". If you don't let the program have access to at least your internal network, you won't be able to do any debugging.

Just as it does when debugging ASP.NET, Visual Studio will start an instance of the web server, in this case Apache. Also, as with ASP.NET, it will pick a somewhat random port and fire off the web browser associated with the project. By default, this is Internet Explorer.

As a clarification, recall when we configured our Drupal installation earlier in this chapter. We accessed the site using simply `http://localhost`, which used the Apache installation that came with the WampServer tool. When you enter debugging mode from Visual Studio, the PHP add-in, VS.Php, will invoke its own version of Apache that has extensions for debugging using Zend. (See Figure 4–30.)

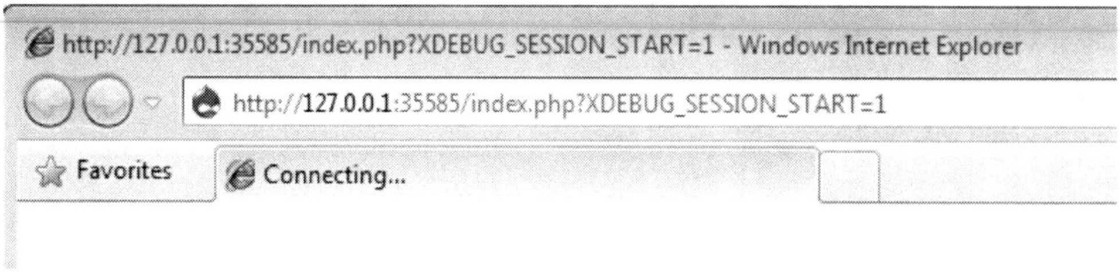

Figure 4–30. Visual Studio spools up a version of Apache on a random port

Visual Studio then attaches to this process so the breakpoints and variable interrogation work inside the tool.

▓ **Tip** If you are using the WampServer version of Apache, you'll access the configuration file, `httpd.conf`, from the WampServer console. However, If you are using VS.Php, the configuration file is at `C:\Program Files\Jcx.Software\VS.Php\2010\httpd-template.conf`. This is copied and a modified version is instantiated whenever a new instance of Apache is fired off from Visual Studio.

In addition, VS.Php also has its own copy of PHP, the configuration file for which is at `C:\Program Files\Jcx.Software\VS.Php\2010\Php 5.2\php.ini`. VS.Php does use the MySQL installation from WampServer, however.

Now that that's out of the way, let's start exploring the Drupal core with the Visual Studio debugger. By this time, the breakpoint you set above has been hit, and Visual Studio is waiting for you to do something. Pressing F11 will step into the `drupal_bootstrap()` function. (See Figure 4–31.)

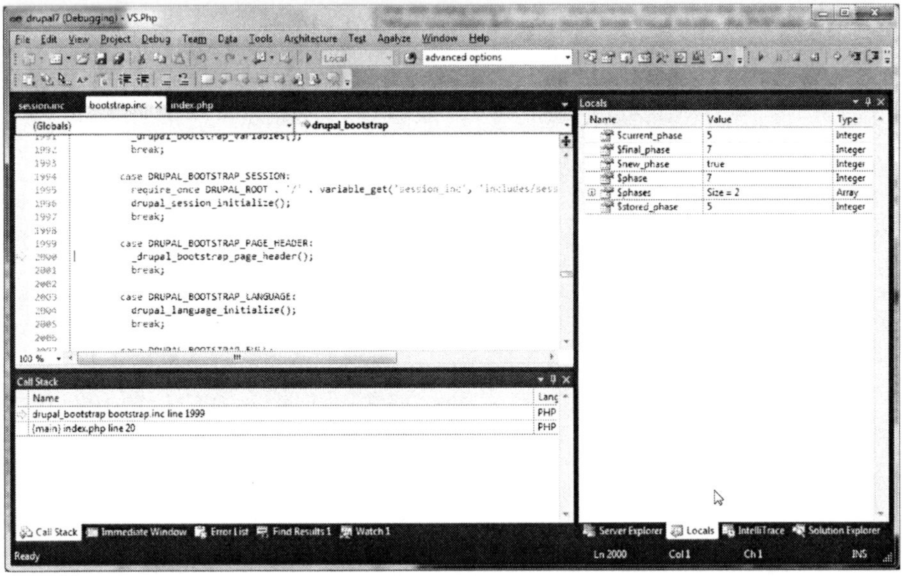

Figure 4–31. *The Visual Studio screen, powered by the VS.Php add-in for PHP debugging*

From here, you can use all of the familiar keys for stepping through the code, plus you can interrogate variable values and automatically display local variables with Visual Studio's Locals window. Of course, all of the other debugging features, like the Call Stack and Watch lists, are available.

So take a while and walk around the code to get a feel for how the Drupal core works.

Summary

In this chapter, we installed the Drupal version 7 core code, created a database, and configured a site using Drupal's installer program. We also loaded the project into Visual Studio using the VS.Php add-in. As I mentioned earlier, there are a lot of development environments you can use for PHP and Drupal, but I like Visual Studio with the VS.Php add-in because Visual Studio is the environment I'm most familiar with. You are certainly free to use whatever environment you'd like, but I'll continue to use VS2010/VS.Php in this book.

In the next chapter, we will create our first module and debug it using Visual Studio.

■ ■ ■

## PART II

Development

CHAPTER 5

■ ■ ■

Module Development

Core concepts in Drupal include blocks, hooks, forms, and menus. Understanding how these things work and interact with each other is critical when you build custom modules.

The main method used to modify the Drupal core or any contributed module is through the hook framework. This is what gives Drupal its flexibility and, frankly, makes things really hard to understand at first. Without inspection tools like tracing debuggers, it is difficult to follow who is grabbing the page, processing it at what point in the page lifecycle, and what they are doing with it.

The Drupal bootstrapping framework takes care of making sure that anyone who needs to have a say in how the page is built gets to have their say.

In order for your module to "have a say," you'll need to create a function with a carefully crafted name inside of a similarly named file in a certain place in the web server file hierarchy. The bootstrapper will interrogate each module to find out who needs to be involved, and invokes the function on all interested parties.

In this chapter, we will create a custom module that will grab from the user the name of some location on earth and pass that to a weather reporting service, which will send us back an XML document containing current weather conditions and a four-day forecast.

This chapter is a hands-on tutorial for creating an entire module, using many of the features you'll use for your own custom module development. Drupal is so rich, however, that we will only touch a small number of all of the features that are available. Still, the information here should help get you through the beginning of the learning process to the point where you can start to make sense out of the incredible amount of support information that's available from the Drupal community on the Internet.

This tutorial will be using modules, blocks, hooks, menus, and web services.

Blocks

Before we get started on the code, you should understand what a Drupal block is. Essentially, a block is a chunk of content that gets placed in a region on a page.

A page consists of a number of regions—based on your site's theme—that can hold dynamic content, static material, or forms. Regions have names like Header, Content, Footer, and so on. If you develop themes, you can create your own set of regions and name them whatever you want, but there are certain guidelines and customs you should follow. For more information on how regions are created and named, see Chapter 7.

The theme-based regions provide a very flexible method of building and customizing a page. You do this by placing a block into a region. Blocks are created by modules and they provide fundamental things we are interested in. For example, there's a block called "Recent content" that contains a list of content that was recently added to the site. A block called "Who's online" contains a list of currently connected users.

Blocks are created by modules and regions are created by themes. Assigning a block to a region is accomplished by going to the Blocks page, which is accessible from the Structure tab on the main menu. (See Figure 5–1.)

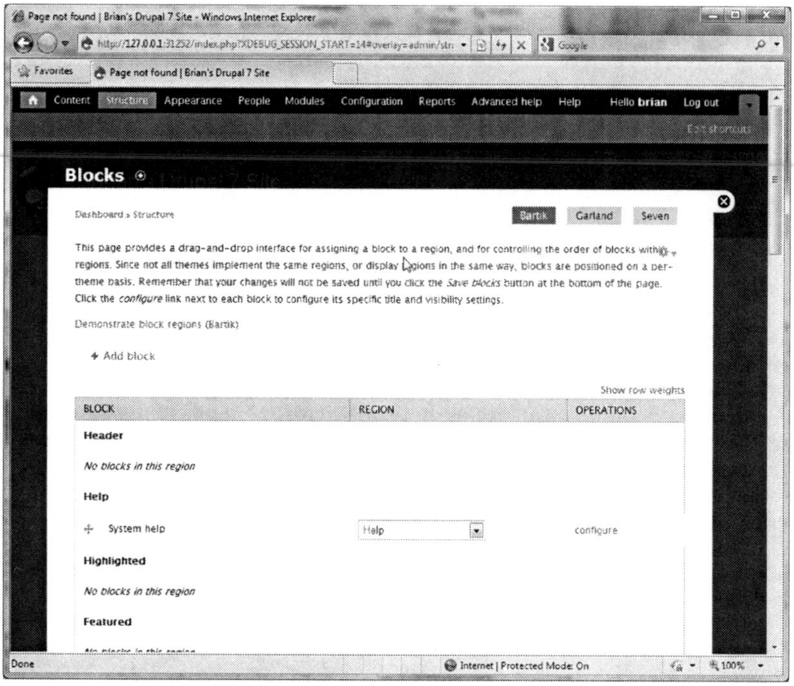

Figure 5–1. *The Blocks page allows certain content items to be placed at various locations on the page.*

On this page, you'll see all of the blocks that are available to you. These are defined by the various modules you've installed and enabled. You'll see how a block is created as we work through this tutorial.

To see your page with the block regions highlighted, click "Demonstrate block regions". (See Figure 5–2.)

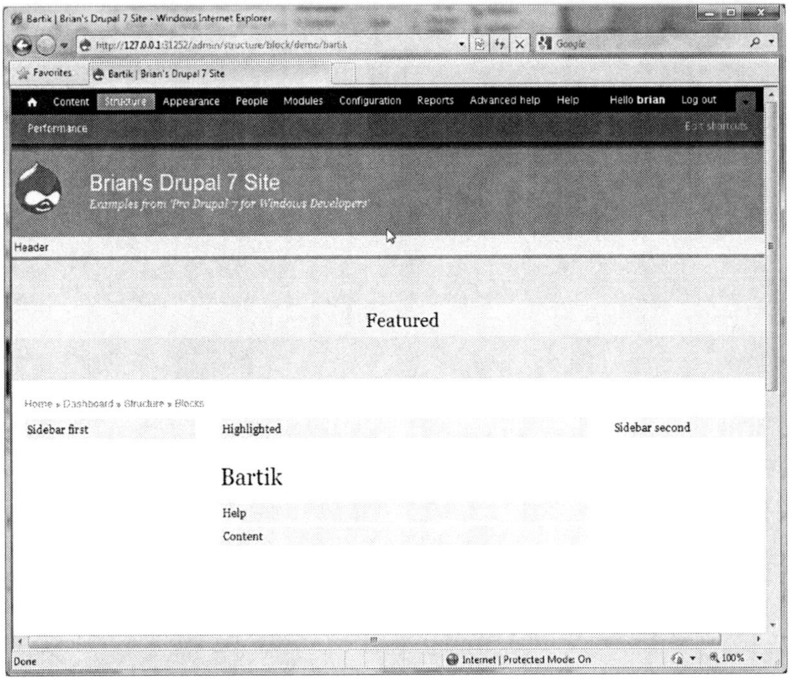

Figure 5–2. Available block regions are highlighted in yellow

Notice the Header, Sidebar first, and Sidebar second regions. Blocks can be assigned to these regions, and you can use this page to indicate what goes where and how they are ordered.

Back on the Blocks page, you can see all of the blocks that are available to be placed into these regions, as shown in Figure 5–3.

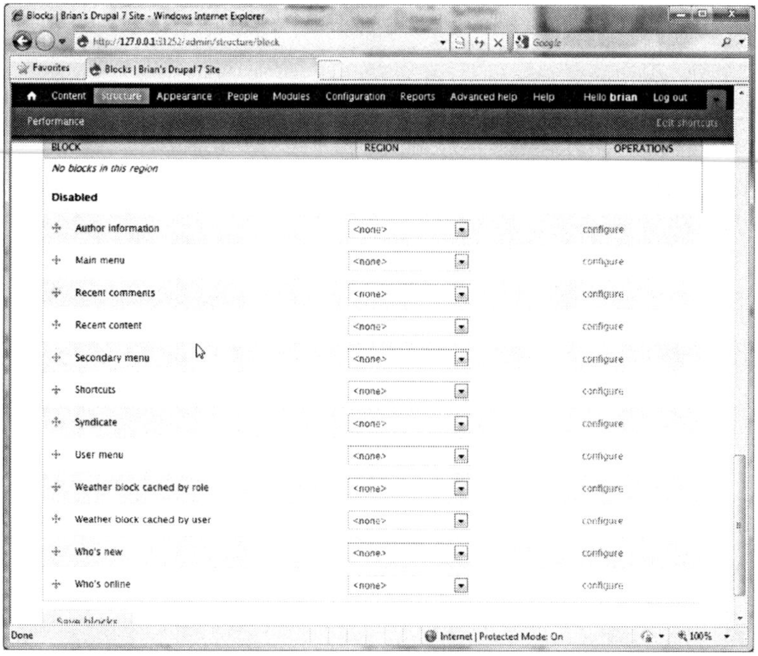

Figure 5–3. *Blocks that are available to place in page regions*

Notice that for each block, there is a pull-down menu that repeats all of the regions that are available. This page provides a graphical way of declaring what block goes in which region, and allows you to move them around using a drag-and-drop interface. Just be sure to hit the "Save blocks" button at the bottom before moving on.

There are six default regions in a Drupal theme:

- Left sidebar
- Right sidebar
- Content
- Header
- Footer
- Help

As you would probably expect, you can define your own regions, and many themes do just that. For now, that's not important. Our task is to create our own custom block that will display in any region that is available.

Modules

We will be creating a new module from scratch. We will do this by adding some files to the hierarchy that was defined when we installed Drupal. The first thing we need to do is to create a directory to hold our code. Under the document root directory of your site is a directory called "sites."

■ **Note** Drupal allows for a so-called "multi-site" configuration, where you can have as many different sites as you want all share the same server and IP address. Drupal interrogates the URL to figure out where the request should go and invokes the appropriate logic.

First, we need to tell Visual Studio that some nonstandard file extensions should be identified and associated with the PHP editor.

The main PHP program file for Drupal has the extension, .module. A second required file that contains metadata about the module has the extension .info. To make Visual Studio identify these extensions and behave accordingly, you can add them in Visual Studio at Tools➤Options➤Text Editor➤File Extension, as shown in Figure 5–4.

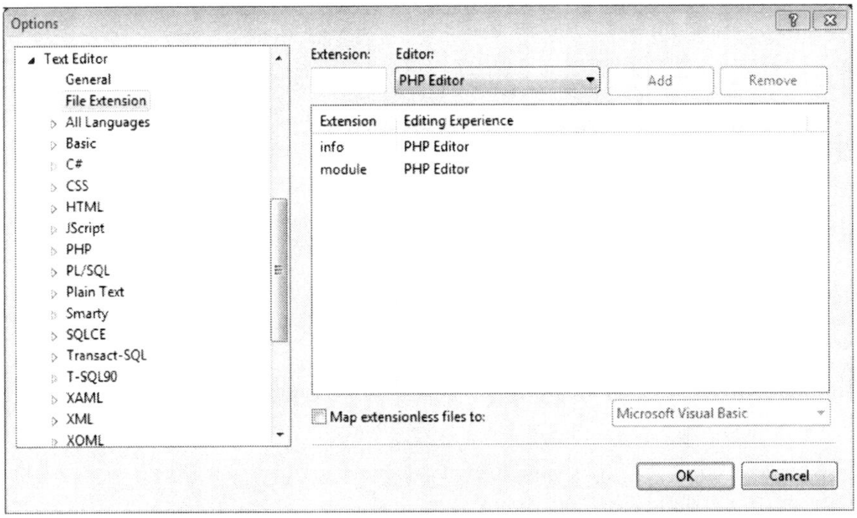

Figure 5–4. Setting .info *and* .module *extensions to be read by the PHP editor*

Click OK and go back to the Solution Explorer. You'll notice that there's a directory called all under the sites directory. If you have features you'd like to share among all sites, this is where you'd put your site.

Since we are creating our site in a development environment, let's just put our modules and themes in that directory.

Using Visual Studio, create two new directories if they don't already exist, modules and themes. And then, under the modules directory, create a directory that will hold our custom module, weather_info.

The Drupal community has published some guidelines for naming modules.

- You should use only letters and underscores in your module's name.

- Don't give your module the same name as any existing core or contributed module. You can check the list at http://drupal.org/project/usage.

- You shouldn't use a core or contributed module's name in the beginning of your module name.

In the weather_info directory, create three files:

- weather_info.info

- weather_info.inc

- weather_info.module

When you're done, your directory structure should look like the one in Figure 5–5.

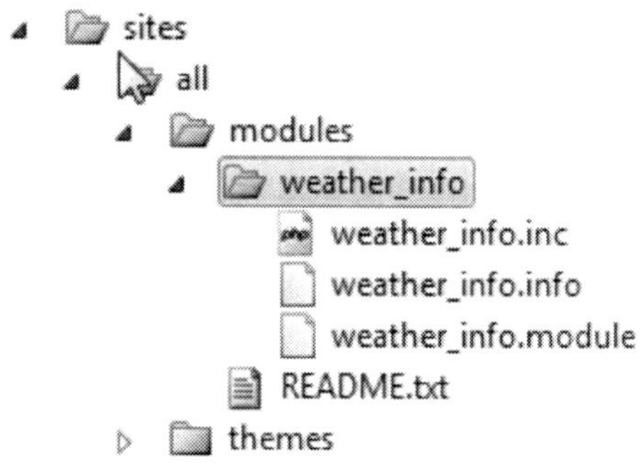

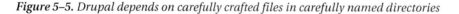

Figure 5–5. *Drupal depends on carefully crafted files in carefully named directories*

The .info file is required for any Drupal project. It is used to tell Drupal some helpful things. At a minimum, the .info file should have some descriptive information to help Drupal when the module is enabled. (See Listing 5–1.)

Listing 5–1. *The .info File Tells Drupal Important Information about a Module*

```
; $Id$
name = Weather information
description = A block that shows current weather for a particualr location.
package = Cool stuff from Brian
core = 7.x
files[] = weather_info.module
version = 7.x-0.as-alpha-as-it-gets
```

The .info file must contain a name, description, core, and files array. The version and package lines are optional. The files array indicates all of the files that will be included in the module. We'll be adding more as we go along.

Let's open the module file now and start coding.

- `http://api.drupal.org/api/7` is a good place to start.

- `http://api.drupal.org/api/functions/7` lists functions.

- `http://api.drupal.org/api/function/hook_block_view/7` describes the `block_view` hook we are about to use.

First, we'll create a rudimentary block. This is done by utilizing a hook that will be called as part of the hook processing logic. In `weather_info.module`, create the `weather_info_block()` hook function shown in Listing 5–2.

Listing 5–2. A Basic Module File for Declaring a Block

```php
<?php
// $Id$

function weather_info_block_info() {
  $blocks['user_custom'] = array(
    'info'    => t('Weather block custom for each user'),
  );
  return $blocks;
}

function weather_info_block_view($delta='') {
  $block['subject'] = t('Get Weather');
  $block['content'] = t('Initial content goes here.');
  return $block;
}
```

The important things to note here are:

- The names of the functions are critical so that Drupal can find them. A name consists of the name of the module (weather_info), followed by the type of hook, (_block_info and _block_view). The Drupal bootstrapper will search for all registered modules and then look for any hooks that a module may have. Eventually it will find them if the names are crafted properly.

- The comment //Id is optional for now, but it provides a place for the revision control system to attach version information should you go that route.

- The variable $blocks['user_custom'] will be used in the list of blocks available for adding to page regions. We can define any number of different blocks, each with a different name and set of parameters.

- The $block['subject'] and $block['content'] variables contain the information we actually want to render on the block when the page is built.

- The logic that calls this hook understands that it will be receiving a block with certain values set, so that's what we give it.

- You'll notice that all text strings are enclosed in a function called t(). This is Drupal's translate function. It is good programming practice to use this so your programs can be translated into other languages.

■ **Tip** Even if you don't think your program ever will be translated into another language, the t() function provides some other nice features, such as string sanitizing and variable replacement. You should get into the habit of using it.

Another reason to use the translate function is that even if you don't want to localize your module, someone else might. For more information on how the Drupal community supports localization, check out http://localize.drupal.org/.

That's the minimum to get us started. Let's enable the module and add the block. First, set a couple breakpoints to your code so we can watch as things progress. You do this just as you would in any other Visual Studio language: click in the breakpoint margin or put the cursor on the line and press F9. (See Figure 5–6.)

```
 4  function weather_info_block_info() {
 5      $blocks['user_custom'] = array(
 6          'info'    => t('Weather block custom for each user'),
 7      );
 8      return $blocks;
 9  }
10
11  function weather_info_block_view($delta='') {
12      $block['subject'] = t('Get Weather');
13      $block['content'] = t('Initial content goes here');
14      return $block;
15  }
16
```

Figure 5–6. Breakpoints set in PHP code

Press F5 to start the debugging session. Drupal will start its bootstrapping process. For more information on how the Drupal bootstrap function works, see Chapter 2. Note that you might get the User login screen and wonder why you need to login again, as shown in Figure 5–7.

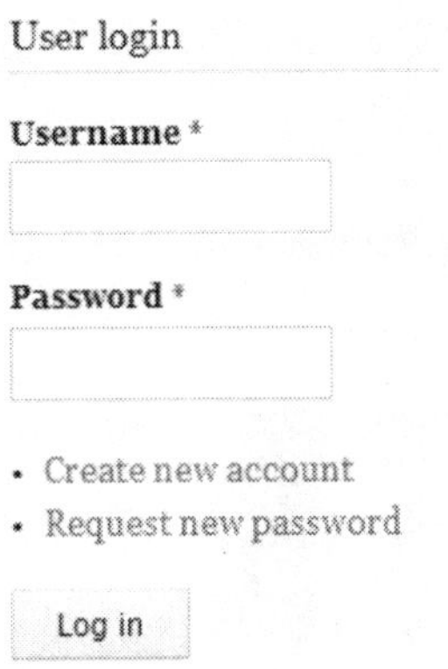

User login

Username *

Password *

- Create new account
- Request new password

Log in

Figure 5–7. The user login screen

The reason is this: even if you logged in and had your browser save your username and password, every time VS.Php starts a debugging session, it picks a random port and starts the web server. Even if your browser saved the username and password the last time, it thinks you were on a different site. So get accustomed to signing in a lot.

■ **Note** There is a way to avoid this problem. In Visual Studio, under Project➤Properties➤Configuration Properties➤Advanced, you can set "Apache port number" to some positive non-zero integer to indicate the port you'd like to use. This will disable dynamic port selection and use the same port each time.

Now we need to enable the module we just created. From the administrator menu, select Modules. Drupal will look at each directory under /sites/all/modules (among others) and look for any .info files that match the name of the directory they are in. If you did everything right, it'll find your new weather_info module. (See Figure 5–8.)

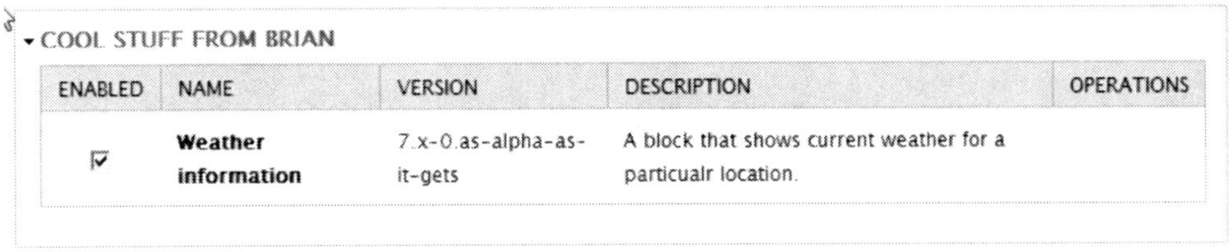

▾ COOL STUFF FROM BRIAN

ENABLED	NAME	VERSION	DESCRIPTION	OPERATIONS
☑	**Weather information**	7.x-0.as-alpha-as-it-gets	A block that shows current weather for a particualr location.	

Figure 5–8. The modules page shows information declared in the .info file.

Notice that the screen shows the information as it was listed in the .info file, including the typo. The module placed the line under the "Cool stuff from Brian" area, and it grabbed the name, version, and description just the way we put it in the .info file.

Now all we need to do is to click the checkbox in the "Enabled" column and then scroll to the bottom and click "Save configuration" as shown in Figure 5–9.

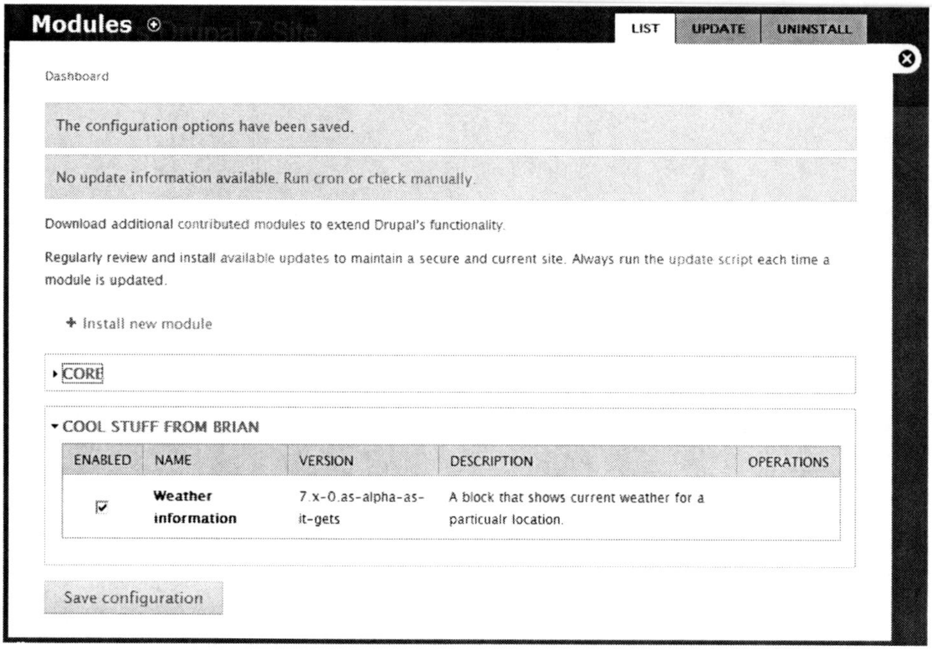

Figure 5–9. Configuration confirmation happy screen

We get the happy screen with a green notice indicating that our module has been added to the site's list of enabled modules.

Now, click on Structure in the main menu, and then Blocks. Notice that the breakpoint caught the weather_info_block_info() hook. (See Figure 5–10.)

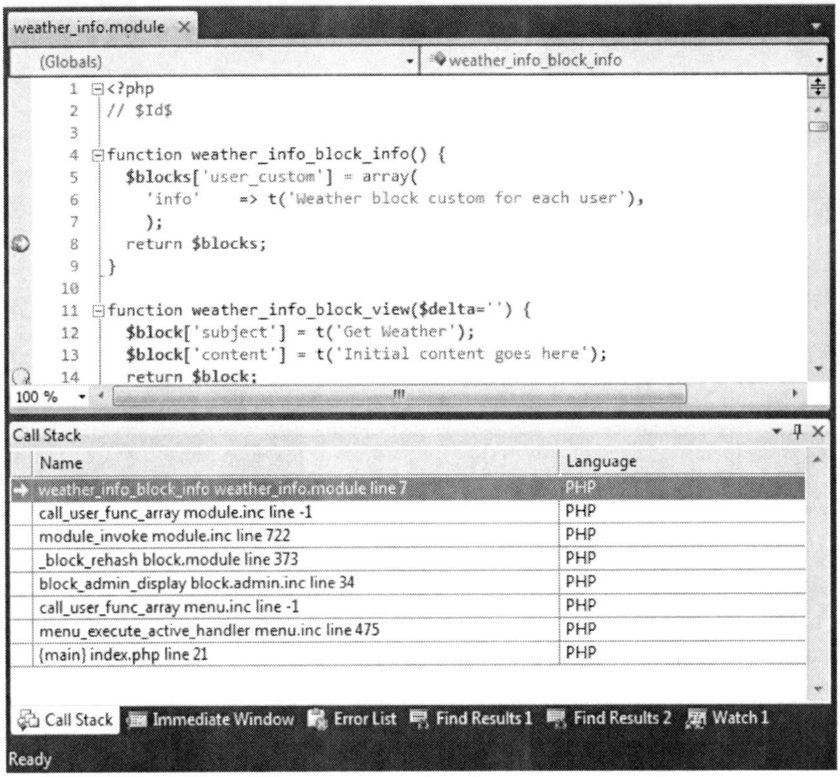

Figure 5–10. Breakpoint caught by the debugger

This was executed by someone who called `module_invoke_all('block_info')`. For more information on how the Drupal page is built, see Chapter 2.

Press F5 to continue executing. You'll see the Block screen. Scroll down to see our new block (Figure 5–11).

Figure 5–11. The weather block appears on the screen, but is not yet assigned to a region.

Notice that the name of the region, "Weather block custom for each user" was set by the `'info'` property of the array created in the `weather_info_block_info()` function. In the pull-down next to Weather information, select "Sidebar second" and then scroll up to see where it landed. (See Figure 5–12.)

111

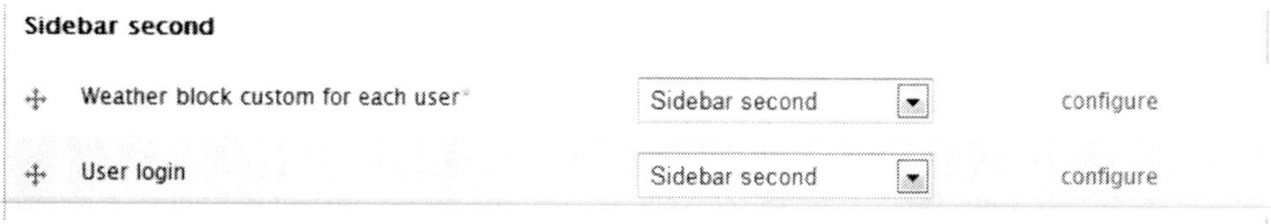

Figure 5–12. *The block shows up in the selected region.*

Notice that the background is a light yellow. This screen is designed so you can drag and drop the blocks to various regions, but nothing is saved until you click "Save blocks" at the bottom of the screen. When you do, the `weather_info_lock_info()` hook breakpoint will be hit again. Press F5 to continue execution. Close the administration window by clicking the X in the top right of the overlay.

This time you'll see that the breakpoint you set on the `weather_info_lock_info()` hook will be hit. This is because Drupal now wants to load your block content in the region as it builds the page. Press F5 to continue execution.

When the page appears, you'll see your new block on the right sidebar. (See Figure 5–13.)

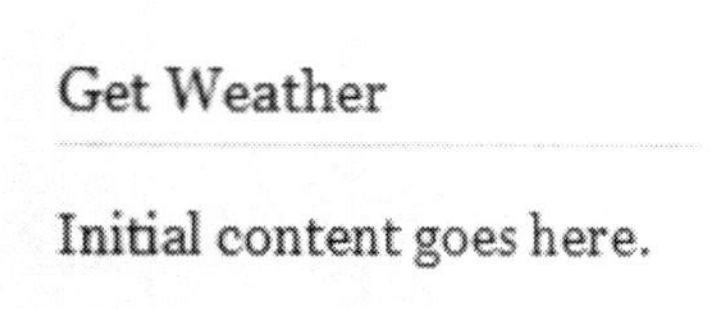

Figure 5–13. *A basic block appears in the second sidebar.*

I hope you can see exactly what's happening here, because this is the steepest part of the learning curve. From here, it's just more of the same, building piece by piece, until you understand the inner workings of Drupal.

We'll continue to build this module by getting data from an external source and then making it look good. But first, let's talk about how the hook mechanism does its work.

Hooks

At certain times in the Drupal page lifecycle, the page-building engine goes through a list of modules that have been enabled, and checks to see if there are any functions with names crafted like the one we just created. The internal process is called `module_invoke_all()` in `module.inc`. It looks like the code shown in Listing 5–3.

Listing 5–3. *The invoke_all() Function from the Drupal Core*

```
function module_invoke_all() {
  $args = func_get_args();
  $hook = $args[0];
  unset($args[0]);
  $return = array();
  foreach (module_implements($hook) as $module) {
    $function = $module . '_' . $hook;
    if (function_exists($function)) {
      $result = call_user_func_array($function, $args);
```

```
    if (isset($result) && is_array($result)) {
      $return = array_merge_recursive($return, $result);
    }
    elseif (isset($result)) {
      $return[] = $result;
    }
    }
  }
}

  return $return;
}
```

The module_implements() function queries the database for all modules that have been enabled using the Modules page.

Running this right now, I can see that 32 modules are currently enabled. They are shown in Table 5–1.

Table 5–1. A ll Currently Enabled Modules

Module Name	File Name
block	modules/block/block.module
color	modules/color/color.module
comment	modules/comment/comment.module
contextual	modules/contextual/contextual.module
dashboard	modules/dashboard/dashboard.module
dblog	modules/dblog/dblog.module
field	modules/field/field.module
field_sql_storage	modules/field/modules/field_sql_storage/field_sql_storage.module
field_ui	modules/field_ui/field_ui.module
file	modules/file/file.module
filter	modules/filter/filter.module
help	modules/help/help.module
image	modules/image/image.module
list	modules/field/modules/list/list.module
menu	modules/menu/menu.module

Module Name	File Name
node	modules/node/node.module
number	modules/field/modules/number/number.module
options	modules/field/modules/options/options.module
overlay	modules/overlay/overlay.module
path	modules/path/path.module
profile	modules/profile/profile.module
rdf	modules/rdf/rdf.module
search	modules/search/search.module
shortcut	modules/shortcut/shortcut.module
system	modules/system/system.module
taxonomy	modules/taxonomy/taxonomy.module
text	modules/field/modules/text/text.module
toolbar	modules/toolbar/toolbar.module
update	modules/update/update.module
user	modules/user/user.module
weather_info	sites/all/modules/weather_info/weather_info.module
standard	profiles/standard/standard.profile

Once it has a list of all loaded modules, the module_implements() function executes a native PHP function, function_exists(), to see if a function called {module_name}_{hook} exists anywhere in the code, where {module_name} is the name of the module (that is, the name of the directory in the modules directory and the name of the PHP code file with the extension .module in that same directory) and {hook} is the name of the particular hook we are looking for. Now you can see why names must be carefully crafted and placed in the proper locations.

> ■ **Note** In the Drupal documentation and in other places where Drupal developers talk among themselves, you'll notice a nomenclature that looks like this: hook_validate. That's the generic way of talking about a particular hook. In this case, it's the validate hook. So if you want to register code that is to be executed when the hook-processing mechanism is performing a form validation, you'd call your function module_name_validate, where module_name is the name of your module. This makes it easy when you are searching the tubes for information on a particular hook.

The hook mechanism is illustrated in Figure 5–14.

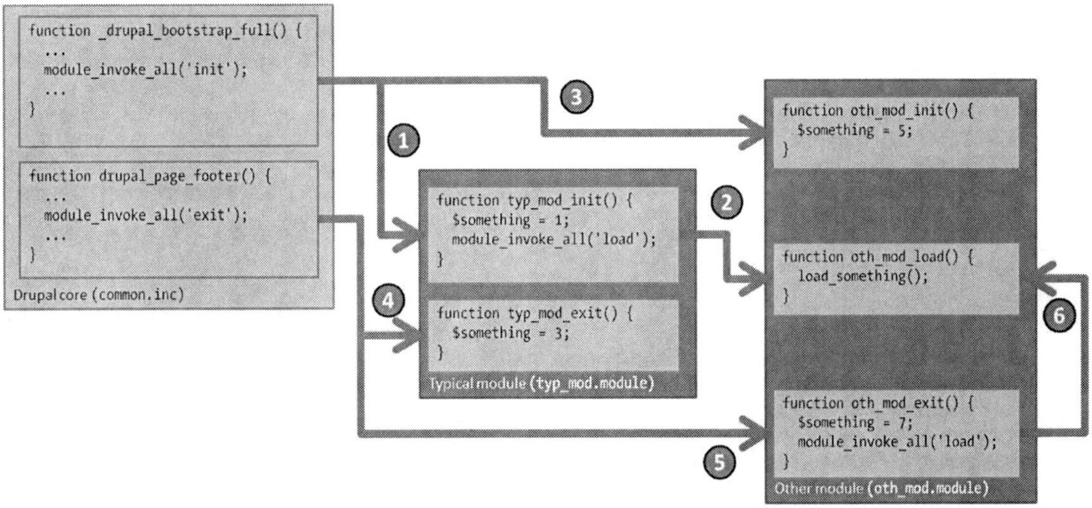

Figure 5–14. *The Drupal hook mechanism*

Let's walk through this a step at a time.

We start in the Drupal core file, common.inc, which contains a function that's called from the bootstrapper and executed in index.php. The function _drupal_bootstrap_full() calls, among other things, the module_invoke_all() function, passing the value 'init'. That function queries the database for all loaded modules and then starts to invoke the _init hook on every module that has an appropriately named function.

1. First, typ_mod_init() is called. The modules typ_mod.module and oth_mod.module are user-created modules.

2. Notice that typ_mod.module also has a module_invoke_all() call. So you can see you can make use of the hook model just like the Drupal core does. The typ_mod_init() function passes the 'load' hook to module_invoke_all(), which invokes the oth_mod_load() function.

3. When the `typ_mod_init()` function finishes, control is returned to the `module_invoke_all()` process of `_drupal_bootstrap_all()`, which looks for the next init hook to invoke, which is `oth_mod_init()`.

4. Other things happen in the building of the page, but at some point, the `drupal_page_footer()` function is called. This function also calls `module_invoke_all()`, passing the 'exit' parameter, which causes `typ_mod_exit()` to be invoked.

5. Next, `oth_mod_exit()` is invoked because that function has the specially crafted name recognized as an exit hook.

6. Notice that `oth_mod_exit()` also calls `module_invoke_all()` with the 'load' parameter. It will call the same `oth_mod_load()`function as `typ_mod_init()`did. This last step is pretty contrived, as you probably would not invoke a load hook while you are exiting, but the capability is there.

This just goes to show that anything can call anything else, and that you should be careful to understand the ramifications of using the `module_invoke_all()` function. With great power comes great responsibility, Peter Parker.

I encourage you to use this knowledge and the Visual Studio step debugger and watch the process as it happens. This investigation should give you basic insight into Drupal's core page processing engine, which will be helpful as you develop modules.

When you're done with your travels with the debugger, let's build more of the weather information block.

Forms

Two basic types of content will appear on your page, nodes and forms. Nodes are the main content, such as blog posts, stories, or custom types. Forms are the same as forms in any typical web application. That is, they are something in which the user can enter information and post it back to the server.

In the case of our weather information module, we want to get a small piece of information from the user, the location for which they are seeking weather information.

Our form will consist of a text input box and a submit button. The Drupal steps required to make this happen include:

- Create the form itself with two fields.

- Create a function to validate the information.

- Create a submit function to process the request after the validation process is successful.

First, let's create our form and then tell it as we build the block where we want to put it.

Building a Drupal form requires creating a specially crafted array with the information that Drupal's form-building code will use. So, in the `weather_info.module` file, we'll create the form function shown in Listing 5–4.

Listing 5–4. A Drupal Form for Getting a Piece of Information from the User

```
function weather_location_form($form_in, &$form_state) {
  $form['wx_info_title'] = array (
    '#value' => t('Location'),
  );
```

```
$form['wx_info']['weather_location'] = array (
  '#type' => 'textfield',
  '#size' => 20,
  '#maxlengh' => 20,
);

$form['wx_info']['weather_location_submit'] = array (
  '#type' => 'submit',
  '#value' => t('Search'),
);

$form['#action'] = '/';

return $form;
}
```

As you can see, this is a multi-dimensional array with a common first index, wx_info. The second index can be used to identify each element in the form when we process it on postback.

Note The sharp-eyed reader will notice an error in one of the form attributes of the text field. If you don't see it, that's OK; we will discover it in Chapter 8.

Once we have the form, we need to include it in our block. We do that by calling the form with the drupal_get_form() function and then rendering it. The revised version of the weather_info_block_view() hook is shown in Listing 5–5.

Listing 5–5. Grabbing a Form and Rendering It as HTML Output

```
function weather_info_block_view($delta='') {
  $block['subject'] = t('Get Weather');

  $temp = drupal_get_form('weather_location_form');
  $block_content = drupal_render($temp);
  $block['content'] = $block_content;

  return $block;
}
```

This will render in the block as a familiar HTML form (see Figure 5–15).

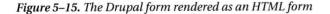

Get Weather

Search

Figure 5–15. The Drupal form rendered as an HTML form

117

There are many different values for #type, which roughly correspond to the familiar HTML form elements, as shown in Table 5–2.

Table 5–2. *Drupal Form Element Types*

Element	Description
button	Formats a submit button, which sends the form to Drupal where it is validated and rebuilt. The submit handler is not invoked.
checkbox	Formats a checkbox.
checkboxes	Formats a set of checkboxes that are related.
date	Formats a date selection box.
fieldset	Renders a box around a group of form items.
file	Formats a file upload field.
form	A form containing form elements.
hidden	Stores data in a hidden form field that renders to the HTML page.
image_button	Formats a form submit button with an image.
item	Generates a display-only form element with an optional title and description.
markup	Generates markup for display inside forms. This the default type, so there is no need to declare a form element as #type = 'markup'.
password	Formats a single-line text field that does not display its contents visibly.
password_confirm	Formats a pair of password fields, which do not validate unless the two entered passwords match.
radio	Formats a single radio button.
radios	Format a set of mutually exclusive radio buttons.
select	Formats a drop-down menu or scrolling selection box.
submit	Formats a form submit button. This sends the form to Drupal, where it is validated, and then invokes the submit handler.
textarea	Formats a multiple-line text field.
textfield	Formats a single-line text field.
token	Stores token data in a hidden form field. A token element is automatically added to each Drupal form so you don't generally have to add one yourself; it is designed for security, preventing the repeated resubmission of the form.
value	A form value that is internal to the form and never displayed to the screen.
weight	Indicates the relative location of the item.

The Drupal Forms API is available at http://api.drupal.org/api/group/form_api/7.

Form Validate Hook

So now we have a form with a submit button and we need to do something with the information the user entered on the form. Drupal provides a two-step process.

First, we need to make sure the data is valid. Second, we need to process the data based on our rules. If the data doesn't validate, there's no reason to process the data.

The type of validation that is used will vary based on what the form is doing. For example, if a start date and end date are entered for some query, the validator might just check to see if the end date is greater than or equal to the start date. Or it might check to see if a field that is supposed to be entered as an integer is, in fact, an integer.

Our end result is to take the location information entered in the form and pass it to a service that returns current weather information and a four-day forecast. This service will take just about any text and try to figure out if it is a location for which it can get the weather conditions. The only way to validate that it is a proper location is to make the actual call to the service. We'll do that a little later.

We can, however, check for at least one obvious validation factor—whether the field has any text in it. Since we know that an empty request will end up as an error, that's an obvious check.

The task, then, is to utilize a hook to accept the call made by the form validator logic. This is called a validate hook, which we will name weather_location_form_validate() in our program. We create this function and declare the parameters we expect to get from the forms engine. That function is shown in Listing 5–6.

Listing 5–6. *Our hook_validate Function*

```
function weather_location_form_validate($form, $form_state) {
  $location = trim($form_state['values']['weather_location']);
  if (!$location) {
    form_set_error('weather_location', t('Location cannot be blank.'));
  }
}
```

The values of the form fields come back in the $form_state parameter inside the 'values' array item. The function removes leading and trailing whitespace characters and checks to see if the field is blank. If it is, it sets an error with the form_set_error() function. This prevents the submit hook from firing and immediately returns to the form with an error to the user. It also outlines in red the field that was listed as the first parameter. (See Figure 5–16.)

Figure 5–16. *The hook_validate function returns an error to the calling screen.*

If the validate hook function (weather_location_form_validate()) executes without setting the error, the submit hook will execute. Let's create that now.

Form Submit Hook

If the validate hook processes without setting the form_set_error() function, the submit hook will be called. The Drupal form-processing mechanism passes the same $form and $form_state variables to the submit hook, where we can interrogate them. Again, we need to create a carefully crafted function name consisting of the name of our form and the hook it is looking to grab, plus the parameters it is expecting to receive. Our function is shown in Listing 5–7.

Listing 5–7. Our form_submit Function

```
function weather_location_form_submit($form, $form_state) {
  $location = trim($form_state['values']['weather_location']);
  variable_set('current_location', $location);
}
```

In this case, all we need to do is to save the current location in a persistent place. To do this, we use Drupal's variable facility. The variable_set(), variable_get(), and variable_del() functions maintain persistent data in your site's variables table. This is an easy way to set something that must be used later, but it comes at a price; setting or deleting a variable dirties the cache and performance could suffer as a result, especially for larger sites where caching is a requirement.

For now, though, let's use the variable facility and we'll explore another way to do it a little later.

XML Data Source

Google provides a "secret" weather information service. It is largely undocumented, but has worked for years and I imagine it will continue to work for a while. There are other free services that return weather information, so if Google doesn't work for you, I'm sure you can find another one that does.

The URL is http://www.google.com/ig/api?weather=, followed by some location. The location can be anything that Google will be able to interpret as a valid geographical place.

- Zipcodes work:

  http://www.google.com/ig/api?weather=94107

  shows up as

  `<city data="San Francisco, CA" />`

- Place names do, too:

  http://www.google.com/ig/api?weather=paris

  returns

  `<city data="Paris, Ile-de-France" />`

- The location must be URL-friendly:

  http://www.google.com/ig/api?weather=san%20luis%20obispo

  finds

  <city data="San Luis Obispo, CA" />

- If Google can't find a location, we get an error:

  http://www.google.com/ig/api?weather=notaplace

  returns

  <problem_cause data="" />

First, let's look at the XML returned from the Google weather service.

```xml
<?xml version="1.0"?>
<xml_api_reply version="1">
  <weather module_id="0" tab_id="0" mobile_row="0" mobile_zipped="1" row="0" section="0" >
    <forecast_information>
      <city data="Paris, Ile-de-France"/>
      <postal_code data="paris"/>
      <latitude_e6 data=""/>
      <longitude_e6 data=""/>
      <forecast_date data="2010-06-08"/>
      <current_date_time data="2010-06-08 18:31:43 +0000"/>
      <unit_system data="US"/>
    </forecast_information>
    <current_conditions>
      <condition data="Mostly Cloudy"/>
      <temp_f data="68"/>
      <temp_c data="20"/>
      <humidity data="Humidity: 68%"/>
      <icon data="/ig/images/weather/mostly_cloudy.gif"/>
      <wind_condition data="Wind: S at 10 mph"/>
    </current_conditions>
    <forecast_conditions>
      <day_of_week data="Tue"/>
      <low data="58"/>
      <high data="72"/>
      <icon data="/ig/images/weather/rain.gif"/>
      <condition data="Showers"/>
    </forecast_conditions>
    <forecast_conditions>
      <day_of_week data="Wed"/>
      <low data="62"/>
      <high data="65"/>
      <icon data="/ig/images/weather/rain.gif"/>
      <condition data="Showers"/>
    </forecast_conditions>
    <forecast_conditions>
      <day_of_week data="Thu"/>
      <low data="59"/>
      <high data="71"/>
      <icon data="/ig/images/weather/rain.gif"/>
      <condition data="Showers"/>
    </forecast_conditions>
```

121

```
<forecast_conditions>
  <day_of_week data="Fri"/>
  <low data="57"/>
  <high data="72"/>
  <icon data="/ig/images/weather/rain.gif"/>
  <condition data="Showers"/>
</forecast_conditions>
</weather>
</xml_api_reply>
```

Hmmm. A rainy week in Paris. PHP comes with several different ways of processing an XML document, but I'd say that the easiest way is with the SimpleXMLElement object. When you load a string containing well-formed XML markup into the SimpleXMLElement object, it immediately becomes available to the programmer. The SimpleXMLElement object is a hierarchical representation of the structure of an XML document, allowing the programmer to use the element and attribute names to navigate through the document.

We are interested in the city name and the forecast in the weather information above. Getting to the city name requires just the following code (assuming $weather is the name of the SimpleXMLElement object that contains the document above):

```
$city_name = $weather->weather->forecast_information->city['data'];
```

Elements are accessed using object accessors and attributes are accessed using array index notation. You can also iterate over sub-elements using standard PHP control structures.

Now that we understand the interface, let's incorporate it into a function. PHP, being a web-savvy programming language, has a rich collection of features that provide access to the World Wide Web. Two features we'll take advantage of are file_get_contents() function and the SimpleXMLElement object.

Helper Functions

The function that will call Google's web service could be used by other modules, so we'll include it as a separate file.

Like almost every computer language, PHP has the ability to include code from different files. In fact, PHP has four different methods.

- include ('file_to_be_included.inc'); This includes and evaluates a file at that point in the source. All source will be treated as if it were written exactly at the point where the include is specified, even if it is inside a function. If file_to_be_included.inc is not found, a warning is generated.

- require ('file_to_be_included.inc'); This works the same as include, except that if the file is not found, PHP will issue a fatal error and halt processing.

- include_once ('file_to_be_included.inc'); This works the same as include, except that it will do nothing if the file has already been included in the current processing run. If file_to_be_included.inc has not been included yet and is not found, a warning is generated.

- require_once ('file_to_be_included.inc'); You can probably figure out this one by its name. If the file hasn't been included and can't be found, PHP will issue a fatal error and halt processing.

I like to put function calls that don't have much to do with Drupal's processing, or functions that are called by several different modules, in include files. It helps to organize things. We will be creating a function that calls the Google weather service from one of our hook functions. This is a good place to set up an include file.

Create a new file in the same directory as weather_info.module and call it weather_info.inc. Unlike the module files that Drupal is looking for, there are no naming requirements for included files; they will just be included in the calling module or theme files.

■ **Note** Before we go much farther, we'll need to add the included file into the .info file for our project. Add it to the files array following the weather_info.module line: files[] = weather_info.inc Your .info file should now look like this:

```
; $Id$
name = Weather information
description = A block that shows current weather for a particualr location.
package = Cool stuff from Brian
core = 7.x
files[] = weather_info.module
files[] = weather_info.inc
version = 7.x-0.as-alpha-as-it-gets
```

Listing 5–8 shows the function to call the weather. Put it in weather_info.inc. According to Drupal's programming guidelines, a function name should begin with the module name to avoid naming conflicts, but this is not a requirement to get the function to work.

Listing 5–8. The weather_info_get_weather Helper Function

```
function weather_info_get_weather($location, $language) {
  $requestAddress = sprintf('http://www.google.com/ig/api?weather=%s&hl=%s',
    url($location), $language);
  try {
    $xml_str = utf8_encode(file_get_contents($requestAddress, 0));
    $weather = new SimplexmlElement($xml_str);

    if (isset($weather->weather->problem_cause)) {
      throw new Exception (t("Can't load %loc", array('%loc' => $location)));
    }

    if(!$weather) {
      throw new Exception ('weather failed');
    }
  } catch (Exception $err) {
    watchdog ('weather_info', 'Cannot get weather for %location: %message',
      array('%location' => $location, '%message' => $err->getMessage()),
      WATCHDOG_ERROR);
    return null;
  }

  return $weather;
}
```

Note that our location could have spaces or other URL-unfriendly characters. Thus we use the sprintf() function so we can substitute a URL-encoded string. This function will make sure the string is properly formatted.

Notice as well that there's a string for the language parameter, hl. For now, we'll always pass 'en'. Later, we'll set a configuration variable so we can change it for each user.

The get_file_contents() function is pretty versatile. It can be used to return a string with the contents of a file on our machine or, as in this case, it can intercept the stream coming from an HTTP GET request and load it into a string. The SimpleXMLElement object requires a string to be encoded in UTF-8 format, but the data coming back from Google is in Unicode. The utf8_encode() function does the transformation.

This encoded string is immediately loaded into a SimpleXMLElement object. As I mentioned earlier, if the service can't parse the location string or can't find the location in its database, it will return an XML document that looks like the example in Listing 5–9.

Listing 5–9. XML Document Returned with an Unfound Location

```
<?xml version="1.0"?>
<xml_api_reply version="1">
  <weather module_id="0" tab_id="0" mobile_row="0" mobile_zipped="1" row="0" section="0" >
    <problem_cause data=""/>
  </weather>
</xml_api_reply>"
```

We first check for the existence of the problem_cause element before proceeding. If there's an error, we tell the Drupal watchdog service. Watchdog writes to the log database and is accessible from the "Recent log entries" page at /admin/reports/dblog, as shown in Figure 5–17.

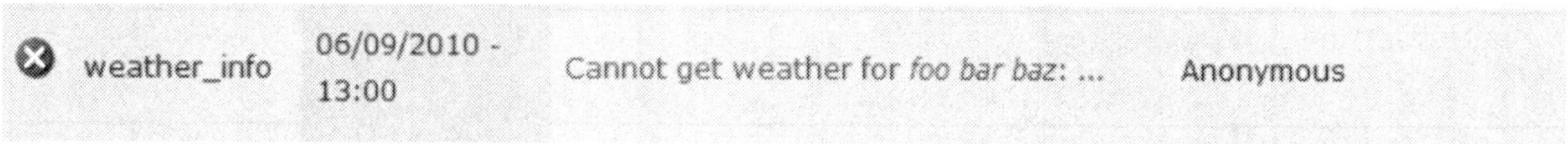

| ✕ | weather_info | 06/09/2010 - 13:00 | Cannot get weather for *foo bar baz*: ... | Anonymous |

Figure 5–17. A line from the logging database

Clicking on the link will provide you with as much information as Drupal has on the topic. This is shown in Figure 5–18.

Details

Type	weather_info
Date	Wednesday, June 9, 2010 - 13:00
User	Anonymous
Location	http://127.0.0.1:16390/index.php?XDEBUG_SESSION_START=1
Referrer	http://127.0.0.1:16390/index.php?XDEBUG_SESSION_START=1
Message	Cannot get weather for *foo bar baz*: *Cannot load foo bar baz*
Severity	error
Hostname	127.0.0.1
Operations	

Figure 5–18. A detailed error log entry

If everything goes fine, the $weather object| is returned, ready to be consumed. So let's write the code that calls this function. Back to the form.

While we're in weather_info.inc, there's one more function we need to write. I call it weather_info_temp() and it will return the temperature, along with the degree symbol and the measuring unit.

■ **Caution** All function names in a PHP program must be unique. While it seems easy to keep track of this, remember that dozens or hundreds of programs may be loaded in a typical page. A function with a name like "temp" is pretty obvious, and there will likely be someone else who wants to use it. That would cause a function naming conflict and a critical error. Therefore, you should prefix your helper functions with the name of your module, which you have already determined is unique.

We need to pass the unit system that will indicate whether the units are returned in metric (SI) or British (US) units. This is hardcoded to "US" for now, but we will have to deal with it later when we change the language of the request.

The weather_info_temp() function goes in weather_info.inc and is shown in Listing 5–10.

Listing 5–10. The weather_info_temp Helper Function

```
function weather_info_temp($in_temp, $unit, $unit_system) {
  return sprintf('%s&deg;%s', $in_temp, $unit);
}
```

Building the Block

When we last saw the form hook, we had created a text box and a submit button and had processed the form using the validate and submit hooks, which set the current_location variable. At that point, the weather_location_form_validate() function could only check to see if the location was blank. Now we have the ability to check whether the location is valid according to the weather service.

So we add a call to the function we just created to the validate hook as shown in Listing 5–11.

***Listing 5–11.** The Form Validation Hook That Checks to See if the Location Is Valid*

```
include_once ('weather_info.inc');

function weather_location_form_validate($form, $form_state) {
  $location = trim($form_state['values']['weather_location']);
  $weather = weather_info_get_weather($location, 'en');
  if (!$weather) {
    form_set_error('weather_location', t('Location %location not found.',
      array('%location' => $location)));
  }
}
```

Notice the include_once() directive at the top; remember that the function that gets the weather is in a different source file. We can test this by entering a location in the block form that can't be found and see what the validation function does. (See Figure 5–19.)

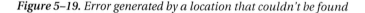

Location *foo bar baz* not found.

***Figure 5–19.** Error generated by a location that couldn't be found*

Now that we know the weather helper is working, it's time to modify the block hook to render the forecast above the text box and submit button. We'll do this by grabbing the XML file from the service and walking over it to find the pieces of information we need. And then, in order to make it look nice, we'll throw some HTML tags around it so we can style it later.

The new weather_info_block_view() function is shown in Listing 5–12.

***Listing 5–12.** The block_view Hook with a Call to the Weather Service and Formatting*

```
function weather_info_block_view($delta='') {
  $block = null;
  $block_content = null;

  $unit = 'F';
  $language = 'en';
  $location = variable_get('current_location', null);
  if ($location) {
    $weather = weather_info_get_weather($location, $language);
    if ($weather) {
      $unit_system = 'US';
      $current = $weather->weather->current_conditions;
      $block_content .= '<div class="currentConditions">';
      $block_content .= "<img src='http://www.google.com/{$current->icon['data']}'/>";
      $block_content .= "<br/>";
      $block_content .= sprintf('%s, %s<br/>',
        $current->condition['data'], weather_info_temp($current->temp_f['data'], $unit,
        $unit_system));
      $block_content .= $current->wind_condition['data'] . '<br/>';
      $block_content .= $current->humidity['data'];
      $block_content .= '</div>';

      $day = 1;
```

```
    foreach($weather->weather->forecast_conditions as $new) {
        $high = weather_info_temp((int)$new->high['data'], $unit, $unit_system);
        $low = weather_info_temp((int)$new->low['data'], $unit, $unit_system);

        $block_content .= "<div class='forecast-" . $day++ . "'>";
        $block_content .= "{$new->day_of_week['data']}<br/>";
        $block_content .= "<img src='http://www.google.com/{$new->icon['data']}'/><br/>";
        $block_content .= "{$high}/{$low}<br/>";
        $block_content .= '</div>';
    }
    $block['subject'] = $weather->weather->forecast_information->city['data'];
}
else {
    form_set_error('weather_location',
        t('Location @loc not found.', array('@loc' => $location)));
    variable_set('current_location', null);
    $block['subject'] = t('Get Weather');
}
}

$temp = drupal_get_form('weather_location_form');
$block_content .= drupal_render($temp);
$block['content'] = $block_content;
return $block;
}
```

First, we grab the location from the variable table, then call the function we wrote earlier.

Assuming all is well and the location is found, it's time to build the HTML that will show the weather forecast. SimpleXMLElement is a hierarchical object that can be looped over depending on its structure. There are only a few items we need from the XML file—the current conditions, the forecast, and the city that was located.

First, we'll grab some pieces from the current_conditions element.

```
$current = $weather->weather->current_conditions;
```

This loads only the <current_conditions> element, along with all of its descendants, as shown in Listing 5–13.

Listing 5–13. *A Single Element and Its Descendants*

```
<current_conditions>
    <condition data="Mostly Cloudy"/>
    <temp_f data="68"/>
    <temp_c data="20"/>
    <humidity data="Humidity: 68%"/>
    <icon data="/ig/images/weather/mostly_cloudy.gif"/>
    <wind_condition data="Wind: S at 10 mph"/>
</current_conditions>
```

From here, it's easy to grab the values of individual properties, $current->wind_condition['data'] for example. Our code puts an HTML DIV wrapper with a class name so we can set CSS style properties later in our theme.

Next, we'll collect all of the forecast_conditions objects and loop over them:

```
foreach($weather->weather->forecast_conditions as $new)
```

Once we have the $new variable, it's pretty simple to access the objects inside. Just remember that attribute values are accessed as if they were keyed arrays: <day_of_week data="Tue"/> is accessed with $new->day_of_week['data']. The city name is accessed using the same technique.

Once we are finished with the looping, we have a nice little HTML div to stick in the block, as shown in Listing 5–14.

Listing 5–14. HTML Generated from the block_view Hook

```
<div class="currentConditions">
    <img src='http://www.google.com//ig/images/weather/sunny.gif'/><br/>
    Rain, 57&deg;F<br/>
    Wind: W at 8 mph<br/>
    Humidity: 100%
</div>
<div class="forecast-1">
Fri<br/>
    <img src='http://www.google.com//ig/images/weather/mostly_sunny.gif'/><br/>
    60&deg;F/51&deg;F<br/>
</div>
<div class="forecast-2">
    Sat<br/>
    <img src='http://www.google.com//ig/images/weather/mostly_sunny.gif'/><br/>
    69&deg;F/50&deg;F<br/>
</div>
<div class="forecast-3">
    Sun<br/>
    <img src='http://www.google.com//ig/images/weather/chance_of_storm.gif'/><br/>
    75&deg;F/53&deg;F<br/>
</div>
<div class="forecast-4">
    Mon<br/>
    <img src='http://www.google.com//ig/images/weather/chance_of_storm.gif'/><br/>
    77&deg;F/59&deg;F<br/>
</div>
```

When we append the text box and submit button using the drupal_get_form() function and set the subject by setting the $block['subject'] array item, we get a nice display once the block is rendered. (See Figure 5–20.)

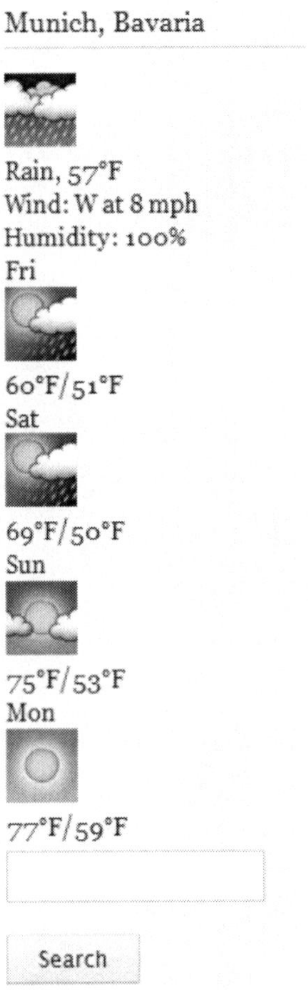

Munich, Bavaria

Rain, 57°F
Wind: W at 8 mph
Humidity: 100%
Fri

60°F/51°F
Sat

69°F/50°F
Sun

75°F/53°F
Mon

77°F/59°F

Search

Figure 5–20. The HTML fragment rendered in the browser

The content showed up just fine, but I'm not too happy about how it looks right now. I'd rather have all of the icons in a single horizontal row, but we'll deal with that when we theme the block.

Menus

So far, we've displayed a pretty simple block using the results from a web service call. We've actually done some pretty advanced work for the morning!

But there's more to do. I'd like to have a setting where we can indicate whether we want to see the temperatures in Fahrenheit (the default) or Celsius. While we're at it, we might as well tickle our nerd fancy and provide Kelvin and Rankine units as options. Plus, I'd like to set a default location that will be used until someone enters something else, and also specify which language we'd like see.

We'll need to create another form and a way to access it. You can access most data in Drupal is through the menu interface, so we'll need to write a menu hook function that will be found when the Drupal hook engine is searching for interested parties. The menu hook is shown in Listing 5–15.

Listing 5–15. The Menu Hook for weather_info

```
 1 function weather_info_menu() {
 2    $items['admin/config/weather_info'] = array (
 3      'title' => 'Weather Info Configuration',
 4      'description' => 'Configuration settings for the Weather Information block.',
 5      'page callback' => 'system_admin_menu_block_page',
 6      'file' => 'system.admin.inc',
 7      'file path' => drupal_get_path('module', 'system'),
 8      'access arguments' => array('administer weather info'),
      );

 9    $items['admin/config/weather_info/settings'] = array (
10      'title' => 'Weather Information settings',
11      'description' => 'Set defaults and unit types for weather display.',
12      'page callback' => 'drupal_get_form',
13      'page arguments' => array('wx_admin_settings'),
14      'access arguments' => array('administer weather info'),
      );

15    return $items;
    }
```

Let's take this a line at a time to see what's happening.

1.   This is the function that declares the menu hook.

2.   The $items array will contain a list of all menu items defined by this function. The key of the array is the path of this particular object. All administrative items are in the /admin hierarchy. Configuration information is in the /config hierarchy just below that. Finally, we create our specific menu name, weather_info.

3.   The title will appear in the configuration block.

4.   The description does not appear in the configuration block, but is available to various administrative functions.

5.   We want this item to appear on the administration menu as a block along with related administrative functions. We need to indicate the name of a function that that will process our block on the page. This is called the page callback function.

6.   The file indicates the program file where the callback function is located.

7.   The file path is the location on the server where the file containing the callback function is located.

8.   Only people with the proper permissions can access this information, which you specify using access arguments. We will cover roles and permissions in Chapter 6.

9.   This item will display information and then load our custom form when it is clicked. The second item is a child of the first. We know that because the first part of the path (admin/config/weather_info) is the same.

10. The title will appear on the configuration screen and will be a link to the form.

11. The description also appears on the configuration screen

12. The form is a standard Drupal form, which is accessed with the standard drupal_get_form function. We can create a custom callback to deal with the menu, but we'll just use the default handler for now.

13. This is the name of the function that returns our form, which is described in detail below.

14. Users must also have the proper permissions to access this item.

15. The menu hook must return an array with menu items.

When we put this in our module, the hook is called and the configuration block shown in Figure 5–21 is displayed on the main configuration screen.

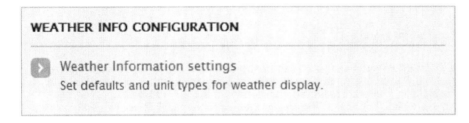

Figure 5–21. Weather configuration block showing on the main configuration screen

On line 13, the form wx_admin_settings is specified. That form is defined as a function that returns a standard Drupal form array. This is shown in Listing 5–16.

Listing 5–16. The Weather Administration Form

```
function wx_admin_settings() {
  $form['wx_settings'] = array (
    '#type' => 'fieldset',
    '#title' => t('Weather defaults')
  );

  $form['wx_settings']['default_location'] = array (
    '#type' => 'textfield',
    '#title' => t('Default location'),
    '#default_value' => variable_get('default_location', null),
    '#size' => 20,
    '#maxlengh' => 20,
    '#description' => t('Enter a location on earth to act as the default for the site.'),
  );

  $form['wx_settings']['default_units'] = array (
    '#type' => 'radios',
    '#title' => t('Default units'),
    '#options' => array(
      'F' => t('Fahrenheit'),
      'C' => t('Celsius'),
      'K' => t('Kelvin'),
      'R' => t('Rankine'),
    ),
    '#default_value' => variable_get('default_units', 'F'),
    '#description' => t('Select the units desired for display of temperature.'),
  );
```

```
$form['wx_settings']['default_language'] = array (
    '#type' => 'select',
    '#title' => t('Language'),
    '#options' => array(
        'en' => t('English'),
        'fr' => t('French'),
        'it' => t('Italian'),
        'de' => t('German'),
        'es' => t('Spanish'),
        'tr' => t('Turkish'),
    ),
    '#default_value' => variable_get('default_language', 'en'),
    '#description' => t('Select the language desired.'),
    );

$form['#submit'][] = 'wx_admin_settings_submit';
return system_settings_form($form);
}
```

The first entry is a fieldset, which means it acts as a container for other items on the form. The form processing function will know which items are its children by looking at the array structure. In this case, everything that is a child of ['wx_settings'] will be contained in the fieldset.

The next is a textfield, which is similar to the one we created in the block form. This will translate into a standard HTML element, <input type="text">.

You can probably figure out the next one, default_units. It will display a list of radio button controls that are linked. The #options parameter is an array with a list of all of the different radios to be rendered. The key is the value to be passed back to the server, and the value is what will be rendered on the form. The #default property allows the form to select one of the values. If this is not set, all four radios would be unselected. By the way, I'm starting a trend to express temperature using the Rankine scale. I think everyone should know how many degrees Fahrenheit they are above absolute zero. I hope it catches on.

Finally, we have a select box to hold languages and a submit button to make sure we can post back the information in the form for processing.

The last two lines require some explaining. The first form we created was the one that collected location information from the user. We created a single textbox and a submit button, and then created validate and submit hooks to process the form. That's pretty much a normal, standard form.

For administrative forms, Drupal provides a nice service that places a couple of buttons at the bottom of the form and then uses a built-in submit hook to do certain automatic processing. One of the things it does is to set variables with the same name as each of the fields on a form and it sets them to the values the user entered. By passing our $form through system_settings_form(), we get such niceties. Because of this automated processing, the normal submit hook is not called.

By adding the $form['#submit'][] = 'wx_admin_settings_submit';, we add our submit hook to the list of hooks that are called when the form is processed.

That's about it for the definition of the form. We just need to return the form to the menu system so it can be built. Selecting the Weather Information settings link from the block on the Configuration menu, or navigating directly to admin/config/weather_info/settings will display the form, as shown in Figure 5–22.

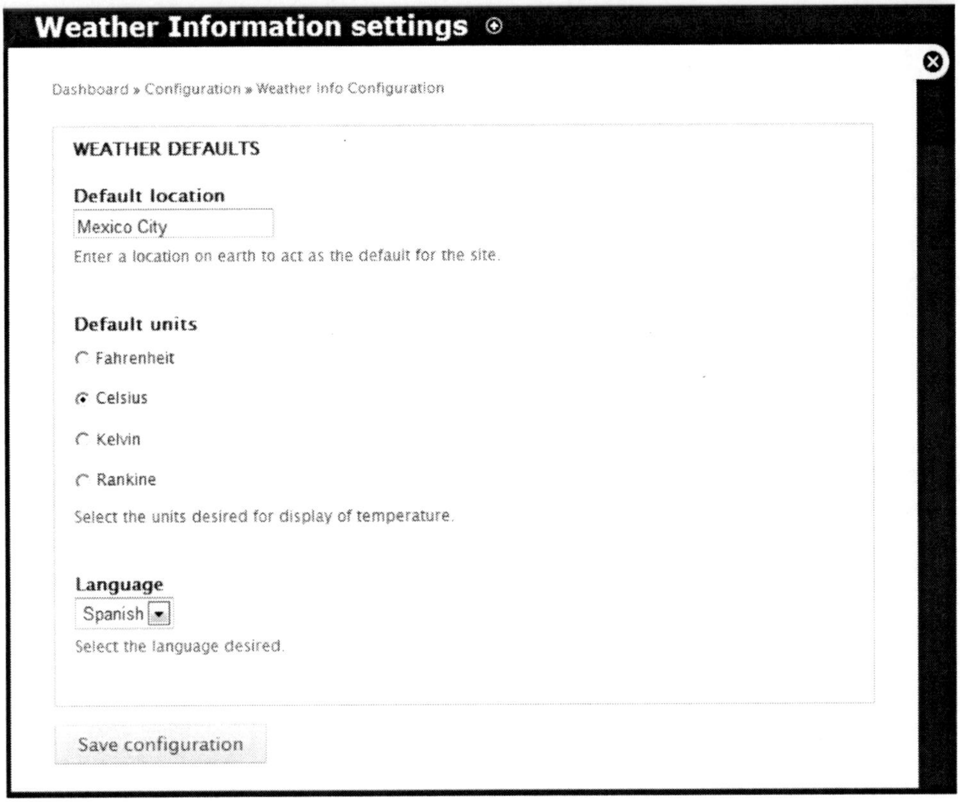

Figure 5–22. The weather info settings form

As with the form in the block above, we need to write two functions to process the data when it comes back from our form. These are the validate and submit hooks.

The name of our form is wx_admin_settings and so the submit and validate hooks must be similarly named. (See Listing 5–17.)

Listing 5–17. Validate and Submit Hooks for the Weather Administration Settings Form

```
function wx_admin_settings_validate($form, &$form_state) {
  $location = $form_state['values']['default_location'];
  if ($location) {
    $weather = weather_info_get_weather($location, 'en');
    if (!$weather) {
      form_set_error('default_location', t('Location %location not found.',
        array('%location' => $location)));
    }
  }
  else {
    form_set_error('default_location', t('Location cannot be blank.'));
  }
}

function wx_admin_settings_submit($form, &$form_state) {
```

```
    variable_set('default_units', $form_state['values']['default_units']);
    variable_set('default_language', $form_state['values']['default_language']);
    variable_set('default_location', $form_state['values']['default_location']);
    variable_set('current_location', $form_state['values']['default_location']);
}
```

The validate hook will simply check for a blank value for location and do pretty much just what it did when we entered a blank value in the block. That is, it will put a scary red error at the top of the page and highlight the offending field. It will rerender the form and not call the submit hook. Likewise, if the location is not found by the service, the appropriate error is listed. (See Figure 5–23.)

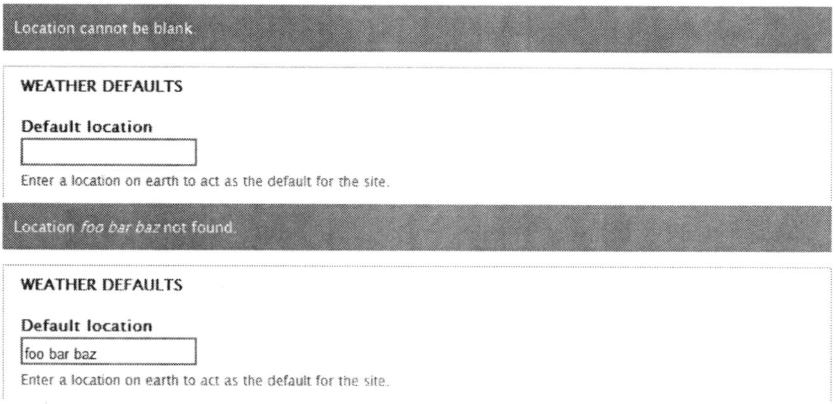

Figure 5–23. *Errors generated by the validation hook*

When a happy path is made through the validate hook, the submit hook will be called, which sets to variables that we can use later. At that point, all of the work has been done and the confirmation screen will appear. (See Figure 5–24.)

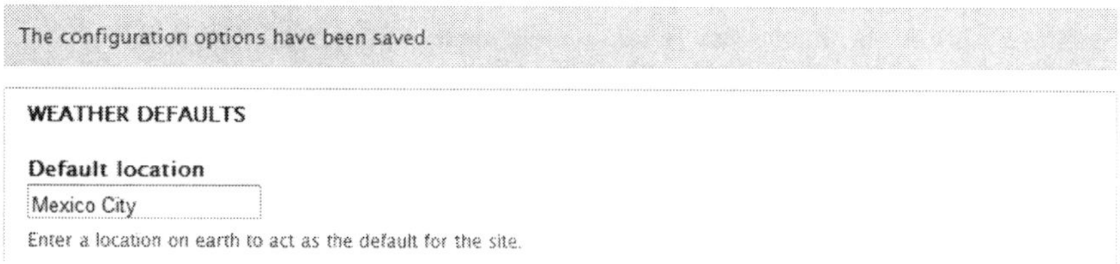

Figure 5–24. *Weather administration happy path*

And, since we changed the current_location, we can see right away the new location's forecast when we return to the home screen.

■ **Note** In the function `wx_admin_settings_submit`, there are four calls to `variable_set`. The purpose of setting these variables is to make sure they are available on a persistent basis. However, three are not necessary. As I mentioned earlier, the three variables that have the same names as the fields in our form (`default_language`, `default_location`, and `default_units`) are automatically set by the `system_settings_form` function. The function would work just the same as the following:

```
function wx_admin_settings_submit($form, &$form_state) {
  variable_set('current_location', $form_state['values']['default_location']);
}
```

Now let's use those default settings to configure our display. One of the settings, `default_units`, will be used to display the temperature in whatever unit the user wants. By default, the temperature comes through in Fahrenheit. We need some functions to convert from Fahrenheit and Celsius into the other units we support.

```
function weather_info_f_to_c($degrees_f) {
  $celsius = ($degrees_f - 32) * 5 / 9;
  return round($celsius);
}

function weather_info_c_to_f($degrees_c) {
  $fahrenheit = ($degrees_c * 9 / 5) + 32;
  return round($fahrenheit);
}

function weather_info_f_to_k($degrees_f) {
  $kelvin = weather_info_f_to_c($degrees_f) + 273.15;
  return round($kelvin);
}

function weather_info_c_to_k($degrees_c) {
  $kelvin = $degrees_c + 273.15;
  return round($kelvin);
}

function weather_info_f_to_r($degrees_f) {
  $rankine = $degrees_f + 459.69;
  return round($rankine);
}

function weather_info_c_to_r($degrees_c) {
  $rankine = weather_info_c_to_f($degrees_c) + 459.69;
  return round($rankine);
}
```

Now we can update the `weather_info_temp()` function to call the appropriate conversion function according to the value of $unit and $unit_system. When the weather service returns the weather for a particular location, it also returns the system of measurement that the location natively uses. It is returned as `<unit_system data="US"/>`. For example, for London or San Francisco, the data attribute would be "US", but for Paris or Tokyo, it would come back as "SI", from the French *Système international d'unités*. The French have different words for everything and put "everything" in italics. The

$unit_system variable can be only one of two values, "SI", or "US". The reason we care about this is that the temperature values in the forecast section of the XML file will adhere to that unit system. So when unit_system is US, the <low> and <high> temperatures will be expressed in Fahrenheit. When unit_system is "SI", the temperatures will be Celsius. Oddly, for the current conditions, both Fahrenheit and Celsius values are present. While this is handy for most people, it clearly shows the anti-Rankine discrimination present in so many places.

The new temp function is shown in Listing 5–18.

Listing 5–18. *The Temp Function Enhanced to Call the Proper Conversion Function*

```
function weather_info_temp($in_temp, $unit, $unit_system) {
  switch ($unit) {
    case 'C':
      if ($unit_system == 'SI') {
        $out_temp = $in_temp;
      }
      else {
        $out_temp = weather_info_f_to_c($in_temp);
      }
      break;
    case 'F':
      if ($unit_system == 'SI') {
        $out_temp = weather_info_c_to_f($in_temp);
      }
      else {
        $out_temp = $in_temp;
      }
      break;
    case 'K':
      if ($unit_system == 'SI') {
        $out_temp = weather_info_c_to_k($in_temp);
      }
      else {
        $out_temp = weather_info_f_to_k($in_temp);
      }
      break;
    case 'R':
      if ($unit_system == 'SI') {
        $out_temp = weather_info_c_to_r($in_temp);
      }
      else {
        $out_temp = weather_info_f_to_r($in_temp);
      }
      break;
  }
  return sprintf('%s&deg;%s', $out_temp, $unit);
}
```

Next, we need to read the value of default_units and send that to the weather_info_temp() function. In the view case of the weather_info_block function, there's a line

```
$unit = 'F';
```

It should be changed to

```
$unit = variable_get('default_units','F');
```

The last thing for this phase is to pass the appropriate language to the weather web service call. In the weather_info_block() function we hard-coded the language.

```
$language = 'en';
```

Like the default_units case above, we need to set the $language variable to get the default_language variable from our database.

```
$language = variable_get('default_language', 'en');
```

Finally, we need to grab the $unit_system value from the XML document when it comes back:

```
$unit_system = $weather->weather->forecast_information->unit_system['data'];
```

At this point, we should be able to set all three variables and have them reflected on our display. (See Figure 5–25.)

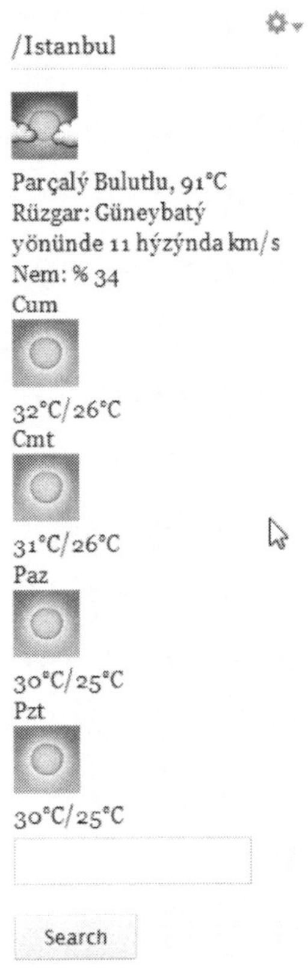

Figure 5–25. Temperatures, units, and language are all reflected in the block display.

Since we made a lot of changes to the weather_info_block function, here's the final version, shown in Listing 5–19.

Listing 5–19. The completed weather information block

```
function weather_info_block_view($delta='') {
    $block = null;
    $block_content = null;
```

```
$unit = variable_get('default_units', 'F');
$language = variable_get('default_language', 'en');
$location = variable_get('current_location', null);
if ($location) {
  $weather = weather_info_get_weather($location, $language);
  if ($weather) {
    $unit_system = $weather->weather->forecast_information->unit_system['data'];
    $current = $weather->weather->current_conditions;
    $block_content .= '<div class="currentConditions">';
    $block_content .= "<img src='http://www.google.com/{$current->icon['data']}'/>";
    $block_content .= "<br/>";
    $block_content .= sprintf('%s, %s<br/>',
      $current->condition['data'], weather_info_temp($current->temp_f['data'],
      $unit, $unit_system));
    $block_content .= $current->wind_condition['data'] . '<br/>';
    $block_content .= $current->humidity['data'];
    $block_content .= '</div>';

    $day = 1;
    foreach($weather->weather->forecast_conditions as $new) {
      $high = weather_info_temp((int)$new->high['data'], $unit, $unit_system);
      $low = weather_info_temp((int)$new->low['data'], $unit, $unit_system);

      $block_content .= "<div class='forecast-" . $day++ . "'>";
      $block_content .= "{$new->day_of_week['data']}<br/>";
      $block_content .= "<img src='http://www.google.com/{$new->icon['data']}'/><br/>";
      $block_content .= "{$high}/{$low}<br/>";
      $block_content .= '</div>';
    }
    $block['subject'] = $weather->weather->forecast_information->city['data'];
  }
  else {
    form_set_error('weather_location',
      t('Location @loc not found.', array('@loc' => $location)));
    variable_set('current_location', null);
    $block['subject'] = t('Get Weather');
  }
}

$temp = drupal_get_form('weather_location_form');
$block_content .= drupal_render($temp);
$block['content'] = $block_content;
return $block;
}
```

If you can see how the hooks interact with the core and how the validate and submit callbacks all work, you are most of the way toward understanding how Drupal does its basic work.

Summary

In this chapter, we created a module that used hooks to tie into the Drupal page-building process. We also used PHP to grab an external data source and display it in a block.

In the next chapter, we will continue this example and add permissions and a custom content type. And later we'll apply output formatting to the block by using the theming layer. After that, we'll write tests against the helper functions and the block to assure that everything is working as we intend.

CHAPTER 6

■ ■ ■

Content Types and Permissions

The main purpose of a content management system (CMS) is to manage content. That's true, but what exactly is content? And what does it mean to manage it?

In a modern, web-based CMS, content is generally thought of as the words that are displayed on the screen for people to read. This includes such elements as front-page stories on a newspaper web site, blog entries on a political pundit's site, or forum posts.

For each of these examples, the content differs slightly. For example, a newspaper article might have a piece of text called a headline, plus information such as a dateline, a byline, and possibly an abstract. After that might be a combination of paragraphs, quotes, illustrations, and links to other content. A blog post usually has a similar format, except the name of the person who wrote it is usually indicated by author or blogger instead of byline. And a forum post typically has some indication of its relation to the parent forum and its place in the current thread.

Drupal formalizes the differences between these and calls them *content types*. A content type is a classification of a particular kind of information, and defines different fields based on the purpose of the content. And since each piece of information on a site adheres to one particular content type, it can be treated in a way that is appropriate to that content type.

Drupal comes with a number of predefined content types:

- **Blog entry:** A single post to an online journal. For blog sites, this is the principal content type used by authors on the site who want to share their ideas with others. Blog entries are generally promoted to the top of the front page as they are written so the most current information is at the top. A Blog entry can be just a sentence or two, or it can be much longer; there is really no particular size limit.

- **Book Page:** A book is a collection of related information that has a predefined flow. A Book Page is a single page in that flow. Drupal displays Book Pages as a table of contents. When a Book Page is accessed, Drupal provides links to move to the next or previous pages. This provides a simple navigation system for organizing and reviewing structured content.

- **Forum topic:** A forum can be created where users can post a topic and others can reply, creating a thread of posts. The Forum topic is the basic content type for creating a forum.

- **Basic Page:** A Basic Page content type provides a simple method for creating and displaying information that rarely changes. Consider a common page on many web sites, the "About us" page. This changes rarely and is probably not something you'd want to show your user when he or she first comes to your site. The Page content type usually provides this type of static content.

- **Poll:** Drupal has a simple polling ability where an author can ask a question and provide a list of possible answers. Answers are collected and users can see the results once they've answered the question.

- **Article:** Am Article is similar to a blog entry in that several can be listed on a single page, with the most recent usually appearing at the top. Articles and blog entries can actually appear together on the same page, usually sorted by the date each was created with the most current showing on the top.

Each of these content types has fields that are required in order to work correctly. The default installation of the Drupal core only enables the Article and Basic Page content types. To get the others, you just need to enable them on the Modules page.

■ **Note** Even though these content types are predefined with the core installation of Drupal, their purpose is only suggested. You can, for example, have a site with blog-type content, article-type content, and other content for a particular purpose, and use only the Article content type.

All content is stored in the database in a normalized manner that allows for efficient access and for keeping many different revisions of a piece of content as it goes through its editorial lifecycle.

Creating Content

Creating content of a particular type is just a matter of navigating to the appropriate place in the administrative section. Let's start with an About Us page.

From the front page, click on "Add new content". You'll get a list of all of the content types that are currently available on your system. (See Figure 6–1.)

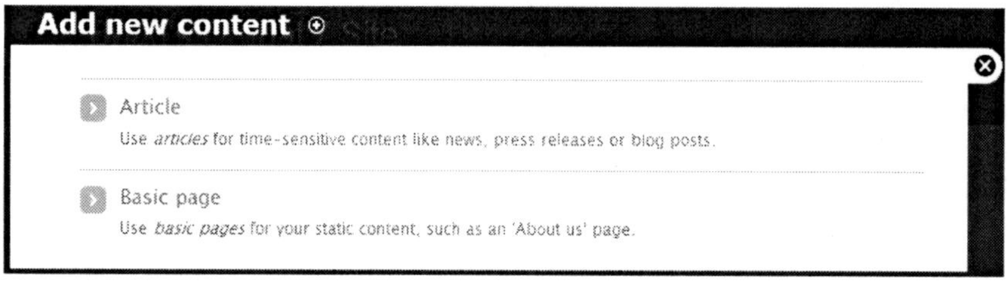

Add new content ◉

> Article
Use *articles* for time-sensitive content like news, press releases or blog posts.

> Basic page
Use *basic pages* for your static content, such as an 'About us' page.

Figure 6–1. Content types available

This page will contain all of the content types that are currently installed and enabled on your system.

■ **Tip** To enable more content types, Click "Modules" from the administration menu and enable the content types you desire.

Clicking "Basic page" presents the screen shown in Figure 6–2, where you'll see two fields, "Title" and "Body."

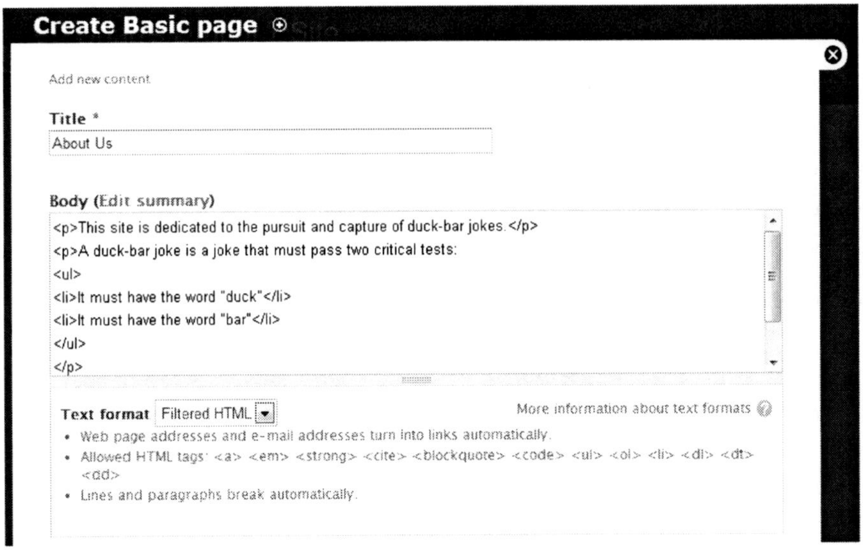

Figure 6–2. Form to create a basic page

The Title and Body fields are standard Drupal features for most content types. Notice the orange asterisk next to the Title field. This indicates that the field is required to contain content.

Notice as well the small number of HTML tags that can be placed inline. These will be interpreted according to the input filters listed just below the body field.

Drupal comes with two filters: Filtered HTML and Full HTML. You can create more filters if you like, and some contributed modules create their own filters for specific purposes.

■ **Tip** Filtered HTML, by default, is very restricted and therefore pretty safe. But your users might not find what they need. For example, Filtered HTML does not even allow the HTML image tag.

Full HTML, on the other hand, is probably way too enabling. If you enable Full HTML on your site and accidentally make it available to anonymous users, you'll probably be hacked in short order. You should use this option only with completely trusted users.

I usually create my own filter that looks a lot like Filtered HTML but adds the image tag and perhaps one or two more tags, depending on what I'm doing.

To understand why filters are necessary, you need to think about the different types of content you create. For example, if your module is designed to send e-mail to your subscribers, you might want a filter that only allows HTML tags that are e-mail-friendly, or one that allows no HTML tags at all for text-only messages.

At the bottom of the page, you'll see some buttons, Save and Preview. Clicking the Preview button lets you see the content before actually publishing it. This is a good idea, particularly as you are learning how the system works, because posting something—especially if you are hand-coding your HTML tags—could result in exposing information publicly before you can check for errors.

Because previewing is so important, it is possible to define content types such that the user will not be able to see the Save button until the post has been previewed first. (See Figure 6–3.)

The trimmed version of your post shows what your post looks like when promoted to the main page or when exported for syndication. You can insert the delimiter "<!--break-->" (without the quotes) to fine-tune where your post gets split.

Preview trimmed version

About Us

This site is dedicated to the pursuit and capture of duck-bar jokes.
A duck-bar joke is a joke that must pass two critical tests:

- It must have the word "duck"
- It must have the word "bar"

The sharp-eyed observer will notice that it is not a requirement that the joke be funny, as you will see as you browse this site.

Read more

Preview full version

About Us

This site is dedicated to the pursuit and capture of duck-bar jokes.
A duck-bar joke is a joke that must pass two critical tests:

- It must have the word "duck"
- It must have the word "bar"

The sharp-eyed observer will notice that it is not a requirement that the joke be funny, as you will see as you browse this site.

Figure 6–3. *Preview of a basic page*

Notice that the HTML tags have been interpreted to format the text. That is, the title has turned into an HTML header and the <ul> and <li> tags have been turned into a list. Notice, also, that there are two versions, "trimmed" and "full." Drupal saves both versions and uses each where appropriate. For example, if a number of articles are to appear on the front page of a site, the trimmed version will be shown. This is also called a teaser. Whenever a teaser is shown, there is usually a "Read more…" button to get to the entire entry.

Drupal makes a guess at where you want the teaser separated from the rest of the content, but if you'd like to indicate, for example, just the first couple paragraphs, you can insert an XML processing instruction, <!--break-->, at the point where you'd like to separate the teaser from the body of the content.

If you'd rather have different text displayed as the teaser, you can click the "Edit summary" link, which will give you another box for entering this text.

Notice the area near the bottom of the page that lists a number of settings you can add for this particular page. The menu settings allow you to add the page to a particular menu hierarchy. In this case, let's add it to our primary links menu so we can display it on every page. (See Figure 6–4.)

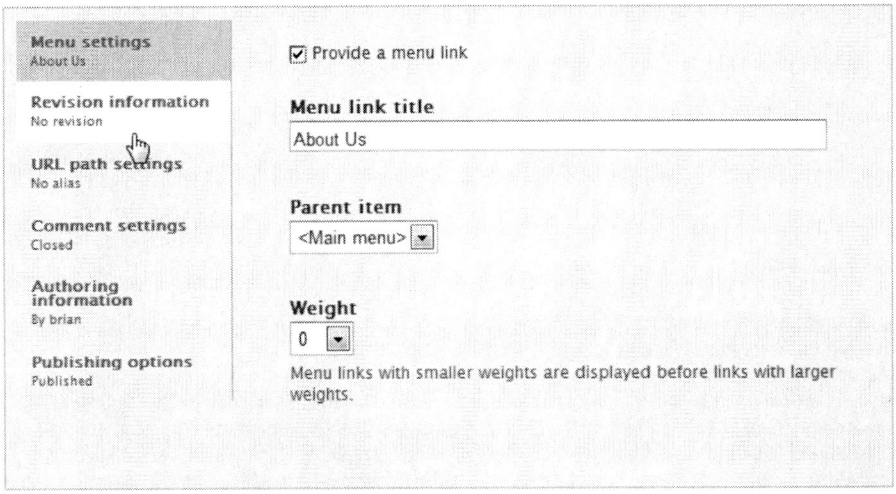

Figure 6–4. Creating a Main menu entry

The revision information area indicates whether you want to keep revisions for this page. Since this is a new page, the only version is the original. In other words, no revision. But if you were to come back and modify this page and click the "Create new revision" box, the original version of the page would be saved, as well as a new revision. If you need to revert back to the original, it thus becomes trivial.

By default, a page is accessed by its node number. If we were to save this page right now, we would access it with the URL http://mysite.com/node/1. While that might be sufficient for accessing forum topic number 60,456, we would like to see something more appropriate for a page used as often as the "About us" page. That's where the URL path settings page comes in. Clicking that link displays a text box where you can type an alias for the path that's more appropriate for the content. (See Figure 6–5)

Figure 6–5. *Setting the URL path*

The text is what your user will type after `http://mysite.com/`. The text can also have paths, so if you set the URL alias field to `content/about/marketing`, you could publish the URL as `http://mysite.com/content/about/marketing`.

Drupal's comment framework provides a way for users to post comments on virtually any piece of content on the site. Commenting is turned off by default for pages, but can be turned on for any page.

The role-based permissions engine allows you to specify which types of users have the ability to create, delete, edit, or even view comments. For example, anonymous users might be given the ability to read comments that have been posted, but only authenticated users who have created an account can add new comments. And only administrators or authors are able modify or delete comments. I'll cover the permissions framework later.

The authoring information block allows you to specify the person who created the content. By default, this is the currently logged-in user.

Given the proper permissions, you can change this to any user on the site. You can also indicate when the post was authored. Leaving it blank specifies the current time, but you can change this if you'd like.

Finally, the Publishing options block will allow you to specify how the content is to be treated when you save it.

By default, pages are not promoted to the front page, but stories and blog entries have that box checked by default. Publishing content allows it to be read by your users (based on permissions).

■ **Note** Promoting to the front page is applicable only when the default front page is used. You can set whatever page you want to be the front page. If it is not the default (/node), though, then the "promoted to the front page" checkbox will not promote the content to that new front page.

Unchecking the Published box lets you save the content, but it will be marked as a draft and users won't be able to see it. This is handy, for example, if you are working on a post but you are not ready to give it to users.

Making a post sticky causes it to appear at the top of any list of content where it would otherwise appear in reverse chronological order. This is useful when you have content that all users should see, like site policies or frequently asked questions.

Pressing the Save button publishes the page and it will appear in the browser, as shown in Figure 6–6.

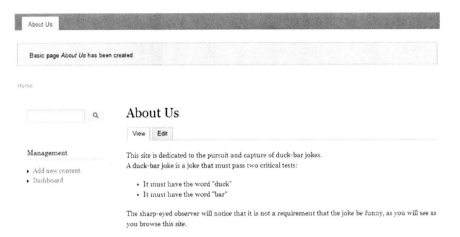

About Us

Basic page *About Us* has been created.

Home

Management

▸ Add new content
▸ Dashboard

About Us

View | Edit

This site is dedicated to the pursuit and capture of duck-bar jokes.
A duck-bar joke is a joke that must pass two critical tests:

- It must have the word "duck"
- It must have the word "bar"

The sharp-eyed observer will notice that it is not a requirement that the joke be funny, as you will see as you browse this site.

Figure 6–6. *The create page happy screen*

Notice at the very top of the page that the "About Us" link appears in the upper left. That's because we added the page to our Main menu. This is a quick way to create several important pages that your users will probably expect to see on your site. Plus, you can access the page with the URL, http://mysite.com/about directly.

WYSIWYG Editing

We just created a page using Drupal's default editing environment, which is just a simple HTML <textarea> element. For any but the most rudimentary pages, you'll probably want a more robust editor that allows for the creation of rich content without the need for hand-coding HTML tags.

There are a number of WYSIWYG editors available for Drupal. The selection of an editor can be a contentious issue, since some people are advocates for one editor or another. My favorite is CKEditor because it is simple to install and provides enough flexibility for most users.

CKEditor wasn't written specifically for Drupal. It's a general purpose JavaScript-powered tool that runs in the user's browser. There is a contributed module that provides an integration bridge between Drupal and the CKEditor code. To integrate it with Drupal, we need to add this module to our site, and then add the CKEditor bits.

First, we'll load a Drupal contributed module that provides an administrative interface for the editor. This module, titled "Wysiwyg," provides an interface for a number of different JavaScript-powered editors.

To add a new module to our site, we can use our site's administration modules page. Click "Modules" on the administrative menu, then click "Install new module". You'll see the page shown in Figure 6–7.

145

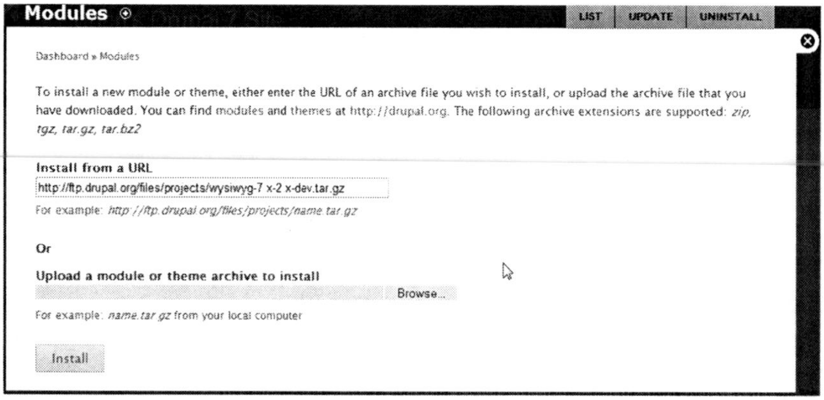

Figure 6–7. Installing a module from a URL

Enter the URL for the WYSIWYG project. At the time of this writing, the most current version is 7.x-2.x-dev. The version will probably be more advanced by the time you read this, so enter the URL that reflects the current version. You can also upload a module archive from your local machine.

■ **Tip** To find the URL for a module you want, go to the Drupal site that tracks all contributed modules, http://drupal.org/project/modules. From here, you can search the database. Once you find the module, grab the link to the one that interests you and paste it into the install module screen.

That process will write the module to the modules directory on your site. If you go to the Modules page from the administration menu, you'll see the new module. Enable it and save the configuration. (See Figure 6–8)

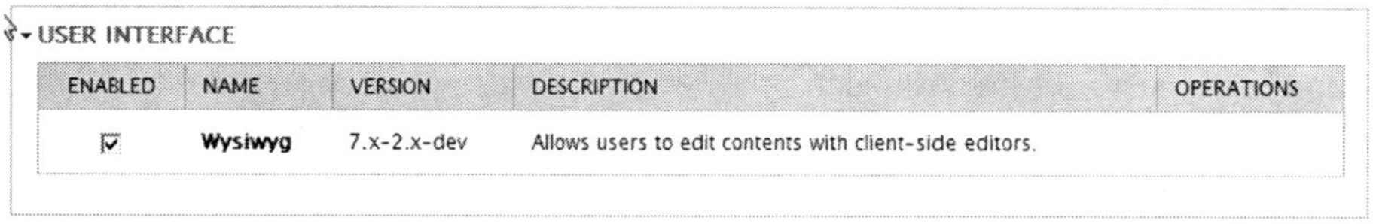

Figure 6–8. Enabling the Wysiwyg module

Now it's time to set up some profiles. Click Configuration and then Wysiwyg profiles in the Content Authoring block (see Figure 6–9).

Figure 6–9. Wysiwyg profiles

Whoops! The resulting screen, shown in Figure 6–10, indicates that something is missing.

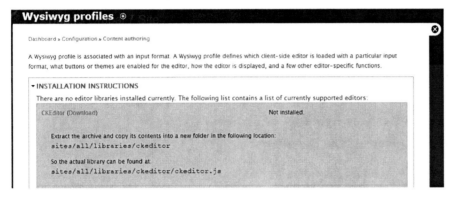

Figure 6–10. No Wysiwyg editors have been loaded yet.

You'll see on that page that the Wysiwyg module supports many different editors and supplies information on how to install each one.

So let's download the JavaScript code for CKEditor and make it available to Drupal. The JavaScript bits for CKEditor are available at http://ckeditor.com/download. Get the .zip archive and unzip it into a new directory, libraries, which will be a sibling of your modules and themes directories. (See Figure 6–11.)

Figure 6–11. The CKEditor bits go in the libraries directory.

Now go back to the Wysiwyg profiles page and refresh it. You should see the happy path screen indicating that it found the CKEditor bits. (See Figure 6–12.)

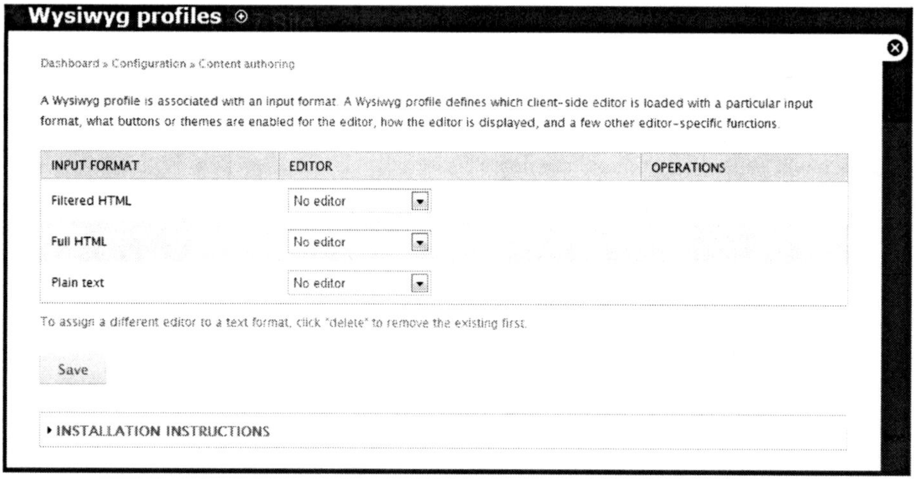

Figure 6–12. Configuring the editor for various input formats

This screen shows us the various filters that are available on our site, and gives us a chance to specify a different editor for each one. For example, we might want to use our fancy new CKEditor to do full-blown HTML editing, but for plain text we might just want to use a standard text box. Or we might have a special content type that requires a graphical XML editor. There are a lot of editors available that provide functionality for various tasks.

The Wysiwyg profiles screen is where we can create different configurations for each input format. For now, let's just create one for Filtered HTML. (See Figure 6–13.)

Figure 6–13. *Establishing CKEditor as the editor for Filtered HTML*

Once you've saved this, you'll notice "Edit" and "Delete" links to the right. Click "Edit" to specify the types of tools exposed to the user (see Figure 6–14). If you don't indicate any tools, your user will see them all, which might expose a security risk.

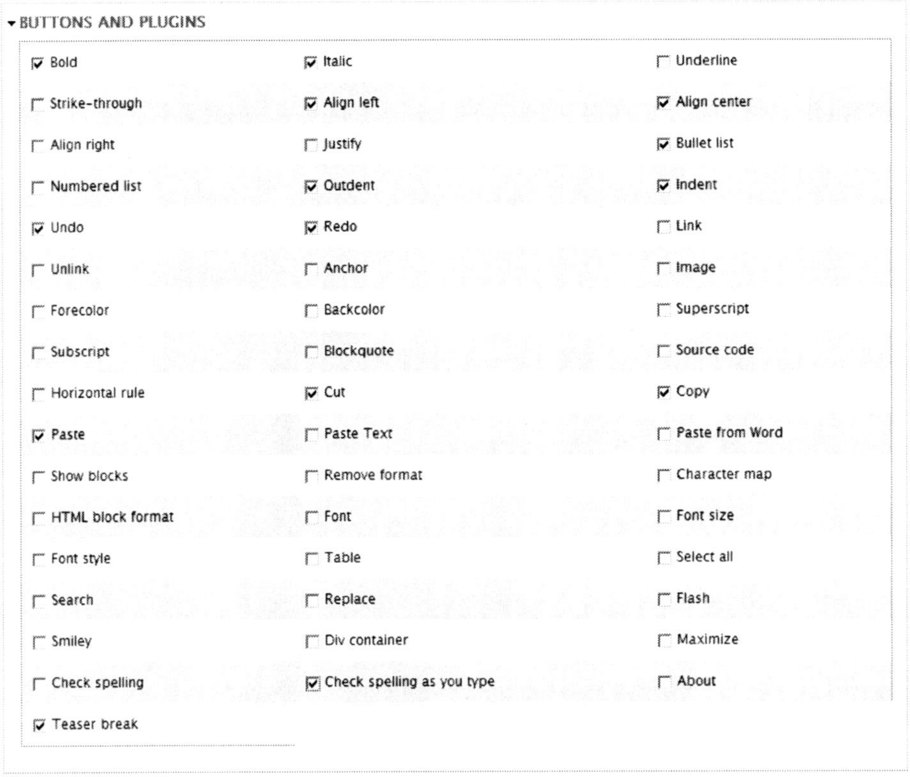

Figure 6–14. *Configuring the Wysiwyg editor*

Check the appropriate boxes and save the configuration. You can always come back later and add or remove features.

■ **Note** If you are using the Filtered HTML input format, you might confuse your users: CKeditor will correctly format all tags it recognizes, but when the user saves the document, the filter will remove all elements not allowed by the filter. Here are the tags CKEditor supports:

```
<a> <p> <span> <div> <h1> <h2> <h3> <h4> <h5> <h6> <img> <map> <area> <hr> <br> <br /> <ul>
<ol> <li> <dl> <dt> <dd> <table> <tr> <td> <em> <b> <u> <i> <strong> <del> <ins> <sub> <sup>
<quote> <blockquote> <pre> <address> <code> <cite> <embed> <object> <param> <strike> <caption>
<tbody>
```

There are modules available (ckeditor, wysiwyg_filter, htmlpurifier, htmLawed) that will help you to configure your Wysiwyg editor to work effectively with input formats. The issue of configuration is both confusing and important. If you will be relying heavily on your users creating content with a Wysiwyg editor, you owe it to yourself to master the care and feeding of input formats.

Now let's take it for a spin! Add content like you did before when we created a page, except this time create an article. You'll see the Create Article page with the new editor where the old text box was, as shown in Figure 6–15.

Figure 6–15. The Wysiwyg editor embedded in the content creation page

You can play with the editor now—enter some text. Notice that I've turned on spell-checking and put a teaser break after the first paragraph. I've also added an image. This particular image is not part of the Wysiwyg editor, but is an artifact of the Article content type.

Now save the article and go to the front page of the site. (See Figure 6–16.)

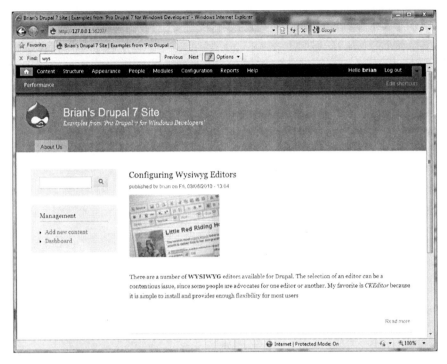

Figure 6–16. Article published to the front page

This is the default action for the Drupal content type, Article. Notice that it has it has been published to the front page, and only the first paragraph is shown, with a "Read more" link. That's because of the content break we put after the first paragraph.

If there were more articles, the first few would appear on this page in their trimmed version. As you'd expect, clicking "Read more" takes you to a page that displays the entire article.

Custom Content

Now that you've seen the basics of content creation, you might be wondering if it's possible to create content types beyond what's shipped with Drupal. The answer to that is yes! You can create custom content types using Drupal's Field framework.

■ **Note** The Field UI is just one way to add new fields to existing content types or to create entirely new content types. You can do both of these tasks by writing modules, and you'll want to do this as part of an install script, for example, if your module requires a new content type or new fields added to one of the core content types.

Field, and the companion module, Field UI, are enabled by default.

■ **Note** In researching Drupal, you might have heard about the module called "Content Construction Kit," or CCK. This was originally a module contributed and maintained by the Drupal community. In versions of Drupal prior to version 7, it was a separate download. CCK turned out to be so stable and popular that it was included as part of the Drupal 7 core and renamed "Field." CCK still exists as a contributed module, containing some features that were not ported to the Drupal core, but the most commonly used parts of CCK have been moved into the core.

Let's create a new content type called "Joke". This will have some special fields that don't exist in any other content type.

From the "Structure" menu, select "Content types," and then "Add content type." Enter information for the new content type. (See Figure 6–17)

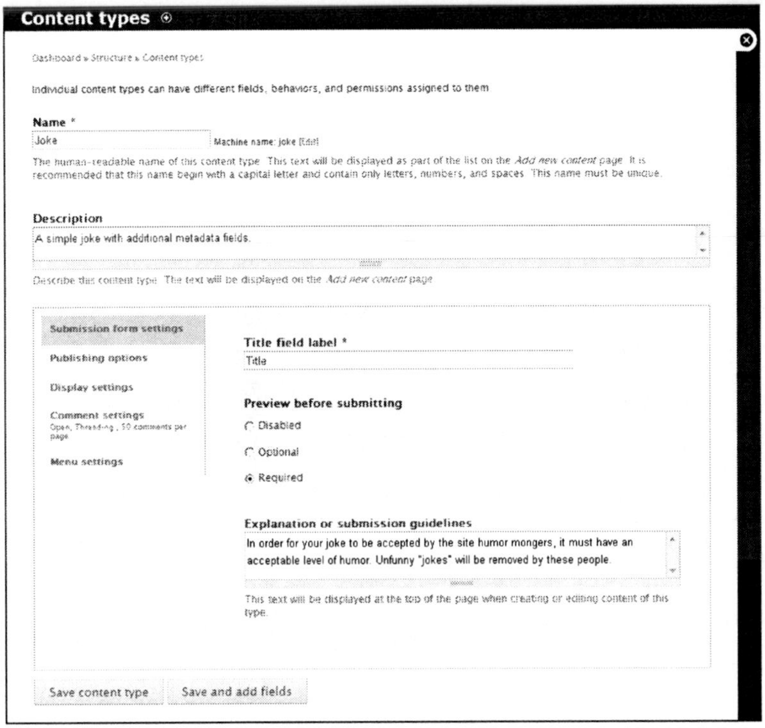

Figure 6–17. Custom content type using the Field UI

Every Drupal content type has two fields, Title and Body. If you don't like those names, you can change them, but Drupal still calls them Title and Body internally. In this case, we're happy with Title, so we leave the default.

We want to let users preview their jokes before printing, so we click the appropriate setting. This will display only the "Preview" button when they author their documents. Only after they've seen the preview will the "Save" button be displayed.

There is also a place you can communicate submission guidelines for this type of content. Various parts of the Drupal core and contributed modules use this when the content type is made available to users for creating their content.

Now press "Save and add fields" and we'll add some new fields to our content type. You'll see a screen where you can start adding fields, as shown in Figure 6–18.

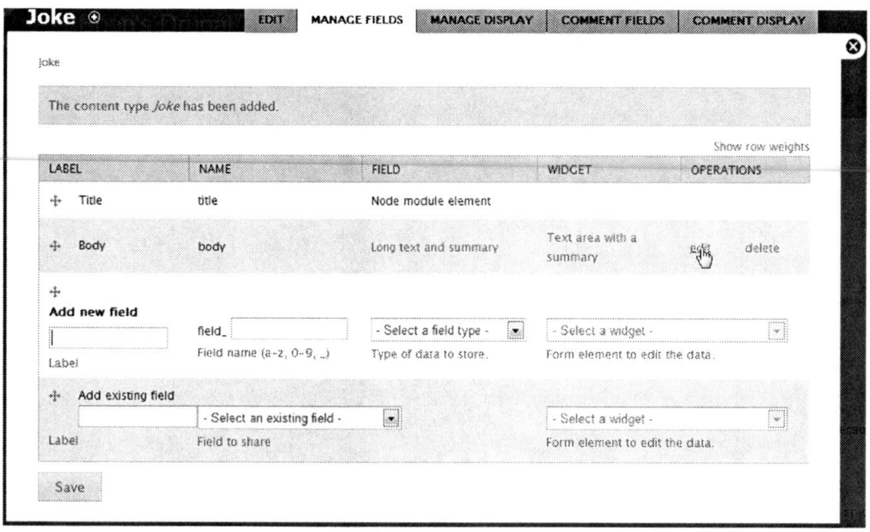

Figure 6–18. Adding fields to a content type

Notice the two standard fields that were created automatically, Title and Body. I like Title, but I'd rather name the Body field "Joke," so click "edit." Here you can rename the field and give some guidelines for entering the values. (See Figure 6–19)

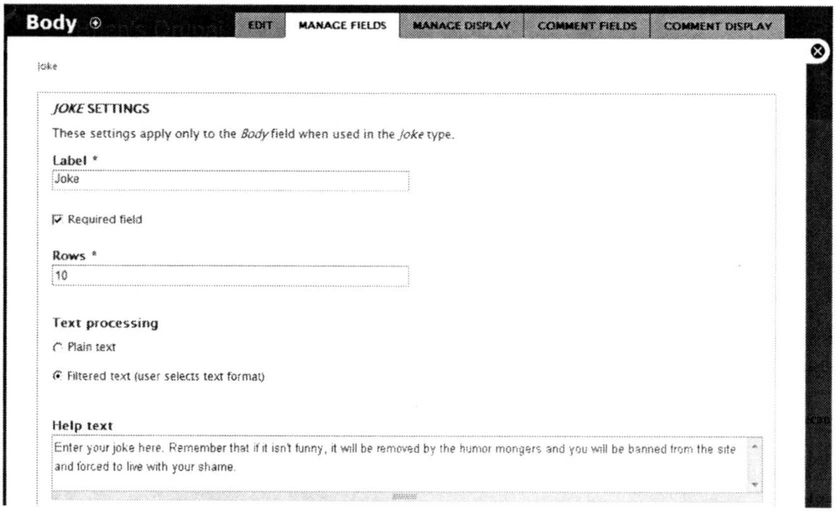

Figure 6–19. Renaming the body field and establishing help guidelines

When you save this, you will go back to the "Manage fields" screen (see Figure 6–20).

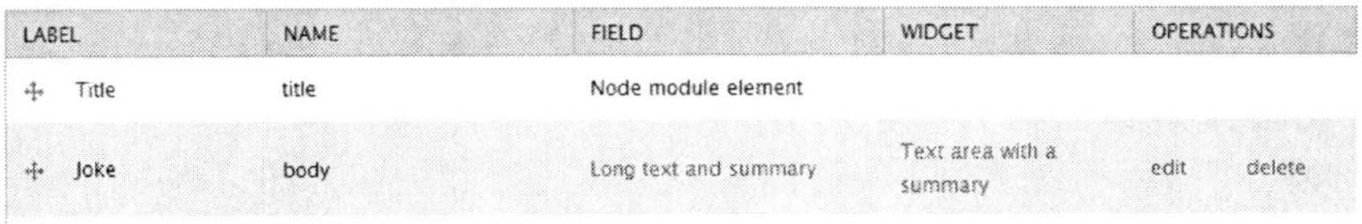

LABEL	NAME	FIELD	WIDGET	OPERATIONS	
✛ Title	title	Node module element			
✛ Joke	body	Long text and summary	Text area with a summary	edit	delete

Figure 6–20. The body field is not renamed.

Notice that, even though you have indicated that you wanted this field to be called "Joke," Drupal's internal name is still "body." This is something that you need to be aware of as you access information in your program.

■ **Tip** Sometimes, it is useful to reuse the body field, but sometimes, because of how themers treat the body, it is better just to disable it and create your own field. The theme template for the body typically includes information, such as author, date created, and comments. If you repurpose the body field, you may have to make changes to the body template. Theming is covered in Chapter 7.

We'll add two more fields, one to allow the author to indicate how funny she thinks her joke is, and another to hold a list of keywords (tags) that categorize the joke (see Figure 6–21).

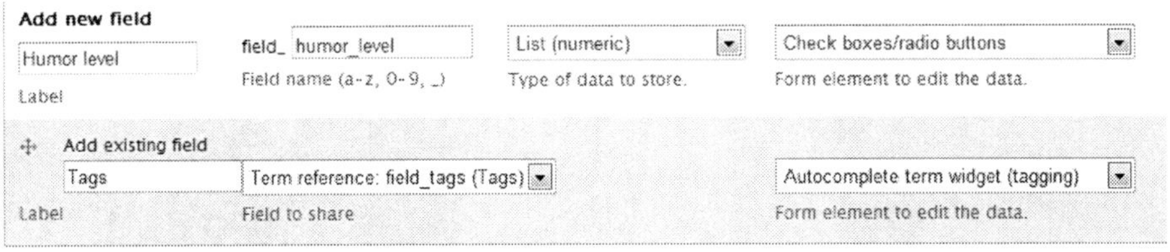

Add new field

Humor level	field_ humor_level	List (numeric) ▾	Check boxes/radio buttons ▾
Label	Field name (a-z, 0-9, _)	Type of data to store.	Form element to edit the data.

✛ **Add existing field**

Tags	Term reference: field_tags (Tags) ▾		Autocomplete term widget (tagging) ▾
Label	Field to share		Form element to edit the data.

Figure 6–21. Adding new fields to a new content type.

The first field to define is the `field_humor_level`. It is specified as a fixed list of numeric values, so we must provide that list. (See Figure 6–22)

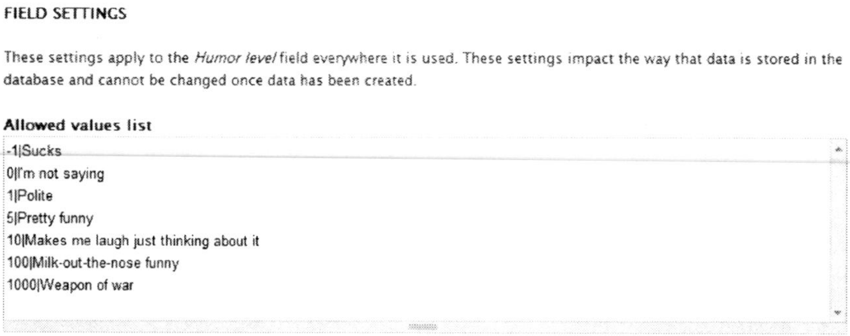

FIELD SETTINGS

These settings apply to the *Humor level* field everywhere it is used. These settings impact the way that data is stored in the database and cannot be changed once data has been created.

Allowed values list

```
-1|Sucks
0|I'm not saying
1|Polite
5|Pretty funny
10|Makes me laugh just thinking about it
100|Milk-out-the-nose funny
1000|Weapon of war
```

Figure 6–22. *Allowed values for our list*

You can enter just numbers here (one per line), or pairs in the form of key|label. The label will appear in the select list, but the key is the value that will be stored in the database. I've chosen the latter for this field type. Saving this screen takes you to another screen where you can establish the default value and provide help text. (See Figure 6–23.)

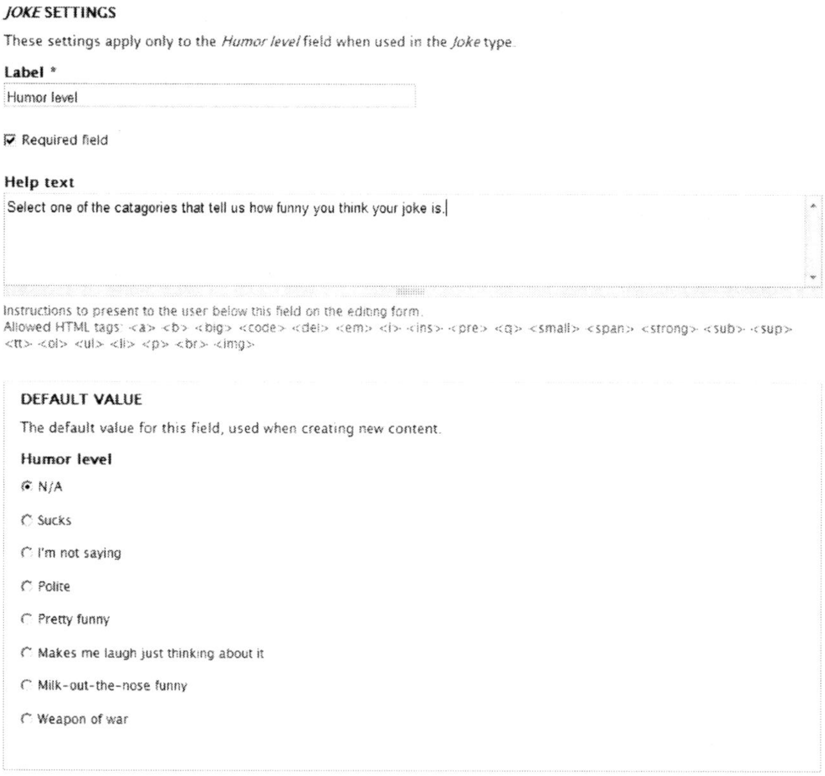

JOKE **SETTINGS**

These settings apply only to the *Humor level* field when used in the *Joke* type.

Label *

```
Humor level
```

☑ Required field

Help text

```
Select one of the catagories that tell us how funny you think your joke is.
```

Instructions to present to the user below this field on the editing form.
Allowed HTML tags: <a> <b> <big> <code> <del> <em> <i> <ins> <pre> <q> <small> <span> <strong> <sub> <sup> <tt> <ol> <ul> <li> <p>
 <img>

DEFAULT VALUE

The default value for this field, used when creating new content.

Humor level

⦿ N/A

○ Sucks

○ I'm not saying

○ Polite

○ Pretty funny

○ Makes me laugh just thinking about it

○ Milk-out-the-nose funny

○ Weapon of war

Figure 6–23. *Settings for the Humor level field*

On the next screen, you can enter settings for the next field, Tags. You'll want to make it a required field and set "Number of values" to "Unlimited". Saving this will bring you back to the main screen for this content type. (See Figure 6–24.)

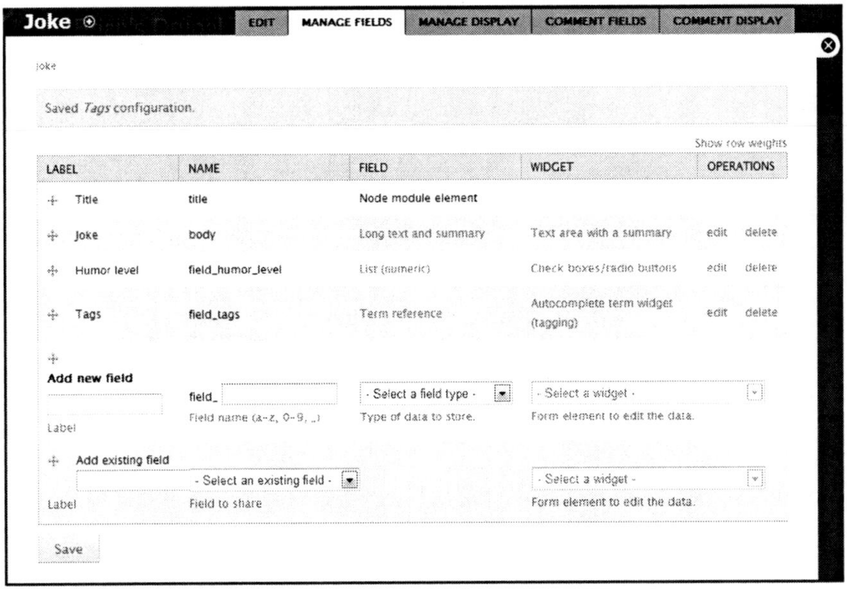

Figure 6–24. Screen showing the two new fields

From here you can add more fields, but let's stop and create some content. From the main menu, click on Content➤Add new content to show the content type we just declared. (See Figure 6–25.)

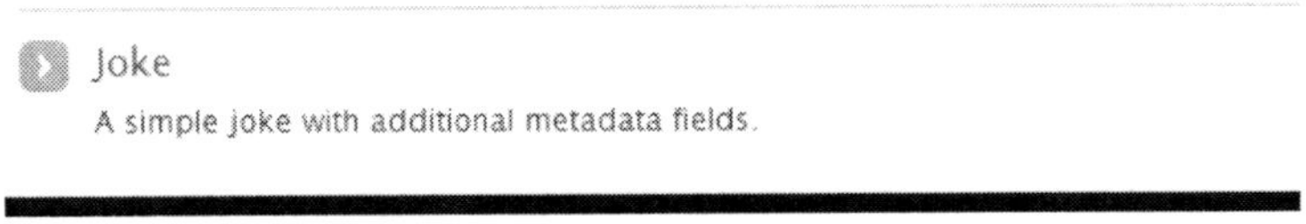

Figure 6–25. New content type

This brings up the content creation page, where we can see the two fields we just defined (see Figure 6–26).

Title *
Food walks in
Joke *(Edit summary)
A cheeseburger and french fries walk into a bar. The bartender says, "We don't serve food here."
body p

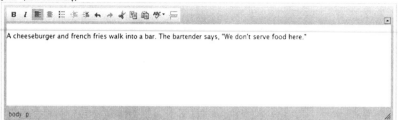

Figure 6–26. Content creation screen

Farther down on the screen, we can see the two extra fields we created, as shown in Figure 6–27.

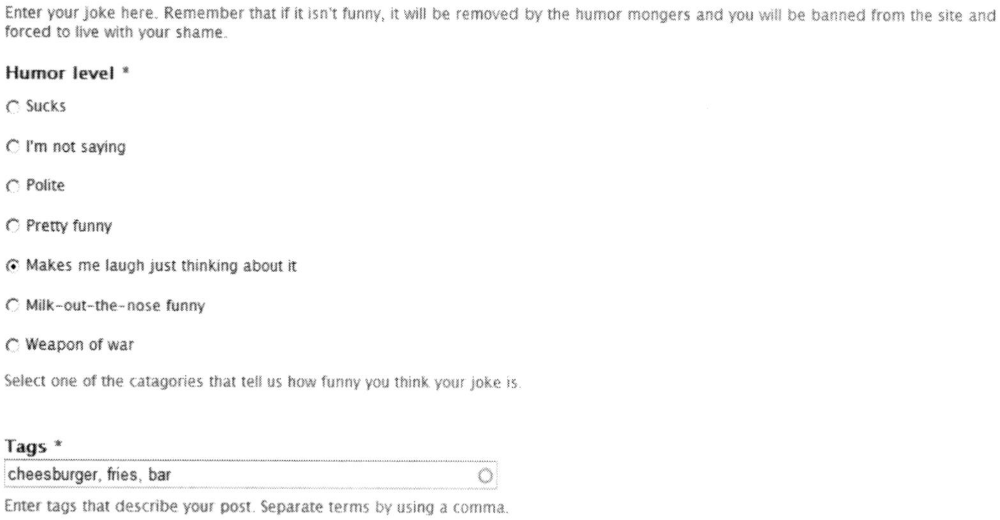
Enter your joke here. Remember that if it isn't funny, it will be removed by the humor mongers and you will be banned from the site and forced to live with your shame.
Humor level *
Sucks
I'm not saying
Polite
Pretty funny
Makes me laugh just thinking about it
Milk-out-the-nose funny
Weapon of war
Select one of the catagories that tell us how funny you think your joke is.
Tags *
cheesburger, fries, bar
Enter tags that describe your post. Separate terms by using a comma.

Figure 6–27. Extra fields to be filled out

Notice the Preview button on the bottom. There is no Save button because we indicated earlier that users must preview their submissions before saving them. This could prevent a posting from going out with unrecognized errors. Clicking Preview will show the trimmed and full versions of the post, and also expose the Save button for committing to the database.

■ **Note** Drupal has the ability to create database tables using the Schema contributed module. If you need to create content types that are not managed by Drupal's content management system, this could be a good alternative. However, if you want all of the goodness that Drupal provides for managed content (comments, revisions, theming, etc.), then custom content types make a lot of sense. I cover the Schema API in Chapter 10.

We'll be using this example later when we do theming. For now, you might want to enter a few more jokes so you have some content to work with. As a start, you can swipe some jokes from my site, DuckBarJokes.com.

Permissions

Drupal has a rich role-based permissions framework. We've already seen some of it as we made some aspects of contributed modules available to certain users. Let's talk more about the permissions framework and how it works.

Each module can specify its own custom permissions to be displayed on the Permissions page. A module programmer can use those custom permissions, or any other permissions, to guide the display, editing, or deletion of various parts of the site.

You can even set permissions on particular nodes based on practically any criteria you'd like. If you want to restrict access to certain users if a piece of content contains the word "McNugget," but only on Fridays when everyone knows you should be eating the Filet-O-Fish, you can write code that will achieve that silly goal.

Users and Roles

Working hand-in-hand with the permissions framework is the concept of user roles. Every user who accesses your site will have one or more roles. Each user has a unique user id, or uid, which is an integer that increments with each new user.

There are two special uids on your site, 0 and 1. When you first configured your site, you entered the username and password of the administrator, who automatically became uid 1. The administrator has access to every single aspect of your site, and does not require any permissions to be set.

At the other end of the spectrum is a user when he first comes to the site. This user is considered "anonymous" and will have a uid of zero.

All other users are considered "authenticated" once they create an account and, optionally, depending on how you configure your site, authenticate that they have a valid e-mail address. Users can create an account by clicking the "Create new account" link under the Log in button.

This will take them to the registration screen, which will only ask for a username and a e-mail address by default. This is shown in Figure 6–28.

Figure 6–28. *New user registration screen*

By default, only a username and e-mail address are required, but you can add more required fields, as we will shortly. By default, the system will send an e-mail to the user requesting her to click on a link. This will verify that the person has entered a valid e-mail address and that the user has access to that e-mail address. This helps to avoid spambots from creating bogus accounts.

Note: if you want more protection against bots, there are a number of bot-fighting modules you can employ, such as CAPTCHA, as shown below:

Username: *

Spaces are allowed; punctuation is not allowed except for periods, hyphens, and underscores.

E-mail address: *

A valid e-mail address. All e-mails from the system will be sent to this address. The e-mail address is not made public and will only be used if you wish to receive a new password or wish to receive certain news or notifications by e-mail.

CAPTCHA

This question is for testing whether you are a human visitor and to prevent automated spam submissions.

What code is in the image?: *

Enter the characters shown in the image.

Create new account

The CAPTCHA module is quick to install in your Drupal enviroment and provides instant discouragement to bots.

The user will see a confirmation that the account was created (see Figure 6–29).

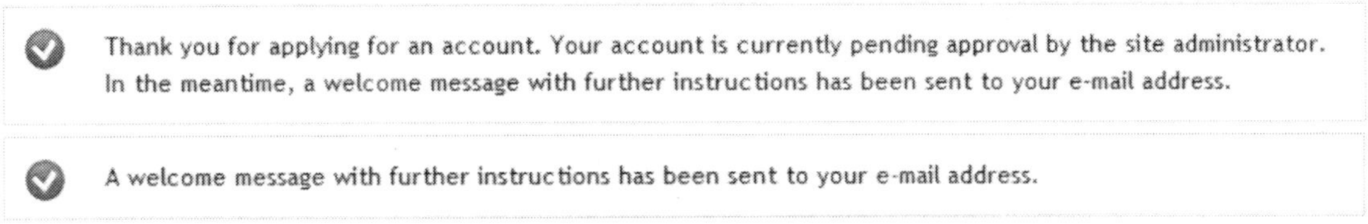

Figure 6–29. The confirmation shown to the user will depend on site approval settings.

As an administrator, you can specify more information that is required on the form at Configuration➤Account settings. That page is shown in Figure 6–30.

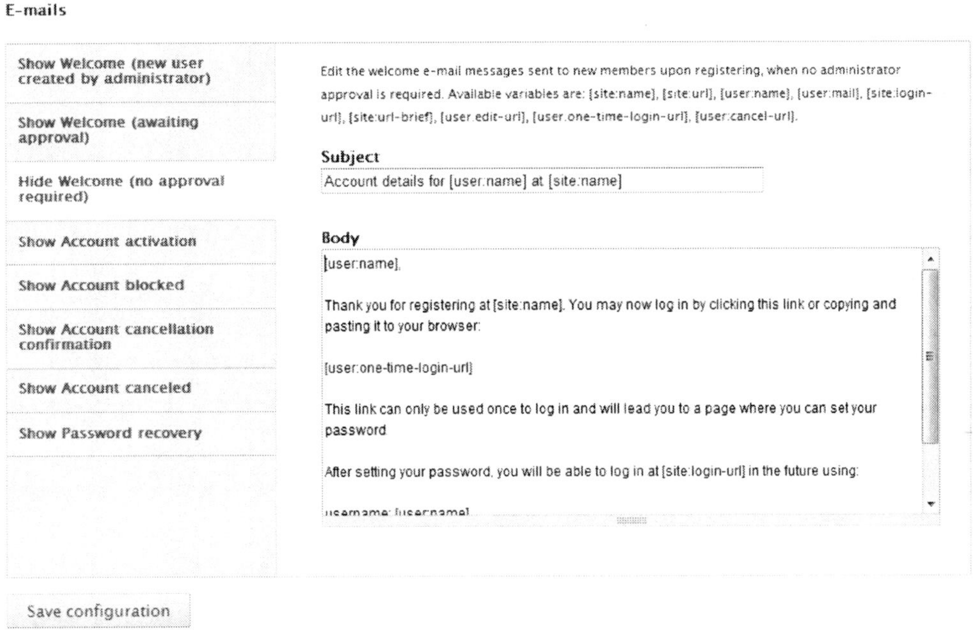

Figure 6–30. In the account settings screen you can craft emails for various purposes.

You can, for example, require that the user respond to an e-mail in order to be authenticated, or that all users be approved by an administrator before being granted access to the system.

On this page, you can also craft e-mail templates for various user management functions:

- Welcome message for a new user created by administrator
- Welcome message for a new user where no approval is required
- Welcome message for a new user who is awaiting administrator approval

- E-mail sent once an administrator approves the account

- E-mail sent when a user asks for password recovery

- E-mail sent to inform a user that his or her account has been blocked

- E-mail sent to inform a user that his or her account has been deleted

These messages have variables available so you can personalize the message to the user. Once a user registers, he or she will get assigned the next available uid. An example e-mail message is shown in Figure 6–31.

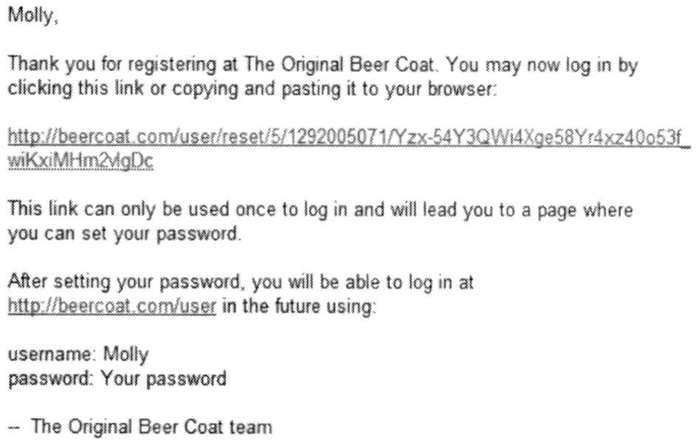

Molly,

Thank you for registering at The Original Beer Coat. You may now log in by clicking this link or copying and pasting it to your browser:

http://beercoat.com/user/reset/5/1292005071/Yzx-54Y3QWi4Xge58Yr4xz40o53f_wiKxiMHm2vlgDc

This link can only be used once to log in and will lead you to a page where you can set your password.

After setting your password, you will be able to log in at http://beercoat.com/user in the future using:

username: Molly
password: Your password

-- The Original Beer Coat team

Figure 6–31. *An message generated to assure a valid e-mail address*

In the case of the site allowing visitors to create their own accounts, the e-mail sent will have the standard link to verify that the e-mail address is correct. It also gives the new user the ability to set a password, as shown in Figure 6–32.

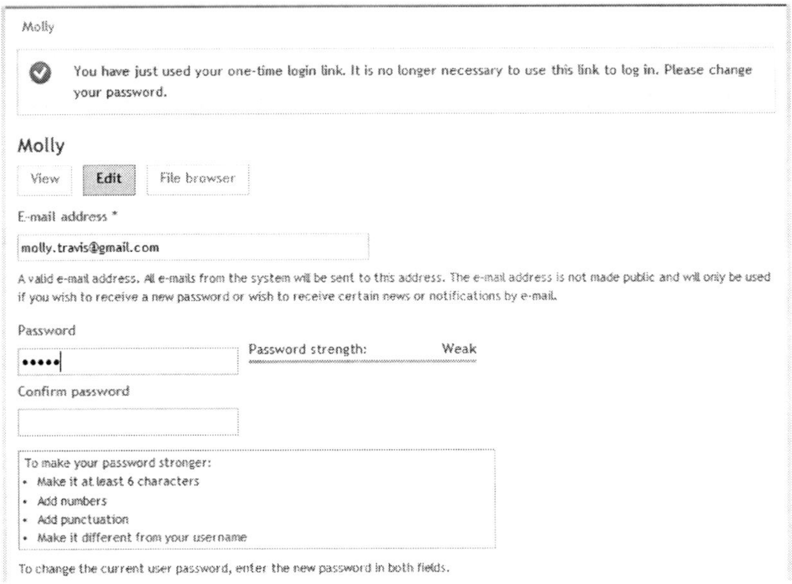

Figure 6–32. Initial user login screen

Once authenticated, either by administrative approval or e-mail verification (or immediately if user authentication is turned off), the user can access the system.

The site administrator can also manually authenticate a user by changing Status from Blocked to Active.

Adding a Role

Your site can have as many different roles as necessary. Let's create a new role for authenticated users on our site whom we have chosen to write blog entries. Let's call the role "blogger." Before doing this, make sure the Blog module is enabled (from the Modules menu).

Access the roles page by navigating to People➤Permissions➤Roles. (See Figure 6–33.)

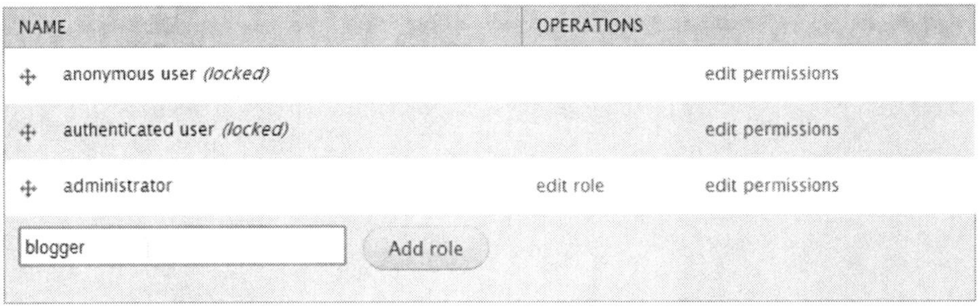

NAME	OPERATIONS	
✛ anonymous user *(locked)*		edit permissions
✛ authenticated user *(locked)*		edit permissions
✛ administrator	edit role	edit permissions
blogger	Add role	

Figure 6–33. Adding a new role

Type "blogger" and click "Add role". Once the screen comes back, click "edit permissions" to get to the permissions page shown in Figure 6–34.

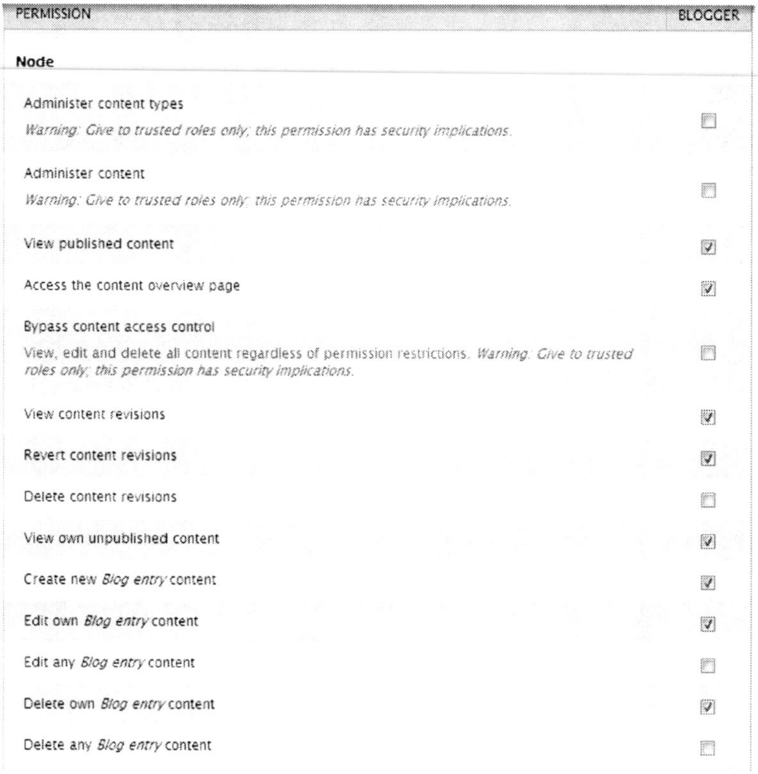

PERMISSION	BLOGGER
Node	
Administer content types	☐
Warning: Give to trusted roles only; this permission has security implications.	
Administer content	☐
Warning: Give to trusted roles only; this permission has security implications.	
View published content	☑
Access the content overview page	☑
Bypass content access control	☐
View, edit and delete all content regardless of permission restrictions. *Warning: Give to trusted roles only; this permission has security implications.*	
View content revisions	☑
Revert content revisions	☑
Delete content revisions	☐
View own unpublished content	☑
Create new *Blog entry* content	☑
Edit own *Blog entry* content	☑
Edit any *Blog entry* content	☐
Delete own *Blog entry* content	☑
Delete any *Blog entry* content	☐

Figure 6–34. *Permissions page for new user*

When you go to the user permissions page you'll see the new role with nothing checked. Check the appropriate permissions and click "Save permissions".

Finally, we'll need to assign a role to a user. When a user creates an account, she is granted the default role, "Authenticated user." If we want to create a user, let's say a "blogger," we can add a new user, or just have that user create her own account, and then promote her afterwards. That's usually the easiest first step for creating a user with different roles. Once the user account is present, you add it to other roles by accessing the account under the People tab on the administration menu. (See Figure 6–35.)

Status

○ Blocked

◉ Active

Roles

☑ authenticated user

☐ administrator

☑ blogger

Figure 6–35. *Activating a user and adding roles*

The user now has the combined permissions of anyone who is an authenticated user or a blogger. Now that the permissions are in place and the user has been assigned a role, how can we take advantage of them in our modules? You've probably guessed that one of the answers has to be hooks.

Programming Permissions

To create entries on the permissions page, you need to write a hook function in your module. For this exercise, I'll be using the weather block module we developed in Chapter 5.

Let's say we have three different settings we want to control:

1. Administer the weather information. This will allow us to set the default location, units, and language for the weather module.

2. View the default weather information, that is, the location, units, and language we established on a site-wide basis with the weather administration function we wrote in Chapter 5.

3. Get weather for any location. This will display the weather location in put box and "Get weather" button on our weather information block.

The Permission Hook

First we need to create these permissions so they will appear on the permissions form. We can do this with the permission hook shown in Listing 6–1.

Listing 6–1. *The Permissions Hook*

```
function weather_info_permission() {
  return array(
    'administer weather info' =>  array(
      'title' => t('Administer weather information'),
      'description' => t('Set global site information for language, units, and location.'),
    ),
    'view weather info' =>  array(
      'title' => t('View weather information'),
      'description' => t('View the site-wide weather information on pages.'),
    ),
    'change weather location' =>  array(
```

```
        'title' => t('Change weather location'),
        'description' => t('Change the current location for weather information.'),
      ),
    );
}
```

Once we've created this in our code, we will immediately see it when we go to the permissions page, as Figure 6–36 shows.

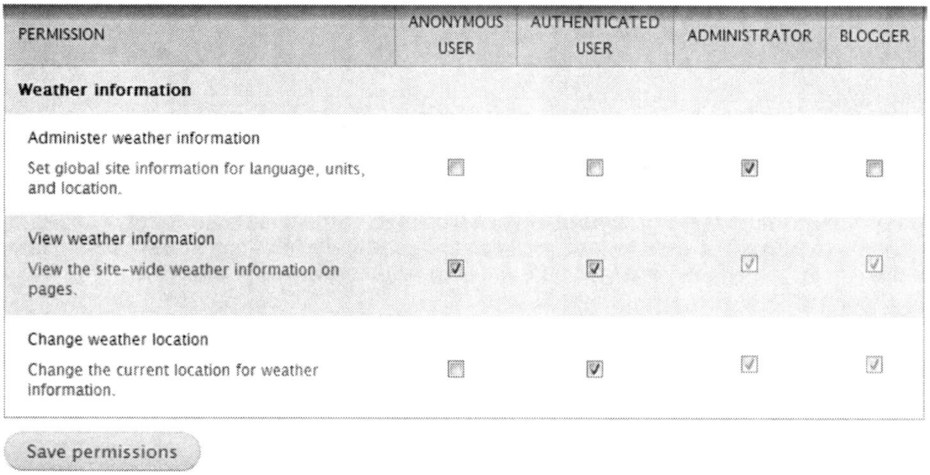

PERMISSION	ANONYMOUS USER	AUTHENTICATED USER	ADMINISTRATOR	BLOGGER
Weather information				
Administer weather information				
Set global site information for language, units, and location.	☐	☐	☑	☐
View weather information				
View the site-wide weather information on pages.	☑	☑	☑	☑
Change weather location				
Change the current location for weather information.	☐	☑	☑	☑

Save permissions

Figure 6–36. *Permissions screen for weather information*

Notice that the entries on the page were generated by the contents of the array in the hook function we just wrote. Also, see that the block title is the same as our module name. And you can see the new role, Blogger, that we just created, as well as the three that were already defined.

In determining who gets access to what, you can see that only the administrator gets the permission to change the site-wide settings, but everyone, even anonymous users, can see the weather for that site-wide location. And authenticated users can change the location, but they can't change the language or units settings.

Also notice that the page knows that the administrator and blogger roles are also authenticated users, so when I check the authenticated user box, the administrator and blogger boxes automatically get set, and they become grayed so I can't uncheck them.

Set the permissions as you see fit and click "Save permissions". Of course, just having those permissions there does absolutely nothing. In order for them to work, we need to incorporate the permissions engine into our module.

Creating roles and assigning permissions doesn't change anything in our module. The task now is to tell our module how to handle access to the information based on roles and permissions. This is done with the access hook.

Access Hook

The user_access() function checks to see if the currently logged-on user has the checkbox set for a particular permission. So at the top of our Weather information module code, we'll want to see if the user has the ability to even display the block at all. Listing 6–2 checks to see if a user has that permission.

Listing 6–2. Checking User Access

```
function weather_info_block_view($delta='') {
  if (!user_access('view weather info')) {
    return null;
  }
  ...
```

This might seem unnecessary, since we've already said that everyone, including anonymous visitors, can view the site-wide weather information. However, we might want to change that policy at a later date. If we don't have this check in our code, we won't have the flexibility to make that change.

■ **Note** the user_access function requires a string that indicates the permission setting. This string must be the key of the array declaring the permission, not the title or description.

Then, as we move down the code, we'll want to see if the user has permission to get the weather for any location. If so, we will want to place the textbox and submit button. Otherwise, we'll just print the current conditions and forecast if we can find it. This is shown in Listing 6–3.

Listing 6–3. Checking Whether a User can Change a Location

```
if (user_access('change weather location')) {
  $temp = drupal_get_form('weather_location_form');
  $block_content .= drupal_render($temp);
}
```

This simple change allows users who don't have the "change weather location" permission to still see the current weather defaults, but the weather location form will not appear on their screens.

Finally, we have our administrative permission. Back in Chapter 5 we created the menu function for the administrative settings. One of the lines was

```
'access arguments' => array('administer weather info'),
```

The access arguments parameter uses the same string as the user_access function.

■ **Tip** You can set permissions for any level of granularity you desire, but be careful not to overburden the permissions page. Note that there is a checkbox for every role and for every permission. You should plan your roles to cover your needs, but don't create a whole new role when a simple permission will do. Don't create a new permission when an existing one will do. Your administrator users will thank you.

Of course, if you create a permission string for every little aspect of your module, the administration could become unwieldy. On the other hand, if you set permissions too broadly, you might not be able to restrict current or future users to the level you desire. As with many aspects of programming, the happy place is found in the middle.

Now that we know how to assign a user a role and set permissions for that role, let's work on making the user's experience more personalized. To do this, we can set up a separate profile for each user.

Attached Fields

Earlier in this chapter, we created a content type, Joke, that took advantage of the concept of fields. Because it's a content type, it has all of the goodies that content types have. For example, Drupal will keep multiple revisions of the content and make available comments if you desire. It will also display the content in summary form on a page or in full form, depending on how you set things up.

We created a new content type by attaching fields to Drupal's "node" type. The concept of "attached fields" is new to Drupal 7, and is baked into the core code. Accessing the goodness of fields is done with the new Field API. And with the Field API comes some terms:

- **Field**: A field defines a particular type of data that can be attached to a fieldable entity type.

- **Fieldable entity type**: An object you can attach fields to. There are four fieldable objects in the Drupal core: node, taxonomy term, comment, and user. The Field CRUD API is used to create, query, update, and delete fields from the fieldable entities.

- **Field instance**: A field that is attached to a bundle.

- **Bundle**: A set of fields that are treated as a group by the Field Attach API. In the Joke structure we created earlier in this chapter, the Humor level and Tags objects are field instances that were attached to the bundle called Joke. Earlier, I called "Joke" a content type, but "bundle" is the term that is used in the Field API jargon. When the node system uses the Field Attach API to load all fields for a Joke node, it passes the node's entity type (which is "node") and content type (which is "joke") as the node's bundle. The `field_attach_load()` function then loads the `field_humor_level` and `field_tags` fields because they are both attached to the "node" bundle "joke".

- **Widget**: A field type has an inherent structure and can be represented in the UI depending on that structure. For example, a list of options can be represented as a pull-down list or a set of checkboxes. A text field can be presented as a text field or a text area. An image might be represented as an upload object with a thumbnail showing the current image. A widget is the thing that is used to present your field to the user. When you create a field type, you also provide a list of widgets that are appropriate for that field type.

- **Field storage**: The storage of attached fields is managed by the Field Storage API. The default storage for fields is the database, but you can write your own storage backend to store your bundles. This is an incredibly powerful concept that is new to Drupal 7. Say, for example, you have a field type that is a PDF document. Storing that in the MySQL database would be cumbersome, so you can create a hook that will put these field types in the file system, or even in a PDF-friendly engine, such as Documentum, PaperVision, or SharePoint. Or you might want to set up a set of web services to store and retrieve certain entity types. The Field Storage API allows you to do this.

If this new vocabulary seems confusing, don't worry; it will become clearer as we move through an example. Let's go back to the weather information code we were working on earlier and make it so each user can set up his or her own location. We will be taking an existing fieldable entity type, user, and attach some new fields to it, creating a bundle that can be managed.

There are two basic ways to create our bundle. We can do it programmatically with the Field API, or we can take advantage of the Administrative UI we used earlier in the chapter. For now, let's use the UI and later, in Chapter 10, we'll use the Field API when we create our installation program.

To attach fields to the user entity type, go to Configuration➤Account settings, and then Manage Fields, as shown in Figure 6–37.

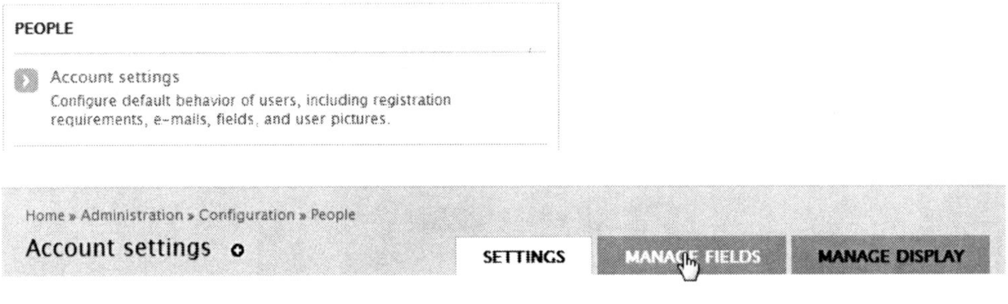

Figure 6–37. Starting the process of attaching fields to an entity type

This brings up the familiar Field UI we saw earlier (see Figure 6–38). The difference is that now we see the existing fields for the user entity type, instead of the node type.

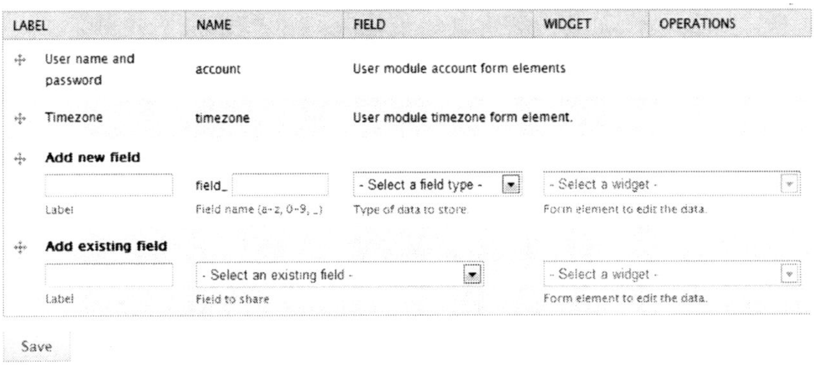

Figure 6–38. The Field user interface

We create the fields the same way as with the Joke content type above, first supplying a label and a field name, and then picking the field type and widget. See Figure 6–39.

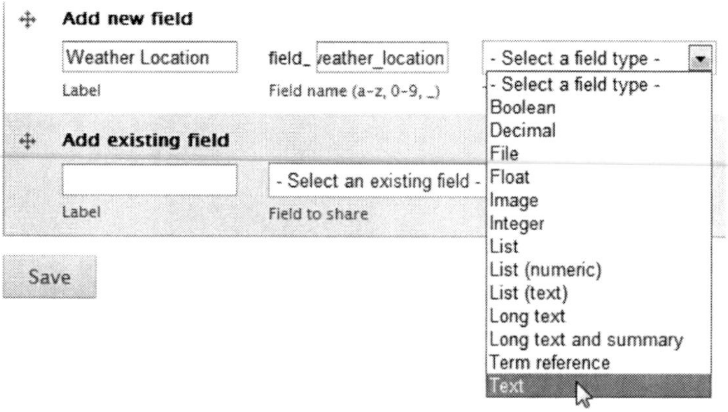

Figure 6–39. Creating a field

The rest of the screens are pretty self-explanatory. You'll want to set the maximum length of the location field to 20, as shown in Figure 6–40.

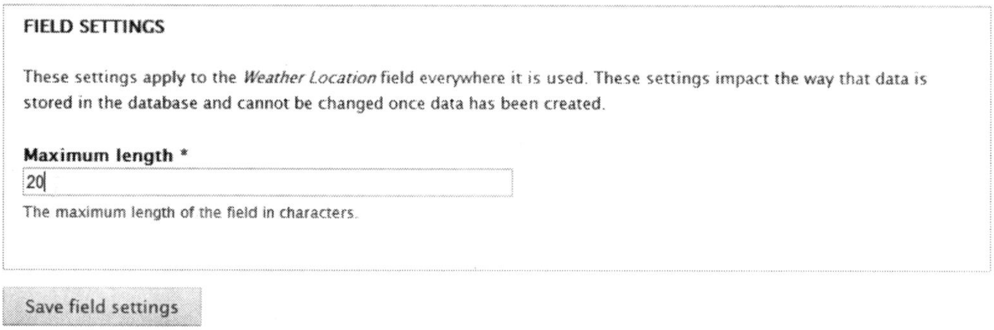

Figure 6–40. Field settings for length

And there are more settings. Notice the "Size of textfield" field in the next screen, shown in Figure 6–41.

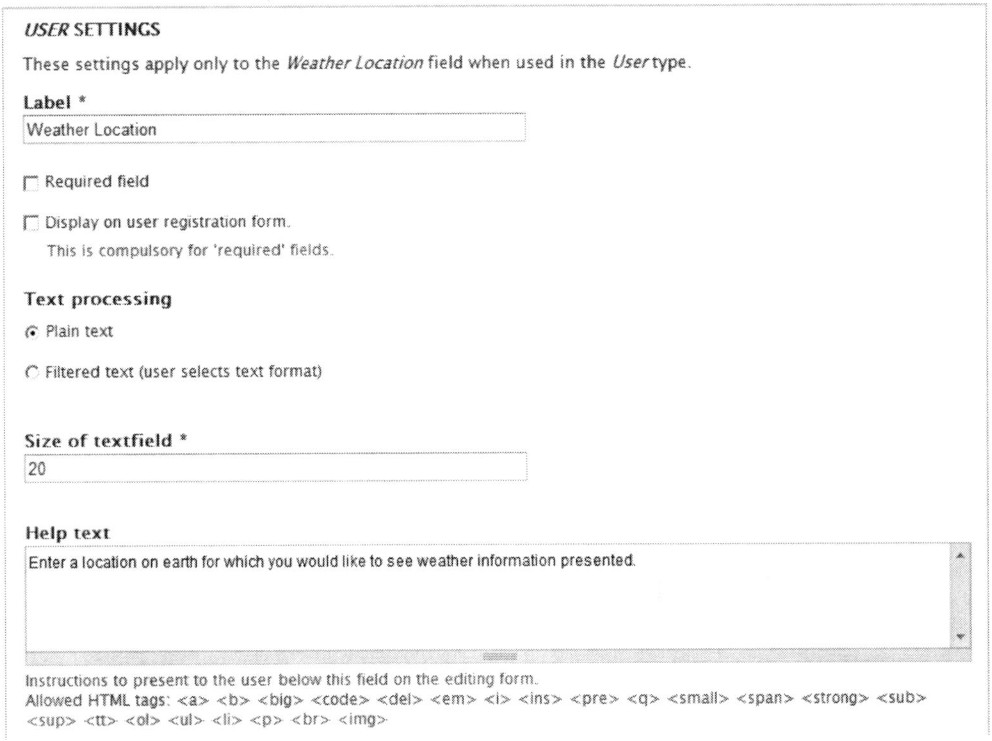

USER SETTINGS

These settings apply only to the *Weather Location* field when used in the *User* type.

Label *

Weather Location

☐ Required field

☐ Display on user registration form.
  This is compulsory for 'required' fields.

Text processing

◉ Plain text

○ Filtered text (user selects text format)

Size of textfield *

20

Help text

Enter a location on earth for which you would like to see weather information presented.

Instructions to present to the user below this field on the editing form.
Allowed HTML tags: <a> <b> <big> <code> <del> <em> <i> <ins> <pre> <q> <small> <span> <strong> <sub>
<sup> <tt> <ol> <ul> <li> <p>
 <img>

Figure 6–41. More field settings

Compare this with the previous screen and the field labeled "Maximum length". The maximum length of the field determines how much space is allocated in the database for the string. "Size of textfield" indicates the size of the field widget that will be presented to the user when the value of the field is required. You may, for example, want to reserve 255 characters for the field in the database, but only have a 25-character text box to present to the user.

This screen also has a place for Help text to prompt the user for what to enter as the value. Clicking the Save settings button will bring you back to the field list.

The next field will be a text list containing all of the supported language codes. (See Figure 6–42).

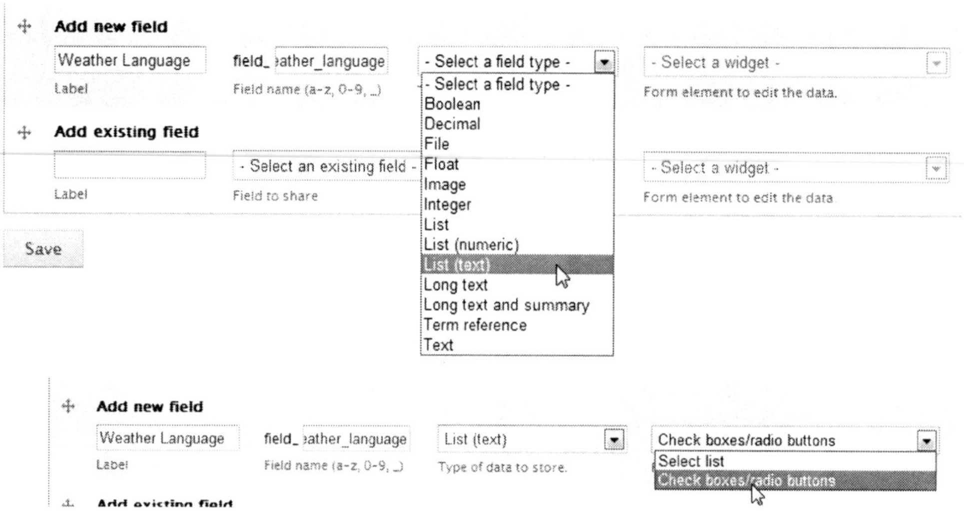

Figure 6–42. Creating a list of values

There are two options for the widget this time—a select-style pulldown list and a series of checkboxes. Either one will work, and can be changed later.

Like in the joke example, the options are listed in a set of key|value pairs (See Figure 6–43.)

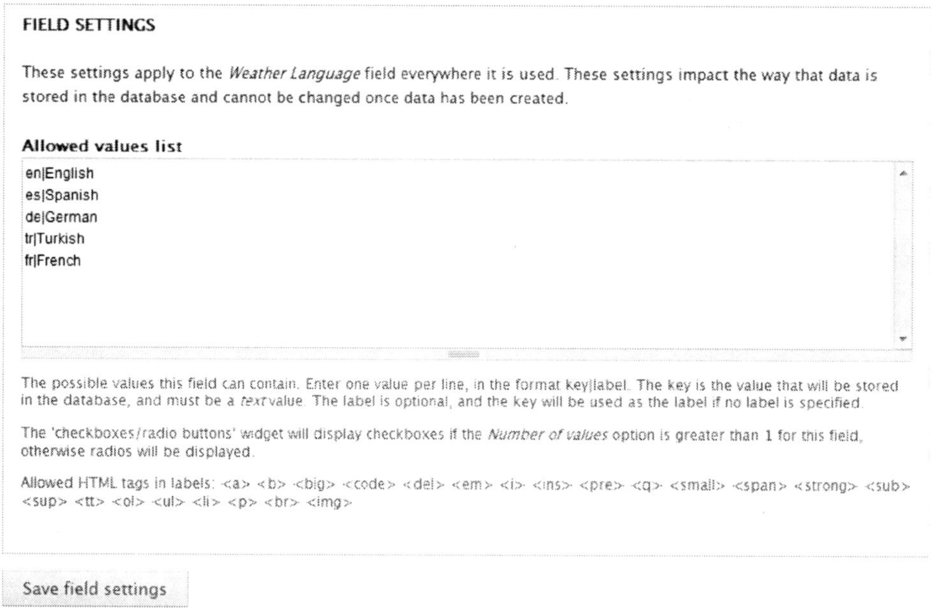

Figure 6–43. Creating a set of options

The next screen lets you indicate the help text and default value from the list. After that, we can create a text list for unit and see the results on our field list screen (see Figure 6–44).

LABEL	NAME	FIELD	WIDGET	OPERATIONS
⊹ User name and password	account	User module account form elements		
⊹ Timezone	timezone	User module timezone form element.		
⊹ Weather location	field_weather_location	Text	Text field	edit delete
⊹ Weather language	field_weather_language	List (text)	Check boxes/radio buttons	edit delete
⊹ Weather units	field_weather_unit	List (text)	Select list	edit delete

Figure 6–44. Three fields ready for processing

These three fields must be created before our weather information module can work properly. In Chapter 10 we'll write an installation program that creates these fields programmatically so our users don't have to deal with the details of the Field UI.

Now we'll enter some values and customize our weather display for each logged-in user. Under the People tab, find a user and click "Edit". (See Figure 6–45.)

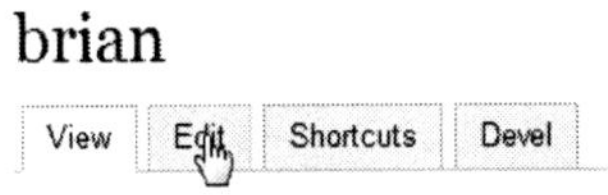

brian

| View | Edit | Shortcuts | Devel |

Figure 6–45. Editing the user's fields

That takes us to the user's profile screen. At the bottom, we can see the three fields we created and attached to the user entity type (see Figure 6–46).

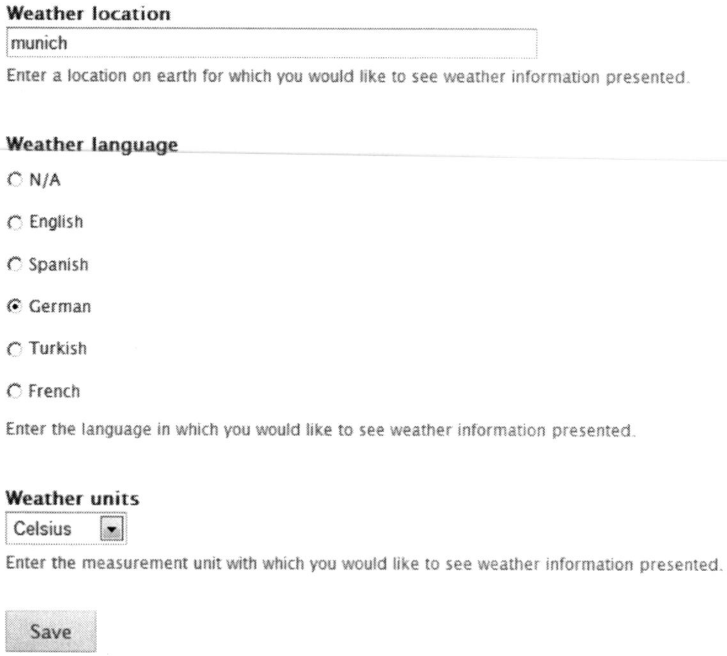

Weather location

munich

Enter a location on earth for which you would like to see weather information presented.

Weather language

○ N/A

○ English

○ Spanish

● German

○ Turkish

○ French

Enter the language in which you would like to see weather information presented.

Weather units

Celsius ▼

Enter the measurement unit with which you would like to see weather information presented.

Save

Figure 6–46. *New fields attached to the user entity type*

Notice the two different types of widgets. The weather language field uses the check boxes/radio button widget, and the units field uses the select list widget. You'd probably want to make these consistent; I show them here just so you can see how each is presented to the user.

We've just created three fields and attached them to the user entity type. This is a powerful concept in Drupal, and one that will be getting a lot of attention as people learn about this feature. The Field API has calls that let you create your own custom field types, along with widgets and validators that are invoked when a user creates an instance of the field. For example, you might want to create a field that represents a color. This field would save the three values for red, green, and blue and might have a color picker as its widget. And perhaps a validator would determine if the particular color chosen was renderable in a basic CSS color profile.

Creating a custom field is the first step, and then you can attach it to certain entity types, which can then be managed as bundles.

Form Alter

The weather location can be a valid location, or it could be something that is not acceptable to the weather service we are using. If we have a bad value in that field, it doesn't make sense to load it into the database, as the user would get an error next time she refreshed the page.

We can use the validate hook to verify that the location is correct before submitting the form. We did this back in Chapter 5, but there's a difference with how we deal with the fields we attached to the user entity. When we hooked into the validate function, we owned the form and named the validate function in a way that the form processor was expecting.

With the way we are adding our fields to the standard user profile screen, however, we don't own the form, Drupal does. With a little investigation, I found that the name of the function that creates the form is user_profile_form(). According to the naming conventions for hooks, we would expect that we just need to create a function called user_profile_form_validate() to be called by the form submission logic, right?

But it's not quite that easy. You see, the user_profile_form() function belongs to the User module, which already has a function called user_profile_form_validate(). If we created a function with that same name, we'd get a PHP error.

So how can we hook into the validate functionality of the user_profile_form() function without violating PHP's rules? We can do this by altering the form before it is displayed, and creating our own validation function.

Let's first create a function that validates the field (see Listing 6–4).

Listing 6–4. Element Validation Function

```
function weather_info_profile_weather_location_validate($element, &$form_state) {
  $location = $form_state['values']['field_weather_location']['und'][0]['value'];
  if (variable_get('default_location') != $location) {
    $weather = weather_info_get_weather($location, 'en');
    if (!$weather) {
      form_set_error('field_weather_location[und][0][value]',
        t('Cannot get weather for %location.',
        array('%location' => $location)));
    }
  }
}
```

This function takes an element, which is a single field on the form, and the same form state structure that is passed to any validation hook. The code grabs the location submitted on the form, and then checks to see if it is different from the one already in our variable store. There's no reason to check for validity if the value is already there.

So how do I know that the name of the field we are interested in is field_weather_location[und][0][value]? The most straightforward way is to have the page render in the browser and then view the source. You'll see something like this:

```
<input name="field_weather_location[und][0][value]" type="text" .../>
```

You can also use a browser debugging tool to highlight the field and check out its properties.

■ **Note** Notice the und array key. This is reserved for language. It is conceivable that you have a multilingual site that has a collection of different translations for a particular field. This array key is where each language will be specified. The value und means "undetermined".

This function gets the location from the form and then calls the weather service to see if it will return a valid report. If there's a problem, it sets the form error, which will keep the submit hook from firing.

Now that we have this function, we need to tell the form, which is owned by someone else, that we want our validation function added to the list of functions to be called when the form is submitted. We do this by writing a function that hooks into Drupal's form-alter mechanism.

Our form-alter function will be called after the form that's being altered has been built, but just before it is to be rendered. That way, all of the fields and settings of the form are available to our function, and we can add, delete, or change whatever we want.

The trick in creating a function to alter an existing form is in properly naming the hook function. The format is:

```
{your module name}_form_{the id of the form you are altering}_alter
```

Our module name is weather_info. The name of the form we are altering is user_profile_form. So we need to create a function with a mouthful of a name: weather_info_form_user_profile_form_alter(). The function is shown in Listing 6–5.

Listing 6–5. *The Form-Alter Function*

```
function weather_info_form_user_profile_form_alter(&$form, &$form_state) {
  $form['profile_weather_location']['#element_validate'][] =
    'weather_info_profile_weather_location_validate';
}
```

This just adds the name of our validation function to the list of functions the form will have to call before it can be considered valid.

So now that we have the field name, we can set the #element_validate property to the validation function we just created. The #element_validate property is an array of all of the validation functions that are to operate on the element. The field is usually null, since the form validation logic will probably do the validation of all fields on the form as necessary.

Now, after the form function is called, Drupal will look around for functions that alter it. Our alter hook function will be hit, which will add the name of our validate function to the list of functions that must all give their nod that a field is valid before the form will be accepted as validated. Then, when the user enters information and submits the form, our function will be called.

Try it. Enter a bad location into the form and click Save. (See Figure 6–47.)

Weather location

```
foo bar baz
```

Enter a location on earth for which you would like to see weather information presented.

Figure 6–47. *Entering bad information into a form*

If you are running in Visual Studio and have the debugger running, you can set breakpoints to see exactly what is happening when.

When we get to the validation function, the weather service will return a null object, which will set the form error and prevent us from saving the information. It will also put our error text at the top of the screen and highlight the offending field. (See Figure 6–48)

❌   Cannot get weather for *foo bar baz.*

Figure 6–48. *The error is caught by the element validation function*

The form_alter() hook is a very powerful tool to have, as it allows you to customize any form in the system, whether it is part of the Drupal core or a contributed module.

Accessing Fields

Once the attached field information has been entered for your user, it is accessible as part of the $user object. The code in Listing 6–6 shows how to get the profile information for the user, and then how to get the values.

Listing 6–6. Accessing Field Information for the Current User

```
global $user;
$user_profile = user_load($user->uid);
if (isset($user_profile->field_weather_unit['und'][0]['value'])
  && ($user_profile->field_weather_unit['und'][0]['value'] != '')) {
    $unit = substr($user_profile->field_weather_unit['und'][0]['value'], 0, 1);
}
else {
    $unit = variable_get('default_units', 'F');
}
```

The global $user variable does not always contain the attached fields information, so to make sure you get it, just call the user_load() function and load all of the user information, including attached fields, into the new variable. From there, you can access the attached fields.

■ **Note** There seems to be an anomaly when loading user information this way. You can read more about it at http://drupal.org/node/57287. One way to deal with it is shown at http://drupal.org/node/361471. I use a more local technique here.

In this case, we will use the values in the profile information to set the location, language, and units for our weather block if they exist. If they are not in the profile, we will use the site defaults.

Listing 6–7 shows the full version of the weather information block view hook.

Listing 6–7. The Weather Information Block View Function

```
function weather_info_block_view($delta='') {
  if (!user_access('view weather info')) {
    return null;
  }

  $block = null;
  $block_content = null;

  global $user;

  $user_profile = user_load($user->uid);
  if (isset($user_profile->field_weather_unit['und'][0]['value'])
    && ($user_profile->field_weather_unit['und'][0]['value'] != '')) {
      $unit = substr($user_profile->field_weather_unit['und'][0]['value'], 0, 1);
  }
  else {
      $unit = variable_get('default_units', 'F');
  }

  if (isset($user_profile->field_weather_language['und'][0]['value'])
    && ($user_profile->field_weather_language['und'][0]['value'] != '')) {
```

```
      $language = substr($user_profile->field_weather_language['und'][0]['value'], 0, 2);
    }
    else {
      $language = variable_get('default_language', 'en');
    }

    if (isset($user_profile->field_weather_location['und'][0]['value'])
        && ($user_profile->field_weather_location['und'][0]['value'] != '')) {
      $location = $user_profile->field_weather_location['und'][0]['value'];
    }
    else {
      $location = variable_get('default_location', null);
    }

    if ($location) {
      $weather = weather_info_get_weather($location, $language);
      if ($weather) {
        $unit_system = $weather->weather->forecast_information->unit_system['data'];
        $current = $weather->weather->current_conditions;

        $block_content .= theme('current',
          array(
            'img' => $current->icon['data'],
            'condition' => $current->condition['data'],
            'temp' => $current->temp_f['data'],
            'unit' => $unit,
            'wind' => $current->wind_condition['data'],
            'humidity' => $current->humidity['data'],
            )
          );

        foreach($weather->weather->forecast_conditions as $new) {
          $block_content .= theme('forecast',
            array(
              'day' => $new->day_of_week['data'],
              'img' => $new->icon['data'],
              'high' => weather_info_temp($new->high['data'], $unit, $unit_system),
              'low' => weather_info_temp($new->low['data'], $unit, $unit_system),
              )
            );
        }
        $block['subject'] = $weather->weather->forecast_information->city['data'];
      }
      else {
        form_set_error('weather_location',
          t('Location @loc not found.', array('@loc' => $location)));
        variable_set('current_location', null);
        $block['subject'] = t('Get Weather');
      }
    }

    if (user_access('change weather location')) {
      $temp = drupal_get_form('weather_location_form');
      $block_content .= drupal_render($temp);
    }
    $block['content'] = $block_content;
    return $block;
}
```

Attached field information is integrated into the Drupal core, making it easy to write functions that require such information.

Updating Field Information

There's one more topic to cover, and that's the updating of attached field information in the database. As we've seen, the Drupal $user variable contains basic information about the user as defined by the core. But we extended the user by attaching fields to the entity type, which caused Drupal to create some database tables, and entries in some other tables, to hold our field information, and metadata to allow the Field API to access everything.

If we want to update the user information, there's a save_user() function that's pretty straightforward. However, updating the values of attached fields requires a different function.

In the scenario detailed above, the user set the three variables, location, language, and unit, by changing them on the account page. But now, suppose the user is on the move and wants to check the weather for another location. This is done by entering a location on the weather information form (see Figure 6–49), which we placed in the second sidebar region of our page.

Figure 6–49. *The weather information block*

Let's make the assumption that, if a user enters a new location on the weather information block, the new location becomes the user's preferred location. I know this is a stretch, as it might just be a temporary query, but making that assumption makes it easier to explain what I want to do here.

Currently, when we enter a new location on the weather information form, the data is validated using the weather_location_form_validate() function, and then processed using the weather_location_form_submit() function. The latter is shown in Listing 6–8.

Listing 6–8. *The Location Submit Function as It Is Currently Written*

```
function weather_location_form_submit($form, $form_state) {
  $location = trim($form_state['values']['weather_location']);
  variable_set('current_location', $location);
}
```

This code not only fails to take into account each user's individual location, but it also sets the global variable to what the user entered. Any user who changes the location will change it for everyone who is currently logged on—not really what we want.

We need to change that logic to update the profile of the current user instead of updating the current location variable for all users. In order to change the user's profile, we use the field_attach_update() function, which is part of the Field Attach API. The code to do that is shown in Listing 6–9.

Listing 6–9. Refactoring the Submit Form to Handle Updating a User's Profile

```
function weather_location_form_submit($form, $form_state) {
    $location = trim($form_state['values']['weather_location']);
    global $user;
    $user_profile = user_load($user->uid);
    $user_profile->field_weather_location['und'][0]['value'] = $location;
    field_attach_update('user', $user_profile);
}
```

The field_attach_update() function requires an array containing a list of the attached fields. In order to give this, we grab the user information and convert it into an array. Once we change the weather location, we can pass it to the function and update our fields.

As you can see, it's possible to programmatically change just about any aspect of the system, even if we don't own the data or the code. For this reason, it becomes important to be sure that your code does not adversely affect other modules and has the effect on the system that you intend. A lot of this can be assured by adopting a test-driven development mindset and running tests on your module and the entire system whenever you change something.

Chapter 8 covers test-driven development and Drupal's Simpletest unit and system test environment.

Summary

In this chapter, we have covered Drupal's role functionality and looked at how roles can be used to allow or restrict access to any level of granularity the programmer wishes to accommodate. We also saw how to build custom content types and customize core content types, as well as add and programmatically access profile information to a special content type, users.

In Chapter 7, we will learn about how to make our system generate HTML to get just the right look and feel to our pages. This is done through the theming process.

CHAPTER 7

■ ■ ■

Theming

Theming is the process of taking page content that has been created by the Drupal engine and turning it into something pleasing and useful to the end user. This chapter discusses the hook and theming concepts and offers suggestions on how to trace your code so you can see what's going on.

Creating a theme for your site can be as easy as using one of the core themes that comes with Drupal, or it can be as difficult as you want to make it. A theming project can require a team of designers, programmers, and marketing people and take months, depending on the complexity of the content and the design of the site. Or, it could take you just a few hours to create your own simple theme or tweak an existing one.

When you create your first site, you'll probably want to explore themes available from the community at http://drupal.org/project/themes. I also like Theme Garden, http://themegarden.org, where you can see previews of each theme. Many themes are free, but some are commercially available for a price.

As with most things, you generally get what you pay for; a commercial product will probably have more direct support if you have a problem or questions, but the free themes, like the freely available modules, are typically very well built and the developers are responsive to errors in their code. Remember, though, as with any open source software, the people writing the code are probably doing it on a part-time basis and if you have a problem with the code, you might just have to fix it yourself.

A theme is far more than just adding style information in a CSS style sheet. The theming layer is a full-blown programming framework with the same hook processing functionality as in module development.

Don't be intimidated by the complexity, however; creating a good-looking site might only require that you tweak the CSS files of a theme you like.

The Theme Layer

Since the theming layer has the ability to do the same hook-based processing as the module layer, it is tempting to do some processing in the theme layer. This brings up the issue of separating logic from presentation in your application. I've always had a bit of trouble with this one, as I'm sure you have if you've been developing applications that have a user interface component. There really aren't many hard-and-fast rules about what constitutes business logic and what constitutes presentation.

■ **Tip** When it comes to deciding if something is in the business logic layer or the presentation layer, my general rule is that if your function touches or updates the database, it is probably business logic. If it touches the eyeballs of the user, it's probably presentation.

In any case, there are always exceptions. The important thing is to make sure your code is in the appropriate place and is maintainable by someone else—or by you three years from now when you've forgotten why you did that silly thing with the presentation layer that makes no sense now.

Things to know as you build your themes:

- For better performance, the theme system caches the template files containing the theme functions that should be called. There are certain places where this can cause problems, so you should make a habit of rebuilding your theme registry every once in a while, particularly if you make a change and it doesn't seem to appear on your screen.

- Drupal stores a cache of the data in .info files. We'll cover subthemes in a minute, but you should know that if you modify any line in your subtheme's .info file, you must refresh the cache by visiting the Configuration➤Performance page and clicking "Clear all caches."

- One handy way to increase performance is by using Drupal's ability to optimize CSS and Javascript files. Rather than gather the sometimes dozens of individual CSS and Javascript files together on each page build, Drupal will combine them into single files that are cached. This greatly increases performance. On the Performance settings page (Configuration➤Performance), you can see the Bandwidth optimization area. (See Figure 7–1.)

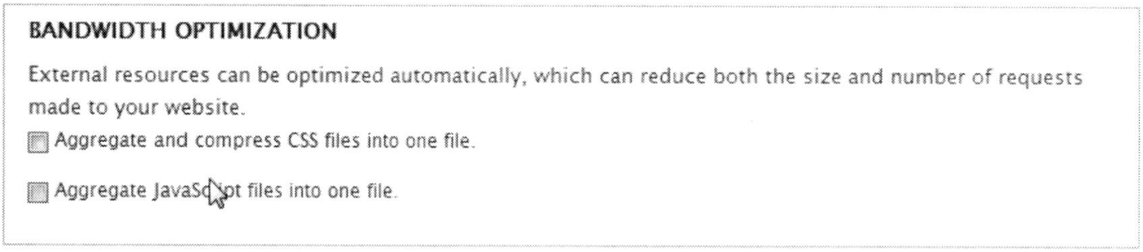

BANDWIDTH OPTIMIZATION

External resources can be optimized automatically, which can reduce both the size and number of requests made to your website.

☐ Aggregate and compress CSS files into one file.

☐ Aggregate JavaScript files into one file.

Figure 7–1. Drupal provides an administration page to optimize performance settings for your situation.

By default these are disabled, so you probably haven't turned them on. However, when you need to make any changes to your theme, do yourself a favor and make sure both of these are disabled. You'll thank me when you don't have to spend hours trying to figure out why your changes aren't updating to the page.

■ **Tip** The performance page has other cache settings as well. It's probably best to turn off all caching when doing any kind of module development. It will slow things down, but you are guaranteed to get the most recent code changes if you have all caching off. Later, when you have a better understanding of how these optimizations work, you can turn off only the ones that affect what you are currently working on, or you can get into the habit of only flushing the cache when it is necessary. You can do this using the menu system or Drush. (Drush is covered in Appendix A.)

Subtheme Creation

If you've been following along with the creation of my site, you've seen that we are still using Bartik, the default theme that came with Drupal 7. Rather than create new complexity, I've stuck with this theme. But now we need to make some changes, particularly in the weather module. As I mentioned earlier, I don't like the way the default theme lists the four-day weather forecast vertically. I'd like to see the days listed next to each other horizontally, and I'd also like to make some minor typographical changes, as shown in Figure 7–2.

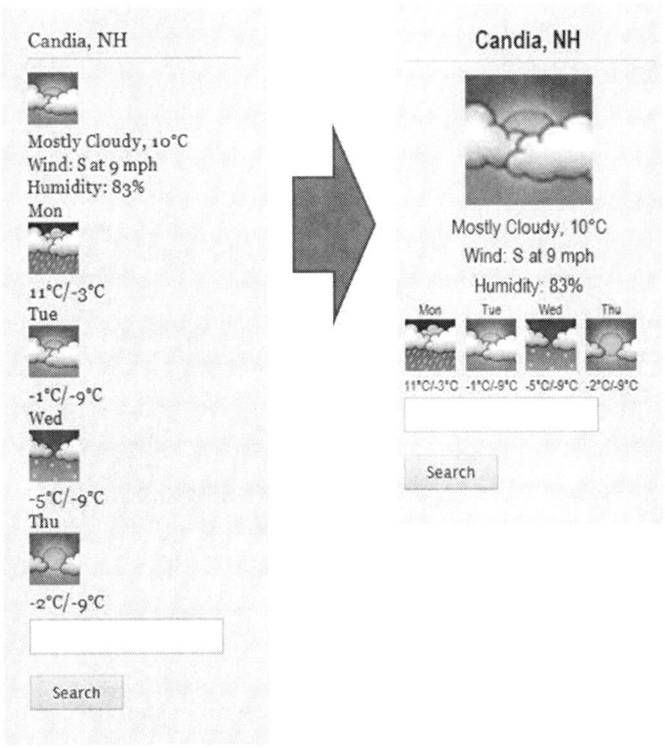

Figure 7–2. Our task is to style the weather block

Since we're already using the Bartik theme, we could just go into its CSS file and make a few small changes. However, this would mean modifying a theme that came with the Drupal core code.

It is not a good idea to make any modifications to the core because any code changes that come later on will overwrite the changes you made. And besides, it is well-known that whenever you hack the core, God kills a kitten. (Artist's rendition shown in Figure 7–3.)

Figure 7–3. Go kitty!

You don't want that on your conscience, do you?

So how do we take an existing theme and make changes to it? We could just copy the theme code to our site directory and make changes there. We would have to change the name of the theme to avoid naming conflicts, but then we could change whatever we want and still get all of the code that came with the original theme.

But there's a better way. We can make a subtheme of a theme we like. Making a subtheme gives us the advantage of all of the nice things the base theme has to offer, plus the custom tweaks we want for our particular site.

■ **Tip** For performance reasons, a subtheme isn't always the best choice. If you have a site where performance is critical, it is probably better to create a new theme without the overhead of a subtheme.

There are various ways to make a subtheme. I'll show you the way I do it so that you can see what's happening behind the scenes.

Since this is our first theme, we need to create a subdirectory in the appropriate place. When we created a new module, we created the modules directory under sites/all. Our custom themes need to be in a directory that's a sibling to that one, so create a directory called sites/all/themes, and then another one, first_subtheme, under that. If you are using Visual Studio and VS.Php, you'll see the structure in your Solution Explorer, as shown in see Figure 7–4.

Figure 7–4. A subtheme must be in the themes directory.

Now, create a .info file with the same name as the new theme's directory. In this case, call it first_subtheme.info. The items shown in Listing 7–1 need to be in this file.

Listing 7–1. The Theme's .info file Must Specify Certain Required Parts

```
name = My First Subtheme
description = My first subtheme, based on Bartik.
core = 7.x
base theme = bartik

regions[header] = Header
regions[help] = Help
regions[page_top] = Page top
regions[page_bottom] = Page bottom
regions[highlight] = Highlighted

regions[featured] = Featured
regions[content] = Content
regions[sidebar_first] = Sidebar first
regions[sidebar_second] = Sidebar second

regions[triptych_first] = Triptych first
regions[triptych_middle] = Triptych middle
regions[triptych_last] = Triptych last

regions[footer_firstcolumn] = Footer first column
regions[footer_secondcolumn] = Footer second column
regions[footer_thirdcolumn] = Footer third column
regions[footer_fourthcolumn] = Footer fourth column
regions[footer] = Footer
```

Notice that a number of regions have been declared here; they are declared in the base theme's `.info` file and are required in the subtheme. The `regions` array indicates the name of the region (the array key) and the description of each region (the array value). The region name will be used internally by Drupal and has the same naming constraints (letters and underscores, basically), while the description is what is shown to the user on the Blocks administration page.

You can also hide regions from the Blocks administration interface, though they still remain available to modules. To do this, you just populate the `regions_hidden` array with the names of the regions you want to hide, as shown in Listing 7–2.

Listing 7–2. Hiding Regions from the Blocks Administration Page

```
regions[content] = Content
regions[help] = Help
regions[page_top] = Page top
regions[page_bottom] = Page bottom
regions[indicators] = Indicators
regions_hidden[] = indicators
```

Why would you want to hide regions? Probably because you want your module to be able to access a new region you are creating, but you don't want the administration users to be able to put whatever they want there.

▓ **Note** If you are familiar with Drupal 6, you're probably used to the idea that if a subtheme has the same regions as the base theme, you don't need to include them in your subtheme's `.info` file. With Drupal 7, however, you do need to indicate all regions in your subtheme file.

If you don't indicate any regions in your subtheme file, you'll get only the default regions: header, help, content, sidebar_first, sidebar_second, footer. However, if you define any regions at all, they will be available—but they'll override the defaults.

Next, you need to create the style sheet. Let's call it `first_subtheme.css`. For Drupal to use this style sheet, we need to add it to the `.info` file, as shown in Listing 7–3.

Listing 7–3. All Style Sheets Must Be Included in the `.info` File.

```
name = My First Subtheme
description = My first subtheme, based on Bartik.
core = 7.x
base theme = bartik

stylesheets[all][] = first_subtheme.css

regions[header] = Header
regions[help] = Help
...
```

The `stylesheets` array in the `.info` file indicates the CSS style sheet you want to use. This adds your style sheet to the list of style sheets that are normally loaded. Since the style sheets in this list will be loaded after all of the others, you have the last chance to override (cascade) any settings in the style sheets that are loaded earlier.

For now, let's just add a single style to deal with the class we created in the weather_info module. (See Listing 7–4.)

Listing 7–4. The CSS File Defines Classes

```
.currentConditions {
  font-family:Arial Narrow;
  text-align:center;
  font-size:12pt;
}
```

That's the minimum we need to create our subtheme. To enable it, go to the Appearance page (/admin/build/themes), enable the theme and make it the default. (See Figure 7–5.)

My First Subtheme

My first subtheme, based on Bartik.

Enable | Enable and set default

Figure 7–5. Before a theme can be used, it must be enabled and set to the default.

When you save the settings, you'll see that the subtheme looks almost exactly like the base theme. There is one difference that sticks out right away, though, as shown in Figure 7–6.

Figure 7–6. A subtheme does not inherit the logo of the base theme.

You can add a site logo by going to Appearance➤{your subtheme}➤settings➤Logo image settings. There are two images that can be specified, the logo and the shortcut icon. (See Figure 7–7.)

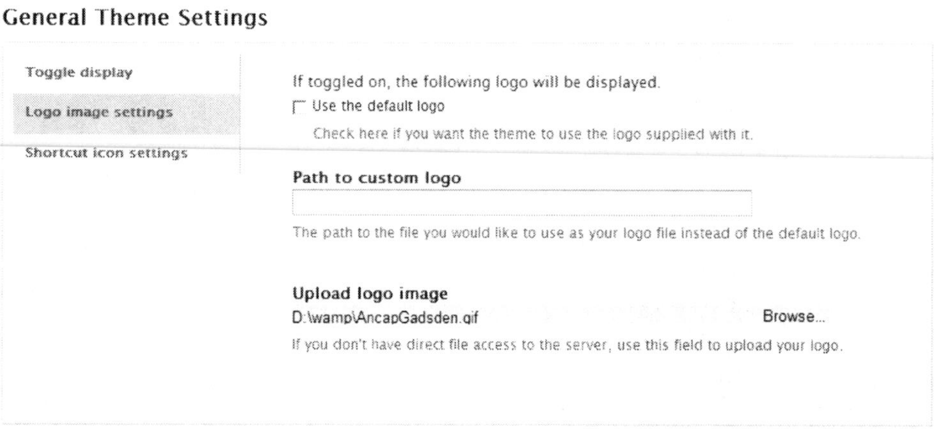

General Theme Settings

Toggle display

Logo image settings

Shortcut icon settings

If toggled on, the following logo will be displayed.

☐ Use the default logo

   Check here if you want the theme to use the logo supplied with it.

Path to custom logo

The path to the file you would like to use as your logo file instead of the default logo.

Upload logo image

D:\wamp\AncapGadsden.gif   Browse...

If you don't have direct file access to the server, use this field to upload your logo.

Figure 7–7. You can use the default logo and icon or specify your own.

The logo image is the one that appears on the top of the site. I should say it usually appears there. It is available to the theme designer to do with as he or she pleases. The Bartik theme, from which we created our subtheme, puts it at the top. The shortcut icon image appears on the tab, but it is also available to the theme designer. (See Figure 7–8.)

♠ Content Structure Appearance People Modules Configuration Reports Help   Hello **brian** Log out

Edit shortcuts

Brian's Drupal 7 Site

Examples from 'Pro Drupal 7 for Windows Developers'

Figure 7–8. A custom logo appears at the top of all pages (by default).

Scroll down a bit and see if our first CSS rule has taken affect. It should set the three lines under the current conditions image in 12pt Arial Narrow centered. Mine looks like the image in Figure 7–9.

Candia, NH

Cloudy, 10°C
Wind: SE at 11 mph
Humidity: 82%

Figure 7–9. Proof that the CSS has been loaded and read

If you get something else, you'll probably want to clear the theme cache.

Now that we've created our subtheme and adjusted our logos, we can do the serious theme work. We just need to do a little tweaking to the subtheme to get our weather icons to show up horizontally instead of vertically.

Theme Debugging Tools

When it comes to creating visual representations in a graphical user interface, you need a different set of debugging tools than when you are writing code and developing and testing algorithms. You can still use the step debuggers in Visual Studio for some parts of your theme development, but you'll probably want to see exactly what kind of code is being sent to your browser so you can tweak things to make them look like you or your designer intended.

Microsoft's Internet Explorer, Google's Chrome, and Mozilla's Firefox all have developer tools that allow you to look at various aspects of the page, such as the name of form elements, CSS classes, even formatting for a particular class once it has gone through its cascading process. This type of debugging information is vital when you are trying to figure out how to get something on the page to look just right.

Internet Explorer has "Developer Tools" that can be accessed from the menu or by pressing F12. (See Figure 7–10.)

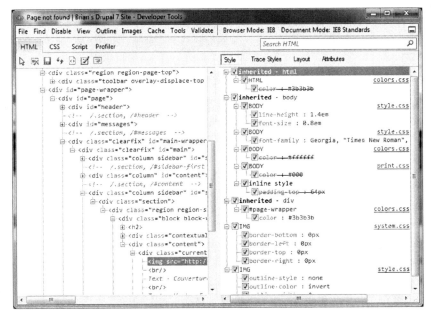

Figure 7–10. Internet Explorer 8 has built-in developer tools for inspecting theming properties.

You'll find rich information about the element's properties, names, computed style, and other handy data. What we want to focus on right now are the names of the classes of the elements we want to style. Of course, since we developed the code to generate this output, we already know the names of the classes, but the functionality of this tool is perfect for changing the current style of objects on a page, and for writing new style code.

There are two more handy tools that work on your site from inside Drupal. The Devel suite of tools provides some goodies that will track things as they happen while the page is being built. The tool can trap all SQL statements, display a page timer, memory usage, and other handy metrics. It also exposes some nice debugging functions, such as dumping the values of variables on the screen so you don't have to rely on the step debugger as much. (See Figure 7–11.)

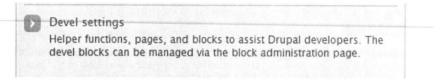

Figure 7–11. The Devel module provides information to the developer.

The Theme developer module is an add-on to the Devel module. It tracks theming information as your page goes through the rendering process and makes it available to you on the rendered page. The Theme developer module can also show you a list of theme templates and functions which may have been used for a given page. See Figure 7–12.

Figure 7–12. The Theme developer module provides some nice features for the theming process

As a page is rendered, various functions and templates act on the page. The Theme developer module can keep track of which artifacts touch the page, which helps you debug your theme. This information is kept in a theme log and can be displayed at the bottom of the page in chronological order. (See Figure 7–13.)

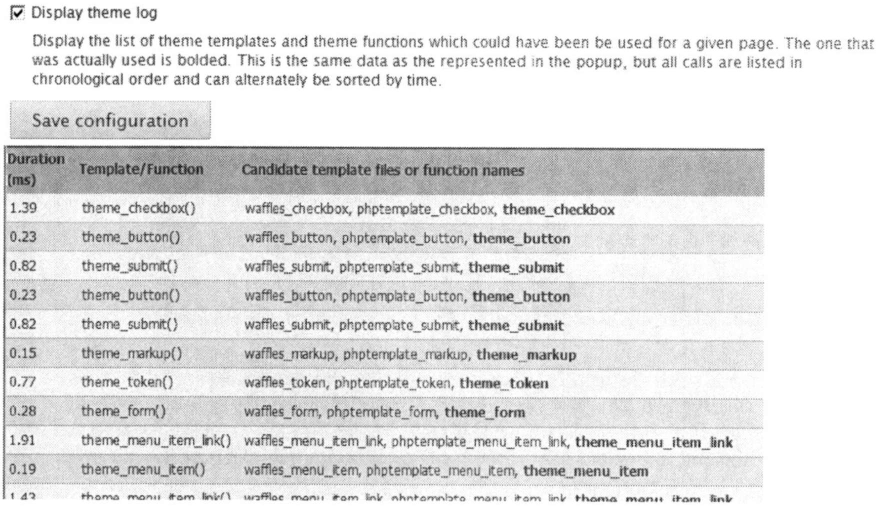

☑ Display theme log

Display the list of theme templates and theme functions which could have been be used for a given page. The one that was actually used is bolded. This is the same data as the represented in the popup, but all calls are listed in chronological order and can alternately be sorted by time.

Save configuration

Duration (ms)	Template/Function	Candidate template files or function names
1.39	theme_checkbox()	waffles_checkbox, phptemplate_checkbox, **theme_checkbox**
0.23	theme_button()	waffles_button, phptemplate_button, **theme_button**
0.82	theme_submit()	waffles_submit, phptemplate_submit, **theme_submit**
0.23	theme_button()	waffles_button, phptemplate_button, **theme_button**
0.82	theme_submit()	waffles_submit, phptemplate_submit, **theme_submit**
0.15	theme_markup()	waffles_markup, phptemplate_markup, **theme_markup**
0.77	theme_token()	waffles_token, phptemplate_token, **theme_token**
0.28	theme_form()	waffles_form, phptemplate_form, **theme_form**
1.91	theme_menu_item_link()	waffles_menu_item_link, phptemplate_menu_item_link, **theme_menu_item_link**
0.19	theme_menu_item()	waffles_menu_item, phptemplate_menu_item, **theme_menu_item**
1.43	theme_menu_item_link()	waffles_menu_item_link, phptemplate_menu_item_link, **theme_menu_item_link**

Figure 7–13. The theme log provides more information about which theming functions touched your page.

Finally, there is an interactive aspect to the Theme developer module that allows you to access information about any rendered object on your screen. Clicking the Themer info button at the bottom of the screen enables the interactive window, then clicking on any object will display the template that was called, along with any functions that were involved in creating that object. (See Figure 7–14.)

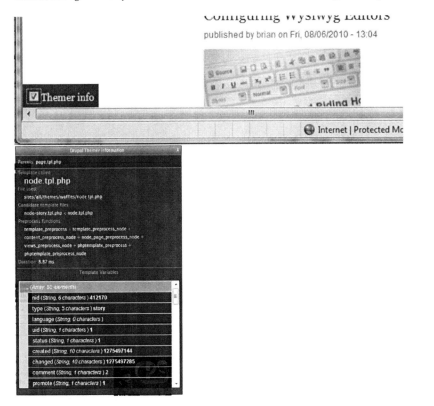

Figure 7–14. *The Theme developer module has an interactive theme interrogation function.*

It's pretty clear that there are many tools available for the Drupal developer. Now let's continue theming our page by adding some style.

CSS Classes

Our small task right now is to change the four-day forecast from a vertical list to a horizontal one. While we're at it, let's also magnify the current conditions graphic and change the type sizes.

We will use only CSS for this task. Going over the details of CSS syntax is beyond the scope of this book, but there are plenty of resources available for learning CSS if you don't know it already.

So let's go back to the CSS file we created when we set up our subtheme— first_subtheme.css. We need to create CSS rules for several different classes based on what we see in the HTML our site generated. Listing 7–5 shows what I came up with.

Listing 7–5. CSS Styles in Drupal Rely Heavily on Classes

```
.block-weather-info.block {
    padding-left:5px;
    padding-right:5px;
}

.block-weather-info h2 {
  font-family:Arial Narrow;
  font-size:14pt;
  font-weight:bold;
  text-align:center;
}

.currentConditions {
  font-family:Arial Narrow;
  text-align:center;
  font-size:12pt;
}

.currentConditions img {
  width:100px;
}

.forecast-2, .forecast-3, .forecast-4 {
  font-family:Arial Narrow;
  font-size:8pt;
  text-align:center;
  float:left;
  margin-left:6px;
}

.forecast-1 {
  font-family:Arial Narrow;
  font-size:8pt;
  text-align:center;
  float:left;
}
```

Saving first_subtheme.css and refreshing the browser provides the style we're looking for. (See Figure 7–15.)

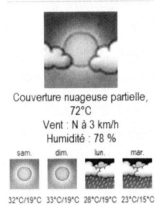

Lyon, Rhône-Alpes

Couverture nuageuse partielle,
72°C
Vent : N à 3 km/h
Humidité : 78 %

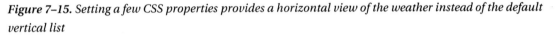

sam.	dim.	lun.	mar.
32°C/19°C	33°C/19°C	28°C/19°C	23°C/15°C

Figure 7–15. Setting a few CSS properties provides a horizontal view of the weather instead of the default vertical list

What you've seen is the basic process for styling your page: identify the classes, IDs, or elements that are of interest, and then create or modify the theme's CSS file to get what you want. As you might expect, there is a lot more richness built into Drupal, but you've just learned the basics.

The Theme Function

The main goal of the presentation layer is that it does all of the presentation. One goal of the theme system is that it takes care of all HTML coding. There are some pretty good reasons for this. If you hard-code the HTML in your module's code, it becomes more difficult to perform any runtime tweaking of the output to make it compatible with various output formats. For example, what if a new browser comes out that interprets some HTML differently from other browsers? This happened, for example, when browser makers starting paying attention to the W3C HTML standards rather than just doing what seemed to work at the time. What will happen when HTML5 comes out? Or some reduced subset of HTML for mobile computing?

Your goal should be, then, to produce modules that don't create a single line of HTML that is not in a theme implementation. That way, upgrading to a different flavor of HTML—or supporting multiple flavors simultaneously—is easier because the code is all in one place.

To make this happen, your module should do as much of the data processing as possible, and then hand off the data to the presentation layer. In your module, you'll need to register the theme functions that will do the theming and then just let the presentation layer do the work.

For these reasons, it's a good idea to separate your presentation from any processing on the data. Drupal has a provision to do this—the theme hook.

The Theme Hook

First, we'll create the theme function that will generate the HTML, then we'll register that function so Drupal can find it.

The place to put a theme function is in your module file (or in an included file).

Let's create two theme functions, one to generate output for the current conditions and one to create output for each forecast day. We can simply take the code from the module where it was embedded and make a couple modifications. The first one is a theme function called 'current', but since it is a theme function, we need to put the keyword theme_ before it. (See Listing 7–6.)

Listing 7–6. A Theme Function Is a Convenient Place to Generate HTML

```
function theme_current($variables) {
  $img = $variables['img'];
  $condition = $variables['condition'];
  $temp = $variables['temp'];
  $unit = $variables['unit'];
  $wind = $variables['wind'];
  $humidity = $variables['humidity'];

  $content = null;
  $content .= '<div class="currentConditions">';
  $content .= "<img src='http://www.google.com{$img}'/><br/>";
  $content .= sprintf('%s, %s<br/>',
    $condition, weather_info_temp($temp, $unit, 'US'));
  $content .= $wind . '<br/>';
  $content .= $humidity;
  $content .= '</div>';
  return $content;
}
```

Notice the argument to the function call. All variables we need will be passed in a single keyed array, with the key being the name of the variable and the value of the array being the value of the variable.

Now here's the second theme function, forecast, shown in Listing 7–7.

Listing 7–7. Another Theming Function

```
function theme_forecast($variables) {
  static $day = 0;

  $day_of_week = $variables['day'];
  $img = $variables['img'];
  $high = $variables['high'];
  $low = $variables['low'];

  ++$day;
  $content = null;
  $content .= "<div class='forecast-{$day}'>";
  $content .= "{$day_of_week}<br/>";
  $content .= "<img src='http://www.google.com{$img}'/><br/>";
  $content .= "{$high}/{$low}<br/>";
  $content .= '</div>';
  return $content;
}
```

These functions are now in our program, but how does Drupal know where they are or how to call them? We need to create a theme hook. This code goes in your module. (See Listing 7–8.)

Listing 7–8. The Module's Theme Hook Is the Place to Register Theme Functions

```
function weather_info_theme() {
  return array(
    'current' => array(
      'arguments' => array(
        'img' => NULL,
```

```
        'condition' => NULL,
        'temp' => NULL,
        'unit' => NULL,
        'wind' => NULL,
        'humidity' => NULL,
      )
    ),
    'forecast' => array(
      'arguments' => array(
        'day' => NULL,
        'img' => NULL,
        'high' => NULL,
        'low' => NULL,
      )
    ),
  );
}
```

This is a theme hook, so the name of the function is carefully crafted, consisting of the name of the module with the suffix '_theme'. The theme hook returns an array with all of the theme functions that can be called. In this case, it contains information about our two theme functions along with the variables with which they will be called. The arguments array contains the names and their default values. All arguments must be given default values since there is no way to assure that a theme call will provide the proper information. If you are not sure as to what the default value should be, use NULL.

So now we've created the theme functions and registered them in our module. All that's left is to call them in our code. In the case of our weather information block, we will call them in the 'view' case of the block hook function. This will involve rewriting the code that we moved down to the theme functions. (See Listing 7–9.)

Listing 7–9. Code inside the Block Hook Rewritten to Use the Theme Functions

```
if ($weather) {
  $unit_system = $weather->weather->forecast_information->unit_system['data'];
  $current = $weather->weather->current_conditions;

  $block_content .= theme('current',
    array(
        'img' => $current->icon['data'],
        'condition' => $current->condition['data'],
        'temp' => $current->weather_info_temp_f['data'],
        'unit' => $unit,
        'wind' => $current->wind_condition['data'],
        'humidity' => $current->humidity['data'],
      )
    );

  foreach($weather->weather->forecast_conditions as $new) {
    $block_content .= theme('forecast',
      array(
        'day' => $new->day_of_week['data'],
        'img' => $new->icon['data'],
        'high' => weather_info_temp($new->high['data'], $unit,
          $unit_system),
        'low' => weather_info_temp($new->low['data'], $unit,
          $unit_system),
      )
    );
  }
  $block['subject'] = $weather->weather->forecast_information->city['data'];
}
```

Notice the theme() function. The first argument is the name of the theme function without the 'theme_' prefix. This can be kind of confusing, but it makes sense once you start to get a feeling for how Drupal's module and function naming conventions are used.

Following the name of the theme function is an array containing all of the variables we created in the function and declared in the theme hook.

Now that we have everything running, you can load the page and it should look exactly the same.

■ **Tip** When you develop themes, you need to realize that theme functions are cached. This means that when you change something in your code, it might not show up on your site—which can be very frustrating, to say the least. However, there are ways to clear the theme cache, and you should get used to doing so whenever you create a new theme function or change the name or signature. I use `drush cc theme` to clear the theme cache.

Using theme functions solves two problems. First, it makes the code easier to write, read, and maintain because we just pass data somewhere else instead of building up a bunch of finicky strings. Second, it solves the problem of separating our data logic from our presentation.

Templates

Drupal's theme engine relies heavily on templates to know where to put certain content and other design elements.

All template files in Drupal end in `.tpl.php`. If you choose to create any template files, they should all be in a directory called `templates` inside your theme directory.

Templates are used to direct the placement of certain pieces of content that Drupal's content management function builds as a result of a page call. These templates are retrieved as part of the page rendering function, after the content is collected into a set of arrays and objects. There are several templates that come with Drupal, but any and all can be overridden by similarly named templates in your module or theme hierarchy.

Figure 7–16 shows the relationship of certain core templates.

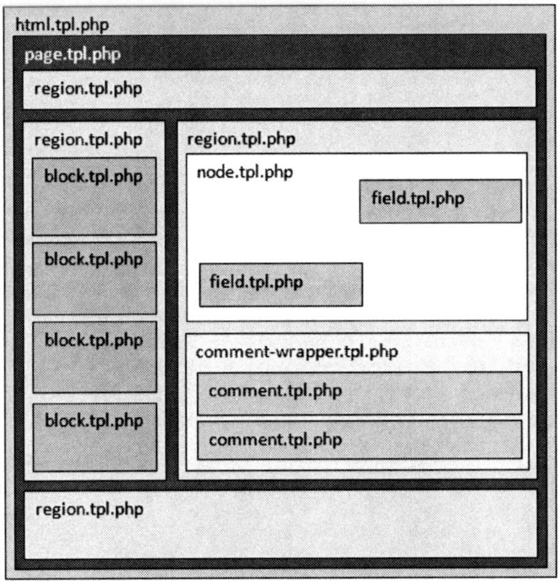

Figure 7–16. Templates that can be used to customize the rendering of the page.

Notice the hierarchical nature of the templates. We'll see how they all work together in a bit.

The HTML Template

Starting at the outermost level, we have the HTML template. This is fairly small and is used to bootstrap the rendering process. If you are familiar with the ASP.NET page model, you might think of the Drupal HTML template as analogous to ASP.NET's master page. The Drupal core has a default HTML template called html.tpl.php, which is shown in Listing 7–10. It mixes HTML with PHP code to specify where content and style objects are to be rendered.

Listing 7–10. The Default HTML Template

```
<!DOCTYPE html PUBLIC "-//W3C//DTD XHTML+RDFa 1.0//EN"
  "http://www.w3.org/MarkUp/DTD/xhtml-rdfa-1.dtd">
<html xmlns="http://www.w3.org/1999/xhtml"
  xml:lang="<?php print $language->language; ?>"
  version="XHTML+RDFa 1.0"
  dir="<?php print $language->dir; ?>"<?php print $rdf_namespaces; ?>>

<head profile="<?php print $grddl_profile; ?>">
  <?php print $head; ?>
  <title><?php print $head_title; ?></title>
  <?php print $styles; ?>
  <?php print $scripts; ?>
</head>
<body class="<?php print $classes; ?>" <?php print $attributes;?>>
  <div id="skip-link">
    <a href="#main-content"><?php print t('Skip to main content'); ?></a>
```

```
    </div>
    <?php print $page_top; ?>
    <?php print $page; ?>
    <?php print $page_bottom; ?>
</body>
</html>
```

Template files are a lot like ASP files in that they are mostly an HTML file that will be sent to your browser. However, you can mix PHP code inside the HTML by using the <?php…?> markers. All of the variables that are printed from the template are created in the module. We'll see how to create those and pass them to a template a little later.

You don't need to create your own HTML template if the default template will do what you need. If you want to create an HTML file that is different, just call it html.tpl.php and put it in the templates directory of your theme's directory and Drupal will use it instead of the default HTML template.

Notice the variables that are printed at various points on the page. These are called "template variables" and they are created in your module as members in an array variable called, $variables[]. Before we go any farther, let's see how to get information from our module into the theming engine as template variables.

Template Variables

Before you start working with templates as a developer, it's helpful to understand where these variables are set. That way, you can add your own—or just be satisfied with the joy of knowledge.

There is an array, $variables[], that is set as part of the theming stage. This array is built in theme.inc in the core directory structure. By the time it gets to your template, the array contains a list of variables, and the key of each is the name of the actual variable. The theming engine converts that single array with multiple values into a set of variables you can use in your template.

To give you an idea of what Drupal is doing under the covers, Listing 7–11 shows some lines from theme.inc.

Listing 7–11. Standard Members of the $variables Array

```
$variables['footer_message']    = filter_xss_admin(variable_get('site_footer', FALSE));
$variables['head']              = drupal_get_html_head();
$variables['language']          = $GLOBALS['language'];
$variables['language']->dir     = $GLOBALS['language']->direction ? 'rtl' : 'ltr';
$variables['logo']              = theme_get_setting('logo');
$variables['mission']           = isset($mission) ? $mission : '';
$variables['css']               = drupal_add_css();
$variables['styles']            = drupal_get_css();
```

During the theming process, this array is converted so that you have $footer_message, $head, $language, and so on available to you.

The Drupal core (in theme.inc) provides a default set of variables that can be used in your page template. These are shown in Table 7–1.

Table 7–1. Drupal's Default Variables (source: Drupal.org)

Variable	Description
$id	The placement of the template. Each time the template is used, it is incremented by one.
$zebra	Either "odd" or "even". Alternate each time the template is used.
$directory	The theme path relative to the base install. Example: "sites/all/themes/myTheme"
$is_admin	Boolean returns TRUE when the visitor is a site administrator.
$is_front	Boolean returns TRUE when viewing the front page of the site.
$logged_in	Boolean returns TRUE when the visitor is a member of the site, and is logged in and authenticated.
$db_is_active	Boolean returns TRUE when the database is active and running. This is only useful for theming in maintenance mode where the site may run into database problems.
$user	The user object containing data for the current visitor. Some of the data contained here may not be safe. Be sure to pass potentially dangerous strings through check_plain.

This is the absolute minimum set. Most themes create many more variables, and you can create any others you like using the technique shown above.

Now what if you need to create a variable that you want to have available when the template gets rendered? It's pretty straightforward, actually. Like all things in Drupal, you just need to know where to look. In your theme or subtheme directory, open the template.php file or create a new one. (See Figure 7–17.)

Figure 7–17. The template.php file is where we can put PHP code to theme our site

In `template.php`, create a function that intercepts the preprocess hook. That hook gives you a reference to the $variables array, where you can add an item with a key and value. (See Listing 7–12.)

Listing 7–12. Hooking into the Page Preprocessor from a Theme Template

```
function first_subtheme_preprocess(&$vars) {
  $vars['theme_secret_word'] = 'duck';
}
```

The preprocess hook is a handy device for the themer, as it gives pretty much any interested party a chance to do something with the page. Suppose you want to access the variables from your module. All you need to do is to create a hook function in the module file, as shown in Listing 7–13.

Listing 7–13. Hooking in to the Page Preprocessor from a Module

```
function weather_info_preprocess(&$variables) {
  $variables['module_secret_word'] = 'goose';
}
```

When this is done, we will have two more variables available in the page template. Locate the place in your HTML template where the content is rendered and put references to the two variables (See Listing 7–14).

Listing 7–14. Including Variables in a Template File

```
<?php print $page_top; ?>
<i><?php print "(html.tpl.php)The secret word (from theme) is: $theme_secret_word" ?></i><br/>
<i><?php print "(html.tpl.php)The secret word (from module) is: $module_secret_word" ?></i><br/>
<?php print $page; ?>
```

■ **Tip** Whenever you make changes to the themes, particularly when creating new templates, it is important to clear the theme registry. You can do this from Configuration➤Performance➤Clear all caches. You can also use the command `drush cc theme`.

As Figure 7–18 shows, this will render the variables on the page.

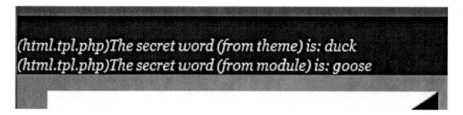

Figure 7–18. Variables defined in the module and the theme can be rendered using the page template.

The preprocess hook will set the variables for pretty much any context. There are other, more specific places you can hook into the theme engine to set variables.

- **template_preprocess_html(&$variables)**: Preprocess variables for html.tpl.php.

- **template_preprocess(&$variables, $hook)**: Adds default helper variables for variable processors and templates. This comes in before any other preprocess function, so it can be used in default theme implementations (non-overridden theme functions.

- **hook_preprocess_HOOK(&$variables)**: Preprocess theme variables for a specific theme hook. This hook allows modules to preprocess theme variables for a specific theme hook. It should only be used if a module needs to override or add to the theme preprocessing for a theme hook it didn't define.

- **template_preprocess_page(&$variables)**

  - Preprocess variables for page.tpl.php.

  - Most themes utilize their own copy of page.tpl.php. The default is located in modules/system/page.tpl.php. Look there for the full list of variables.

  - Uses the arg() function to generate a series of page template suggestions based on the current path.

  - Any changes to variables in this preprocessor should also be made in template_preprocess_maintenance_page() to keep all variables consistent.

- **template_preprocess_node(&$variables)**

  - Process variables for node.tpl.php.

  - Most themes utilize their own copy of node.tpl.php. The default is located in modules/node/node.tpl.php. Look there for the full list of variables.

  - The $variables array contains the following arguments:

      - $node
      - $view_mode
      - $page

- **template_preprocess_block(&$variables)**

  - Process variables for block.tpl.php.

  - Prepares the values passed to the theme_block function to be passed to a pluggable template engine. Uses block properties to generate a series of template file suggestions. If none are found, the default block.tpl.php is used.

  - Most themes utilize their own copy of block.tpl.php. The default is located in modules/block/block.tpl.php. Look there for the full list of variables.

  - The $variables array contains the following argument:

      - $block

- **template_preprocess_field(&$variables, $hook)**

  - Theme preprocess function for theme_field() and field.tpl.php.

- **template_preprocess_region(&$variables)**

- Preprocess variables for `region.tpl.php`.

- Prepares the values passed to the `theme_region` function to be passed into a pluggable template engine. Uses the region name to generate template file suggestions. If none are found, the default `region.tpl.php` is used.

- `template_preprocess_comment(&$variables)`

  - Process variables for `comment.tpl.php`.

- `template_process_html(&$variables)`

  - Process variables for `html.tpl.php`.

  - Performs final addition and modification of variables before passing them to the template. To customize these variables, call `drupal_render()` on elements in `$variables['page']` during `THEME_preprocess_page()`.

- `template_process(&$variables, $hook)`

  - A default process function used to alter variables as late as possible.

- `template_process_field(&$variables, $hook)`

  - Theme process function for `theme_field()` and `field.tpl.php`.

It is customary for the template designer to place a list of all available variables at the top of the template. For example, the default region theme template, `region.tpl.php`, contains the following comment:

```
/**
 * @file
 * Default theme implementation to display a region.
 *
 * Available variables:
 * - $content: The content for this region, typically blocks.
 * - $classes: String of classes that can be used to style contextually through
 *   CSS. It can be manipulated through the variable $classes_array from
 *   preprocess functions. The default values can be one or more of the following:
 *   - region: The current template type, i.e., "theming hook".
 *   - region-[name]: The name of the region with underscores replaced with
 *     dashes. For example, the page_top region would have a region-page-top class.
 * - $region: The name of the region variable as defined in the theme's .info file.
 *
 * Helper variables:
 * - $classes_array: Array of html class attribute values. It is flattened
 *   into a string within the variable $classes.
 * - $is_admin: Flags true when the current user is an administrator.
 * - $is_front: Flags true when presented in the front page.
 * - $logged_in: Flags true when the current user is a logged-in member.
 *
 * @see template_preprocess()
 * @see template_preprocess_region()
 * @see template_process()
 */
```

Processing in the other templates happens in pretty much the same way, as the Drupal theming process works its way down the hierarchy. Each template exposes different variables using the technique I just described. For a list of variables exposed by each of the Drupal core templates, see Appendix C.

Page Rendering

When Drupal renders a page, it goes through a complex but predictable series of steps to turn your structures into HTML. Once they are all rendered, there is a final construction phase that puts all of the HTML snippets where they need to go. The templates help guide that process. Let's take a look at how a typical page is rendered.

Consider a page that has a number of regions, into which blocks are placed using Drupal's Structure➤Blocks administration panel. The regions for our template, Bartik, are shown in Figure 7–19.

Figure 7–19. *Available regions for a typical template*

The only required block is Content, which we have placed in the region titled Content (see Figure 7–20).

Figure 7–20. The Content block in the Content region

There are several nodes to be rendered on our page, but we'll just focus on nodes in the Content region. The basic flow that works with any Drupal page is shown in Figure 7–21.

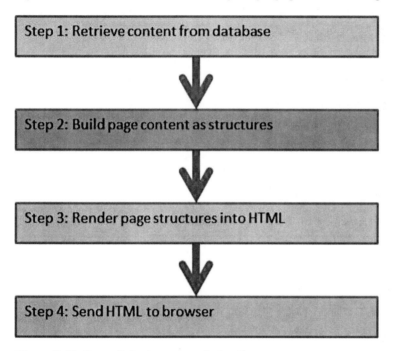

Figure 7–21. Drupal's basic page rendering flow

Let's start with the page that was rendered and sent to the browser. Figure 7–22 shows the content region of the page as it is rendered.

Food walks in

published by brian on Fri, 08/06/2010 - 14:22

A cheeseburger and french fry walk into a bar. The bartender says, "We don't serve food here."

Read more

Configuring Wysiwyg Editors

published by brian on Fri, 08/06/2010 - 13:04

There are a number of **WYSIWYG** editors available for Drupal. The selection of an editor can be a
contentious issue, since some people are advocates for one editor or another. My favorite is *CKEditor* because
it is simple to install and provides enough flexibility for most users

Read more

***Figure 7–22.** Segment of a page as shown in the browser*

Starting with step 1, Drupal's content management engine will get all content from the database
and start building the content arrays with regard to various current conditions, such as the user's
permissions, the need for comments or revisions to be displayed, and the existence of cached data. The
process used is illustrated in Figure 7–23.

1. All requests start at index.php. First, the system is bootstrapped. This includes
   starting a connection to the database, checking for cached data, setting up a
   session, registering the language, plus a few other things. The page lifecycle is
   described in more detail in Chapter 2. After bootstrapping, the
   menu_execute_active_handler() function is called.

2. The menu_execute_active_handler() function checks to make sure the site is
   online and then calls menu_get_item(), which returns a router item that it gets
   from the menu_router table in the database. A router item is an array that is used
   internally. It contains information about the object, such as the function to be
   executed (called back) when the page is to be loaded, the access information for
   the current user, and certain theme information. The callback page information
   is what we will use for the next step.

3. The call_user_func_array() function is called with the callback and arguments
   properties of the router array. The call is
   call_user_func_array($router_item['page_callback'],
   $router_item['page_arguments']); which resolves to
   call_user_func_array('node_page_default', ''); .

205

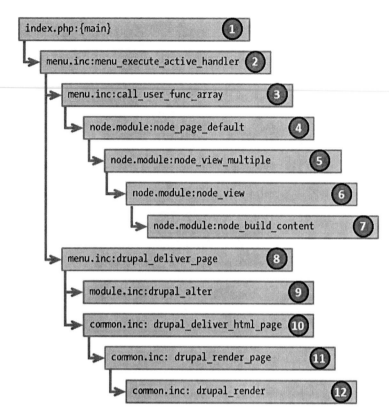

Figure 7–23. *The flow required to create page content*

4. The node_page_default() function makes a call to the database to find all of the nodes that are to be built. In this case, there are two nodes with node identifiers (nid) of 3 and 2. Node 3 is our joke, and node 2 is an article on WYSIWYG editors. After retrieving the list of nids, the function retrieves the nodes with $nodes = node_load_multiple($nids); . The function then calls node_view_multiple() to build the view.

5. The node_view_multiple() function calls the node_view() function once for each node in the array, then returns an array of built nodes ready for rendering.

6. The node_view() function calls the node_build_content() function to do the actual building of the node for display, and then invokes drupal_alter() to give other modules an opportunity to modify the view. This ability to alter nodes after they are built is a very powerful (and potentially scary!) feature of Drupal.

7. The node_build_content() function calls the field_attach_view() function, which does the heavy lifting of creating the node. The field_attach_view() function calls module_invoke_all() to give all modules a chance to have their say into the building of the node.

8. Now that the nodes that are to be included in the region have been built, it's time to render them into HTML for delivery back to the browser. The `drupal_deliver_page()` function is called to start that process. It is called with an array, `$page_callback_result`, which contains a pager and the node information. A pager is a standard Drupal feature that enables the rendering of multiple pages of long lists of items. Since we only have two items, the pager won't be rendered on our page.

   First, the function calls `drupal_alter()` to give all modules one last chance to do anything to the content before finally delivering it.

9. The `drupal_alter()` function is called with the `'page_delivery_callback'` argument.

10. The `$delivery_callback` variable contains the string `drupal_deliver_html_page`, which is called at this point. This function makes a last check to see if the page should be rendered by checking to see if the item was not found, or if the user doesn't have access, or if the site is offline. What? Shouldn't we have checked this already? While it seems like a waste to build the whole page, only to decide at the last moment that the user doesn't have access, this check is pretty important. Remember the calls to `drupal_alter()`? It is conceivable that one of the functions might have decided to punt and mark the page as not renderable for some reason. It would be rude to render the page after one of the modules has said not to.

11. Now that all of the data for the page has been collected and we've gotten the green light to render the page, it's time to build the HTML. The `drupal_render_page()` function calls all `page_build` hooks and a last `drupal_alter()` is called for all page hooks.

12. Finally, the general-purpose `drupal_render()` function is called to create the actual HTML. This function is called from many different places, and acts to find the appropriate style sheets, template files, and other theme information. The `drupal_render()` function is recursive, since there will certainly be objects inside the page that need to be rendered, and there will be objects inside those objects that need to be rendered, and so on.

At this point, HTML is generated and sent to the browser. Easy as pie.

Template Interaction

I mentioned that templates can be thought of as hierarchical. That is, templates can be contained in other templates. Figure 7–24 displays the HTML code that was generated to show the page.

1. First, the HTML template, `html.tpl.php`, is called. Think of this as the master page that drives all other functionality. When the line `<?php print $page; ?>` is encountered in the HTML template, the page template is invoked.

2. The page template, `page.tpl.php`, starts with the page-wrapper div. The page template creates divs within divs until it reaches the line, `<?php print render($page['content']); ?>`. At this point, the page content is rendered, which means our friend `drupal_render()` is called recursively to process the objects in `$page['content']`. During the theming process, as the rendering function is rendering the content, it discovers that there is a "theme wrapper" that is to encapsulate the nodes. The code, in `drupal_render`, looks like this:

```
        if (isset($elements['#theme_wrappers'])) {
          foreach ($elements['#theme_wrappers'] as $theme_wrapper) {
            $elements['#children'] = theme($theme_wrapper, $elements);
          }
        }
```

Figure 7-24. HTML code that created the page rendered to the browser

From here, we can see how the various template files interacted to create the HTML during the `drupal_render()` process described above.

3. The variable `$theme_wrapper` evaluates to 'region', which sets off a series of events, culminating in a call to `$render_function($template_file, $variables);`, where `$render_function` evaluates to `theme_render_template` and `$template_file` evaluates to `modules/system/region.tpl.php`. A simple include, `include DRUPAL_ROOT . '/' . $template_file;`, causes `region.tpl.php` to load. It is just a simple wrapper:

    ```
    <div class="<?php print $classes; ?>">
      <?php print $content; ?>
    </div>
    ```

    Magically, the `$content` variable has already been rendered by hierarchical calls to the templates within, as shown in the next few steps.

4. Inside the region there is a block that was configured using the administrative screens. Now it is time to call the template file for blocks, `block.tpl.php`. The block template will output a title if we set it up in the block configuration page. In the case of our nodes, there is no title, so the block template acts pretty much as a simple wrapper.

5. The node template, `node.tpl.php`, is called, which outputs some classes and prepares to receive the content rendered by the field content generator. The node template actually does a lot of work to get the default node just right. It places information that is meaningful, such as the author, publishing date, and title, plus it can render helpful links for administrators and authors to allow them to edit or delete the node.

6. The field wrapper is generated by the `theme_field` function in the field module. This function plays the role of default field theming if a theme template file for field, `field.tpl.php`, is not found. There is a default field template file, but it will not be used; it is included in the Drupal core as a starting point for creating your own field template file if you want to do that.

7. Finally, as part of the node template, if there are any links to be rendered, they are put here. In this case, the only link is "Read more," which takes us to a page that has the contents of this node in its entirety.

So that's the inside scoop on creating a simple front page for our site. As you can see, there are many steps, but once you understand the general flow of things, the design becomes logical and it gets easy to master the concepts.

Other Templates

In addition to the standard templates described here, you can have a template for just about any content type, and even a single instance of a content type. Suppose, for example, you want to create a page template for the front page, and a different template for all other pages. This is a pretty common practice so there's a provision in Drupal to do this. If the file `page-front.tpl.php` is present in the current theme's directory, it will be used when the front page is called, and `page.tpl.php` will be called for all other pages.

You can also create page templates for certain URL paths. For example, if you want a different template for when you add a content node, the URL looks like this: `http://yoursite.com/node/add`; you just need to create a page template that has the path, replacing the slashes with hyphens: `page-node-add.tpl.php`.

The most common template, besides page, is node. Bartik's node template (`node.tpl.php`) is shown in Listing 7–15. A node template indicates where node-related content is to be rendered.

Listing 7–15. A Typical Node Template

```
<div id="node-<?php print $node->nid; ?>" class="<?php print $classes; ?> clearfix"<?php print
$attributes; ?>>

  <?php print render($title_prefix); ?>
  <?php if (!$page): ?>
    <h2<?php print $title_attributes; ?>>
      <a href="<?php print $node_url; ?>"><?php print $title; ?></a>
    </h2>
  <?php endif; ?>
  <?php print render($title_suffix); ?>
```

```php
<?php if ($display_submitted): ?>
  <div class="meta submitted">
    <?php print $user_picture; ?>
    <?php
      print t('published by !username on !datetime',
        array('!username' => $name, '!datetime' => $date));
    ?>
  </div>
<?php endif; ?>

<div class="content clearfix"<?php print $content_attributes; ?>>
  <?php
    // We hide the comments and links now so that we can render them later.
    hide($content['comments']);
    hide($content['links']);
    print render($content);
  ?>
</div>

<?php
  // Remove the "Add new comment" link on the teaser page or if the comment
  // form is being displayed on the same page.
  if ($teaser || !empty($content['comments']['comment_form'])) {
    unset($content['links']['comment']['#links']['comment-add']);
  }
  // Only display the wrapper div if there are links.
  $links = render($content['links']);
  if ($links):
?>
  <div class="link-wrapper">
    <?php print $links; ?>
  </div>
<?php endif; ?>

<?php print render($content['comments']); ?>

</div>
```

The node.tpl.php template will be used for all nodes, unless a more specific template is found.(See below for how specific templates are chosen.) If you want to use a generic node template for all nodes, but you want the story content type to use a different template, you can create a file called node-story.tpl.php.

Getting even more specific, you can create a template for a particular node, referenced by its node identifier (nid). To do this, you create a file in the theme's directory with the name node-123.tpl.php, where 123 is the nid. While this is rarely used and comes with the usual disclaimers of non-portability, it's nice to know it's available.

Template Specificity

When the Drupal core theming engine is looking for the most appropriate template to use, it goes through a process called "template suggestions." During this process, Drupal makes a list of all possible templates that could be chosen at that point. It then goes down the list until it finds one of the choices.

For example, in order to edit node 123, the URL looks like this: `http://mysite.com/node/123/edit`. Drupal builds a list with all possible template names:

```
page-node-edit.tpl.php
page-node-123.tpl.php
page-node.tpl.php
page.tpl.php
```

After the list is created, Drupal will look in the theme directory for a template and will stop when the template is found. It is possible to modify this list to affect the order of the suggested templates, but that's advanced topic beyond the scope of this book. If you need to do that, check the Drupal documentation for details.

Summary

The Drupal theming process is incredibly rich. That's a good thing, unless you are just learning to do theming "the Drupal way." I hope that after reading this chapter, you have at least a basic understanding of the theming process and can start up that learning curve. Having a step debugger is a great help in understanding how all of the pieces fit together.

Once you get the basics, you'll want to spend some time at `drupal.org` to get into the intricacies of the theming engine as you need to know more.

Appendix B is a working case study that shows how to theme a fairly complex site from scratch, using a Photoshop design and the Omega theme system. In the next chapter, we'll cover the important task of testing.

In the next chapter, we will go over a very important topic, Testing.

CHAPTER 8

■ ■ ■

Testing

One area of software development that has gotten more attention lately is testing. From unit testing to user interface testing to full system testing, this subject is finally getting the attention I think it deserves. Of course, we all test our code to some extent, but automated testing tools and integration into the IDE have made the nasty task of testing much more palatable.

A formalized test strategy requires creating code that programmatically exercises every single line of your program to assure that it works as it is supposed to. Programmers have traditionally tended to avoid developing formalized test harnesses for their programs, mostly because of the extra time involved in writing the tests. This time does not directly tie into their deliverables since the testing code never leaves the developers' workstations.

I used to think the same way. Who wants to spend time writing boring tests when they know their code works? How demeaning!

Over a few small and one large projects recently, I have come to embrace the idea of unit and system testing and to see how building a formalized test suite and coding to the tests really does shorten the development cycle. I've really been able to see how this can save time and money in the long term—and create a better product with fewer defects. The value of that is incalculable.

Dries Buytaert is the original creator and project lead of Drupal. He had this to say about testing during the development of the Drupal 7 code:

> For well over a year now, core development has used a test-driven development strategy combined with automated testing. I think all core developers working on Drupal 7 will unanimously agree when I say that our test infrastructure has drastically improved our velocity and effectiveness. Overall, patches get accepted faster.
>
> The automated tests allow us to focus on the architectural and the algorithmic changes introduced by a patch, rather than having to worry about unexpected side-effects. This helps both patch reviewers and core developers contributing patches. Furthermore, thanks to the tests, we have a much better feel about the stability and the health of Drupal 7.
>
> I am optimistic that our code freeze period for Drupal 7 could be shorter than prior releases. As the project lead, our test framework helps me sleep better at night. The stability and health of our code base is important to me, but frankly, it is at least as important for the many Drupal users, or for those people and organizations looking to adopt Drupal.

Before Drupal 7, there was a plague of incidents where someone would fix a bug in core or a contributed module, test it and solve the problem in one place, only to find out after releasing the fixed code that it broke something else in another module. Just consider the form alter hook we saw in Chapter 6, which allows us to alter a form we don't own. It would be possible for me to write code that

213

broke your module without even touching your code. This was a very frustrating situation for everyone in the community.

There was a test module, SimpleTest, available for Drupal version 6. It never really took off, partly because there wasn't a testing zeitgeist present in the developer community. Plus, the Drupal 6 version of SimpleTest required a hack to the core. Naughty, naughty. Suffice it to say that SimpleTest did not get much traction in Drupal 6.

Fortunately, the attitude toward testing has changed in the development community, and the SimpleTest module has not only been embraced, it has been included in core. Moreover, all core modules are required to have a test suite that assures that the module works as designed.

To drive home the value of testing in Drupal, here's one more quote, this from the testing page on drupal.org:

> *SimpleTest is Drupal's custom testing framework. During the Drupal 7 development cycle SimpleTest has become an integral part of the workflow, and has been moved into core as the Testing module. It has significantly enhanced the way core is developed and made it possible to make major API enhancements with confidence.*
>
> *Drupal 7 HEAD is much more stable than any release we [have] ever had. -chx*
> *Drupal 7 has seen major benefits from embracing the testing framework.*

So I suggest that your module have full test coverage and that you run all tests against the core and your module before you release it.

Getting Started

Before you do any testing in Drupal, you must do some configuration. The Testing module is installed as part of the Drupal 7 core, but you need to enable it just like you would any other module—under Modules as shown in Figure 8–1.

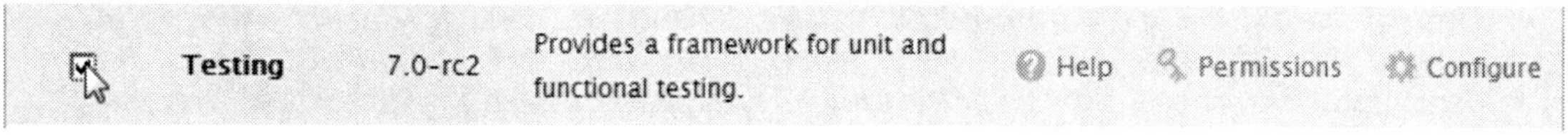

Figure 8–1. Enabling the Testing module

Save the configuration and hope for the best. If you get the banner, "The configuration options have been saved.", you're all set. But chances are you'll have a problem, as shown in Figure 8–2.

Figure 8–2. The Testing module requires the PHP cURL library

cURL is a tool used to transfer data from or to a server using a number of different protocols. The cURL functionality comes in two flavors: a command-line tool that we don't care about here, and a library that has been packaged into a PHP library called php_curl.dll. Before we run our web-based testing, we must enable the cURL library.

Installing the cURL library is pretty straightforward, but it is complicated a bit by the fact that we are running in a Windows environment using Visual Studio.

First, let's create a PHP file that gives us the status of PHP and tells us what is loaded. There is a PHP command, phpinfo(), that will print out the status of the loaded PHP interpreter and let us know the version numbers and lots of other helpful information.

Create a new file, phpinfo.php, using Visual Studio in the same directory as Drupal's index.php. It should contain just two lines, as shown in listing 8–1.

Listing 8–1. The PHP Information Page

```php
<?php
phpinfo();
```

Now, set that to the default page for debugging. VS.PHP uses its own instance of PHP. To see where php.ini is loaded, we need to run this PHP script from Visual Studio. In the property pages as shown in Figure 8–3 (Project▶{your project} Properties▶Debug), set the Start page parameter to phpinfo.php.

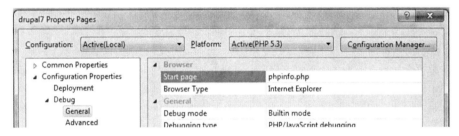

Figure 8–3. Setting the initial Start page property to test PHP installation

Installing cURL requires making a change to the PHP initialization file, php.ini. Our PHP add-in, VS.PHP, has its own version of php.ini, which it copies to the web directory every time you start a debugging session. This is designed to give you a fresh copy of the initialization file each run. However, the cURL libraries are not loaded. The VS.PHP initialization file does not have cURL enabled by default, so we must create our own version of php.ini and enable cURL.

On the property pages for your project, go to the Advanced page and set the php.ini path as shown in Figure 8–4.

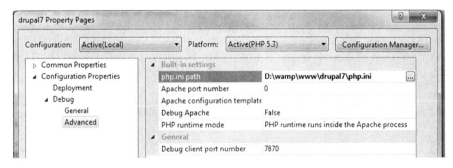

Figure 8–4. Setting a custom path for the PHP initialization file

Note that the path should be where your index.php file is. Click OK and press F5 to start debugging. You'll see the PHP information in your browser, as shown in Figure 8–5, and you'll notice that the path identified with "Loaded Configuration File" is set to the path you indicated on the property page.

PHP Version 5.3.2

System	Windows NT SHUTTLE 6.1 build 7600 ((null)) i586
Build Date	Mar 3 2010 19:38:00
Compiler	MSVC6 (Visual C++ 6.0)
Architecture	x86
Configure Command	cscript /nologo configure.js "--enable-snapshot-build" "--disable-isapi" "--enable-debug-pack" "--disable-isapi" "--without-mssql" "--without-pdo-mssql" "--without-pi3web" "--with-pdo-oci=D:\php-sdk\oracle\instantclient10\sdk,shared" "--with-oci8=D:\php-sdk\oracle\instantclient10\sdk,shared" "--with-oci8-11g=D:\php-sdk\oracle\instantclient11\sdk,shared" "--enable-object-out-dir=../obj/" "--enable-com-dotnet"
Server API	Apache 2.0 Handler
Virtual Directory Support	enabled
Configuration File (php.ini) Path	C:\Windows
Loaded Configuration File	D:\wamp\www\drupal7\php.ini

Figure 8–5. PHP Information showing the configuration file path

All is good so far. If you search for the string "curl", you probably won't find it. We first need to enable the extension by removing a comment from the PHP initialization file.

Using any text editor, open the php.ini file that has been copied to your home directory and search for the string "php_curl.dll". You'll notice a semicolon in front of it, which indicates a commented line. Remove the semicolon as shown in Figure 8–6.

```
; Windows Extensions
; Note that ODBC support is built in, so no dll is needed for it.
; Note that many DLL files are located in the extensions/ (PHP 4) ext/ (PHP 5)
; extension folders as well as the separate PECL DLL download (PHP 5).
; Be sure to appropriately set the extension_dir directive.
;
;extension=php_bz2.dll
extension=php_curl.dll
;extension=php_dba.dll
```

Figure 8–6. Removing the semicolon before the cURL extension enables the extension.

Now save the file and restart your debugging session using Ctrl+Shift+F5. You'll see the PHP Information screen again, but now when you search for "curl", you'll see that the extension has been enabled and is working properly. It should look something like Figure 8–7.

curl

cURL support	enabled
cURL Information	7.20.0
Age	3
Features	
AsynchDNS	Yes
Debug	No
GSS-Negotiate	No
IDN	No
IPv6	Yes
Largefile	Yes
NTLM	Yes
SPNEGO	No
SSL	Yes
SSPI	Yes
krb4	No
libz	Yes
CharConv	No
Protocols	dict, file, ftp, ftps, http, https, imap, imaps, ldap, pop3, pop3s, rtsp, smtp, smtps, telnet, tftp
Host	i386-pc-win32
SSL Version	OpenSSL/0.9.8l
ZLib Version	1.2.3

Figure 8–7. The cURL library extension information

Once the cURL library is loaded properly, we can start creating and executing tests.

■ **Tip** The phpinfo.php page is handy, but you should definitely not put it on your production machine as it contains information that could be helpful to a hacker. The same goes for php.ini. And it should not be present in the same directory as your index.php file. Rather, it will be placed in some location defined by your system administrator (which could be you, of course!).

You should probably change the start page back to index.php for the next steps.

Testing Fundamentals

The Drupal test subsystem provides the ability to do unit testing like many other systems (including Visual Studio Team Edition), but it also allows more integrated testing of the entire system.

The three typical categories of software testing are: unit, integration, and system. Unit testing is pretty straightforward. A unit test suite is designed to identify (usually) small portions of code and test to see if they work. Actually, a good unit test suite will also test the boundaries of a particular piece of code to make sure that the proper errors are handled if expected inputs are not made available. Unit testing only concerns itself with the basic blocks that make up the code, usually on a function-by-function basis. As such, the unit test harness must be intimately involved with the internal capabilities of the code in order to exercise them properly.

Integration testing, on the other hand, is more concerned about how all of the individual functions operate together to provide a working system. In Drupal, we have little functions that do certain small things, but there are many tasks that require the larger system to do something before they can work. Consider the simple act of creating a node. Once a user logs in and has the right privileges to create a node, she can click a link to add a certain type of content and then be presented with a screen to enter the title, body, and whatever else the node requires.

Now, let's automate that process. Carl Sagan, in his wonderful series *Cosmos*, said, "If you wish to make an apple pie from scratch, you must first invent the universe." It's sort of that way with Drupal testing.

Before creating a node, the automated test routine must first log in as a user that has the rights to create a node, and then the node creation can be on its way. But before we can even create the node, it might be necessary to enable some modules, create a role, set permissions, even create the content type if it's not one that is included in the Drupal core.

One way to do this user-emulated testing would be to put a robot at the keyboard to replace the human, but that could get quite cumbersome.

Fortunately, the Drupal 7 Testing module provides an API to do integration testing without the expense of a physical robot. In the above scenario, we must first emulate the logging in of a user. But which user? Do we need to create a user for testing? Good question, and the answer is no.

Drupal's testing framework allows you to create a user with a random name and specific roles. It then lets you log in as that user, perform any necessary tasks, and then delete anything that was created along with the temporary user. All along, the testing framework is keeping track of what the virtual user did, and the responses Drupal returned. We can test expected responses against what was returned to assert that everything is working as designed.

After unit and integration testing, the next level of testing, system, involves a comprehensive test of the entire system, including networks, hardware, and sometimes novice or experienced users. The testing that Drupal's test framework performs is somewhere between integration testing and system testing, but provides a nice way to automate our system so I'm not going to quibble about where it falls on the continuum.

Test-Driven Development

Developing any nontrivial application requires some level of testing. Over the last few years, there's been a lot of talk about test-driven development—that is, developing tests first and then using those tests to define and guide the development of the application. Yeah, that sounds good, but it seems like way too much bureaucracy for my anarchist brain. Why can't I just write my program?

If you are reading this book, Drupal is probably new to you, and PHP is probably new as well. When you are learning a new technology or two, insisting on developing a test suite first can be a real buzz-kill. When you're just learning, sometimes it's best just to play around for a while to see what happens in box 2 when the red button in box 1 is pressed. Testing be damned!

In fact, that's just what I have been doing so far in this book. You get a pass for not developing tests while you are learning a technology. But once you master the technology, doing test-driven development becomes a lot easier, and is definitely preferable for more complex systems.

Ward Cunningham is the inventor of the wiki. He maintains a wiki on test-driven development that is very accessible. He boils test-driven development down to a simple list.

- Think about what you want to do.

- Think about how to test it.

- Write a small test. Think about the desired API.

- Write just enough code to fail the test.

- Run and watch the test fail. Now you know that your test is going to be executed.

- Write just enough code to pass the test (and pass all your previous tests).

- Run and watch all of the tests pass. If anything doesn't pass, you did something wrong, fix it now since because it's still fresh in your mind.

- If you have any duplicate logic, or inexpressive code, refactor to remove duplication and increase expressiveness—this includes reducing coupling and increasing cohesion.

- Run the tests again; you should still see all tests pass. If you get a failure, you made a mistake in your refactoring. Fix it now and rerun.

- Repeat the steps above until you can't find any more tests that drive writing new code.

Ward points out that the first step is the most difficult, followed by the second step. Everything else is pretty easy.

Now that I've gone over the importance of test-driven development, we are about to break those rules. In this book, we've been developing a module that will provide the weather conditions and forecast for a particular location on earth. We built the module without creating any formal automated tests, but now it's time to develop those tests. This is not a total waste; having an automated test suite will allow us to be confident should we change the code or add functionality.

It's never too late to develop a test harness.

Developing Tests

We will be creating two types of tests for our weather information module. First, we'll invoke the unit testing facility of the Drupal Testing module. This will simply exercise stand-alone functions to see if they provide the expected output for a given input. Plus, we'll do some boundary checking to see if we can get it to break by providing bad input data. Unit testing is done by instantiating the DrupalUnitTestCase class.

After that, we'll invoke the DrupalWebTestCase class to do more in-depth integration and system testing.

By now, you've probably figured out "the Drupal way" of building applications. There's a heavy emphasis on coding standards, naming conventions, and metadata. Developing a test harness for your application is an application in itself and, as such, incorporates those same development philosophies.

Tests are typically contained in a directory under the module directory that is being tested. To get started, create a directory called tests under the weather_info directory, which is under sites/all/modules. The hierarchy is shown in Figure 8–8.

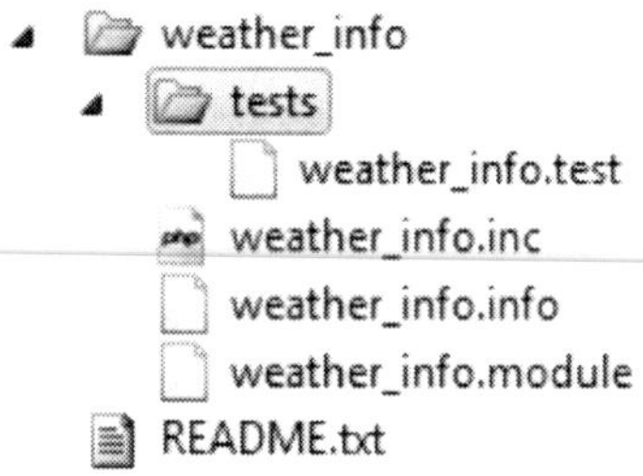

Figure 8–8. Adding a directory for tests

As you might expect, we need to give Drupal some information about our test suite. We can do this by adding some lines to our project's `.info` file. The module's `.info` file should already exist in your `weather_info` directory. You'll need to add the bold line shown in Listing 8–2.

Listing 8–2. The Information File Additions for a Test Suite

```
; $Id$
name = Weather information
description = A block that shows current weather for a particular location.
package = Cool stuff from Brian
core = 7.x
files[] = weather_info.module
files[] = weather_info.inc

files[] = tests/weather_info.test

version = 7.x-1.x
```

The file, `tests/weather_info.test`, is the Drupal module that contains all tests for the weather module. Next, we need to create the unit test harness.

Developing a Unit Test Harness

Unit tests are developed by extending the `DrupalUnitTestCase` class and overriding the `getInfo()` function. We will first be testing the temperature functions of our weather information module. We will start by calling the `weather_info_temp()` function, which calls the various conversion functions: `weather_info_f_to_c()`, `weather_info_c_to_f()`, `weather_info_c_to_k()`, etc.

The skeleton for our unit test class is shown in Listing 8–3.

Listing 8–3. Skeleton for a Unit Test Case

```
class WeatherTempTest extends DrupalUnitTestCase {

  public static function getInfo() {
    return array(
      'name' => 'Temperature tests',
      'description' => 'Tests temperature conversions.',
      'group' => 'Weather info',
      );
  }
// tests go here
}
```

Like all things Drupal, there is plenty of descriptive metadata to help build the screens and report progress. It's important to declare a `getInfo()` function, as the test framework will execute this when running the tests.

Everything else in the class will be considered a single test case that will be executed by the testing engine. For our simple test, we will call the `weather_info_temp()` function with various parameters and then assert that the resulting output returns what we expect. An example test is shown in Listing 8–4.

Listing 8–4. *Sample Test Case for Temperature*

```
$out_temp = weather_info_temp(32, 'C', 'US');
$this->assertEqual($out_temp, '0&deg;C', 'F to C conversion.');
```

Look at the second line. The `DrupalUnitTestCase` class has a number of assertions for checking the output. In this test, we are passing the integer value 32 to the function. The second parameter is the unit we want the temperature converted to, and the third parameter is the unit system, either 'US' for British measure, or 'SI' for metric measure. In this case, we are sending a value representing 32 degrees Fahrenheit and asking the function to return the corresponding value in Celsius. As you'll recall from earlier chapters, the `weather_info_temp()` function returns a handy string ready for us to output to the browser. This includes the degree entity and the unit returned.

So the `assertEqual()` function will compare the first parameter to the second and check to see if they are equal. If they are, the test will be considered a success. If not, it will be deemed a failure. The third parameter is a string that will be printed on reports to indicate the nature of the test.

We have several different temperature conversion combinations to test. The complete test case for this function is shown in Listing 8–5.

Listing 8–5. *A Unit Test Suite to Exercise the Temperature Conversion Functions*

```
class WeatherTempTest extends DrupalUnitTestCase {

  public static function getInfo() {
    return array(
      'name' => t('Temperature tests'),
      'description' => t('Tests temperature conversions.'),
      'group' => 'Weather info',
      );
  }
  function testFtoC() {
    $out_temp = weather_info_temp(32, 'C', 'US');
    $this->assertEqual($out_temp, '0&deg;C', t('F to C conversion.'));

    $out_temp = weather_info_temp(32, 'F', 'US');
    $this->assertEqual($out_temp, '32&deg;F', t('F to F conversion.'));

    $out_temp = weather_info_temp(10, 'C', 'SI');
    $this->assertEqual($out_temp, '10&deg;C', t('C to C conversion.'));

    $out_temp = weather_info_temp(32, 'K', 'US');
    $this->assertEqual($out_temp, '273&deg;K', t('F to K conversion.'));

    $out_temp = weather_info_temp(10, 'K', 'SI');
    $this->assertEqual($out_temp, '283&deg;K', t('C to K conversion.'));

    $out_temp = weather_info_temp(32, 'R', 'US');
    $this->assertEqual($out_temp, '492&deg;R', t('F to R conversion.'));

    $out_temp = weather_info_temp(10, 'R', 'SI');
    $this->assertEqual($out_temp, '510&deg;R', t('C to R conversion.'));
  }
}
```

Let's run the tests! Get to the Configuration page and find the Testing module under Development (See Figure 8–9).

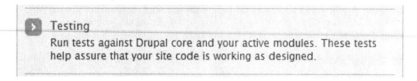

Figure 8–9. Access the testing module under the development group on the configuration page.

You will see a page with the available tests. All of the core modules contain tests, so you'll see them all listed. We are interested only in the Weather Info tests right now, so scroll down to see the tests as shown in Figure 8–10.

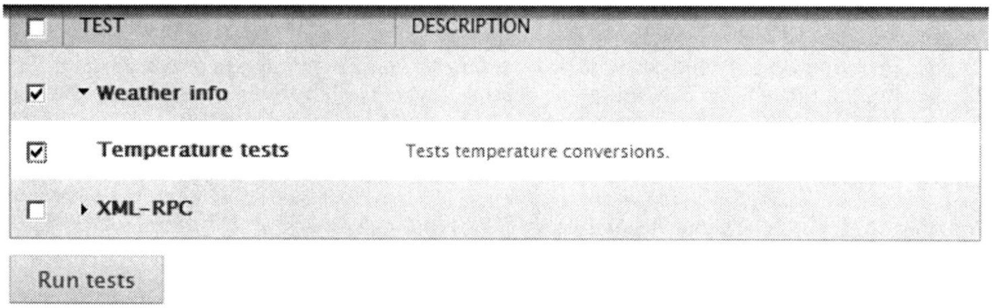

☐	TEST	DESCRIPTION
☑	▾ **Weather info**	
☑	**Temperature tests**	Tests temperature conversions.
☐	▸ **XML–RPC**	

Run tests

Figure 8–10. The weather information tests

Under the Weather info group you'll see all of the test cases that inherited the test case classes. Right now, there is only one but we'll be creating more later. Click the Run tests button to start the tests.

You will see the throbber going as the tests are run and Drupal is communicating with the browser using AJAX. (See Figure 8–11.)

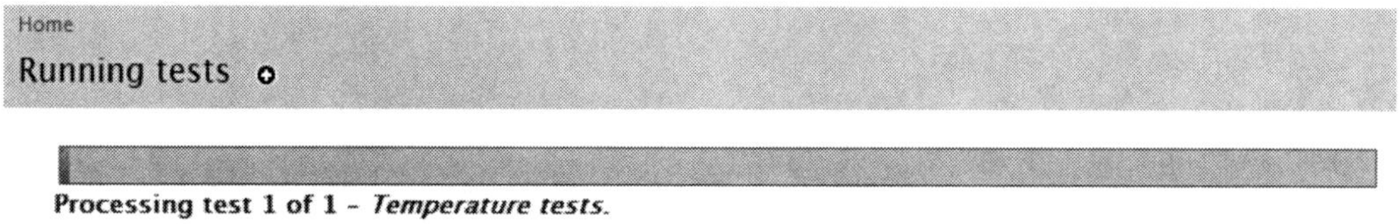

Home
Running tests ○

Processing test 1 of 1 – *Temperature tests*.

Figure 8–11. The page displays the test-processing progress

Unit tests run pretty quickly, so you won't see this for long. Don't worry, though, you'll spend a lot of time looking at this screen once we get into web testing.

After the tests are complete, you will see a screen that displays the test results as shown in Figure 8–12.

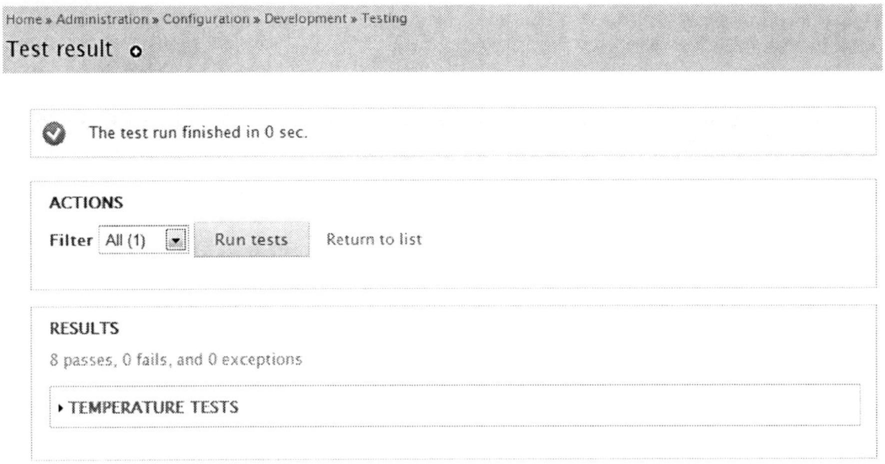

Figure 8–12. Test results screen

If you want to see the details of the tests, you can click the TEMPERATURE TESTS link (see Figure 8–13).

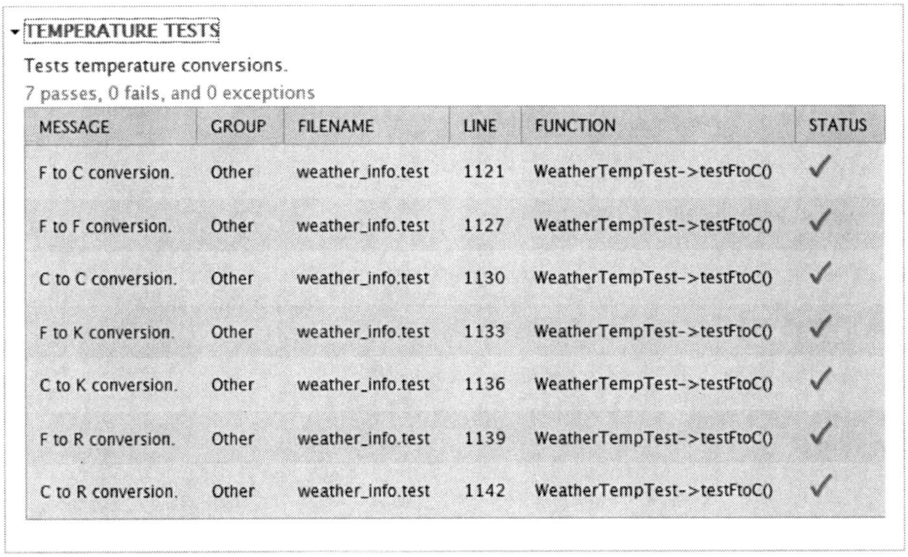

Figure 8–13. Result of the unit test processing

From this, you can see the relationship between the code in our test case and the report as it is displayed in the browser.

This will exercise the code, but I'm not quite happy with the coverage yet. What we've done here is pretty safe. What would happen, for example, if we passed a string to the function? It is designed to take an integer, but is it smart enough to provide some kind of error if the wrong data type is sent?

Let's suppose we think the function should return a null if it doesn't understand the temperature sent to it. Listing 8–6 shows how I would write that function.

Listing 8–6. *Testing Incorrect Data Type Input*

```
$out_temp = weather_info_temp('thirty-two', 'C', 'US');
$this->assertNull($out_temp, 'F to C conversion with bad type.');
```

I'll add this to the test case and run the tests again. The results are shown in Figure 8–14.

▾ TEMPERATURE TESTS

Tests temperature conversions.
7 passes, 1 fail, and 0 exceptions

MESSAGE	GROUP	FILENAME	LINE	FUNCTION	STATUS
F to C conversion.	Other	weather_info.test	1121	WeatherTempTest->testFtoC()	✓
F to C conversion with bad type.	Other	weather_info.test	1124	WeatherTempTest->testFtoC()	✗
F to F conversion.	Other	weather_info.test	1127	WeatherTempTest->testFtoC()	✓
C to C conversion.	Other	weather_info.test	1130	WeatherTempTest->testFtoC()	✓
F to K conversion.	Other	weather_info.test	1133	WeatherTempTest->testFtoC()	✓
C to K conversion.	Other	weather_info.test	1136	WeatherTempTest->testFtoC()	✓
F to R conversion.	Other	weather_info.test	1139	WeatherTempTest->testFtoC()	✓
C to R conversion.	Other	weather_info.test	1142	WeatherTempTest->testFtoC()	✓

Figure 8–14. *Whoops! The function did not fail correctly.*

Now we're starting to test the waters of test-driven development. We have an expected return, but our function is not returning it. So we need to go into the code and do the right thing. Listing 8–7 shows a modification to the function that will check for the proper data type.

Listing 8–7. *Modifying our Function Will Produce the Expected Result*

```
function weather_info_temp($in_temp, $unit, $unit_system) {
  if (is_string($in_temp)) {
    return null;
  }

  switch ($unit) {
  ...
```

Now we can run the tests again and get the output shown in Figure 8–15.

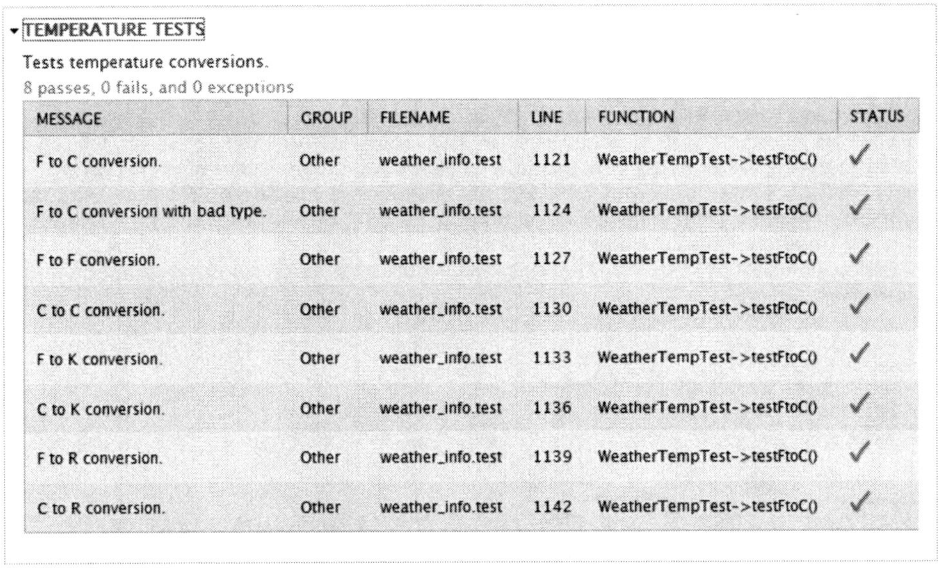

Figure 8–15. Our test was successful in driving the development of our function.

There are other tests that should be written in order to test the functionality of our system completely. It is up to you to come up with a list of tests and implement them in the test suite. You might consider testing a function's out-of-range condition or the presence of an array item that doesn't exist. There are many tests that can be performed on any piece of code. Like Ward said of his list, the first two steps are the hardest. Trying to figure out how to test something can be challenging, but the time spent is invested well for the time it will save you down the road.

For now, let's move on to a more complex form of testing that can invoke the entire Drupal experience, web testing.

Web Testing

Automated unit testing is a powerful development and debugging tool, but it can only take us so far. As I mentioned before, there are many places where unit testing doesn't allow us to do the kind of complex testing that exercises Drupal's operations.

For this, there is the `DrupalWebTestCase` class. Developing test cases using this class is quite a bit more complex simply due to the nature of the tests that will be conducted. The class inheritance is shown in Listing 8–8.

Listing 8–8. Creating an Instance of the `DrupalWebTestCase` Class

```
class WeatherBlockTest extends DrupalWebTestCase {
...
}
```

To get started with web test cases, you must think of a completely blank Drupal installation. That is, just the default core modules enabled. No blocks set in regions. No users. Default theme. Get the picture? A blank slate.

The testing engine creates a copy of every table in the database and sets the state as if the site has just been installed.

From here, you must invent the universe. You can build exactly what you want, isolated from other distractions. Only then can you get a fair, repeatable test that isolates only those things that you want to test. Fortunately, the test case class provides tools to do this difficult task pretty easily.

In our case, we will check various aspects of the weather information block. First, we will initialize our blank slate by enabling the weather_info module. Then we will create a user with certain permissions and profile information. Finally, we will add the block to a region on the page. And that will get us just to the point when we can start making our apple pie. OK, I'll stop with the Sagan quote. You can start testing the functionality of the block.

Listing 8–9 shows the setUp() function that does the initial creation of our environment.

Listing 8–9. *Creating the Initial Environment*

```
public function setUp() {
  // Enable any modules required for the test
  parent::setUp(array(
    'weather_info',
    'block',
  ));
```

The inherited (parent) class contains a setUp() function that takes an array as an argument. This array contains names of all modules that need to be enabled for the test to proceed. In our case, the weather_info and block modules must be enabled. If the modules we enable have any dependencies, the testing framework will automatically enable them.

Next, the drupalCreateUser() function is called. That function creates a temporary role with the permissions that are listed, and then creates a temporary user and assigns the user to that role. This code is shown in Listing 8–10.

Listing 8–10. *Creating a Test User and Logging In*

```
  // Create and log in our privileged user.
  $this->test_user = $this->drupalCreateUser(array(
    'view weather info',
    'change weather location',
    'administer weather info',
    'administer site configuration',
    'administer users',
    'access user profiles',
    'administer blocks',
    'access administration pages',
  ));
  $this->drupalLogin($this->test_user);
```

Finally, the user is logged in with the appropriate password. The effect of this setup is an environment that can be leveraged to do whatever testing we need.

Listing 8–11 shows the extended class for our skeleton.

Listing 8–11. *Extending the DrupalWebTestCase Class*

```
class WeatherBlockTest extends DrupalWebTestCase {

  public static function getInfo() {
    return array(
      'name' => t('Weather block tests'),
      'description' => t('Tests the weather block.'),
      'group' => 'Weather info',
```

```
    );
  }

  public function setUp() {
    // Enable any modules required for the test
    parent::setUp(array(
      'weather_info',
      'block',
    ));
    // Create and log in our privileged user.
    $this->test_user = $this->drupalCreateUser(array(
      'view weather info',
      'change weather location',
      'administer weather info',
      'administer site configuration',
      'administer users',
      'access user profiles',
      'administer blocks',
      'access administration pages',
      ));
    $this->drupalLogin($this->test_user);

  function testDoNothing() {
    $this->assertNull(null, 'just a stub');
  }

  //... actual tests go here
}
```

Notice the testDoNothing() function. This is required by the test class. If there are no tests, the setup does not work.

Now to the test. The test framework makes a copy of all Drupal tables as they are when Drupal is first installed. If everything goes according to plan, they are all removed when the tests are finished. If something wrong happens, however, they hang around and can affect the next test. The system also caches the tests that are to be performed in your test suite.

Whenever you change any code in your tests, or when a test is aborted or something else goes wrong, it is a good idea to clean up the test environment using the button on the test list screen. (See Figure 8–16.)

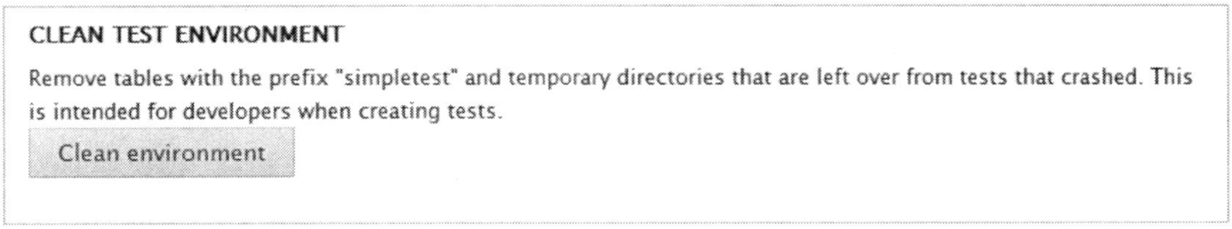

CLEAN TEST ENVIRONMENT

Remove tables with the prefix "simpletest" and temporary directories that are left over from tests that crashed. This is intended for developers when creating tests.

Clean environment

Figure 8–16. Cleaning the test environment creates a clean base from which to run tests.

If there were any testing artifacts left around, the status area would detail the clean-up that was done. (See Figure 8–17.)

- Removed 73 leftover tables.
- Removed 3 temporary directories.
- Removed 1 test result.

Figure 8–17. Cleaning a dirty environment

Don't worry about cleaning the test environment; if it is already clean and you clean it, nothing bad will happen; it will just indicate that nothing needed to be cleaned, as shown in Figure 8–18.

- No leftover tables to remove.
- No temporary directories to remove.
- Removed 0 test results.

Figure 8–18. No cleaning necessary

Since we changed our test suite, however, we definitely need to clean the environment. Doing so rereads the test module and displays it on the list of tests. (See Figure 8–19.)

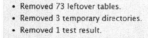

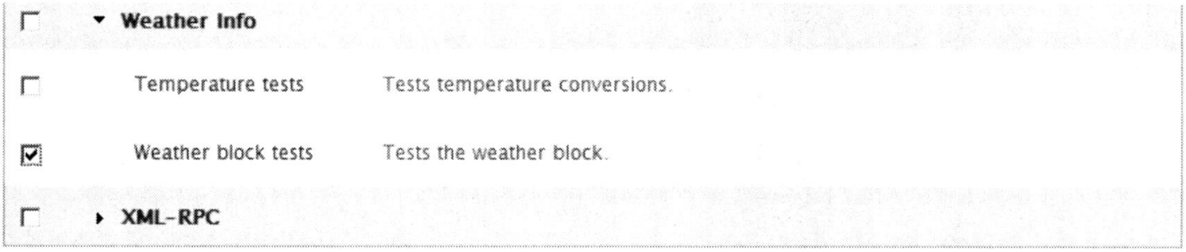

□	▼ **Weather Info**	
□	Temperature tests	Tests temperature conversions.
☑	Weather block tests	Tests the weather block.
□	▶ **XML–RPC**	

Figure 8–19. The new web test case shows up

Start the test and let's see what happens. We can see the report in Figure 8–20.

WEATHER BLOCK TESTS

Tests the weather block.

9 passes, 0 fails, 0 exceptions, and 2 debug messages

MESSAGE	GROUP	FILENAME	LINE	FUNCTION	STATUS
Created role of name: tbQB5VRY, id: 4	Role	weather_info.test	1091	WeatherBlockTest->setUp()	✓
Created permissions: view weather info, administer weather info, administer site configuration, administer blocks, access administration pages	Role	weather_info.test	1091	WeatherBlockTest->setUp()	✓
User created with name *aS17b2Zs* and pass *ZUxi5KPyTE*	User login	weather_info.test	1091	WeatherBlockTest->setUp()	✓
GET http://127.0.0.1:12347/user returned 200 (5.7 KB).	Browser	weather_info.test	1092	WeatherBlockTest->setUp()	✓
Valid HTML found on "http://127.0.0.1:12347/user"	Browser	weather_info.test	1092	WeatherBlockTest->setUp()	✓
Verbose message	Debug	weather_info.test	1092	WeatherBlockTest->setUp()	⚠
GET http://127.0.0.1:12347/user/2 returned 200 (5.53 KB).	Browser	weather_info.test	1092	WeatherBlockTest->setUp()	✓
Valid HTML found on "http://127.0.0.1:12347/user/2"	Browser	weather_info.test	1092	WeatherBlockTest->setUp()	✓
Verbose message	Debug	weather_info.test	1092	WeatherBlockTest->setUp()	⚠
User *aS17b2Zs* successfully logged in.	User login	weather_info.test	1092	WeatherBlockTest->setUp()	✓
just a stub	Other	weather_info.test	1097	WeatherBlockTest->testDoNothing()	✓

Figure 8–20. Web test case report

You can see the progress as the system creates a role with permissions, then creates the user and logs in with the temporary credentials. Notice the two entries labeled "Verbose message." The Drupal test engine creates a virtual browser that you can interact with. Whenever a screen is created, it will capture this screen and save the parameters in the database so you can see exactly what the testing framework "sees."

The first screen, for example, is the logon screen, which was exposed to the electronic robot. The screen is represented in Figure 8–21.

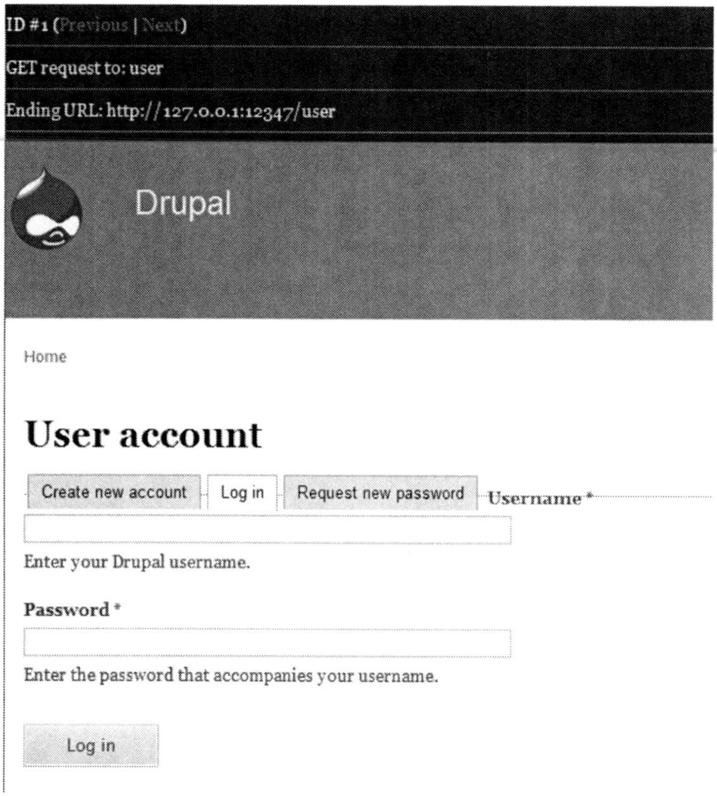

ID #1 (Previous | Next)

GET request to: user

Ending URL: http://127.0.0.1:12347/user

Drupal

Home

User account

Create new account · Log in · Request new password · Username *

Enter your Drupal username.

Password *

Enter the password that accompanies your username.

Log in

Figure 8–21. The Drupal testing framework takes pictures of screens as it encounters them.

To recap, then, what have we done? Well, nothing substantial yet. It's as if we just started DOS; we've loaded the kernel and now we've got a C: prompt sitting in front of us. What can be done? Answer: plenty.

Assign a Block to a Region

Our first task is to fire up the weather_info module as a block and assign it to the second sidebar region. Then we'll ask our virtual user to type in a location and have the module retrieve the information and display it on the screen.

The testing framework creates a virtual page and then acts on that page based on the input we give it in our test case. The best way to find out what we want this virtual page to do is to see how we interact with the real page. In order to build our test case, we need four pieces of information:

1. The name of the button to click to start the posting process

2. The address of the form we are posting to

3. The names of all of the fields we will need to set and the values we want to set them to

4. The happy text created when the form submission was a success

We know that there is a pull-down menu that allows us to set the region in which we want to place the weather information block. To refresh your memory, that pull-down is on the Structure Blocks page as shown in Figure 8–22.

Figure 8–22. The weather information block can be assigned to a region.

The first piece of information we need is right there in front of us. It's the button we use to submit the form back to the server, "Save blocks".

To get the second and third required pieces, we'll need to take a look at the HTML that was generated by Drupal. From the browser, you can "Show Source" and look for the `<form>` tag. Specifically, we are looking for the `action` attribute. This is shown in Figure 8–23.

```
103    <div class="content">
104       <form action="/admin/structure/block"  method="post" id="block-admin-display-form"
105    <div><table id="blocks" class="sticky-enabled">
```

Figure 8–23. The value of the `action` attribute is where we will be posting.

Next, we need to find the field to set. We can search the HTML source for what we know, "Weather block custom for each user". This is shown in Figure 8–24.

```
452         <td class="block">Weather block custom for each user</td>
453      <td><div class="form-item form-type-select form-item-blocks-weather-info-user-custom-region">
454      <label class="element-invisible" for="edit-blocks-weather-info-user-custom-region">Region for Weather block
         custom for each user block </label>
455      <select class="block-region-select block-region--1 form-select" id="edit-blocks-weather-info-user-custom-region"
         name="blocks[weather_info_user_custom][region]"><option value="-1">- None -</option><option
         value="header">Header</option><option value="help">Help</option><option
         value="highlight">Highlighted</option><option value="featured">Featured</option><option
         value="content">Content</option><option value="sidebar_first">Sidebar first</option><option
         value="sidebar_second">Sidebar second</option><option value="triptych_first">Triptych first</option><option
         value="triptych_middle">Triptych middle</option><option value="triptych_last">Triptych last</option><option
         value="footer_firstcolumn">Footer first column</option><option value="footer_secondcolumn">Footer second
         column</option><option value="footer_thirdcolumn">Footer third column</option><option
         value="footer_fourthcolumn">Footer fourth column</option><option value="footer">Footer</option></select>
456      </div>
457      <input type="hidden" name="blocks[weather_info_user_custom][theme]" value="first_subtheme" />
458      </td>
```

Figure 8–24. The HTML source will tell us what values to assign to which fields.

Notice the select element, `<select>` with the attribute `name="blocks[weather_info_user_custom][region]"`. That's the pull-down box we want. And then we can see all of the options that populate the box. The one we want is `<option value="sidebar_second">Sidebar second</option>`.

▓ **Tip** Rather than viewing the HTML source as an entire page, you can use your browser's debugging mode. In Internet Explorer, pressing F12 brings up the Developer Tools. You can point to an element on the page and the tool will take you right to the source where you can interrogate the code.

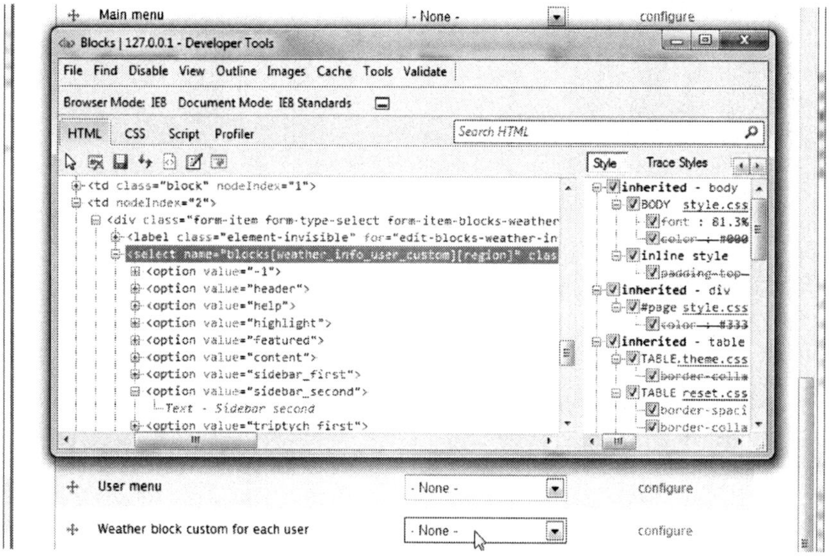

Google Chrome has a similar feature, which is accessed with Ctrl-Shift-I, and there is an extension for Firefox, Firebug, that provides even more functionality for the developer.

Finally, we need to tell the testing engine how to know if the settings have been done correctly. Return to the browser, set the value of the pull-down to "Sidebar Second" and click the "Save blocks" button. You should see, at the top of the page, the familiar green banner shown in Figure 8–25.

Figure 8–25. The successful update happy banner

The fourth piece of information we need is the text on this banner. Now we have all the information we need to create a new test case. See Listing 8–12.

Listing 8–12. Posting to a Form and Eevaluating the Results

```
$edit = array (
  'blocks[weather_info_user_custom][region]' => 'sidebar_second',
  );

$this->drupalPost('admin/structure/block', $edit, 'Save blocks');
$this->assertRaw(t('The block settings have been updated.'),
  t('Check that configuration is saved'));
```

Notice the value of the $edit array. This array is sent to the drupalPost() function as a command to set the values of certain form fields. This is where we set the value of 'blocks[weather_info_user_custom][region]', to 'sidebar_second'. This array can have as many members as you need in order to set the values of fields on the form.

The drupalPost() method needs to know the address to which we are posting and the contents of the form to post. The third parameter is the name of the button to press to submit the form.

Calling drupalPost() will cause the testing engine to build the page, set the variables, and submit the fields back to the server. By the time it gets to the next line, we will have assigned the block to the second sidebar region. But to make sure, we need to assert that the happy banner is found. This is done with the assertRaw() method.

Now let's save the test and run it. Don't forget to clean the environment in order to refresh the cache since we made changes to the code.

After running the tests, you should see the report with some new lines, as shown in Figure 8–26.

GET http://127.0.0.1:20974/admin/structure/block returned 200 (56.54 KB).	Browser	weather_info.test	156	WeatherBlockTest->testDisplayLocation()	✓
Valid HTML found on "http://127.0.0.1:20974/admin/structure/block"	Browser	weather_info.test	156	WeatherBlockTest->testDisplayLocation()	✓
Verbose message	Debug	weather_info.test	156	WeatherBlockTest->testDisplayLocation()	⚠
GET http://127.0.0.1:20974/admin/structure/block returned 200 (56.79 KB).	Browser	weather_info.test	156	WeatherBlockTest->testDisplayLocation()	✓
Valid HTML found on "http://127.0.0.1:20974/admin/structure/block"	Browser	weather_info.test	156	WeatherBlockTest->testDisplayLocation()	✓
Verbose message	Debug	weather_info.test	156	WeatherBlockTest->testDisplayLocation()	⚠
Check that configuration is saved	Other	weather_info.test	157	WeatherBlockTest->testDisplayLocation()	✓

Figure 8–26. Report showing the successful block setting

The first "Verbose message" link shows the block configuration screen, and the second shows the after-post screen with the green success banner.

Getting a Page

So far, we've been successful in creating an environment where we can perform our task. Our next test will be to load a page and then check to see if it contains information we are interested in. We will do this with the drupalGet() method. The task will be to check whether the system-wide variables are read, since this is what the weather block uses to display weather to an anonymous user or a user who has not yet set location, language, and unit preferences in her profile.

This test is straightforward and can be specified immediately after we have logged in our test user. The code is shown in Listing 8–13.

Listing 8–13. Calling a Page and Checking the Results

```
function testDisplayLocation() {
  variable_set('default_units', 'R');
  variable_set('default_language', 'de');
  variable_set('default_location', 'san francisco');

  $this->drupalGet('node');
  $this->assertRaw(t('San Francisco, CA'), t('Check that the block displayed'));
}
```

Notice that this function doesn't have any environment setup calls. The testing framework will automatically call the setUp() function before each of the test functions in our test suite.

The drupalGet and drupalPost methods are similar to the HTTP GET and POST methods. That is, while drupalPost() requires an array of form data that is sent to the server, the drupalGet() method just needs an address. Both will cause the Drupal engine to build a page, which we can interrogate using the same assertion methods that we used for drupalPost().

The test results for this function are shown in Figure 8–27.

GET http://127.0.0.1:20974/node returned 200 (7.6 KB).	Browser	weather_info.test	121	WeatherBlockTest->testDisplayLocation()	✓
Valid HTML found on "http://127.0.0.1:20974/node"	Browser	weather_info.test	121	WeatherBlockTest->testDisplayLocation()	✓
Verbose message	Debug	weather_info.test	121	WeatherBlockTest->testDisplayLocation()	⚠
Check that the block displayed	Other	weather_info.test	122	WeatherBlockTest->testDisplayLocation()	✓

Figure 8–27. Test results for a drupalGet method call

■ **Note** The screen in Figure 8–27 shows a report of only the part defined in the testDisplayLocation() function. When you run this test, you will see the entries for creating a new user, logging-in the user, and setting the block. In other words, the steps that are declared in the setUp() function are repeated.

Changing the User Profile

Now let's exercise the weather information block by asking it to get the weather report for a location that's specific for this particular user. The Weather information block provides this functionality by setting each user's location in the user profile we created in Chapter 6.

This task will require another form post, so the process will be similar to what we did when setting the block to a particular region. That is, we do the work manually on the deployed version of our environment, and learn what we need to teach the testing engine in order to perform the task automatically.

As with the previous case, we will need the same four pieces of information. By viewing the source of the page with the weather information block, we can see the code displayed in Figure 8–28.

```
      src='http://www.google.com/ig/images/weather/cloudy.gif'/><br/>55&deg;F/35&deg;F<br/></div><form
      action="/" method="post" id="weather-location-form" accept-charset="UTF-8"><div><div class="form-
      item form-type-textfield form-item-weather-location">
134   <input type="text" id="edit-weather-location" name="weather_location" value="" size="18"
      maxlength="18" class="form-text" />
135   </div>
136   <input type="submit" id="edit-weather-location-submit" name="op" value="Search" class="form-
      submit" /><input type="hidden" name="form_build_id" value="form-
      WplH1ysXTjZjnMVamJWkFVqrmpmncWDsLO3NbsrlW9s" />
137   <input type="hidden" name="form_token" value="GXZ6vdlFNqmcAhXoKQ9n53vkSo3Byedc9lh9c2GdJc4" />
138   <input type="hidden" name="form_id" value="weather_location_form" />
139   </div></form>   </div>
```

Figure 8–28. HTML code produced by the weather information form

From this, we can get the three pieces of information we need to do a drupalPost—the location to be posted to (`<form ... action="/"...>`), the name of the form field where we'll enter the location (`<input ... name="weather_location"...>`), and the value of the submit button (`<input type="submit" ... value="Search"...>`). When we manually enter the information into our live site, we see that we get our fourth piece of required information—the location that has been retrieved from the weather service. The code to perform these tasks is shown in Listing 8–14.

Listing 8–14. Posting to a Form on a Block and Verifying the Results

```
function testUserLocationChange() {
  $edit = array (
    'weather_location' => 'manhattan',
    );
  $this->drupalPost('/', $edit, 'Search');
  $this->assertRaw(t('New York, NY'), t('Check that the location was found'));
}
```

Notice that the location we entered is "manhattan", but that we will be looking for "New York, NY". This is a sure test that the weather service has been called and translated the informal name to the formal one.

Now, save this and rerun the tests. Don't forget to clean the test environment because we changed code.

The outcome will show a failure. You're probably wondering why it failed, and why I subjected you to this display. There's a good reason. Two, actually. First, it took me a while to figure out what was happening, so I wanted to share my pain with you. Second, lessons learned through pain tend to stick.

Figure 8–29 shows the error.

| Verbose message | Debug | weather_info.test | 171 | WeatherBlockTest->testUserLocationChange() | ⚠ |
| Check that the location was found | Other | weather_info.test | 172 | WeatherBlockTest->testUserLocationChange() | ⊗ |

Figure 8–29. Error in setting the user location.

You'll see a clue if you expand the "Verbose message" link or look at the page shown in Figure 8–30.

Figure 8–30. Posted screen that is missing the weather information

Here we see the weather information block with the search button, but there is no weather for New York. To understand why this doesn't work, you need to recall the basics of the DrupalWebTestCase framework. Remember that we start with a completely blank slate. No users, no enabled modules (except the core defaults), and no blocks. In the setUp() method, we enabled the modules and created the user, and then established the block in the appropriate region.

But we didn't attach fields to the user entity and set the values. The Fields module is enabled by default, but we must also do all the work to establish and attach the three fields we created in Chapter 6, and then add values to those fields for our temporary user.

This requires making some calls to the Fields API. The calls are field_create_field() and field_create_instance(). Listing 8–15 shows the code for creating the three fields.

Listing 8–15. Attaching Fields to the User Entity

```
// *
// * Weather location field
// *
$field = array(
  'field_name' => 'field_weather_location',
  'type' => 'text',
  'translatable' => TRUE,
  );
$instance = array(
  'field_name' => 'field_weather_location',
  'entity_type' => 'user',
  'bundle' => 'user',
  'label' => 'Weather location',
```

```
      'widget' => array(
          'type' => 'text_textfield',
          'weight' => '15',
        ),
        'description' => st('Enter a location on earth for which you would like '
          . 'to see weather information presented.'),
      );
field_create_field($field);
field_create_instance($instance);

// *
// * Weather language field
// *
$field = array(
    'field_name' => 'field_weather_language',
    'type' => 'list_text',
    'translatable' => TRUE,
    'settings' => array(
        'allowed_values' => "en|English\nes|Spanish\nde|German\ntr|Turkish\nfr|French\n",
        'allowed_values_function' => '',
      ),
    );
$instance = array(
    'field_name' => 'field_weather_language',
    'entity_type' => 'user',
    'bundle' => 'user',
    'label' => 'Weather language',
    'widget' => array(
        'type' => 'options_select',
        'weight' => '16',
      ),
      'description' => st('Enter the language in which you would like to see '
        . 'weather information presented.'),
      'default_value' => array(
        array(
          'value' => 'en',
        ),
      ),
    );
field_create_field($field);
field_create_instance($instance);

// *
// * Weather units field
// *
$field = array(
    'field_name' => 'field_weather_unit',
    'type' => 'list_text',
    'translatable' => TRUE,
    'settings' => array(
        'allowed_values' => "F|Fahrenheit\nC|Celsius\nK|Kelvin\nR|Rankine",
        'allowed_values_function' => '',
      ),
    );
$instance = array(
    'field_name' => 'field_weather_unit',
    'entity_type' => 'user',
    'bundle' => 'user',
    'label' => 'Weather units',
    'widget' => array(
        'type' => 'options_select',
```

```
            'weight' => '17',
          ),
        'description' => st('Enter the measurement unit with which you would like '
          . 'to see weather information presented.'),
        'default_value' => array(
          array(
            'value' => 'F',
          ),
        ),
      );

// Create the field and instance.
field_create_field($field);
field_create_instance($instance);
```

Once we create the three fields, we need to set some values for the fields in the user profile and see if they take. This is shown in Listing 8–16.

Listing 8–16. Adding Values to the Profile Fields

```
$uid = $this->test_user->uid;

$edit = array (
  'field_weather_location[und][0][value]' => 'san francisco',
  'field_weather_language[und]' => 'en',
  'field_weather_unit[und]' => 'F',
);

$this->drupalPost("user/{$uid}/edit/", $edit, 'Save');
$this->assertRaw(t('The changes have been saved.'),
  t('Check that profile was updated'));
```

First, we get the identifier of the current user. This is the temporary user the test framework created for us. We'll need that in order to craft the URL later. Next, we create the array of fields that we'll be populating. A call to drupalPost() will create the page, passing the field data and pressing the submit button. And then we check for the happy text that the profile was updated. The result is shown in Figure 8–31.

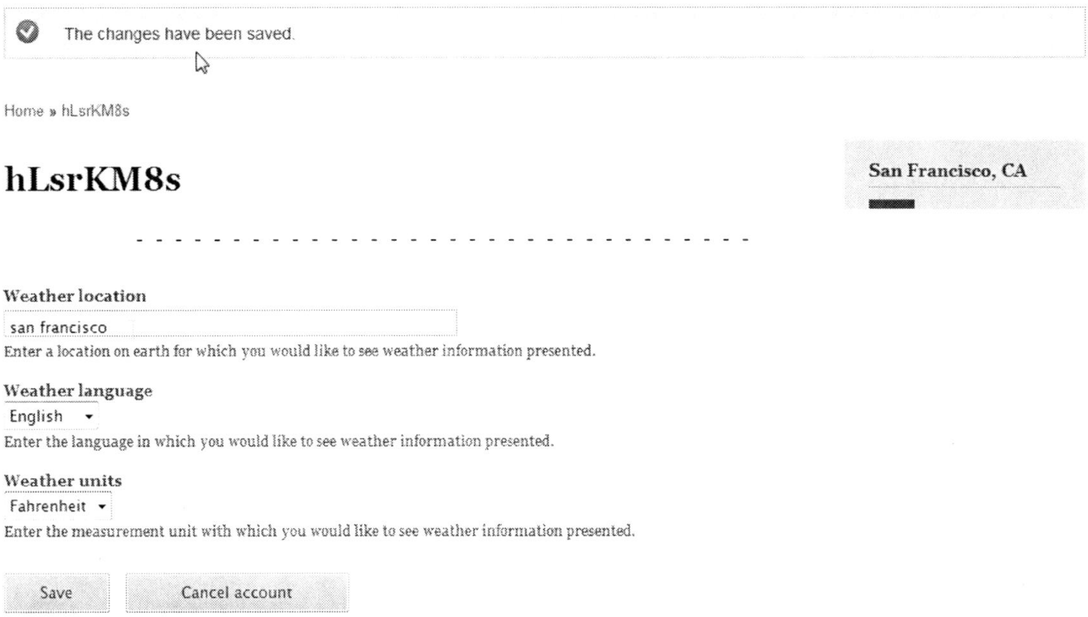

> ✅ The changes have been saved.

Home » hLsrKM8s

hLsrKM8s

San Francisco, CA

- -

Weather location

    san francisco

Enter a location on earth for which you would like to see weather information presented.

Weather language

    English ▾

Enter the language in which you would like to see weather information presented.

Weather units

    Fahrenheit ▾

Enter the measurement unit with which you would like to see weather information presented.

[Save]   [Cancel account]

Figure 8–31. Proof that our test worked

The next step is to see that the block on a normal page is reading the attached fields from the user profile. That's done with the code in Listing 8–17.

Listing 8–17. Testing That the Block Read from the User's Profile

```
$this->drupalGet('node');
$this->assertRaw(t('San Francisco, CA'),
  t('Check that the user location displayed'));
```

The drupalGet() function is called, passing 'node', which displays the front page. If the profile is read properly, the block will show with the proper city and our test will pass. The page, as recorded by the testing framework, shows that it worked. (See Figure 8–32.)

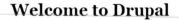

Home

Welcome to Drupal

No front page content has been created yet.

San Francisco, CA

Cloudy, 54°F
Wind: S at 6 mph
Humidity: 96%
Sun

Figure 8–32. *Test passed showing the appropriate weather*

That wraps up the tests on the user side. The key to a successful web test harness is to set up the environment with everything you need to do the test. If you keep this simple rule in mind, your testing will go much better.

Testing Administration Values

There's one more area that needs testing, and that's the code that sets up default values from the administrator's page. As you'll recall, the system administrator can set weather information values globally, which are used by anonymous users and registered users who have not yet created their own custom location. These default fields are entered in the form shown in Figure 8–33.

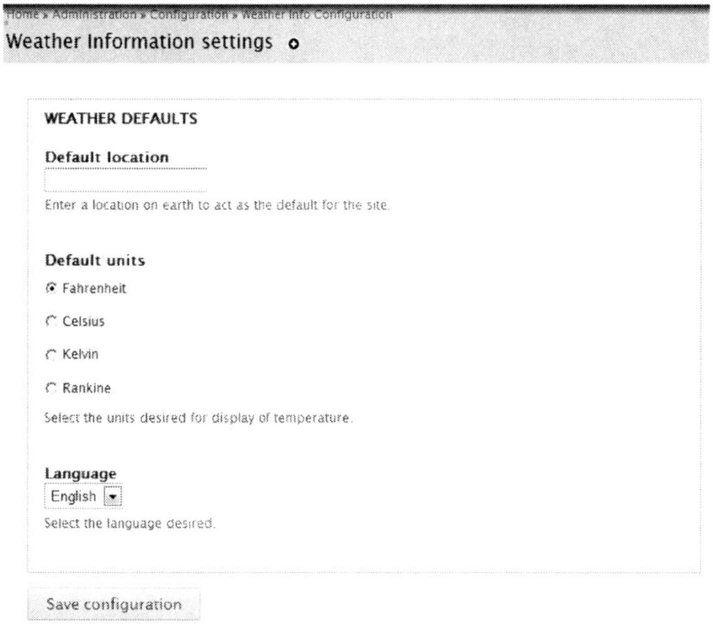

Home » Administration » Configuration » Weather Info Configuration

Weather Information settings o

WEATHER DEFAULTS

Default location

Enter a location on earth to act as the default for the site.

Default units

⦿ Fahrenheit

○ Celsius

○ Kelvin

○ Rankine

Select the units desired for display of temperature.

Language

English ▾

Select the language desired.

Save configuration

Figure 8–33. *Administration screen for setting weather information defaults*

We need to create a test case that exercises this screen so we can be confident that any changes to our code don't break this functionality.

To create the test, we will instantiate the DrupalWebTestCase class. This test doesn't use profiles so the setUp() method is a bit more streamlined, as shown in Listing 8–18.

Listing 8–18. *The Setup Function for Testing Weather Information Settings*

```
class WeatherSettingsTest extends DrupalWebTestCase {

  public static function getInfo() {
    return array(
      'name' => 'Weather default tests',
      'description' => 'Tests default settings and weather display.',
      'group' => 'Weather info',
      );
  }

  public function setUp() {
    // Enable any modules required for the test
    parent::setUp(array('weather_info'));
    // Create and log in our privileged user.
    $this->privileged_user = $this->drupalCreateUser(array(
      'view weather info',
      'administer weather info',
      'administer site configuration',
      'access administration pages',
      ));
    $this->drupalLogin($this->privileged_user);
  }
```

The settings screen takes the values entered in the form variables and writes them as persistent Drupal variables. The first test is to set the defaults on the screen and then check to see if they made it successfully into Drupal variables. The code for this is in Listing 8–19.

Listing 8–19. *Setting Default Values and Checking for Their Persistence*

```
function testWeatherDefaults () {
  $default_location = 'Boise';
  $default_units = 'F';
  $default_language = 'en';

  $edit['default_location'] = $default_location;
  $edit['default_units'] = $default_units;
  $edit['default_language'] = $default_language;

  $this->drupalPost('admin/config/weather_info/settings', $edit, t('Save configuration'));
  $this->assertRaw(t('The configuration options have been saved.'),
    t('Check that configuration is saved'));

  $this->assertEqual(variable_get('default_location'), $default_location,
    t('Default location variable'));
  $this->assertEqual(variable_get('current_location'), $default_location,
    t('Current location variable'));
  $this->assertEqual(variable_get('default_units'), $default_units,
    t('Default unit variable'));
  $this->assertEqual(variable_get('default_language'), $default_language,
    t('Default language variable'));
}
```

Three function variables are set with test values and the form fields are created as an array called $edit. Next, the drupalPost() method is called, posting the values back to the form using the submit button labeled "Save configuration". Finally, some assertions are done to check the four Drupal variables that the form sets. Figure 8–34 shows that it worked.

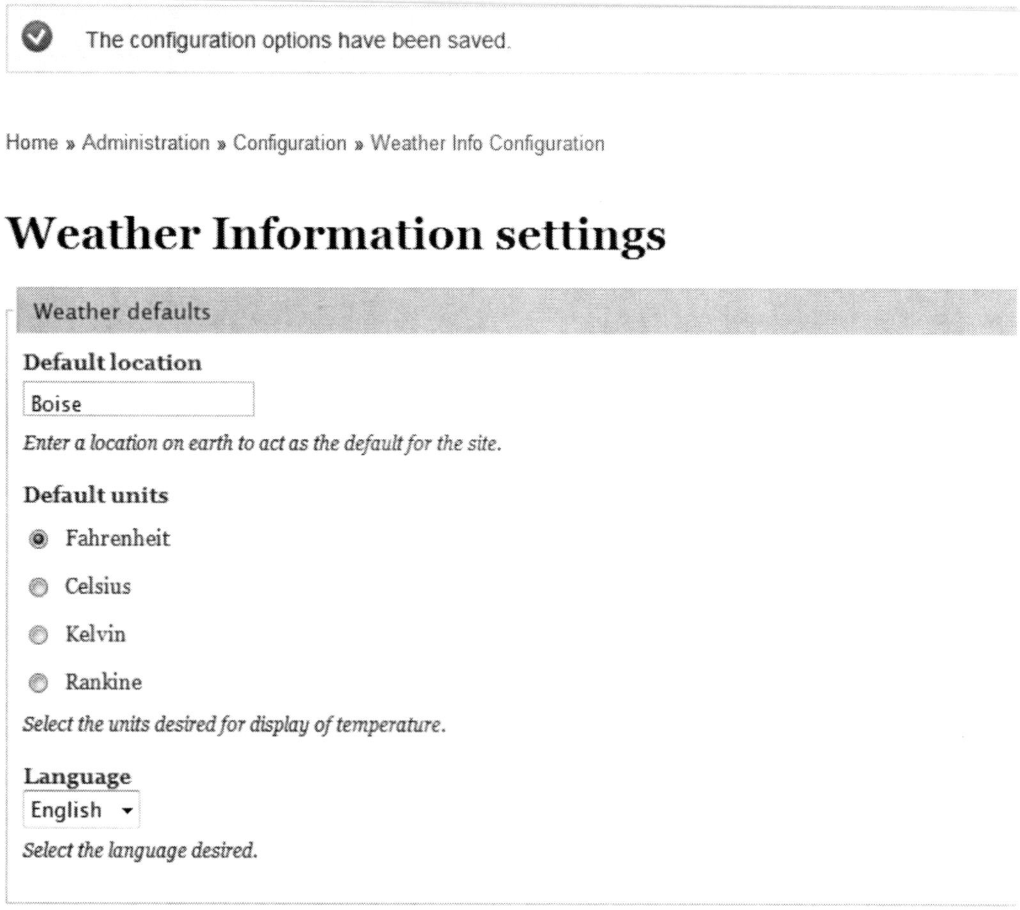

✓ The configuration options have been saved.

Home » Administration » Configuration » Weather Info Configuration

Weather Information settings

| Weather defaults |

Default location

Boise

Enter a location on earth to act as the default for the site.

Default units

◉ Fahrenheit

◯ Celsius

◯ Kelvin

◯ Rankine

Select the units desired for display of temperature.

Language

English ▾

Select the language desired.

Figure 8–34. Test of default settings passed

Here we can see the happy text and the new defaults.

Negative Tests

Our last test intentionally creates an error condition and then interrogates the page to see if the error was reported correctly. In this case, we will test the boundaries of the #maxlength attribute of the location field on the weather information settings page. In Chapter 6, we indicated that the maximum length of the data allowed in the field is 20 characters. The code in Listing 8–20 tests that limit.

Listing 8–20. *Testing the Length of a Field*

```
function testMaxlengthFail () {
  // this should fail because the location is longer than 20 characters
  $default_location = 'San Francisco, California';
  $default_units = 'C';
  $default_language = 'es';

  $edit['default_location'] = $default_location;
  $edit['default_units'] = $default_units;
  $edit['default_language'] = $default_language;

  $this->drupalPost('admin/config/weather_info/settings', $edit,
    t('Save configuration'));
  $this->assertRaw(t('Default location cannot be longer than 20 characters'),
    t('Check length error'));
}
```

Putting this into our `DrupalWebTestCase` class produces the report shown in Figure 8–35.

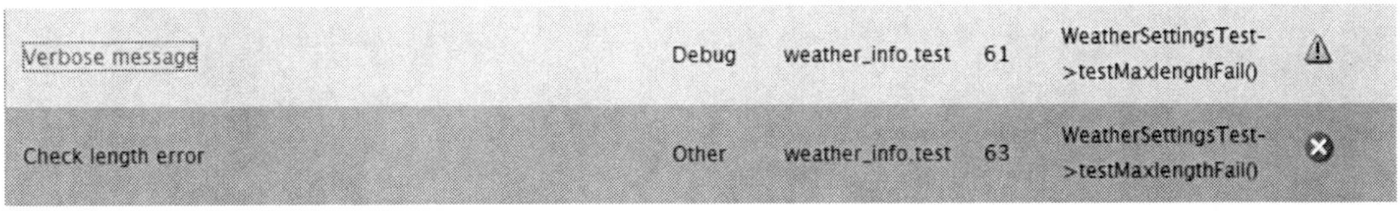

Verbose message		Debug	weather_info.test	61	WeatherSettingsTest->testMaxlengthFail() ⚠
Check length error		Other	weather_info.test	63	WeatherSettingsTest->testMaxlengthFail() ✖

Figure 8–35. *Fail test failed*

Something is wrong here. By checking on the saved screen behind the "Verbose message" link, we can get an idea of what went wrong, as Figure 8–36 shows.

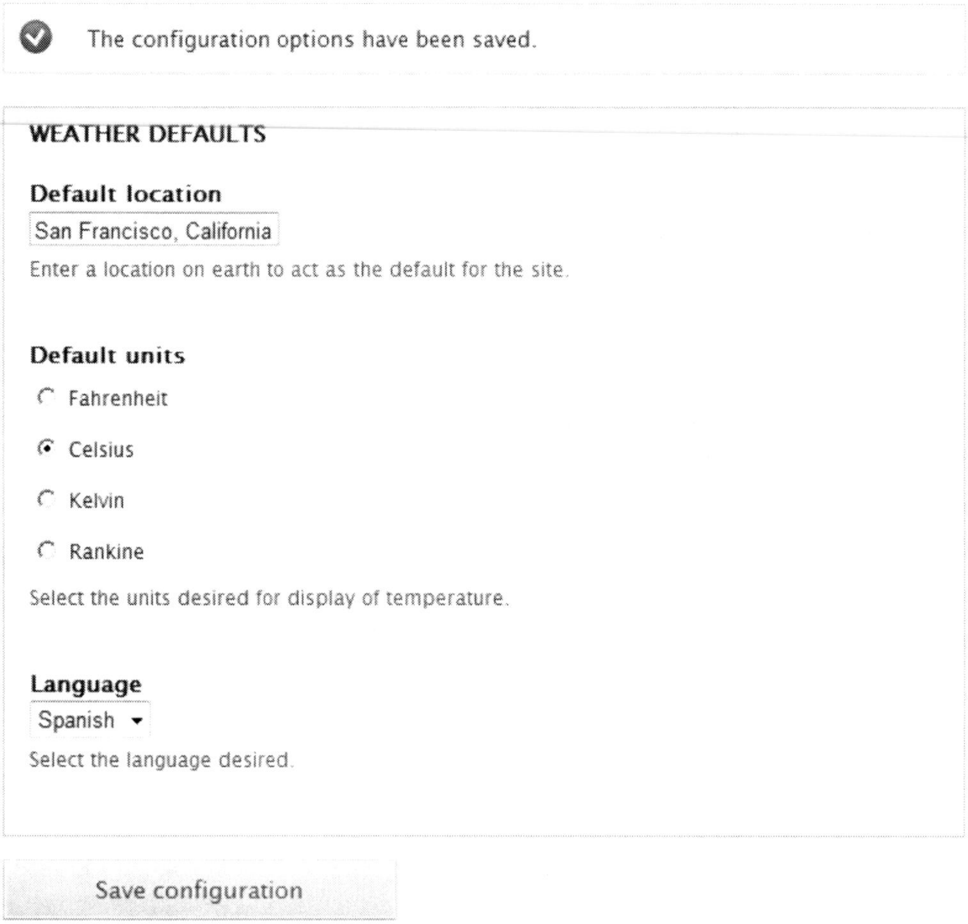

> The configuration options have been saved.

WEATHER DEFAULTS

Default location

San Francisco, California

Enter a location on earth to act as the default for the site.

Default units

○ Fahrenheit

◉ Celsius

○ Kelvin

○ Rankine

Select the units desired for display of temperature.

Language

Spanish ▾

Select the language desired.

Save configuration

Figure 8–36. Evidence of a problem

Notice that the text that should indicate a failure is showing success. I'll save you the debugging chautauqua, but I hinted at the culprit in Chapter 6 when we created this settings page. The offending code is shown in Listing 8–21.

Listing 8–21. Code with a Typographical Error

```
$form['wx_settings']['default_location'] = array (
  '#type' => 'textfield',
  '#title' => t('Default location'),
  '#default_value' => variable_get('default_location', null),
  '#size' => 20,
  '#maxlengh' => 20,
  '#description' => t('Enter a location on earth to act as the default for the site.'),
  );
```

Notice that the attribute, #maxlength is misspelled. This is not recognized as an error by Drupal, which just ignores everything it doesn't recognize. But by not recognizing the attribute, the system default for #maxlength, 128, is used instead. So our 25-character test field was within the boundaries and did not raise an error. Correcting the spelling and rerunning the test gives us the results we sought. See Figures 8–37 and 8–38.

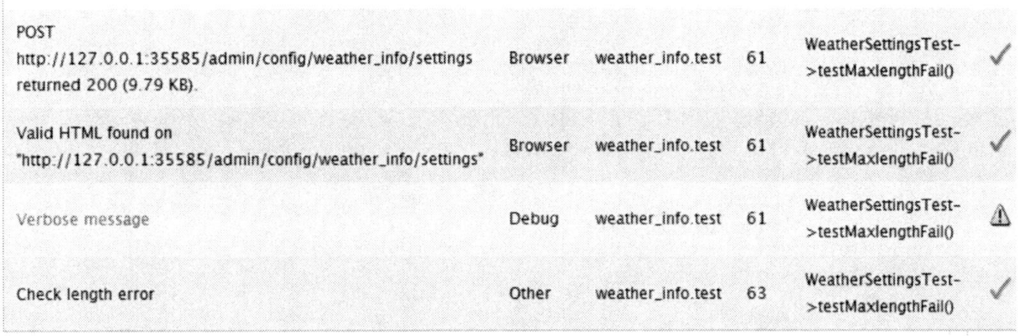

POST http://127.0.0.1:35585/admin/config/weather_info/settings returned 200 (9.79 KB).	Browser	weather_info.test	61	WeatherSettingsTest- >testMaxlengthFail()	✓
Valid HTML found on "http://127.0.0.1:35585/admin/config/weather_info/settings"	Browser	weather_info.test	61	WeatherSettingsTest- >testMaxlengthFail()	✓
Verbose message	Debug	weather_info.test	61	WeatherSettingsTest- >testMaxlengthFail()	⚠
Check length error	Other	weather_info.test	63	WeatherSettingsTest- >testMaxlengthFail()	✓

Figure 8–37. *Test report showing successful failure*

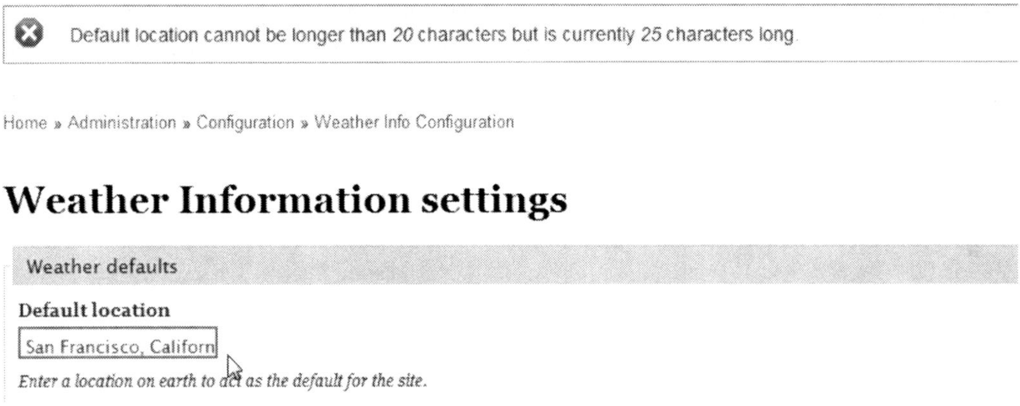

❌   Default location cannot be longer than *20* characters but is currently *25* characters long.

Home » Administration » Configuration » Weather Info Configuration

Weather Information settings

Weather defaults

Default location

San Francisco, Californ

Enter a location on earth to act as the default for the site.

Figure 8–38. *Successful failure*

Code Coverage

Creating tests to drive your code development is important, but it is also important to know that all parts of your code are exercised by the test harness. The term for this is "code coverage." That is, how much of your code has been tested.

Testing code coverage is a tricky business. It requires some sort of agent to keep track of source code as the tests are being run and reporting the results after the test execution finishes.

There are tools that work on PHP to do code coverage, but unfortunately, there is no comprehensive package that plugs into Drupal specifically. The code_coverage module exists, but needs some work as of this writing.

I expect there will be more work done on code coverage, since it is such a vital piece to the entire testing process. For now, just make sure your tests cover your code and that your code works as designed.

Summary

Testing is a critical part of modern software engineering. Before version 7 of the Drupal framework, testing was not taken very seriously. In fact, the testing module required a hack to the core in order to work. With Drupal 7, the developers have really placed testing where it should be: front and center for all development. In fact, no core module will be released without a comprehensive test harness and no code will be accepted without passing all automated test functions.

In this chapter, we continued development of the weather information module by creating tests for it. We even found an honest spelling error in our code that probably would not have been caught if it were not for the development of a test harness for the module.

In the next chapter, I'll delve into the important topic of database access and how to ship installers and updaters as part of your code's deployment.

Databases and Deployment

CHAPTER 9

▪ ▪ ▪

The Database Layer

At its core, Drupal is a tool for creating, maintaining, and displaying information stored in a database. Drupal database management is a crucial part of the entire system, as all aspects of a site are stored in the database.

It's pretty important, then, that the parts of Drupal that touch the database be pretty solid and efficient.

Prior to version 7 of Drupal, the system was pretty much locked into a single database product—MySQL. There were some successful implementations of Postgres/SQL, but virtually all development was done against MySQL and the vast majority of current implementations use MySQL.

In many ways, using Drupal with PHP is similar to the way we created our classic ASP programs. Either we'd write our own data abstraction layer or, more likely, we'd just create direct SQL statements to the database. I remember my first ASP database application—where the underlying database was Microsoft Access. I connected using the ASP `ADODB.Connection` object. If you started that far back, perhaps you'll recognize the code in Listing 9–1.

Listing 9–1. Classic ASP Code Using the ADODB Object

```
<%@ LANGUAGE = "VBScript" %>
<XMLNEWS>
<%
set objConnection = Server.CreateObject("ADODB.Connection")
DBFile = Server.MapPath("data\Newsfeed.mdb")
objConnection.Open("driver={Microsoft Access Driver (*.mdb)}; DBQ=" & DBFile)
set RS = objConnection.Execute("SELECT * FROM News " &
    "WHERE Date > #" & DaysAgo(5) & "# " &
    "ORDER BY Date DESC, Location, Headline")
do until RS.EOF
    %>
    <ITEM DATE="<%=RS("Date")%>" LOCATION="<%=RS("Location")%>">
        <URL><%=RS("Url")%></URL>
        <HEADLINE><%=RS("Headline")%></HEADLINE>
        <ABSTRACT><%=RS("Abstract")%></ABSTRACT>
    </ITEM>
    <%
    RS.MoveNext
Loop
objConnection.Close
%>
</XMLNEWS>
```

This code created an XML document with news information, sort of a precursor to RSS. Notice that the database connection is expressed as a connection to a physical file, and that the SQL select statement is concatenated into a string that is passed to the connection via the execute method.

There are substantial security risks using this approach, the most common of which is SQL injection. SQL injection is the attempt to exploit common shortcuts that programmers take with their code for malicious purposes. The problem is illustrated in Figure 9–1.

Figure 9–1. Sometimes, SQL injection can be used for good (Source gizmodo.com)

Someone looking for exploits would assume that a programmer did not escape any table names, and possibly did not sanitize the input.

In case you're not familiar with how this works, I'll explain. In this license plate example, the end of the banner, the area under the driver's-side headlight, is, I assume, partially obscured. I expect it says TABLE LICENCE; -- (probably using the British spelling).

Someone looking to exploit this vulnerability could make an educated guess that the query is something like:

```
SELECT registration-status FROM licence WHERE plate-num = '%s';
```

The string variable, %s, would be inserted from the OCR performed by the traffic scanner. So the result would be disastrous for the police:

```
SELECT registration-status FROM licence WHERE plate-num = 'ZU 066', 0, 0); DROP DATABASE TABLE
LICENCE; --'
```

This is a sort of humorous example, and the owner definitely gets extra nerd points for this one. But the point is that SQL injection attacks are very common, and are easy to prevent if you just do a little sanitizing.

■ **Tip** Better yet, don't use direct SQL calls at all! I'll discuss this later in the chapter.

The ASP code shown above is pretty primitive by today's standards, but Drupal code before version 7 wasn't much more advanced. Fortunately, things have changed.

Data Abstraction

One of the key goals of Drupal 7 was to abstract the database layer so other database engines could be used without major rewrites of core and contributed modules.

If you are a .NET programmer, you're probably familiar with ADO.NET, a facility that provides an abstraction between your application and your data. It works by establishing an object that represents the data, along with whatever metadata is required to understand the data itself. Getting data out of your database becomes a simple task of establishing a connection to the database, including a connection string, and then executing a set of methods against a DataTable object, which is an abstraction of the underlying database tables or views.

In the Drupal world, the corollary to ADO.NET is PDO, which stands for PHP Data Objects. PDO is a data access object that separates the physical database from the application that uses it. The PDO object provides methods for managing transactions, reporting error conditions, and an interface for preparing and executing statements.

It is important to note, however, that PDO is not a database abstraction layer. PDO does not rewrite any SQL statements or provide emulation for features that might be missing in a particular database implementation. For that, you need to write an abstraction layer that sits on top of PDO. And that's exactly what has been done for Drupal 7.

■ **Note** Versions of Drupal prior to version 7 had a set of functions that were referred to as a data abstraction layer. This was mostly a set of routines to clean up and rewrite SQL statements to normalize for certain installation variables and provide some level of protection against SQL injection. However, this abstraction layer did not provide an easy path to alternative database engines.

The Database API

When you did the initial configuration of your site, the setup program modified Drupal's initialization file, settings.php. One of the things you did was provide the name of your database and the logon credentials. This is the first step in accessing the database from your Drupal installation.

The database connection information is contained in the $databases array, which is loaded from settings.php when the bootstrapper starts your page. The array is represented in Listing 9–2.

Listing 9–2. The $databases Array in settings.php

```
$databases = array (
  'default' => array (
    'default' => array (
```

```
        'driver' => 'mysql',
        'database' => 'drupal7',
        'username' => 'brian',
        'password' => 'super-secret-password',
        'host' => 'localhost',
        'port' => '',
        'prefix' => '',
    ),
  ),
);
```

This is the default structure for the LAMP stack, which includes the MySQL database engine. As you can probably guess, it's possible to define more database instances in the settings file. For example, you might want to set up a master/slave configuration in order to provide some level of high availability or scaling. In this case, your $databases array might look like the code in Listing 9–3.

Listing 9–3. Defining a Master/Slave Configuration

```
$databases['default']['default'] = array(
  'driver' => 'mysql',
  'database' => 'drupal7master',
  'username' => 'username',
  'password' => 'super-secret-master',
  'host' => 'dbserver1',
);
$databases['default']['slave'][] = array(
  'driver' => 'mysql',
  'database' => 'drupal7firstslave',
  'username' => 'firstslave',
  'password' => 'super-secret-slave-one',
  'host' => 'dbserver2',
);
$databases['default']['slave'][] = array(
  'driver' => 'mysql',
  'database' => 'drupal7secondslave',
  'username' => 'secondslave',
  'password' => 'super-secret-slave-two',
  'host' => 'dbserver3',
);
```

Both of these cases use the mysql driver. In Appendix A, I'll show you how to use Microsoft SQL Server as a database engine instead of MySQL.

In the next section, I'll describe the Drupal 7 database layer from the programmer's perspective.

Programming Against the Database API

In this section, I will cover the db_query() function, and then show an alternate technique for accessing data in a database-agnostic way. This assumes your database is configured and connected, and that the Drupal databases have been created using the installation scripts. You should have a nice clean environment ready to develop modules against.

There are two basic ways to select data from the database: static and dynamic.

Static Queries

A static query is a holdover from the days before Drupal 7's database abstraction layer. I recommend you avoid using static queries for reasons I'll mention later, but since there are plenty of static queries in the Drupal 7 core and contributed modules, let's take a look at them here.

The quickest way to get data out of a table is to use the db_query() function and pass a SQL string directly to it, then process the results that come back. This is shown in Listing 9–4.

Listing 9–4. The db_query() Function

```
$result = db_query("SELECT nid AS my_nid, title FROM {node}");
foreach ($result as $record) {
  $nid = $record->my_nid;
  $title = $record->title;
}
```

The result is an object that contains information about the query, including the records that were retrieved from the database.

■ **Note** Drupal has already connected to the database, so the db_query() function has all of the information it needs to get the data you desire. All that's required is a SQL query and you can then process the records.

To get the most out of the db_query() function, you should be aware of some its features. Some of these are optional, but others are required if your code is to have maximum security and extensibility.

Prefixing

In the db_query() function, all table names must be wrapped in curly braces. This is required so that Drupal can add a prefix string to the table name if it needs to. It's possible to share a single database instance with several Drupal installations. In such cases, you can establish a prefix that will be placed on each database table to distinguish which instance uses which set of tables. In your SELECT statement, then, you just need to put the generic name of the table, and if you add curly braces, the db_query() function will apply the appropriate table prefix for your site.

Placeholders

Placeholders are abstractions you can place in your query string to indicate the value of variables that will be replaced when the query string is parsed by the db_query() function. This abstraction allows the database to differentiate between raw SQL syntax and values provided by the user, thereby avoiding SQL injection.

Placeholders are set apart from the query by prefixing a string with a colon. The value of all placeholders must then be defined by creating a keyed array with their values, as shown in Listing 9–5.

Listing 9–5. Placeholders in Action

```
global $user;
$uid = $user->uid;
$result = db_query (
```

```
'SELECT n.nid, n.title, n.created '
. 'FROM {node} n '
. 'WHERE n.uid = :uid AND n.created > :created'
, array(
    ':uid' => $uid,
    ':created' => REQUEST_TIME - 3600,
    )
);

foreach ($result as $record) {
    $nid = $record->nid;
    $title = $record->title;
    $created = $record->created;
}
```

This returns all nodes that have been created in the past hour (3,600 seconds). The REQUEST_TIME variable is a handy shortcut for the time the page is being processed (i.e., now).

Here are some important safety tips when using placeholders:

- You can have virtually any number of placeholders in your query, but make sure they each have a unique name and are given a value in the array.

- The order of the placeholder strings declared in the query need not match the order in which they are defined in the array.

- Placeholders beginning with "db_" are reserved by Drupal for its internal use.

- Placeholders should not be escaped or quoted regardless of their type. Since they are passed to the database separately, the database server can deal with them intelligently.

- You can specify a placeholder that consists of a simple array that will be expanded into a comma-separated list. Listing 9–6 illustrates this feature.

Listing 9–6. *Using Arrays in a Placeholder*

```
$result = db_query (
  'SELECT title, created '
  . 'FROM {node} '
  . 'WHERE uid IN (:uids)'
  , array(
      ':uids' => array(1, 3, 5, 7, 11),
      )
    );

foreach ($result as $record) {
  $title = $record->title;
  $created = $record->created;
}
```

Fetching Result Sets

The most common technique for accessing the record set returned by the query is by using the foreach() loop as in the preceding examples. There are other ways to fetch the records, though, depending on your situation. And there are three different functions to explicitly fetch the next record, depending on how you want to deal with the data.

- $record = $result->fetch();loads a record object just as if you had used the foreach() loop technique.

- $record = $result->fetchObject(); loads the record into a stdClass object.

- $record = $result->fetchAssoc(); loads the record as an associative array.

- $record = $result->fetchField($column_index); loads just the field with the corresponding column number.

- $records = $result->fetchAll();loads all records into an array of stdClass objects.

- $record_count = $result->rowCount(); returns the number of rows in the record set.

Be sure to check that the return value from the fetch functions is not FALSE before proceeding, which indicates you've reached the end of the record set.

One technique you'll see as you explore the Drupal core code is a shortcut made possible by PHP's support for chaining method calls. Listing 9–7 shows an example of how to access just a single field by querying the database and chaining the methods.

Listing 9–7. Chaining Method Calls

```
// Get a keyed array of all nodes
$nodes = db_query("SELECT nid, title FROM {node}")->fetchAllKeyed();

// Extract just the title of a node
$title = db_query(
  'SELECT title FROM {node} '
  . 'WHERE nid = :nid',
  array(':nid' => $nid))->fetchField();
```

Now, why don't I like static queries? Because they send SQL statements from your module to the database. The designers of Drupal's database layer have done a pretty good job of sanitizing the database inputs using the escaped fields, so there's not much to worry about security-wise. But there is the issue of cross-database portability.

Consider a simple query to select the first ten records. For MySQL, the LIMIT keyword is used in the predicate:

```
SELECT title FROM table LIMIT 0, 10
```

For SQL Server, the TOP keyword is used:

```
SELECT TOP 10 title FROM table
```

If you are accustomed to working with MySQL, your query might look like the example in Listing 9–8.

Listing 9–8. Using the LIMIT Keyword

```
$nodes = db_query('SELECT title FROM {node} LIMIT 0, 10')->fetchObject();
```

But what would happen if this query was executed against an underlying SQL Server database? It would break.

For this reason, the database layer has a range query function that can be used to act as a layer between your code and the database engine. The syntax for using the query is shown in Listing 9–9.

Listing 9–9. Using the db_query_range Function

```
$result = db_query_range('SELECT title FROM {node}', 0, 10);
```

Drupal 7 encapsulates this functionality, along with much more, into a more abstract query syntax, dynamic queries, which I'll describe in the next section.

■ **Tip** To maximize the portability of your code, use dynamic queries instead of static queries.

Dynamic Queries

These queries are built dynamically by Drupal and can be optimized for the underlying database engine. They eliminate the problem of cross-database incompatibility and truly make your code database-agnostic. This is important if you are moving to a database other than MySQL.

It is so important that the use of static queries for anything except SELECT queries is deprecated. Use them and some members of the community will be frustrated when you code doesn't work as it should for them.

Dynamic Select Query

You can create dynamic queries for SELECT, INSERT, UPDATE, DELETE and MERGE queries. The API has been written to allow as much reuse as possible between the query types, so let's first take a look at the methods available for SELECT.

■ **Tip** There are a number of specialized functions for retrieving many common pieces of information from the database. For example, the user_load() function gets information about a particular user while the node_load() function gets everything you ever need to know about a particular piece of managed content. I suggest you use these built-in functions if they are available rather than building a db_select() function to do the same thing.

Now that I've said that, you'll see in my examples below that I do exactly what I just told you not to do. The reason is that the tables are available and filled with data on a freshly installed system so I can illustrate these database functions.

Before doing any query, check to be sure that there is not already a specialized function that provides what you need.

Simple Select Query

Creating a dynamic query for a SELECT requires providing the table name and some optional parameters as shown in Listing 9–10.

Listing 9–10. Dynamic Query for SELECT

```
$query = db_select('node', 'n');
$query
  ->condition('n.uid', 0, '<>')
  ->fields('n', array('nid', 'title', 'type', 'created'))
  ->range(0, 5);
$result = $query->execute();

foreach ($result as $record) {
  $title = $record->title;
  $type = $record->type;
  $created = $record->created;
  print($title . ' (' . $type . ') created: '
    . date("D, j M, Y \a\\t G:i", $created) . '<br>');
}
```

This gives us the output shown in Figure 9–2.

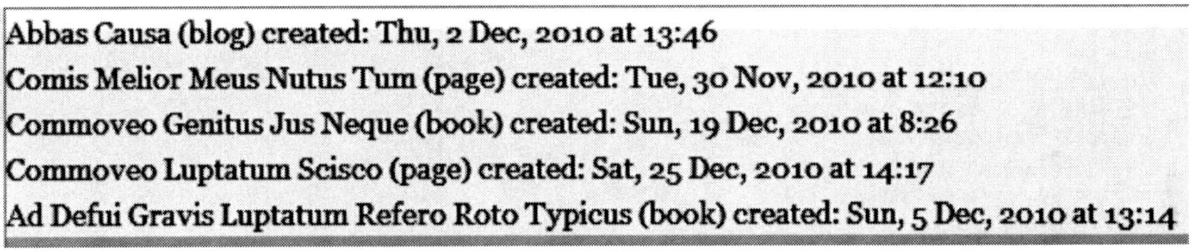

Abbas Causa (blog) created: Thu, 2 Dec, 2010 at 13:46

Comis Melior Meus Nutus Tum (page) created: Tue, 30 Nov, 2010 at 12:10

Commoveo Genitus Jus Neque (book) created: Sun, 19 Dec, 2010 at 8:26

Commoveo Luptatum Scisco (page) created: Sat, 25 Dec, 2010 at 14:17

Ad Defui Gravis Luptatum Refero Roto Typicus (book) created: Sun, 5 Dec, 2010 at 13:14

Figure 9–2. Simple SELECT using a dynamic query

The db_select() function is where we indicate the table we are using. There is no need to wrap the name in curly braces as in the preceding static query because the function already knows that's the table name. The second parameter is an alias for the table.

The condition property is pretty self-explanatory; I want nodes only where the user ID is not zero.

The fields property lists the fields I want returned, and starts with the alias declared in the db_select() function.

Finally, the range property limits the record set to the first five records.

This simple example will produce different SELECT statements depending on the database engine. For MySQL, the query will look like this:

```
SELECT n.nid, n.title, n.type, n.created FROM node n WHERE n.uid <> 0 LIMIT 0, 5;
```

For SQL Server, it will generate a different SELECT statement:

```
SELECT TOP 5 n.nid, n.title, n.type, n.created FROM node n WHERE n.uid <> 0;
```

So we've solved the problem of cross-database incompatibility and made our code easier to read, test, and debug at the same time.

Joins

When you join two or more tables, a number of properties can define how the join is to be done.

- The innerJoin() property does an inner join of two tables. The join() property is a convenience property that does the same thing.

- The leftJoin() property does a left outer join of two tables.

- The rightJoin() property does a right outer join of two tables.

Consider the task of getting information out of the node and user tables, which requires doing a join of two tables. Listing 9–11 shows how to do this with a static query.

Listing 9–11. Static Query with a Join

```
$result = db_query('SELECT u.name, u.mail n.title, n.type '
. 'FROM {node} n '
. 'INNER JOIN {users} u on u.uid = n.uid'
. 'WHERE u.uid=:uid'.
array(':uid' => $user->uid));
```

Listing 9–12 shows the same thing with a dynamic query.

Listing 9–12. Dynamic Query with a Join

```
$query = db_select('node', 'n');
$query
  ->condition('u.uid', $user->uid, '=')
  ->fields('u', array('name', 'mail'))
  ->fields('n', array('title', 'type'))
  ->join('users', 'u', 'u.uid = n.uid');
$result = $query->execute();
```

This gives us the output shown in Figure 9–3.

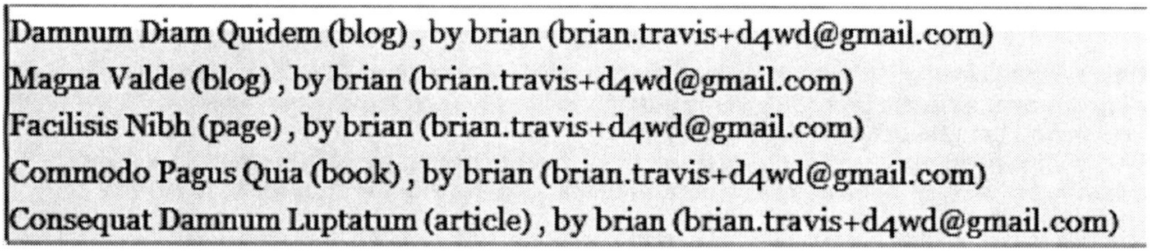

Damnum Diam Quidem (blog), by brian (brian.travis+d4wd@gmail.com)

Magna Valde (blog), by brian (brian.travis+d4wd@gmail.com)

Facilisis Nibh (page), by brian (brian.travis+d4wd@gmail.com)

Commodo Pagus Quia (book), by brian (brian.travis+d4wd@gmail.com)

Consequat Damnum Luptatum (article), by brian (brian.travis+d4wd@gmail.com)

Figure 9–3. Output from a dynamic query with join

There are other combinations and permutations of the joins that you can read about in the Drupal documentation, but this should be enough to get you started.

Fields

In the code in Listing 9–12, you'll notice the `fields()` property. This property is used to indicate the columns you want returned from your query. The alias is specified first, followed by an array of field names corresponding to the column names in your table.

■ **Note** Calling `fields()` without any field names will result in a `SELECT *` clause.

Notice that Listing 9–12 has two `fields()` methods. This is necessary because the query defines two different aliases. There is no room, however, to create field aliases using this syntax. If you want to have field aliases, you can use the `addField()` method for each field as shown in Listing 9–13.

Listing 9–13. Creating Field Aliases Using the `addField()` Method

```
global $user;
$query = db_select('node', 'n');
$query
  ->condition('u.uid', $user->uid, '=')
  ->join('users', 'u', 'u.uid = n.uid');
$query->addField('u', 'name', 'user_name');
$query->addField('u', 'mail', 'user_mail');
$query->addField('n', 'title', 'node_title');
$query->addField('n', 'type', 'node_type');

$result = $query->execute();

foreach ($result as $record) {
  $name = $record->user_name;
  $mail = $record->user_mail;
  $title = $record->node_title;
  $type = $record->node_type;
  print($title . ' (' . $type . ') , by ' . $name . ' (' . $mail . ')' . '<br>');
}
```

This results in the same output as the previous example, and builds a `SELECT` statement as shown in Listing 9–14.

Listing 9–14. SELECT Statement Created Using `addField()`

```
SELECT
  u.name AS user_name,
  u.mail AS user_mail,
  n.title AS node_title,
  n.type AS node_type
FROM
  {node} n
INNER JOIN
  {users} u ON u.uid = n.uid
WHERE
  (u.uid = :db_condition_placeholder_0)
```

▨ **Note** The query placeholder :db_condition_placeholder_0 in Listing 9–14 will be filled in by the execute() method.

Besides being able to assign aliases to fields, the addField() function is handy if you are building a query using some looping construct. Before this capability, you had to use the string concatenation method to build up a list of fields.

The Distinct Property

If you wish to limit your record set to a distinct set of values, you can use the distinct() property as shown in Listing 9–15.

Listing 9–15. Setting the distinct Flag

```
$query = db_select('node', 'n');
$query
  ->fields('n', array('title'));
  $query->distinct();
  $result = $query->execute();
```

Expressions

Expressions can be added to a query if you need to express something that is not otherwise available, as Listing 9–16 shows.

Listing 9–16. Using Expressions to Add Functionality to Your Query

```
$query = db_select('node', 'n');
$query
  ->condition('n.created', time() - (14 * 86400), '>')
  ->fields('n', array('title', 'created', 'type'));
$query->addExpression('created - :offset', 'offset_by_an_hour', array(':offset' => 3600));
$result = $query->execute();

foreach ($result as $record) {
  $name = $record->title;
  $type = $record->type;
  $created = $record->created;
  $offset = $record->offset_by_an_hour;
  print($name . ' (' . $type . ')'
    . ' created: ' . date("D, j M, Y \a\\t G:i", $created)
    . ' hour before: ' . date("D, j M, Y \a\\t G:i", $offset)
    . '<br>');
}
```

This inserts a computed field that is the value of the created timestamp minus one hour, and returns all nodes created in the past fortnight (14 * 86400). (See Figure 9–4.)

Abico Feugiat Iriure Te (blog) created: Mon, 20 Dec, 2010 at 11:39 hour before: Mon, 20 Dec, 2010 at 10:39
Camur Eros Patria Sino (book) created: Tue, 21 Dec, 2010 at 9:36 hour before: Tue, 21 Dec, 2010 at 8:36
Imputo Inhibeo Zelus (page) created: Wed, 22 Dec, 2010 at 4:26 hour before: Wed, 22 Dec, 2010 at 3:26
Ideo Proprius Vicis Ymo (book) created: Wed, 22 Dec, 2010 at 22:32 hour before: Wed, 22 Dec, 2010 at 21:32
Abdo Antehabeo Appellatio Vulpes (book) created: Sun, 26 Dec, 2010 at 5:00 hour before: Sun, 26 Dec, 2010 at 4:00
Aptent Eu Sagaciter Vulputate (book) created: Tue, 28 Dec, 2010 at 0:36 hour before: Mon, 27 Dec, 2010 at 23:36
Luctus Neque Te (page) created: Fri, 31 Dec, 2010 at 5:23 hour before: Fri, 31 Dec, 2010 at 4:23
Ideo Quae (page) created: Fri, 31 Dec, 2010 at 23:46 hour before: Fri, 31 Dec, 2010 at 22:46

Figure 9–4. Output from the query that used an expression

■ **Caution** Since you can insert expressions that are SQL functions, it's possible to use a function that is available on one database engine but not on another. Using this feature may therefore cause your application to be platform-dependent.

The other side of this story is that you will also be depending on other programmers who create or modify core or contributed modules. If someone does something that makes her module platform-dependent, and doesn't see that it fails on your platform, you should file a bug report as soon as you find the problem. This will do at least two things: First, it will notify the programmer that she did something that broke your system. Second, it is a form of reporting that other members of the community will see and it will help them realize the importance of being platform-independent.

This is especially important for readers of this book, who might be using databases other than the default MySQL engine.

Ordering

You use the orderBy() method to specify the collation order of a record set. Listing 9–17 shows an example.

Listing 9–17. Ordering a Record Set

```
$query = db_select('node', 'n')
  ->condition('n.created', time() - (14 * 86400), '>');
$query->fields('n', array('title', 'type', 'created'));
$query->orderBy('title', 'ASC');
$result = $query->execute();

foreach ($result as $record) {
  $name = $record->title;
  $type = $record->type;
  $created = $record->created;
  print($name . ' (' . $type . ')'
```

```
   . ' created: ' . date("D, j M, Y \a\\t G:i", $created)
   . '<br>');
}
```

This creates the output shown in Figure 9–5.

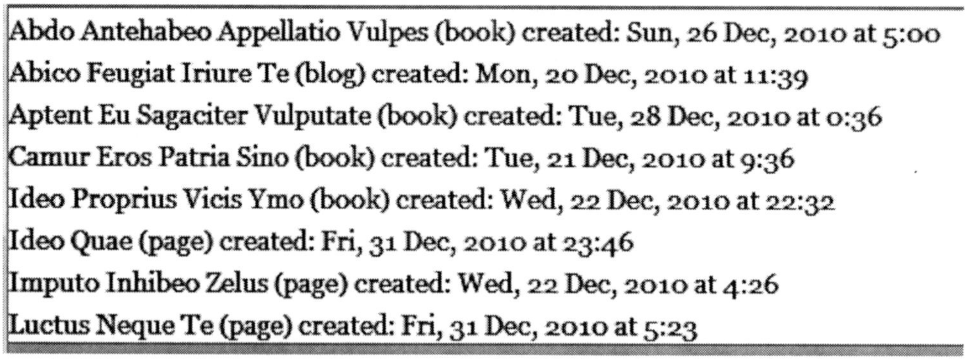

Abdo Antehabeo Appellatio Vulpes (book) created: Sun, 26 Dec, 2010 at 5:00

Abico Feugiat Iriure Te (blog) created: Mon, 20 Dec, 2010 at 11:39

Aptent Eu Sagaciter Vulputate (book) created: Tue, 28 Dec, 2010 at 0:36

Camur Eros Patria Sino (book) created: Tue, 21 Dec, 2010 at 9:36

Ideo Proprius Vicis Ymo (book) created: Wed, 22 Dec, 2010 at 22:32

Ideo Quae (page) created: Fri, 31 Dec, 2010 at 23:46

Imputo Inhibeo Zelus (page) created: Wed, 22 Dec, 2010 at 4:26

Luctus Neque Te (page) created: Fri, 31 Dec, 2010 at 5:23

Figure 9–5. Ordering a result set

You can also specify a random ordering by using the orderRandom() method. It is possible to chain ordering and random ordering together, as shown in Listing 9–18.

Listing 9–18. Chaining Normal and Random Ordering

```
$query = db_select('block', 'b');
$query
  ->condition('b.region', -1, '<>')
  ->fields('b', array('region', 'module', 'delta'));
$query->orderBy('module')->orderRandom();
$result = $query->execute();

foreach ($result as $record) {
  $region = $record->region;
  $module = $record->module;
  $delta = $record->delta;
  print($region . ', ' . $module . ', ' . $delta . '<br>');
}
```

This orders first by region and then randomly orders the records when there are two or more records with the same region, as shown in Figure 9–6.

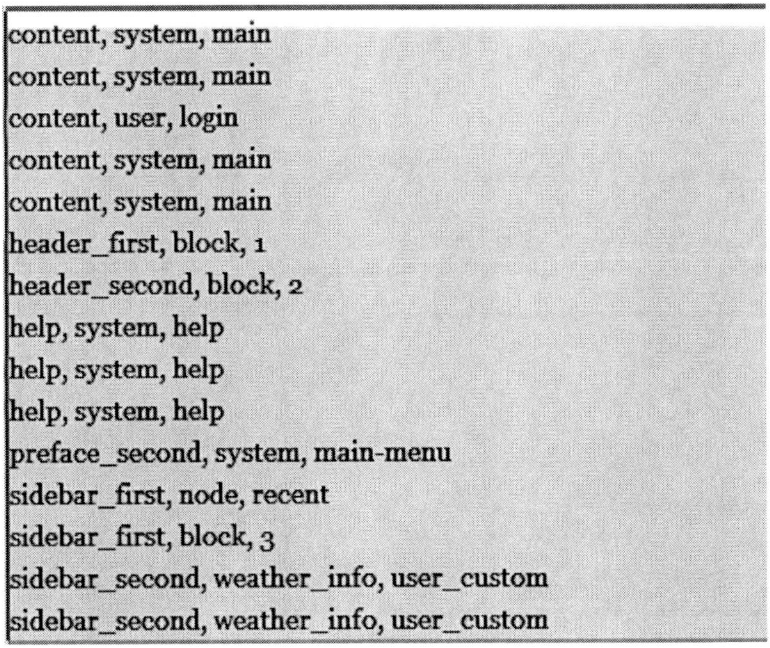

```
content, system, main
content, system, main
content, user, login
content, system, main
content, system, main
header_first, block, 1
header_second, block, 2
help, system, help
help, system, help
help, system, help
preface_second, system, main-menu
sidebar_first, node, recent
sidebar_first, block, 3
sidebar_second, weather_info, user_custom
sidebar_second, weather_info, user_custom
```

Figure 9–6. Output from the random order method

Some notes on the orderBy() method:

- The second parameter may be "ASC" or "DESC" to indicate ascending or descending order. If the parameter is not present, the default is "ASC".

- If you are using an aliased field name, the field name in the orderBy() method should be the alias, not the native column name. You can set an aliased field name by using the addField() method as described above.

- To order by multiple fields, call orderBy() multiple times in the order desired.

Grouping

Use the groupBy() method to group by a given field. This is demonstrated in Listing 9–19.

Listing 9–19. Using the groupBy() Method

```
$query = db_select('block', 'b');
$query
  ->condition('b.region', -1, '<>')
  ->fields('b', array('region', 'module', 'delta'));
$query->addExpression('COUNT(region)', 'count');
$query->orderBy('region');
$query->orderBy('module');
$query->groupBy('region');
$result = $query->execute();
```

```
foreach ($result as $record) {
  $region = $record->region;
  $module = $record->module;
  $delta = $record->delta;
  $count = $record->count;
  print('(' . $count . ') ' . $region . ', ' . $module . ', ' . $delta . '<br>');
}
```

Notice that this example also uses the addExpression() method to add a count of records that are consumed in each group. The output of this code fragment is shown in Figure 9–7.

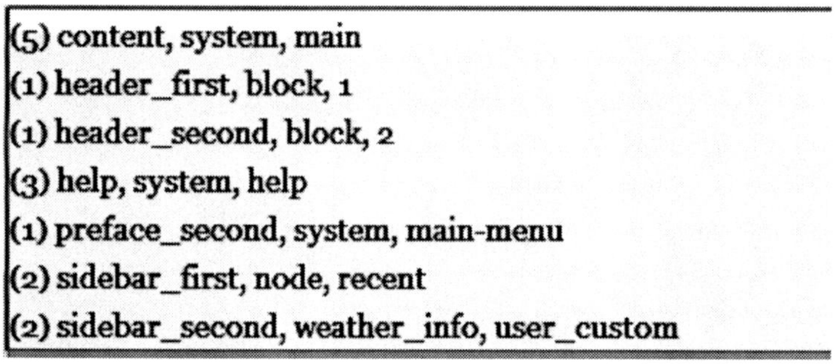

(5) content, system, main

(1) header_first, block, 1

(1) header_second, block, 2

(3) help, system, help

(1) preface_second, system, main-menu

(2) sidebar_first, node, recent

(2) sidebar_second, weather_info, user_custom

Figure 9–7. Output from the groupBy() example

Some notes on the groupBy() method:

- If you are using an aliased field name, the field name in the groupBy() method should be the alias, not the native column name. You can set an aliased field name using the addField() method as described above.

- To order by multiple fields, call groupBy() multiple times in the order desired.

Ranges and Limits

The range() property can be used to limit the query to a certain number of records. It is called with two parameters that indicate the record to start with and the number of records to return from that point. An example is shown in Listing 9–20.

Listing 9–20. Using the range() Property

```
$query = db_select('role', 'r');
$query
  //->condition('p.module', 'node', '=')
  ->condition('r.name', 'administrator', '<>')
  ->fields('r', array('name'))
  ->fields('p', array('permission', 'module'))
  ->join('role_permission', 'p', 'r.rid = p.rid')
;
$query->orderRandom();
//$query->orderBy('name');
//$query->orderBy('module');
```

```
//$query->orderBy('permission');
$query->range(5, 8);
$result = $query->execute();

foreach ($result as $record) {
  print($record->name . ', ' . $record->module . ', ' . $record->permission . '<br>');
}
```

This limits the query to return eight records, starting with the fifth one. The output is shown in Figure 9–8.

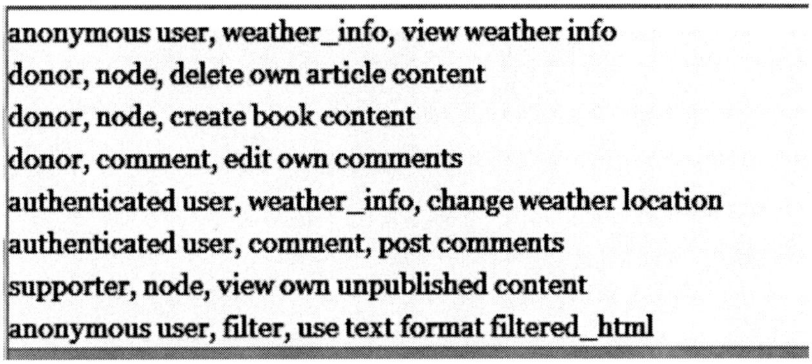

anonymous user, weather_info, view weather info
donor, node, delete own article content
donor, node, create book content
donor, comment, edit own comments
authenticated user, weather_info, change weather location
authenticated user, comment, post comments
supporter, node, view own unpublished content
anonymous user, filter, use text format filtered_html

Figure 9–8. Output from a range-limited query

Some notes on the range() method:

- To return just the first *n* records, set the first parameter to 0: ->range(0,10).

- Calling range() subsequent times will overwrite previously set values.

- Calling range() with no parameters will remove any range restrictions from the query.

Counting

The countQuery() method returns the number of rows returned by any query. Listing 9–21 shows an example.

Listing 9–21. Counting the Records Returned from a Query

```
$query = db_select('role_permission', 'p');
$query
  ->condition('p.module', 'node', '=')
  ->fields('p', array('permission'))
;
$num_rows = $query->countQuery()->execute()->fetchField();
```

This outputs what you'd expect, as Figure 9–9 shows.

Figure 9–9. Counting rows

Query Alteration

Another advantage of dynamic queries over static queries is that other modules can alter the query before it is executed against the database. Since the query is expressed in a Drupal-smart form instead of in raw SQL, we can tag the query with metadata that lets us identify a query that another module might be interested in.

This tagging is done with the addTag() method, as shown in Listing 9–22.

Listing 9–22. The addTag()Method Provides Information for Oher Modules

```
$query = db_select('role', 'r');
$query
  ->condition('p.module', 'node', '=')
  ->condition('r.name', 'administrator', '=')
  ->fields('r', array('name'))
  ->fields('p', array('permission', 'module'))
  ->join('role_permission', 'p', 'r.rid = p.rid')
;
$query->orderBy('name');
$query->orderBy('module');
$query->orderBy('permission');
$query->addTag('get_permissions');
$result = $query->execute();

foreach ($result as $record) {
  print($record->name . ', ' . $record->module . ', ' . $record->permission . '<br>');
}
```

The output, shown in Figure 9–10, displays all node permissions granted to administrator. The query is sorted by name, then module, then permission, all ascending.

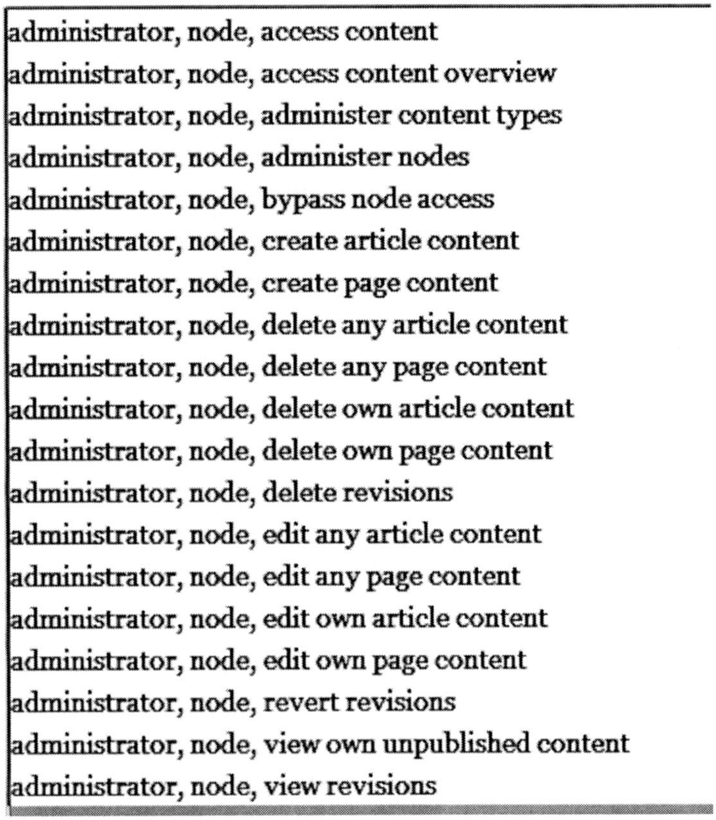

administrator, node, access content

administrator, node, access content overview

administrator, node, administer content types

administrator, node, administer nodes

administrator, node, bypass node access

administrator, node, create article content

administrator, node, create page content

administrator, node, delete any article content

administrator, node, delete any page content

administrator, node, delete own article content

administrator, node, delete own page content

administrator, node, delete revisions

administrator, node, edit any article content

administrator, node, edit any page content

administrator, node, edit own article content

administrator, node, edit own page content

administrator, node, revert revisions

administrator, node, view own unpublished content

administrator, node, view revisions

Figure 9–10. A query before altering

Notice that the tag, 'get_permissions' was added to this query. Tagging the query just marks the query with some descriptive tags and doesn't cause any immediate processing. However, it is possible to create a hook that will be invoked when a tagged query is encountered.

You can put any tag on your query but there are some conventions used in the core modules:

- **node_access:** This query should have node access restrictions placed on it.

- **translatable:** This query should have translatable columns.

- **term_access:** This query should have taxonomy term-based restrictions placed on it.

- **views:** This query is generated by the views module.

All dynamic queries are passed through the query alter hook when the execute() method is called and just before the query string is compiled. That means modules have the opportunity to alter the query before it goes to the database.

The format for the hook is module_name_query_tag_name_alter, where module_name is the name of our module, and tag_name is the name of the tag we added. The hook function that captures the query is shown in Listing 9–23.

Listing 9–23. A Query Alter Hook for a Tagged Query

```
function weather_info_query_get_permissions_alter(QueryAlterableInterface $query) {
  $order =& $query->getOrderBy();
  $order['permission'] = 'DESC';
}
```

This function will modify the ordering parameters, changing the order of 'permission' from 'ASC' to 'DESC'. Notice that the query is passed as a type of QueryAlterableInterface. Even though it is not passed by reference, it acts as though it is because of the way PHP 5 handles objects. It is essential to grab the properties you are looking for using the reference assignment (=&) so that anything that's altered affects the original query string.

■ **Note** Be sure you don't execute the query inside the query alter hook, as this will cause an infinite loop.

Table 9–1 shows the properties that are available to the query alter hook.

Table 9–1. Properties That Can Be Modified on the Select Query Object

Artifact	Description
conditions();	Returns a reference to the conditions in the WHERE clause for this query.
getExpressions();	Returns a reference to the expressions array for this query.
getFields();	Returns a reference to the fields array for this query.
getGroupBy();	Returns a reference to the group-by array for this query.
getOrderBy();	Returns a reference to the order by array for this query.
getTables();	Returns a reference to the tables array for this query.
getUnion();	Returns a reference to the union queries for this query. This includes queries for UNION, UNION ALL, and UNION DISTINCT.
havingConditions();	Helper function to build most common HAVING conditional clauses.

There is no need to take any action inside the query alter hook. As soon as the function is completed, the query engine will look for any other alter hooks that need to be executed, and then it will compile the query string and send it to the database engine.

The result of our query, having been created in our module and altered to change the sort order, is shown in Figure 9–11.

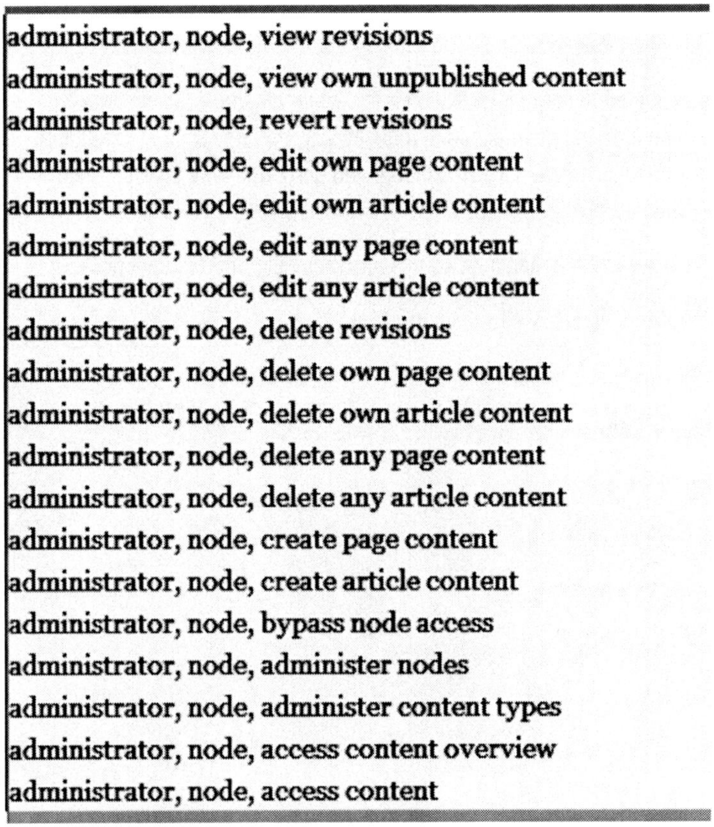

administrator, node, view revisions

administrator, node, view own unpublished content

administrator, node, revert revisions

administrator, node, edit own page content

administrator, node, edit own article content

administrator, node, edit any page content

administrator, node, edit any article content

administrator, node, delete revisions

administrator, node, delete own page content

administrator, node, delete own article content

administrator, node, delete any page content

administrator, node, delete any article content

administrator, node, create page content

administrator, node, create article content

administrator, node, bypass node access

administrator, node, administer nodes

administrator, node, administer content types

administrator, node, access content overview

administrator, node, access content

Figure 9–11. The result of an altered query

In sum, the dynamic query model provides all of the functionality of the static query model, with the added benefit of being cross-database compatible. I believe it's also easier to read and maintain due to its self-documenting mode of expression.

Many of the methods that are available for SELECT queries are also available for other queries, as we will see in the next sections.

Dynamic Insert Query

Inserting records into a database can be done with the db_insert() function, which uses syntax similar to the db_select() function described earlier.

■ **Tip** There are built-in methods that are designed to insert information into certain database tables. For example, the node_save() function writes a node to the database and, if necessary, updates several tables that form the basis of the node hierarchy. If you create a record in the node table and don't update the rest of the tables, you could end up with an unstable system.

The dynamic insert query method should be used with caution, and you should know the interdependencies of all of the data you are inserting before you use this function.

In the following sections, I will be using a table we created using the Schema API, which is described in Chapter 10. Figure 9–12 shows the layout of the table and some sample data.

			hid Primary Key: Unique history entry ID.	**location** Weather location.	**units** Weather unit system.	**language** Language in which weather is displayed.	**uid** The uid of the user making the entry.	**timestamp** A unix timestamp indicating the time the entry was made.
☑	✎	✕	1	Manchester, NH	F	en	1	1291300832
☐	✎	✕	2	Istanbul	C	tr	1	1291300927
☐	✎	✕	3	Paris	K	fr	1	1291300937
☐	✎	✕	4	Munich	C	de	1	1291300955
☐	✎	✕	5	Manhattan	F	en	1	1291300965

Figure 9–12. Sample database table to illustrate the database API

Using the db_insert() function in its basic form requires just specifying the name of the table and the fields and values you want to insert. Listing 9–24 shows an example of the db_insert() function.

Listing 9–24. The db_insert()Function Provides a Database-Agnostic Insert

```
$fields = array(
  'location' => 'San Luis Obispo',
  'language' => 'en',
  'units' => 'R',
  'uid' => 1,
  'timestamp' => REQUEST_TIME,
  );
$hid = db_insert('weather_info')
  ->fields($fields)
  ->execute();
```

Notice the $fields variable. This is a keyed array with the key being the name of the column in the table and the value being the value you want to assign to the column in the new row. Executing the db_insert() function will return, by default, the value of the primary key of the inserted row. This can be changed by setting the return value of the $options parameter, as shown in Listing 9–25.

Listing 9–25. Changing the Options on an Insert

```
$fields = array(
  'location' => 'San Luis Obispo',
  'language' => 'en',
  'units' => 'R',
  'uid' => 1,
  'timestamp' => REQUEST_TIME,
  );
$options = array('return' => Database::RETURN_STATEMENT);
$statement = db_insert('weather_info', $options)
  ->fields($fields)
  ->execute();
```

This example returns the statement that was created by the database abstraction layer instead of the value of the inserted key. The options available are:

- target: This is the database target against which to execute a query. Valid values are "default" or "slave". This is used if you are running a high-availability configuration with more than one database.

- fetch: This element controls how rows from a result set will be returned. Legal values include PDO::FETCH_ASSOC, PDO::FETCH_BOTH, PDO::FETCH_OBJ, PDO::FETCH_NUM, or a string representing the name of a class. If a string is specified, each record will be fetched into a new object of that class. The behavior of all other values is defined by PDO. See http://www.php.net/PDOStatement-fetch for more information.

- return: Depending on the type of query, different return values may be meaningful. This directive instructs the system which type of return value is desired. The system generally sets the correct value automatically, so it is rare that a module developer will ever need to specify this value. Setting the value incorrectly would likely lead to unpredictable results or fatal errors. Legal values include:

    - Database::RETURN_STATEMENT: Returns the prepared statement object for the query. This is usually meaningful only for SELECT queries, where the statement object is how one accesses the result set returned by the query.

    - Database::RETURN_AFFECTED: Returns the number of rows affected by an UPDATE or DELETE query. Note that this means the number of rows that actually changed, not the number of rows matched by the WHERE clause.

    - Database::RETURN_INSERT_ID: Returns the sequence ID (primary key) created by an INSERT statement on a table that contains a serial column.

    - Database::RETURN_NULL: Returns nothing, as there is no meaningful value to return. This is the case for INSERT queries on tables that don't contain a serial column.

- throw_exception: By default, the database system will catch any error on a query as an exception, log it, and then rethrow it so that code further up the call chain can take an appropriate action. To suppress that behavior and return NULL on failure, set this option to FALSE.

Like db_select(), the db_insert() function can be specified in a more compact form, eliminating the need to hold certain values as variables. This is shown in Listing 9–26.

Listing 9–26. Compact Form for the db_insert() Function

```
$returned = db_insert('weather_info', array(
    'return' => Database::RETURN_STATEMENT
))
  ->fields(array(
    'location' => 'San Luis Obispo',
    'language' => 'en',
    'units' => 'R',
    'uid' => 1,
    'timestamp' => REQUEST_TIME,
    ))
  ->execute();
```

Multi-Insert Form

The db_insert() function can be executed with more than one record being inserted at a time. To do this, you must use a "degenerate" form of the query. Listing 9–27 shows the form using the query we've been working with.

Listing 9–27. The Degenerate Form of db_insert()

```
$hid = db_insert('weather_info')
  ->fields(array(
    'location',
    'language',
    'units',
    'uid',
    'timestamp'))
  ->values(array(
    'location' => 'San Luis Obispo',
    'language' => 'en',
    'units' => 'R',
    'uid' => 1,
    'timestamp' => REQUEST_TIME,
    ))
  ->execute();
```

Notice that the fields and values are specified separately. By using this form, we can specify multiple sets of values and then execute them all at once, as shown in Listing 9–28.

Listing 9–28. Executing a Multiple-Record Insert

```
$hid = db_insert('weather_info')
  ->fields(array(
    'location',
    'language',
    'units',
    'uid',
    'timestamp'
    ))
  ->values(array(
```

```
      'San Luis Obispo',
      'en',
      'R',
      1,
      REQUEST_TIME,
      ))
  ->values(array(
      'Cupertino',
      'en',
      'F',
      1,
      REQUEST_TIME,
      ))
  ->values(array(
      'San Diego',
      'es',
      'C',
      1,
      REQUEST_TIME,
      ))
  ->execute();
```

Another way to execute this multi-record insert would be to create an array and then iterate over it using the foreach() control structure, as shown in Listing 9–29.

Listing 9–29. Processing an Array of Values

```
$values = array(
  array('San Luis Obispo', 'en', 'R', 1, REQUEST_TIME),
  array('Cupertino', 'en', 'F', 1, REQUEST_TIME),
  array('San Diego', 'es', 'C', 1, REQUEST_TIME),
  );

$query = db_insert('weather_info')
  ->fields(array(
      'location',
      'language',
      'units',
      'uid',
      'timestamp'
      ));
foreach($values as $record) {
  $query->values($record);
}
$hid = $query->execute();
print $hid;
```

This method is used often in the core as well as in many contributed modules, so you should feel comfortable with it. Note that if you are using the multi-insert technique, the return value is undefined and should not be trusted as it may vary depending on the database driver.

Not only is this method a bit more straightforward than executing three separate inserts, it is potentially safer and more efficient. It is up to the database driver to determine the best way to do this insert. For example, multiple insert statements could be executed together inside a transaction for greater data integrity and speed. Or, if the database engine supports batch inserts, the driver might use that approach instead.

Dynamic Update Query

You can use the db_update() function to update data in a table. Listing 9–30 shows an example.

Listing 9–30. The db_update() Function

```
$rows_updated = db_update('weather_info')
  ->fields(array(
      'language' => 'EN'
      ))
  ->condition('language', 'en', '=')
  ->execute();
```

This function generates the following SQL query:

```
UPDATE weather_info SET language='EN' WHERE language='en';
```

The value returned is the number of rows that are affected, which is not necessarily the same as the number of rows that are actually changed. For example, if there are three rows where the language is 'en' and two where the language is 'EN', the two uppercased rows will be matched, but since they didn't change, they will not be counted in the return value. The function will return a 3.

Dynamic Delete Query

The db_delete() function works similarly to the db_update() function in that it requires a condition and returns the number of records affected. An example is shown in Listing 9–31.

Listing 9–31. The db_delete() Function

```
$rows_deleted = db_update('weather_info')
  ->condition('location', 'San Luis Obispo', '=')
  ->execute();
```

This returns the number of records that were deleted.

Dynamic Merge Query

Merge queries are a special type of hybrid query. A merge query is a combination of an insert and an update. If a given condition is met, usually a row with the primary key, an update query is run. If the specified key is not found, an insert query is run. Although there is a formal specification for merge in the SQL standard, many databases don't implement the feature, so it is the job of the database driver to encapsulate the logic for the Drupal db_merge() function.

The syntax is similar to the other dynamic query functions. Listing 9–32 shows an example.

Listing 9–32. A Dynamic Merge Query Using db_merge()

```
$records_merged = db_merge('weather_info')
  ->key(array('location' => 'San Diego'))
  ->fields(array(
      'location' => 'San Diego, CA',
      'language' => 'es',
      ))
  ->execute();
```

If the merge function finds the location 'San Diego, CA' in one or more of the records, those records will be updated with a new location and language. Otherwise, the function will attempt to insert a new row. Note, however, that if the merge function needs to insert a new row, it will fail. Why? Because the table has fields that don't have a default value and aren't specified in the fields array. To fix that, we need to specify two different sets of fields for the two different conditions that the merge query might encounter. An example of this is shown in Listing 9–33.

Listing 9–33. Adding the updateFields() Object

```
$records_merged = db_merge('weather_info')
  ->key(array('location' => 'San Francisco, CA'))
  ->fields(array(
      'location' => 'San Francisco, CA',
      'language' => 'us',
      'units' => 'F',
      'uid' => 1,
      'timestamp' => REQUEST_TIME,
      ))
  ->updateFields(array(
      'language' => 'es',
      ))
  ->execute();
```

In this case, if the key is not found, the merge function will insert a new record using the `fields()` array. If the record does exist in the database, only the language field will be updated. Note that if there is more than one record that matches the key condition, each of the rows will be updated.

▓ **Tip** When you are using this form of the `db_merge()` function, be sure to specify the `updateFields()` array after the `fields()` array.   .

Expressions

Expressions can be used to do some computation when a record is inserted. An example is shown in Listing 9–34.

Listing 9–34. Using Expressions on the db_merge() Function

```
db_merge('search_index')
  ->key(array(
    'word' => $word,
    'sid' => $sid,
    'type' => $module,
  ))
  ->fields(array('score' => $score))
  ->expression('score', 'score + :score', array(':score' => $score))
  ->execute();
```

This is commonly used where there is some sort of counter that keeps track of similar records in the table. The example in Listing 9–34 is used by the search function. In this case, if the word doesn't exist in the `search_index` table, it is added with the precalculated score value. If it is already there, the score value is incremented by the score value.

Conditional Clauses

The db_select(), db_update(), and db_delete() functions can make use of a conditional clause that is eventually turned into the appropriate conditional clause for the target database server.

There are two basic ways of specifying conditions in your query:

- ->condition():This specifies a condition that defines a field and a value with an operator that says what the relationship is between the two. This is the preferred method because of its abstract nature. A simple example is:

  ```
  $query->condition('timestamp', REQUEST_TIME - 3600, '<');
  ```

- ->where(): For more complex clauses, the where method allows arbitrary SQL as a conditional fragment. This can contain a string that will be placed following a SQL WHERE statement, or it can contain string replacements, as shown below:

  ```
  $query->where("$alias.name <> test.name");
  $query->where('age > :age', array(':age' => 26));
  ```

  This form is deprecated, as it could make your code incompatible with other database engines.

In addition to the simple comparison operators (=, <, >, <=, >=), there are operators that require an array, as shown in Listing 9–35.

Listing 9–35. Array Operators for the condition() Property

```
$query->condition('name',
  array(
    'location', 'language', 'unit',
    ),
  'IN'
);
// Becomes: name IN ('location', 'language', 'unit')


$query->condition('timestamp',
  array(REQUEST_TIME - 7200, REQUEST_TIME - 3600),
  'BETWEEN'
);
// Becomes: timestamp BETWEEN 1291305433 AND 1291309033
```

Nested Conditionals

Conditions can also be nested by specifying multiple condition() properties. This is shown in Listing 9–36.

Listing 9–36. Conditions Can Be Nested

```
$query
  ->condition('field1', array(1, 2), 'IN')
  ->condition(db_or()->condition('field2', 5)->condition('field3', 6));
// Becomes: (field1 IN (1, 2) AND (field2 = 5 OR field3 = 6))
```

The default when specifying multiple conditions is to "AND" them together. We see this with the two conditions that are on separate lines. The db_or() function also takes multiple condition()

properties but returns a SQL string set to "OR" all included conditions together. Combining that with the first condition gives us the desired conditional string.

Null Values

There are two methods for specifying the "nullness" of a field in the query, as shown in Listing 9–37.

Listing 9–37. Determining Nullness

```
$query->isNull('language');
// Becomes (language IS NULL)

$query->isNotNull('language');
// Becomes: (language IS NOT NULL)
```

Error Handling

The database abstraction layer sits on top of Drupal's error-handling framework. This means errors that occur while accessing the database will be displayed and logged, depending on the site-wide settings for error logging.

If an error is detected by the database layer, it is thrown back up to the calling function until someone catches it. You can use `try...catch` structures to deal with problems in an intelligent way. Listing 9–38 shows an example .

Listing 9–38. Trapping Errors Using `try...catch`

```
try {
  $records_merged = db_merge('weather_info')
    ->key(array('location' => 'San Francisco, ZA'))
    ->fields(array(
        'location' => 'San Francisco, CA',
        'language' => 'us',
        ))
    ->updateFields(array(
        'language' => 'es',
        ))
    ->execute();
}
catch(exception $err) {
  drupal_set_message("Whoops! Trouble merging data: $err", 'error');
}
```

This sort of logic doesn't do much; I include it here just as an example. Using `try...catch` to handle errors does have an impact, however, if you are using transactions.

Transactions

The Drupal database abstraction layer supports transactions and includes a provision for creating a transparent fallback for databases that don't support transactions. Transactions can get quite complicated in certain situations, so transaction-processing behavior varies among databases.

In order to deal with nested transactions, the database abstraction layer sets up a framework using constructors and destructors. This is necessary because one PHP function might start a transaction and call another function that also starts a transaction. If the inner function were to end the transaction, it might unwittingly end the calling function's transaction.

Transactions are started using the db_transaction() object. They are committed once in the scope in which the db_transaction() object is created, and can be rolled back if necessary. Once the db_transaction() object goes out of scope, the transaction is committed and is torn down. Listing 9–39 shows an example using a try...catch block.

Listing 9–39. Transactions in Action

```
$txn = db_transaction();

try {
  $records_merged = db_merge('weather_info')
    ->key(array('location' => 'San Francisco, ZA'))
    ->fields(array(
        'location' => 'San Francisco, CA',
        'language' => 'us',
        ))
    ->updateFields(array(
        'language' => 'es',
        ))
    ->execute();
}

catch(exception $err) {

  drupal_set_message('Whoops! Trouble merging data: ' .
    $err->xdebug_message, 'error');
  $txn->rollback();
}
```

The catch will result in the message being sent to the screen, as shown in Figure 9–13.

> ❌ • Whoops! Trouble merging data: PDOException: SQLSTATE[HY000]: General error: 1364 Field
> 'units' doesn't have a default value in D:\wamp\www\drupal7\includes\database\database.inc
> on line 2005 Call Stack: 0.0867 345192 1. {main}() D:\wamp\www\drupal7\index.php:0 0.3705
> 19705208 2. menu_execute_active_handler(???, ???) D:\wamp\www\drupal7\index.php:22
> 0.3726 19870760 3. call_user_func_array(???, ???) D:\wamp\www\drupal7
> \includes\menu.inc:485 0.3726 19870992 4. drupal_get_form(???, ???) D:\wamp\www\drupal7
> \includes\menu.inc:0 0.3726 19871536 5. drupal_build_form(???, ???) D:\wamp\www\drupal7
> \includes\form.inc:188 0.5613 20412288 6. drupal_process_form(???, ???, ???)
> D:\wamp\www\drupal7\includes\form.inc:350 0.5866 20566736 7. drupal_validate_form
> (???, ???, ???) D:\wamp\www\drupal7\includes\form.inc:814 0.5867 20567104 8. _form_validate
> (???, ???, ???) D:\wamp\www\drupal7\includes\form.inc:1079 0.5979 20614664 9. _form_validate
> (???, ???, ???) D:\wamp\www\drupal7\includes\form.inc:1218 0.5980 20618152 10.
> weather_info_profile_weather_location_validate(???, ???, ???) D:\wamp\www\drupal7
> \includes\form.inc:1332 0.6930 20618688 11. weather_info_insert_history(???, ???, ???, ???)
> D:\wamp\www\drupal7\sites\all\modules\weather_info\weather_info.module:230 0.7407
> 20626248 12. MergeQuery->execute() D:\wamp\www\drupal7
> \sites\all\modules\weather_info\weather_info.inc:150

Figure 9–13. Error caught and displayed

When $txn is destroyed, the transaction will be committed. If your transaction is nested inside of another transaction, Drupal will track each transaction and only commit the outermost transaction when the last transaction object goes out of scope, that is, when all relevant queries complete successfully.

Summary

Drupal grew up using the LAMP stack, which utilizes MySQL as its database engine. The Drupal core, as well as most contributed and private modules, assumed that the database was MySQL and there are many instances of SQL statements written directly for that platform.

With version 7 of Drupal, the emphasis is on writing to an abstracted layer instead of assuming MySQL as the underlying data engine. Drupal's database layer now provides a database-agnostic way to manage content.

Even with this abstracted layer, however, you will surely find some code examples that write directly to a database, assuming it is MySQL. This may cause modules to break when they are deployed to a platform that does not use MySQL.

Keep this in mind as you develop your database interactions. Avoid embedding any SQL at all, but if you must, check to make sure that it is compatible with all database engines the code is likely to be deployed to.

In the next chapter, we will see what is required to deliver your module and provide updates as it goes through its lifecycle.

■ ■ ■

Deployment

If you create custom modules or themes, you'll need to provide enough information for yourself or others to deploy the module to the Drupal core. The installer uses two files, one required and one optional, to prepare the system for accepting your module.

The .info File

If your module is self-contained and does not make any changes to the system, you can use a simple .info file. (The file is pronounced "dot info.")

The .info file stores metadata about your module or theme. For a module, the .info file tells Drupal the following:

- That the module exists and what it is called.

- How to control the activation and deactivation of the module.

- How to render the module's information on the Drupal administration pages.

- How to deal with the module in other administrative contexts.

In Chapter 5, you saw a simple .info file for Drupal 7. The code in Listing 10–1 shows that .info file.

Listing 10–1. A Basic .info File

```
; $Id$
name = Weather information
description = A block that shows current weather for a particular location.
package = Cool stuff from Brian
core = 7.x
files[] = weather_info.module
files[] = weather_info.inc
files[] = tests/weather_info.test
dependencies[] = block
configure = admin/config/weather_info/settings
version = 7.x-1.x
```

The .info file must have the same base name as the .module file and be in the same directory in your module hierarchy. In this case, our module is weather_info.module, so our .info file must be weather_info.info. The same goes for the .info file for themes.

▓ **A Note on Names:** The Drupal community has developed a set of naming conventions you should follow in order to be compatible with the community. You'll find a full description at `http://drupal.org/coding-standards#naming`.

Let's cover each of the fields here, and add a few as we go.

- `; $Id$:` All Drupal files should begin with this line so the version control system can replace it with the appropriate metadata.

- `name:` This is the name of the module, which will appear on the administration page and other places. Choose the name carefully as you'll be seeing a lot of it. Drupal conventions state that the name should be descriptive but short, with the first word capitalized and the rest in lowercase. The string does not need to be quoted. The name should not end with a period.

- `description:` The description is limited to 255 characters. It should follow the Drupal capitalization conventions and end with a period. The line should be descriptive enough to tell the user what the module or theme is or does. The description can also have simple HTML markup to, for example, insert a link to online documentation or the author's site:

  ```
  description = The <a href="http://drupal.org/project/omega">Omega
  Theme</a> is a kitchen sink full of features from many of the popular base
  themes available on Drupal.org thrown into an end-all theme for maximum
  flexibility.
  ```

- `package:` This is an optional field meant for integrating a link to your module into the administration page. If the package field is not present, your module will be listed in the "Other" section of the module administration page. This is meant for multi-module packages; if you have a single module that does not relate to any of the common items, leave this out to keep from cluttering the administration page. The following are common items for the package field:

  - Administration
  - CCK
  - Commerce
  - Development
  - Media
  - User interface
  - Video
  - Views
  - Voting

- **core:** This required field indicates which version of the Drupal core is needed to run your program. Modules can only specify the version of the core, not the branch of that version. For example, 7.x is correct, but 7.1 is not.

- **files[]:** This is an array that indicates all of the files your module depends on. You would want to add any include files or testing files if they exist. Note that this is a new requirement for Drupal 7; it was created as a speed optimization feature not present in Drupal 6. Drupal will scan all dependent files every time the module is installed to keep its hook registry up to date.

- **dependencies[]:** This array indicates the other modules that are required for your module to run. The value of the dependencies array is the machine name of the module: that is, `weather_info`, not Weather information. Following the name of the dependent module, you can optionally indicate which version of the module is required. Examples:

  - **dependencies[] = comment:** indicates that any version of the comment module is required.

  - **dependencies[] = votingapi (1.x):** indicates that any branch of version 1 of the Voting API is required.

  - **dependencies[] = wysiwyg (2.1):** indicates that only the 2.1 branch of the Wysiwyg module will satisfy the dependency requirement.

  - **dependencies[] = token (>=7.1-1.2):** indicates that only the 1.2 branch of the Token module is required, and Drupal core 7.1 or greater is required. (Standard evaluation symbols may be used: = or == equals, > greater than, < lesser than, >= greater than or equal to, <= lesser than or equal to, != not equal to)

  - **dependencies[] = simplenews (>1.1, <=2.3, !=2.0):** evaluators can be combined.

- If the dependent files are not enabled and can be enabled, the installer engine will ask if you want to have them installed automatically, as Figure 10–1 shows.

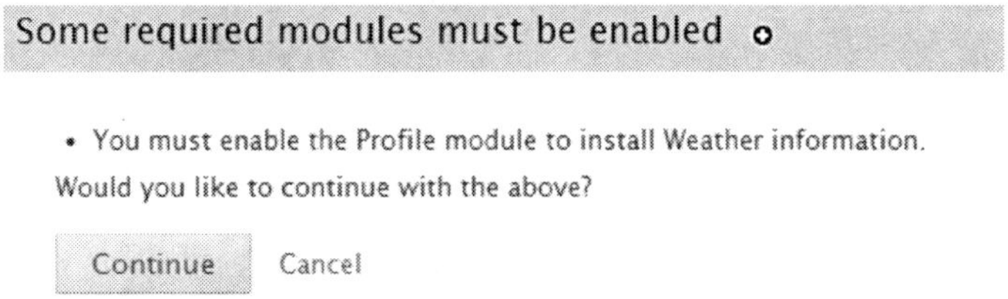

Figure 10–1. Enabling dependent files

- **php:** This optional field indicates the minimum version of PHP required by the module.

- **version:** The version of the module that you'd like to indicate. This field is discouraged as it is added by drupal.org when your module is released and a tarball is packaged. However, if you'll be hosting your module elsewhere or it's not for public use, you'll need to populate this field yourself.

- **configure:** This optional field indicates the path to the module's configuration page. It is the page that will display when the "Configure" link is clicked on the modules overview page (see Figure 10–2).

Figure 10–2. The modules overview page

Be careful not to insert a leading slash in the path:

```
configure = admin/config/weather_info/settings
```

- **required:** This optional field indicates that this module is absolutely required to the functioning of the system and should never be disabled. If required = TRUE, the module will be enabled automatically and the enabled checkmark will be disabled. Be careful with this one, as it was designed for core modules. Your module better be pretty critical to rise to this level for all people who install it.

- **hidden:** This optional field indicates that the module should be hidden from users. When you set hidden = TRUE, the module will not appear on the modules page. This is usually used for testing modules, which the end user should not have access to.

Themes also require a .info file. A typical .info file for a theme is shown in Listing 10–2.

Listing 10–2. Typical .info File for a Theme

```
; $Id: bartik.info,v 1.5 2010/11/07 00:27:20 dries Exp $

name = Bartik
description = A flexible, recolorable theme with many regions.
package = Core
version = VERSION
core = 7.x

stylesheets[all][] = css/layout.css
stylesheets[all][] = css/style.css
stylesheets[all][] = css/colors.css
stylesheets[print][] = css/print.css
```

```
regions[header] = Header
regions[help] = Help
regions[page_top] = Page top
regions[page_bottom] = Page bottom
regions[highlighted] = Highlighted

regions[featured] = Featured
regions[content] = Content
regions[sidebar_first] = Sidebar first
regions[sidebar_second] = Sidebar second

regions[triptych_first] = Triptych first
regions[triptych_middle] = Triptych middle
regions[triptych_last] = Triptych last

regions[footer_firstcolumn] = Footer first column
regions[footer_secondcolumn] = Footer second column
regions[footer_thirdcolumn] = Footer third column
regions[footer_fourthcolumn] = Footer fourth column
regions[footer] = Footer

settings[shortcut_module_link] = 0

; Information added by drupal.org packaging script on 2010-11-14
version = "7.0-beta3"
project = "drupal"
datestamp = "1289694732"
```

> ■ **Note** The last four lines were created by the packaging script that was run on the theme before including it on the `drupal.org` site. If you are going to make your module or theme available on `drupal.org`, these fields should not be specified so they can be added by the packaging script.

The fields that are specific to themes are:

- **regions[]:** All regions defined by your theme must be declared in the `.info` file for the theme if you want to be able to access them with the blocks administrator. If you have a subtheme and are using only the same regions as the base theme, you still need to specify them here.

- **stylesheets[media][]:** All style sheets used by your theme must be declared here or they will not be applied. The first dimension of the array must indicate the style sheet's "media property." Recognized media properties are:

  - **all:** Suitable for all devices.

  - **braille:** Intended for braille tactile feedback devices.

  - **embossed:** Intended for paged braille printers.

- **handheld:** Intended for handheld devices (typically small screen, limited bandwidth).

- **print:** Intended for paged material and for documents viewed on screen in print preview mode.

- **projection:** Intended for projected presentations, for example projectors.

- **screen:** Intended primarily for color computer screens.

- **speech:** Intended for speech synthesizers.

- **tty:** Intended for media using a fixed-pitch character grid (such as teletypes, terminals, or portable devices with limited display capabilities). Authors should not use pixel units with the "tty" media type.

- **tv:** Intended for television-type devices (low resolution, color, limited-scrollability screens, sound available).

▓ **Tip** If you want to override a particular style sheet, just declare that file name in your style sheet area but don't include it in your module directory. This essentially replaces the existing style sheet file with nothing.

- **base theme:** If your theme is a subtheme, this is where you put the name of the theme it is derived from. Note that this is the machine-readable name of the theme, not the human-readable name: base theme = pixture_reloaded.

- **scripts[]:** If your theme includes Javascript files, this is where you specify them. In versions of Drupal before 7, the file script.js is included automatically. In Drupal 7, it is only included if you specify it in the scripts[] parameter.

- **features[]:** Various elements output by the theme can be turned on and off from the theme's configuration page. The features[] array in the .info file controls which of these check boxes display on the configuration page. If you want to suppress the display of a check box, omit the entry for it in the .info file. Realize, though, that if no features are defined, all check boxes will display due to the assumed defaults. The following features are available:

  - features[] = logo

  - features[] = name

  - features[] = mission

  - features[] = node_user_picture

  - features[] = comment_user_picture

  - features[] = favicon

  - features[] = primary_links

  - features[] = secondary_links

- `features[] = comment_user_verification`

- **settings[]:** This optional keyed array is intended to communicate information to the theme. If you are familiar with the .NET application configuration framework, you can think of this:

  `<add key="mykey" value="myvalue" />`

  in `app.config` or `web.config`. The settings are available to the theme module using the `theme_get_setting()` function. The equivalent in your `.info` file would be:

  `settings[mykey] = myvalue`

- **engine:** This required field indicates the theme engine your theme uses. If none is provided, the theme is assumed to be stand-alone, i.e., implemented with a ".theme" file. Most themes should use `phptemplate` as the default engine. Omit this entry only if you know what you're doing.

- **screenshot:** This optional field indicates to the Drupal theme-page engine where it can find a thumbnail image for the theme. If this key is omitted from your `.info` file, Drupal uses the `screenshot.png` file in the theme's directory.

The lines in your `.info` file can appear in any order (except for the `$Id$` line), but most users put the name and description first to make it easy on the human reader or updater.

▓ **Note** The contents of the `.info` file are cached in the database so Drupal won't notice any alteration. To clear it, do one of the following: Click the "Clear all caches" button located at Configuration➤Performance.

By creating the required `.info` file in your module, you give others an instant starting point to learn about your module, as well as providing the information Drupal needs to manage your module and integrate it into the site.

During the deployment process, it is possible to do other things with the system using a special Drupal module called the `.install` file (is pronounced "dot install"). This file has the same name as your module with an extension of `.install`.

The `.install` File

If your module requires new content types, custom databases, or otherwise makes changes to the environment, such as creating directory structures, you'll want to include a `.install` file with your package that the installer can use to prepare the system for accepting your module. You'll also want a `.install` file if you are upgrading your module from one version to another.

The philosophy of an install program is the same in Drupal as it is in Windows or any other platform. That is, you should create everything the user needs in order to use your module, and leave no trace if the user wants to uninstall the module. The `.install` file allows you to do both of those things; the Drupal engine hooks into your `.install` file to set things up and tear them down.

■ **Tip** The `.install` file is a PHP code file, and uses the same coding conventions as any other PHP file. If you are using Visual Studio, you should add `.install` as a valid extension for PHP files so you will get all of the coloring and IntelliSense goodness you expect.

In Chapter 5, we enabled a module using the Modules administration page. When a module is enabled, Drupal goes through the module file, as well as any included files, and makes a list of artifacts it might need later. It stores this information in the database and refers to it when the hook mechanism is executed.

The module-enabling process, then, is really a code-deployment process. During this process, you might need to do other things to the environment so your module has the requisite information it needs to function and so the Drupal installation has everything it needs to make use of your module.

Building the `.install` File

The `.install` file works with Drupal's hook system just like any other Drupal program file. Probably the most common reason for creating a `.install` file is to create a database table or two, which you do using the schema hook. Like all hooks, your function will have the name of your module, followed by an underscore and the hook name, in this case, schema.

Thinking back to the weather information module we created in the second part of this book, recall that it allows the user to specify a custom location, language, and display units for the weather location. We used the user profile module to assure that each user could specify his own information.

But now suppose we'd like to keep track of the locations, languages, and display units of anyone who has entered weather location information. We can access the user profile tables to get information about what our users have specified right now, but that's lost if they make a change. I want to keep track of all information ever entered. For that, we'll need a special table that we can create, manage, and drop if necessary.

The first thing we need to do in our `.install` file is to create a hook function for the schema. That function is called `weather_info_schema()` and appears in Listing 10–3.

Listing 10–3. *A Schema Hook Function for Creating a Table in the Drupal Database*

```
function weather_info_schema() {
  $schema['weather_info'] = array(
    'description' => 'Weather information history.',
    'fields' => array(
      'hid' => array(
        'type' => 'serial',
        'unsigned' => TRUE,
        'not null' => TRUE,
        'description' => 'Primary Key: Unique history entry ID.',
      ),
      'location' => array(
        'type' => 'varchar',
        'length' => 255,
        'not null' => TRUE,
        'default' => '',
        'description' => 'Weather location.',
      ),
```

```
      'units' => array(
        'type' => 'text',
        'length' => 50,
        'not null' => TRUE,
        'description' => 'Weather unit system.',
      ),
      'language' => array(
        'type' => 'text',
        'length' => 50,
        'not null' => TRUE,
        'description' => 'Language in which weather is displayed.',
      ),
      'uid' => array(
        'type' => 'int',
        'not null' => TRUE,
        'default' => '0',
        'description' => 'The uid of the user making the entry.',
      ),
      'timestamp' => array(
        'type' => 'int',
        'not null' => TRUE,
        'default' => '0',
        'description' => 'A unix timestamp indicating the time the entry was made.',
      ),
    ),
    'primary key' => array('hid'),
    'indexes' => array(
      'list' => array('location'),
    ),
  );

  return $schema;
}
```

First, the fields are created and then, optionally, the keys and indexes. The term in the first dimension of the array is the name of the table to be created, in this case weather_info. You can create as many tables as you want in a single schema array by adding first-dimension array items keyed by the name of the table. The definition of the table's fields, keys, and indexes is in an array contained therein.

As with most things Drupal, a description is required, which is the first array item. Then the fields are defined with their own arrays—each item is a table column containing an array of parameters.

Keys and indexes fill out the array. In addition to the items shown in the example in Listing 10–3, you can specify unique keys, foreign keys, and other artifacts. A list of available schema API keys is reprinted in Appendix III.

Notice that the schema is returned from the schema hook function. There is no need to explicitly create the database tables, as the Drupal module installation function will take care of that. In fact, it's best to let Drupal deal with the database because it needs to know about your schemas in case it needs to remove them later.

The Enable and Install Hooks

In Drupal, a module can be enabled, installed, disabled, or uninstalled. Modules are enabled on the module administration page (Modules from the admin menu, or /admin/modules from the URL). Remember that in order for a module to appear on that page, it must appear in the sites directory hierarchy. For more information on this, see Chapter 5.

When the administrator checks the box next to your module and clicks the "Save configuration" button, the installer looks for certain hooks in your .install file. First, it deals with the schema hook and creates your database tables. And then, if the module has not yet been installed (or has been uninstalled), the installer engine will look for the install hook and execute it if it is present. After that, the enable hook is executed. (See Figure 10–3)

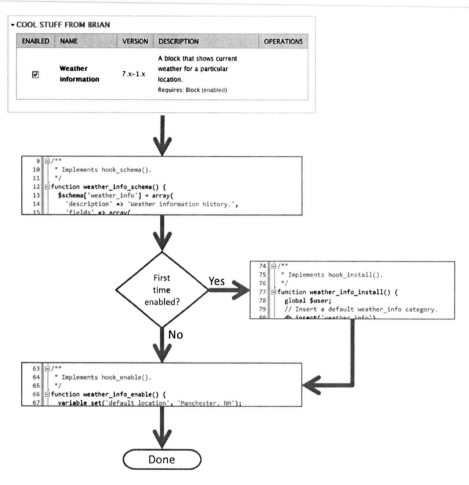

Figure 10–3. The install hook is executed only the first time a module is enabled.

It is in these hooks that you should do everything necessary to make sure your module has what it needs in the environment to function.

The Install Hook

Listing 10–4 shows the install hook for our weather information module.

Listing 10–4. Install Hook That Seeds a Custom Table

```
function weather_info_install() {
  global $user;
  // Insert a default weather_info category.
  db_insert('weather_info')
    ->fields(array(
        'location' => 'Manchester, NH',
        'units' => 'F',
        'language' => 'en',
        'uid' => $user->uid,
        'timestamp' => REQUEST_TIME,
        ))
    ->execute();
  drupal_set_message(st('Weather information table has been created.'));
}
```

■ **Tip** Notice the st() function in this module. In your regular Drupal module, you should use the t() function to provide translatable strings. This is a best practice and will be enforced by community standards. However, during the installation process, the database, theme, or localization subsystems might not be available. The st() function is a functional equivalent to t() for use only in installation programs.

First, an initial record in the database is inserted using the database API function, db_insert(). Recall that the schema array is read first by the installer program, so the table or tables should exist by the time the installer gets to the install hook. This means we are safe to insert our record. If this fails, it usually means there was a problem creating the tables from the schema. If that was the case, however, the error handler would probably prevent us from getting to this point.

The fact that we've gotten this far should mean that everything is good so far.

Next, we need to create the fields that our program depends on. The weather information module depends on certain fields that will be managed as part of the user's profile information. Back in Chapter 6, we created those fields manually. But we don't want to burden our users with this,

The Fields API has a number of functions that allow us to create, retrieve, update, and delete fields. Like any good API, the Fields CRUD API isolates us from the details of the underlying implementation and allows us to get our job done without worrying about how the tables actually look.

Listing 10–5 shows the API call for the first field, field_weather_location.

Listing 10–5. Creating a Field and an Instance with field_create_field()

```
// *
// * Weather location field
// *

$field = array(
  'field_name' => 'field_weather_location',
  'type' => 'text',
  'translatable' => TRUE,
  );
$instance = array(
```

```
  'field_name' => 'field_weather_location',
  'entity_type' => 'user',
  'bundle' => 'user',
  'label' => 'Weather location',
  'widget' => array(
      'type' => 'text_textfield',
      'weight' => '15',
      ),
    'description' => st('Enter a location on earth for which you would like '
      . 'to see weather information presented.'),
    );

// Create the field and instance.
field_create_field($field);
field_create_instance($instance);
```

We use two arrays. The first, $field, provides the name of the field we are creating and its type. This is the field itself, which can be used in many different places. The second, $instance, is one instantiation of a field, which has particulars concerning the actual instance. This seems redundant for this simple field, but you could have a custom field that contains many different facets of a type of information, such as a color with red, green, and blue components, or an address made up of street, city, state, postal code, etc. Defining this field once and instantiating it for particular purposes is more efficient.

Listing 10–6 shows the remaining two fields we need to create.

Listing 10–6. Creating Two More Fields and Instances

```
// *
// * Weather language field
// *

$field = array(
  'field_name' => 'field_weather_language',
  'type' => 'list_text',
  'translatable' => TRUE,
  'settings' => array(
      'allowed_values' => "en|English\nes|Spanish\nde|German\ntr|Turkish\nfr|French\n",
      'allowed_values_function' => '',
      ),
    );
$instance = array(
  'field_name' => 'field_weather_language',
  'entity_type' => 'user',
  'bundle' => 'user',
  'label' => 'Weather language',
  'widget' => array(
      'type' => 'options_select',
      'weight' => '16',
      ),
    'description' => st('Enter the language in which you would like to see '
      . 'weather information presented.'),
    'default_value' => array(
      array(
        'value' => 'en',
        ),
```

```
        ),
    );
field_create_field($field);
field_create_instance($instance);

// *
// * Weather units field
// *

$field = array(
    'field_name' => 'field_weather_unit',
    'type' => 'list_text',
    'translatable' => TRUE,
    'settings' => array(
        'allowed_values' => "F|Fahrenheit\nC|Celsius\nK|Kelvin\nR|Rankine",
        'allowed_values_function' => '',
    ),
);
$instance = array(
    'field_name' => 'field_weather_unit',
    'entity_type' => 'user',
    'bundle' => 'user',
    'label' => 'Weather units',
    'widget' => array(
        'type' => 'options_select',
        'weight' => '17',
    ),
    'description' => st('Enter the measurement unit with which you would like '
        . 'to see weather information presented.'),
    'default_value' => array(
        array(
            'value' => 'F',
        ),
    ),
);

field_create_field($field);
field_create_instance($instance);
```

Notice the allowed_values property for the language and unit fields. Since these are list_text field types, the allowed_values field provides a list that will appear in a drop-down select widget or a radio button list. The newline characters (\n) denote the individual values, and the vertical bar (|) separates the value that will be placed in the database from the text that will be shown to the user.

The Enable Hook

The enable hook is shown in Listing 10–7.

Listing 10–7. *The Enable Hook Sets Up System Variables*

```
function weather_info_enable() {
    variable_set('default_location', 'Manchester, NH');
    variable_set('default_units', 'F');
    variable_set('default_language', 'en');
```

```
  variable_set('current_location', variable_get('default_location'));
  drupal_set_message(st('Weather information default variables have been set.'));
}
```

The only task of the enable hook, in our case, is to set up the four system variables the module depends on. Recall that this hook is called after the install hook, so if there are any tasks you need to do that depend on tables that were created or modified, it's safe to do them in this hook.

That wraps up the tasks necessary for setting up our installer to be ready for our weather information module. Here are some other common tasks you might want to take care of in your install hook:

- **Create custom content types.** The schema hook creates tables that your module alone will manage, but if you need to create a content type that is managed by Drupal's node framework, you can do this using the node_type_save() function.

- **Set the values of persistent system variables.** Drupal's variable table holds values that are available to all users. Your module will probably need to set some of these for access later.

- **Populate your tables with sample data or required parameters.** Your module might contain a few records of reference data or a few thousand. The install hook is where you can populate those tables.

- **Create records in tables maintained by other modules.** This might be necessary if your module has dependencies on other modules and you need to tell the other modules about your newly installed module. You can also modify the system table, giving your module more weight than others, for example. Be careful with this, though, as you might step on other modules' wishes.

- **Create directory structures for storage of temporary or legacy files.** For example, the image module creates a directory structure for temporary storage of thumbnail images and other graphics. You might also need to create such structures and set the permissions appropriately.

- **Establish a connection to an enterprise database source for populating managed tables.** You might need to access information from back-end systems using web services or direct database connections.

- **Grant permissions to certain roles.** The roles are created in your module, but you might want to add permissions to the standard roles, DRUPAL_ANONYMOUS_RID and DRUPAL_AUTHENTICATED_RID.

Of course, there are myriad other things you might want to do to set the system up for your module.

Module Changes

Now that we've created the weather information history table, we'll want to add some functionality to our module that takes advantage of the new table. To start, we will insert a record every time a user changes his profile information in his user profile. The function to insert the record is shown in Listing 10–8.

Listing 10–8. *Inserting a Record into the History Table*

```
function weather_info_insert_history($location, $language, $unit, $weather) {
  global $user;
    $fields = array(
```

```
      'location' => $location,
      'language' => substr($language, 0, 2),
      'units' => substr($unit, 0, 1),
      'uid' => $user->uid,
      'timestamp' => REQUEST_TIME,
      );
  $options = array('return' => Database::RETURN_STATEMENT);
  $returned = db_insert('weather_info', $options)
    ->fields($fields)
    ->execute();
}
```

We will call this function from the validate function of the form where the user enters information on the profile page. The code is shown in Listing 10–9.

Listing 10–9. *Calling the Insert History Function*

```
function weather_info_profile_weather_location_validate($element, &$form_state) {
  $location = $form_state['values']['field_weather_location']['und'][0]['value'];
  $language = $form_state['values']['field_weather_language']['und'][0]['value'];
  $unit = $form_state['values']['field_weather_unit']['und'][0]['value'];
  if (variable_get('default_location') != $location) {
    $weather = weather_info_get_weather($location, 'en');
    if ($weather) {
      weather_info_insert_history($location, $language, $unit, $weather);
    }
    else {
      form_set_error('field_weather_location[und][0][value]', t('Cannot get weather for
%location.',
        array('%location' => $location)));
    }
  }
}
```

This stores the appropriate information into the history table whenever the user makes a change.

The Disable and Uninstall Hooks

The disable and uninstall hooks are used to back out of certain environmental changes you made with the enable and install hooks. They can also be used (particularly the uninstall hook) to remove any information generated in the normal use of your module.

The reason for this two-part process is simple. A user might enable and disable a module several times for any number of reasons. If your module creates and maintains its own database tables or file structures, the user might have entered information that goes in these areas.

Another example is that you, as a developer, might want to try out some new things with a module without harming existing data. Or you might want to just temporarily disable a module during a quick test.

If you were to drop the tables and wipe the directories every time the user disabled your module, the data would be gone the next time it was enabled.

The Disable Hook

The disable hook is executed when a module is unchecked on the Modules page and the page is submitted, as shown in Figure 10–4.

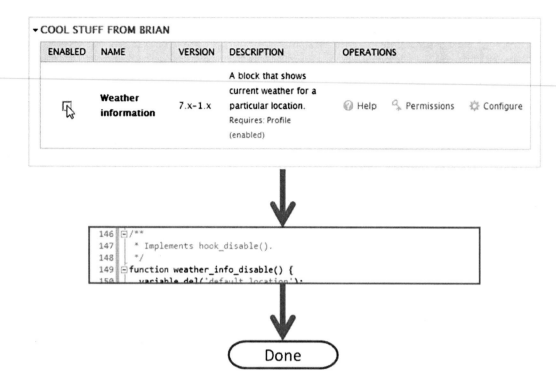

Figure 10–4. *The disable hook*

The disable hook, then, should be used only to put the system in a state where other functions are not affected by its presence. Listing 10–10 shows the weather information disable hook.

Listing 10–10. *Disable Hook Function*

```
function weather_info_disable() {
  variable_del('default_location');
  variable_del('default_units');
  variable_del('default_language');
  variable_del('current_location');
}
```

This function merely deletes the system variables from the variables table. This is probably not necessary because it's unlikely that any other module will be using them, but it is good manners to clean up after yourself. Remember that the disable hook is optional. If you don't include it, your module will still be removed from the list of enabled modules, and its functionality will be unavailable.

The Uninstall Hook

The uninstall hook is executed when the module is checked on the uninstall page and the page is submitted, as shown in Figure 10–5.

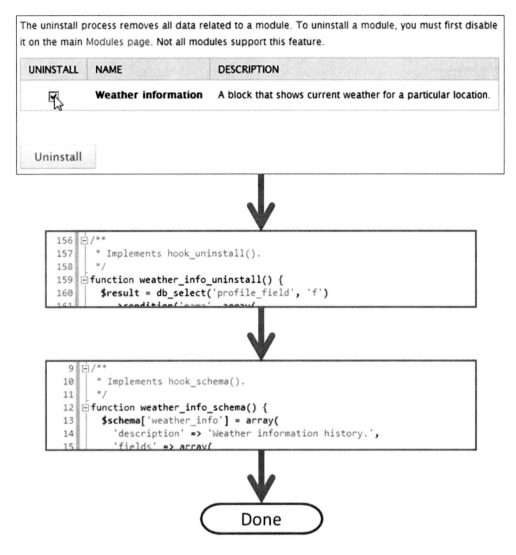

Figure 10–5. The Uninstall Hook

The uninstall hook is where you really clean up all traces of your module—any directories you've created on the site-managed store, or any configuration changes made to the system table, or any number of things you may have done to prepare the system for your module. Listing 10–11 shows the weather information uninstall hook.

Listing 10–11. The Uninstall Hook

```
function weather_info_uninstall() {
  field_delete_field('field_weather_location');
  field_delete_field('field_weather_language');
```

```
field_delete_field('field_weather_unit');

// Flush the cache to get rid of the user profile page entry
drupal_flush_all_caches();
}
```

During the install phase, we created three attached fields that entered information into the database tables that the Field module managed. When we uninstall the module, our uninstall hook function needs to delete all traces of our activities. This is done by deleting the fields, which removes all of the information from the system.

■ **Note** If you have created tables using the schema hook, you need not remove those tables as the uninstall engine will take care of it for you.

There's one last task to perform before we deliver our module. We need to add the .install file to our .info file so Drupal knows about it. Listing 10–12 shows the new .info file.

Listing 10–12. A .info File Showing the .install File as Part of the Package

```
; $Id$
name = Weather information
description = A block that shows current weather for a particular location.
package = Cool stuff from Brian
core = 7.x
files[] = weather_info.module
files[] = weather_info.inc
files[] = weather_info.install
files[] = tests/weather_info.test
dependencies[] = blocks
configure = /admin/config/weather_info/settings
version = 7.x-1.x
```

That covers the installing and uninstalling of modules. Now, what happens if you need to make changes to existing modules and you don't want to require your users to rebuild everything? You can give them the tools to perform an update.

The Update Hook

As development of your module proceeds, you will certainly want to make improvements to it. Drupal has an update manager that periodically checks the Drupal community site, drupal.org, for updates released for all modules loaded on a particular system. If your module is hosted at drupal.org and you release a new version, the update manager on all systems where your module is enabled will inform the administrator that a new version is ready.

This is why you need to think about how the functionality of your module has changed and make it easy for the administrator to update the system.

If you add or remove functionality to your module that affects only the module, then all you need to do is put the new module file in your project directory. It will be distributed to the community and everyone will send you love, respect, and PayPal contributions.

On the other hand, if you add functionality that affects another part of the system, you'll want to include an update hook so the installer engine will know what to do with your new code.

You might need to update the system if you add functionality that captures more information with new database fields. Or you might need to fix a database table that was incorrectly specified in the first place. There could be new directories required to store certain information, or some role permissions might need to be changed. The update hook is where to perform these tasks.

Drupal's update engine is quite ingenious. Not only does it have to understand which update is currently installed, it needs to be able to graciously apply new updates without affecting existing updates or the base installation of the module. It does this by reading through the .install file looking for updates that it needs to apply. Drupal keeps track of each module that has been installed and what the current update version is. When an update for a currently installed module comes along, the Drupal installer will look in the .install file for update hooks with a carefully crafted name indicating the updated version of the module.

■ **Warning:** Note that you must never use the same update number twice. Once you publically issue code with update 7103, for example, then the next update—even if you removed update 7103 as faulty, buggy code—must be 7104. Otherwise, none of your users with the old 7103 installed will see it as a new update to run.

Creating an Update

The project for this book, the weather information block, saves location, language, and unit information in the database table we created with the .install script. As a new revision, I'd like to also save the XML stream that's returned whenever a user selects a new location. Plus, I'd like to make the name of the database table more descriptive.

Changing the name of a table in the database will break all kinds of things that depend on it. In our case, we have encapsulated the access to that table in a single function, so we don't need to make many changes. Listing 10–13 shows the modified function to write to the table and insert the new information.

Listing 10–13. New Function for Writing to the Database

```
function weather_info_insert_history($location, $language, $unit, $weather) {
  global $user;
  $fields = array(
    'location' => $location,
    'language' => substr($language, 0, 2),
    'units' => substr($unit, 0, 1),
    'uid' => $user->uid,
    'timestamp' => REQUEST_TIME,
    'xml' => $weather->asXML(),
  );
  db_insert('weather_info_history')
    ->fields($fields)
    ->execute();
}
```

Notice the asXML() method on the weather object. This is a way to serialize the XML weather object so it can be stored as a text field. We have also changed the name of the table on the db_insert() function to reflect our new table name.

This code works on our system, because we have manually changed the name of the table in our database and added the field. But we don't want our users to have to go through that effort. Plus, we want to take all of the existing data and populate the new field with the XML for the previously stored locations.

Listing 10–14 shows the update function that will do all of that.

Listing 10–14. An Update Hook

```
/**
 * Rename {weather_info} table to {weather_info_history} and add a field to capture
 * raw XML data from the weather service.
 */
function weather_info_update_7100() {
  ... update logic goes here.
}
```

First, notice the Doxygen-style comment before the function declaration. We'll see that a bit later when the module is updated.

Next, see the carefully crafted function name, weather_info_update_7100(). This is a hook that will be found and executed by the update program. It is the name of our module, followed by _update_, followed by a number that indicates information about the particular update. That number is created according to the following rules:

- 1 digit for Drupal core compatibility

- 1 digit for your module's major release version (e.g., is this the 7.x-1.* (1) or 7.x-2.* (2) series of your module?)

- 2 digits for sequential counting starting with 00

▨ **Note** The second digit should be 0 for the initial porting of your module to a new Drupal core API.

The following are examples of update hook names:

- weather_info_update_7100(): This is the first update to get the database ready to run weather_info version 7.x-1.*.

- weather_info_update_7000(): Assuming I had a version of the module running under Drupal 6, this is a required update to bring it up to compatibility with Drupal core API 7.x.

- weather_info_update_7200(): This is the first update to get the database ready to run weather_info version 7.x-2.*.

- weather_info_update_7201(): This is the second update to get the database ready to run weather_info version 7.x-2.*.

Listing 10–15 shows the complete function that will be updating our module.

Listing 10–15. A Complete Update Function

```
/**
 * Rename {weather_info} table to {weather_info_history} and add a field to capture
 * raw XML data from the weather service.
 */
function weather_info_update_7100() {
  db_rename_table('weather_info', 'weather_info_history');
  db_add_field('weather_info_history', 'xml',
    array(
      'type' => 'text',
      'size' => 'normal',
      'description' => 'Raw weather XML returned.',
    )
  );

  // update all existing records
  $result = db_select('weather_info_history', 'h')
    ->fields('h', array('hid', 'location', 'language'))
    ->execute();
  foreach ($result as $record) {
    $weather = weather_info_get_weather($record->location, $record->language);
    if ($weather) {
      db_update('weather_info_history')
        ->fields(array(
            'xml' => $weather->asXML())
          )
        ->condition('hid', $record->hid, '=')
        ->execute();
    }
  }
}
```

The first two functions rename the table and add a new field. Then, the rest of the code reads the existing records and updates each record with the XML generated by a call to the weather service.

Updating Your System

Now that the .install file is ready, let's deliver our package to the users. We just need to modify the .info file first. Since we have a new version of our program, we should update the version number. In this case, the new version number will be 7.x-1.0. Our new .info file is shown in Listing 10–16.

Listing 10–16. A .info File That Updates the Version Number

```
; $Id$
name = Weather information
description = A block that shows current weather for a particular location.
package = Cool stuff from Brian
core = 7.x
files[] = weather_info.module
files[] = weather_info.inc
files[] = weather_info.install
files[] = tests/weather_info.test
dependencies[] = profile
```

```
configure = /admin/config/weather_info/settings
version = 7.x-1.0
```

After we place the new module files in our directory and go to the Configuration page, we'll see the error shown in Figure 10–6.

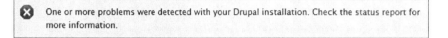

Figure 10–6. The update manager detected a new version.

The error message is displayed by the update manager, which noticed that there is at least one new version of an installed module. Clicking on "status report" provides more information, as shown in Figure 10–7.

❌	Database updates	Out of date

Some modules have database schema updates to install. You should run the database update script immediately.

Figure 10–7. The update manager has detected new updates.

Clicking on "database update script" launches the update program, which starts the wizard shown in Figure 10–8.

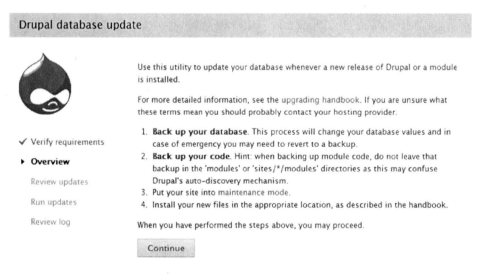

Figure 10–8. The database update wizard

Clicking "Continue" shows all of the updates that are available. (See Figure 10–9.)

Figure 10–9. *Information on a pending update*

You'll notice that the information in our `.install` file is shown here. You can see the information contained in the comment that was entered just before the update function definition. Also, you can see the number of the update, 7100. Clicking "Apply pending updates" causes the updater to run all of the update functions available (in this case, just one). The throbber displays while the process is executing. (See Figure 10–10.)

Figure 10–10. *The module update screen indicates updates in progress.*

Finally, the update happy screen is shown in Figure 10–11.

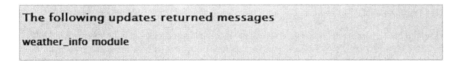

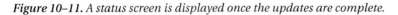

Figure 10–11. *A status screen is displayed once the updates are complete.*

303

There are some important things to keep in mind about the `.install` file and updates:

- When you update your module's schema, the changes should be reflected in the schema hook. Even though your update functions will make changes to the schema, if you have new users who come in after you've made a couple of updates, the functions will load the most current schema and then apply updates from that point.

- Keep all of your updates in your `.install` file. You may have some users who have used your module from the beginning and have applied the updates as they came along. However, other users might have installed your module after you have made a couple of updates and they'll need to start from that point. Also, some users might be a couple updates behind and need to execute them in order.

- Never renumber your update functions. The number at the end of your update function is an incremental value. The highest applied update for your module is stored in the database. If you renumber an update after it has been applied, bad things could happen. Just stick to the numbering conventions and you shouldn't have any problems.

■ **Warning:** Your install code must be current with your module code and vice versa. In this example, we changed the module to update the table name and add a field. If a user installed that new module and tried to run it before running the update script, the module would fail. It is up to the user to run the update script whenever a new module is loaded, and it is up to the programmer to make sure everything is in sync.

- Test, test, test. It is even more important that the update function work flawlessly than the initial installation. Having an update means your users are using your module, and they probably have data that depends on it. If your update program fails, it renders the module useless. Worse, it could orphan your users' data.

Now that you have your module described and instructions for installation, let's talk about the process of delivering your module to your users.

Delivering your Module

By creating the `.info` and `.install` modules, you have described your module to the Drupal core in enough detail for it to do the installation. But there is still more you need to do to help your user understand the module and how to use it.

The Drupal site, drupal.org, provides a service that hosts your module for anyone to access. You've already used this site if you've installed any contributed modules. The site includes a search function that lets users look for modules that contain the features they want, and it gives them a way to download the most recent versions.

The site is available to users and developers for free, but if you want your module listed on the site, you must agree to the site's guidelines, which basically means you must be involved in the maintenance of the module and allow others to join your project to make it better. Just uploading code and forgetting about it will not be tolerated by the community.

> ▦ **Note** Even if you don't want your module hosted on `drupal.org`, you should use these guidelines to help you maintain your module. For a list of compelling reasons why you should list your module on `drupal.org`, see `http://drupal.org/node/648898`.

Getting involved in the Drupal community can take several forms. The book page for the site that explains the different ways to be involved starts at `http://drupal.org/node/281873`.

But regardless of whether you decide to maintain your module on the community site, you should develop certain files while the information is still fresh in your mind.

Documentation

Good documentation is vital for your module to be accepted widely. It will also help your users work with the module's functionality and get the most out of it. This, in turn, improves the chance that your module will be referred, picking up new users. And community recognition is most likely why you are spending all of your valuable time creating something to give a way for free, isn't it?

Here are some guidelines to use when coding modules that will be available in the Drupal contributions repository. These guidelines are a good place to start even if your module will only be used by you or your company.

- **Have a useful README file:** All but the most trivial modules should have a README.txt file in the project directory. This should provide a basic overview of the module and how a potential user might benefit from installing it. The README.txt file from the Services module is about as brief as you'd want to go:

  ```
  // $Id:$

  Goals
  ===============
  - Provide weather information for a geographical location on Earth.
  - Provide a block that can be placed in any region.
  - Allow users to define their own location, language, and display
    units that will be displayed when they log on.

  This module uses the profile module and creates new profile fields
  so each user can specify his or her own location for weather.

  Documentation
  ==============
  http://drupalforwidows.com/docs/weather_info
  ```

- **Use** `hook_help()`**:** All but the most trivial modules should implement the help hook to provide information about the module to the administrator and/or users of your module. The embedded documentation style guide (`http://drupal.org/node/24566`) is a resource for creating effective documentation for your module. At the very least, you should create a help hook that simply displays the README file using a function like:

  ```
  /**
   * Implements hook_help().
   */
  ```

```
function weather_info_help($section) {
  switch ($section) {
    case 'admin/help#weather_info':
      // Return a line-break version of the module README
        return _filter_autop(
          file_get_contents( dirname(__FILE__) . "/README.txt"));
  }
}
```

- **Tell the user what the module does:** The README and help files should give the user an idea of what the module does, what the menu paths are for administration, what file directories created or accessed, and what might impact other modules or the Drupal core. In short, the information should help the user get the most out of your module and let him know what to expect from its interaction with others.

- **Don't name your package unless it is justified:** Remember the package parameter in the .info file? Most modules should not create their own packages as this tends to clutter up the module administration page. Chances are your package does something similar to what other modules are doing and should therefore be placed in a well-known package name. If it is a unique, stand-alone module, just leave the package name out and it will be listed under "Other" on the module administration page.

- **Document your functions properly:** The Drupal community has embraced the Doxygen documentation conventions as a standard way to generate documentation from inline comments. Using Doxygen-style comments allows various scripts to roll up your comments into a standardized form that others in the community are comfortable with. For more information on Doxygen formatting conventions, see http://drupal.org/node/1354.

- **Write and deliver tests:** I can't overemphasize the importance of developing test suites for your module. Chapter 8 goes into depth on creating test suites and executing them against your module and your site.

- **Consider an installation profile:** If you have several modules to install, or if your module requires other modules that might not be installed on potential user sites, you can create a supercharged profile that performs a batch installation of a set of modules and even of the Drupal core itself. You can create an installation profile that contains the core (for systems that don't yet have Drupal installed), or a profile that includes only the modules that makes your profile unique. For more information on creating installation profiles, see http://drupal.org/node/159730.

These should be considered a minimum set of requirements for developing your modules. They will help other users understand your code. Remember, that other user could be you in three years when you have to fix the code!

Summary

Installing and deploying a Drupal module is as critical a task as installing any other program. You need to create an environment that is favorable for your application, and then you need to provide the means to uninstall gracefully and be a good neighbor should your user not want to use your module any more.

APPENDIX A

■■■

Windows Development Environment

For those developers who spend most of their coding time with Microsoft development tools, the world of *nix is probably a scary place. Drupal is written for the so-called LAMP stack, "Linux/Apache/MySQL/ PHP." While it is possible to substitute Windows for Linux, it is a bit more difficult to substitute IIS for Apache, and even harder to substitute SQL Server for MySQL. And don't even think about replacing PHP with C# or Visual Basic. This appendix provides a step-by-step tutorial for setting up a debugging environment on your Windows workstation. My goal was to duplicate the development environment of Visual Studio, and this set-up gets about as close as you can.

Old habits die hard, and if you're like me you've got some.

I've been using a Windows-based computer since Windows was first available as an application that ran under DOS. As with most technologies, Windows and I have a love-hate relationship, but for some reason I keep coming back.

Visual Studio is the perfect development environment. My development editor of choice was once VEdit, an emacs-style editor. I reluctantly switched to Visual Studio to do Visual Basic 6 programming, and learned to love IntelliSense. With Visual Studio 2010 and the .NET reflection-based IntelliSense, I can't imagine coding without it.

After the Windows Vista debacle, I seriously considered switching to Ubuntu or Macintosh. If Microsoft couldn't get its core operating system right, how long would it be until everything else suffered?

Windows 7 changed my mind. From what I see, it is as slick as Macintosh OSX and more secure.[1] It is much better supported than Ubuntu, a Linux distribution that is growing in popularity. Windows 7 runs all of the software I already have, on hardware I already own.

WAMP Stack

Back to Drupal. The LAMP stack (Linux, Apache, MySql, and PHP/Perl) prefers Linux, and most developers have their development environment on some Linux GUI such as Ubuntu. I started there, but found I was missing some things I had become accustomed to in Windows.

Fortunately, I'm not alone; others before me have gotten their Apache/MySQL/PHP stack working on Windows. They call this "WAMP" and it works quite well. I've worked with two different WAMP stacks, XAMPP and WampServer. Both use the same core packages (Apache, MySQL and PHP), but have different control panels. I prefer WampServer simply because it's easy to switch between PHP versions 5.2 and 5.3.

---

[1] http://lifehacker.com/5518787/famous-hacker-calls-windows-more-secure-than-mac

As far as a development environment goes, Microsoft doesn't support PHP out of the box. There has been some talk over the years, and I've even seen some snippet libraries and at least one attempt at making PHP a .NET-compatible language.

Development Environments

I'm not so interested in using PHP as a .NET language because the most likely eventual target for my PHP code will be a Unix-compatible server. All I want is an integrated development environment (IDE) that lets me work quickly and debug, and provides a platform for documentation.

I've explored several different tools, all of which are available on the Windows platform:

- **Eclipse:** Eclipse is an open-source development environment designed for developing in almost any language you can imagine. It is written in Java and was initially designed to attract Java developers. There are hundreds of add-ons available, and that's where I got stuck. Simply configuring an Eclipse environment required such a learning commitment that a lot of the time I had budgeted for learning Drupal was spent just figuring out the differences between all of the competing add-ons, and then getting them to work together.

- **NetBeans:** NetBeans is similar to Eclipse in that it is an open-source solution and its adherents are strong supporters of the platform. Unfortunately, I found the same learning-curve problems with NetBeans as with Eclipse.

- **Komodo IDE:** Komodo is a commercial product made by ActiveState. ActiveState provides support to get you up and running, so you don't have to go through the learning issues to choose which peg fits into which hole. However, Komodo IDE is not free. At the time of this writing, the tool is US$295. That's a pretty cheap price if you consider the time you'd have spent figuring out how to use a "free" tool. Another advantage of Komodo is that it runs on all popular platforms. You need just one license to run its code on Windows, Linux, and Macintosh, and the user experience is similar in all cases.

- **VS.Php:** In doing my investigations, I stumbled onto this add-in for Visual Studio, and it became my preferred environment, by far. It is a commercial product, published by a small company called JCX Software. VS.Php takes advantage of all of Visual Studio's features and provides step debugging, IntelliSense, team collaboration capabilities, and more. At the time of this writing, the software is US$99, but it requires Visual Studio. Fortunately, it can be used with Microsoft's free Visual Studio Shell.

The trick is to get all of these pieces to work together, on your preferred platform, with a development environment that allows you to debug and walk through the code.

In this appendix, I'll cover the prerequisites for getting Drupal running on your Windows development box. I've been using Windows 7, so the screen shots and tools will be for that platform. Adjust for your system.

There are four parts to the LAMP stack, and we will be twiddling with the first three. First, we will replace Linux with Windows and get a system up and running with Apache web server, MySQL database, and PHP. As I mentioned before, this configuration is called WAMP and it is the most stable.

After that, we'll install the same Drupal code, but we'll replace Apache with IIS and MySQL with SQL Server.

WampServer

Many tools are needed to create the WAMP stack on Windows. Fortunately, someone has already put everything together. There are a number of WAMP server collections, all with the same open source pieces: Apache HTTP Server, PHP, MySQL, and phpMyAdmin, a MySQL database administration package. Some packages also have other tools we won't be using here.

The two most popular are XAMPP and the aptly named WampServer. Choosing one is a matter of taste. I like the WampServer collection because it seems to be the easiest to add in different versions of PHP, but you can use whichever feels comfortable to you.

First, you'll want to get the WAMP stack installed and running, a pretty straightforward task. You can get WampServer from `http://wampserver.com`. Download and install it; it's pretty easy.

■ **Tip** If you have Skype, you'll want to turn it off. Users have reported problems installing WampServer with Skype running, possibly because Skype uses port 80 (HTTP) as an alternative for incoming connections. If you want to use WAMP and Skype together, go into the Tools…Options…Advanced Connection panel in Skype and deselect the option, "Use 80 and 443 as alternatives for incoming connections."

Installing WampServer is pretty straightforward. I installed the server on the root of the C: drive, just to make things easier, as shown in Figure A–1.

Figure A–1. Default location for WampServer

I'll be using this directory for all the pieces. When you're done, you'll get the happy screen indicating success (see Figure A–2).

Figure A–2. *WampServer set up complete*

Start the server and make sure it starts. If everything is successful, the WampServer icon will show up in your task tray (Figure A–3).

Figure A–3. *The WampServer icon*

Make sure the WampServer meter is green. If it is some other color, something is wrong.

The most common cause of this problem is that Apache didn't start. The most common reason for Apache not starting is that you have something else controlling port 80. The most common application that controls port 80 is Microsoft Internet Information Server (IIS).

If you encounter this problem, you can check to see who is sitting on port 80 by asking WampServer. Click on the icon to display the WampServer control panel, as shown in Figure A–4.

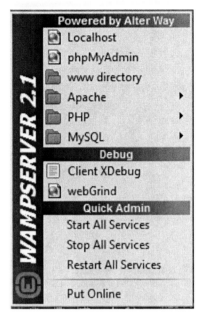

Figure A–4. The WampServer control panel

On the Apache submenu, you'll find a selection to "Test Port 80." (See Figure A–5.)

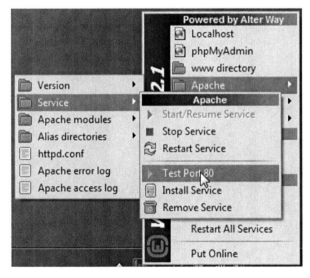

Figure A–5. Testing the HTTP port

This brings up a command window so you can see what is using that port, as shown in Figure A–6.

```
c:\wamp\bin\php\php5.3.0\php.exe
Your port 80 is actually used by :

Server: Microsoft-IIS/6.0


Press Enter to exit...
```

Figure A–6. IIS is using port 80.

If you want to fix this, just to go Computer Management and turn off the default web site—that is, if you have a generic site. Your mileage may vary. To turn off IIS, go to Computer Management. I usually get there by typing "iis" in the "Search programs and files" area of the Start menu. This brings up the IIS control panel. On Windows 7 it looks like the screen shown in Figure A–7.

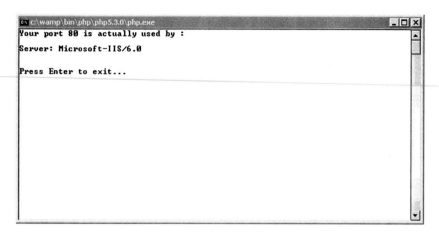

Figure A–7. IIS in Windows 7

Here we can see that, indeed, IIS is using port 80. Clicking "Stop" should release that port so Apache can use it. It is possible to run Apache on a different port, but I don't recommend it, especially while you are learning a new environment.

Having gone through all of that, you'll see that VS.Php has its own version of Apache built in and will use a random port, much like Visual Studio does when debugging ASP.NET. But I like to have Apache controlling port 80 as well, since I sometimes access my site when Visual Studio is not debugging.

Visual Studio and VS.Php

Once you have your WAMP stack running, you'll want to load Visual Studio and the VS.Php add-on, if that's the development environment you have chosen.

I use Visual Studio 2010, but VS.Php supports older versions of Visual Studio as well. Plus, there is a distribution of VS.Php that includes the free Visual Studio Shell in case you don't have a full license for Visual Studio.

Once you've installed a compatible version of Visual Studio, get the VS.Php bits from http://www.jcxsoftware.com/VS.Php and run the installer. It's probably safe to stay with the defaults for now. You should end up with the happy screen shown in Figure A–8.

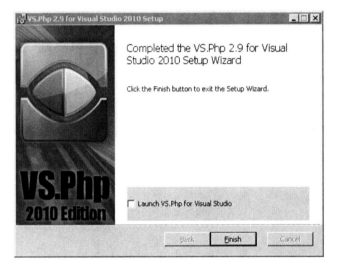

Figure A–8. VS.Php happy screen

Now you can start VS.Php. This will start Visual Studio and VS.Php will then add itself to the development environment. You'll probably get the nag screen (Figure A–9) prompting for a license. You can activate it now if you have it, or just continue.

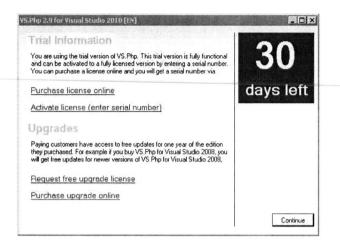

Figure A–9. The VS.Php trial version nag screen

Since you have a new language, you'll want to tell Visual Studio how to handle the source code. The settings below are compatible with Drupal's code formatting conventions. In Visual Studio, go to Tools►Options, and then expand to Text Editor►PHP►Tabs. (See Figure A–10.)

Figure A–10. Make sure tabs are consistent with Drupal tab rules.

Drupal's code formatting conventions require two spaces for indents, and that spaces should be used instead of the tab character. Now let's tell Visual Studio that it should know about some additional file extensions for PHP code files, as shown in Figure A–11.

Figure A–11. Adding file name extensions

Add the `.info` and `.module` extensions and press OK.

MySQL comes packaged with WampServer, which also includes a tool that lets you manage your database server. You can create and delete databases, create and query tables, and manage users and permissions. This tool is called phpMyAdmin and is available from the WampServer console (see Figure A–12). I cover phpMyAdmin in detail in Chapter 4.

Figure A–12. Accessing phpMyAdmin

Clicking phpMyAdmin launches the default browser and presents your MySQL database, as shown in Figure A–13.

Figure A–13. The phpMyAdmin screen

If you'd rather use Visual Studio to manage your database server, you can install the MySQL Connector for .NET, which is available for free at http://dev.mysql.com/downloads/connector/net. The Connector will install itself into Visual Studio and give you the same kind of functionality you're accustomed to with the Visual Studio Server Explorer. See Figure A–14.

Figure A–14. MySQL Connector for Visual Studio

At this point, you are ready to download the Drupal code and start developing. See Chapter 4 to get started. However, if you'd rather install IIS and SQL Server to replace Apache and MySQL, we'll do that in the next section.

IIS and SQL Server

Version 7 is the first release of Drupal that abstracts the data layer to make it easier to plug in databases other than MySQL. The database layer is based on PHP Data Objects (PDO), which allows the decoupling of database engines from the PHP core. This decoupling means a database engine vendor can write a thin layer to translate generic database calls into its engine's protocol.

The leaders of the Drupal 7 development effort have been adamant that all core modules be written to work through this data abstraction layer. Because of this commitment, a project was commenced to write the drivers for Microsoft SQL Server, which takes the form of a PHP extension, php_pdo_sqlsrv.dll. We'll be enabling that, plus some other things written specifically to get SQL Server running.

To learn more about how to program against the database abstraction layer, see Chapter 9.

While PHP has been extended to be friendlier in a Microsoft environment, Microsoft's Internet Information Server (IIS) has been extended to be a little friendlier with the open source world. With the advent of FastCGI and Windows Cache Extension for PHP (WinCache), IIS now plays nicely with PHP. So let's put it all together and see if we can get Drupal running on a WISP (Windows/IIS/SQL Server/PHP) stack.

You can get the bits you need at http://www.microsoft.com/web/drupal. Click the tab on the left that says "Install Drupal 7 with SQL Server" to see the screen shown in Figure A–15.

Figure A–15. Get the bits from Microsoft

■ **Caveat:** Drupal 7 is brand new, and the SQL Server driver is even newer and has had fewer eyes looking at the code. As with any new technology, things change quickly. The instructions below worked as of the alpha1 version of the package released by Microsoft. By the time you read this, things may have changed, so please be flexible. In fact, as this book goes to press, I just learned that Microsoft is about to release a new tool, called "WebMatrix", which makes this process much more streamlined. Before reading the rest of this section, you should go to http://microsoft.com/web/drupal to see what they've done. Such is the reality of publishing books in a web-based world!

Click the "Install" button, shown in Figure A–16.

Prepare your clean Windows installation: Start with a clean Windows Vista or Windows 7 image. Install IIS SQL Server 2008 Express, PHP and SQL Server Driver 2.0 with PDO using the Web Platform Installer

Figure A–16. Invoking the web installer

This presents a User Account Control (UAC) warning. Click "Yes" to continue. You'll see the Microsoft Web Platform Installer as shown in Figure A–17.

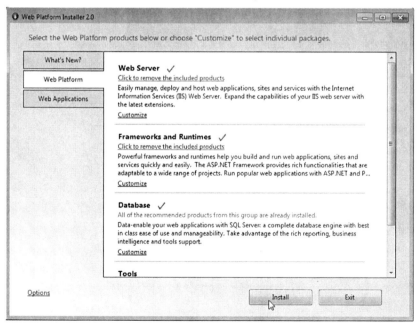

Figure A–17. The Web Platform installer

You'll want to click around this installer and make sure it is set to install the following pieces:

- Web Server
    - CGI
    - Static Content
    - Default Document
    - Directory Browsing
    - HTTP Errors
    - URL Rewrite 2.0
    - Web Deployment Tool 1.1
    - HTTP Logging
    - Logging Tools
    - Request Monitor
    - Advanced Logging
    - IIS Management Console
    - Static Content Compression
    - Request Filtering
- Frameworks and Runtimes
    - .NET Framework 3.5 SP1
    - Microsoft .NET Framework 4
    - Windows Cache Extension 1.1 for PHP 5.2
    - PHP Manager for IIS
    - PHP 5.2.14
- Database
    - Microsoft SQL Server Driver for PHP 2.0
    - SQL Server Express 2008 R2

Click Install and then review the screen shown in Figure A–18.

Figure A–18. *The Web Platform confirmation screen*

Accept the license terms and watch everything load. You should get the happy screen shown in Figure A–19.

Web Platform Installation

✓ **Congratulations! You have successfully installed the following products:**

Static Content
Default Document
Directory Browsing
HTTP Errors
HTTP Logging
Logging Tools
Request Monitor
Request Filtering
IIS Management Console
CGI
Static Content Compression
ISAPI Extensions
ISAPI Filters
Tracing
.NET Extensibility

Finish

Figure A–19. Web Platform Installation happy screen

That's it for the prerequisites. Now let's load the Drupal core bits. Back on the Microsoft Drupal site, click the Download button as shown on Figure A–20 to get the Drupal code.

Custom Drupal 7 package that contains:

• Drupal 7
• SQL Server Drupal Module
• Views Module

Read me file for instructions

Download

Figure A–20. Drupal package for SQL Server

■ **Note** At the time of this writing, the Drupal package customized for SQL Server is still in its alpha stage. I expect that by the time you read this, the released version will be available.

Unzip the contents of the package to your desktop or somewhere convenient. There's no need to put it in the inetpub directory structure, as there is a script that will do that for you. In fact, it should be anywhere except the inetpub directory. In the directory you choose, as shown in Figure A–21, you'll see the executable, DeployDrupalOnSqlServer.exe. Click it to start the process.

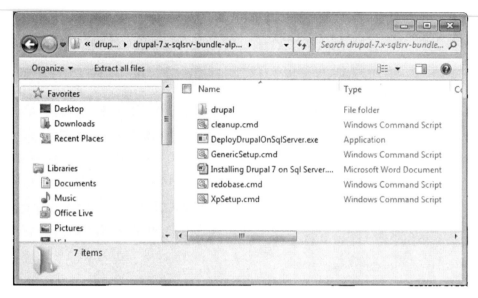

Figure A–21. *Drupal distribution for IIS and SQL Server*

The script calls GenericSetup.cmd, which will create a database on your SQLEXPRESS installation, add some service account rights, and then copy the Drupal modules to the IIS folder hierarchy.

The next step is to load our code into VS.Php and get it running. From Visual Studio, select File➤New➤Php Project from Existing Code. You'll see the new project wizard, shown in Figure A–22.

Figure A–22. *VS.Php's new project wizard*

The next screen, shown in Figure A–23, lets you indicate the location of the existing code.

Figure A–23. *Project location screen*

This is the directory that IIS uses as its default, and the one that the setup script copied all of the Drupal bits to. Give the project a name that feels good to you and press Next to go to the project type screen shown in Figure A–24.

Figure A–24. VS.Php's Project type screen

Select Web project so the appropriate tools are incorporated into the development environment.

▦ **Note** Set the PHP platform to 5.2. Drupal 7 supports PHP 5.2 and 5.3, but the SQL driver has only been tested with PHP 5.2 as of this writing.

The wizard will scan the directory and ask which subdirectories to include in the solution. Since you're in the process of learning Drupal, it is probably best just to include everything for now. (See Figure A–25.) This will allow you to step-debug the entire core so you can see how things work.

Figure A–25. Include the directories you want to be part of the project.

That's the last step. Press Next and then Finish.

The project will load and you'll see the familiar Visual Studio environment. (See Figure A–26.) You are only a couple steps away from starting a debugging session!

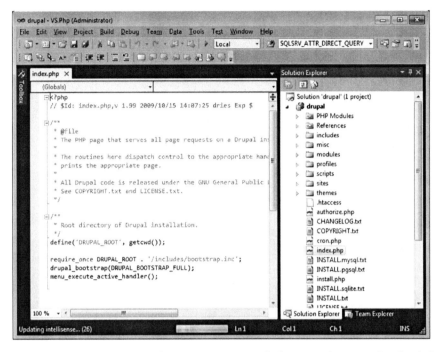

Figure A–26. The Visual Studio project screen with the Drupal PHP project loaded

By default, VS.Php is configured to use its own version of Apache web server to run the code. We need to change that so that IIS will be running it. Get to the project's property pages by selecting Project➤{your project name} Properties. (See Figure A–27.)

Figure A–27. *Project property pages*

We'll change the debugging mode to use IIS. Select "Local IIS web server" from the drop-down menu. This will start a wizard to configure IIS 7, as shown in Figure A–28.

Figure A–28. *The IIS configuration wizard*

We will need to create a new virtual directory, so check the Advanced Settings box and click Next to see the screen in Figure A–29.

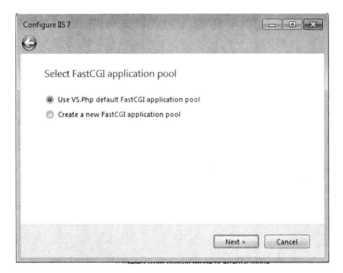

Figure A–29. *Specify the virtual directory name*

Enter the name of a new virtual directory. You might already have a virtual directory named drupal; if so, you can just create another one to distinguish it. Click Next to get to the screen shown in Figure A–30.

Figure A–30. *Application pool selection*

When the platform installer installed FastCGI, it set up an application pool. You can specify another application pool, but it's probably best to stick with the default for now.

Clicking Next displays the review screen, as shown in Figure A–31.

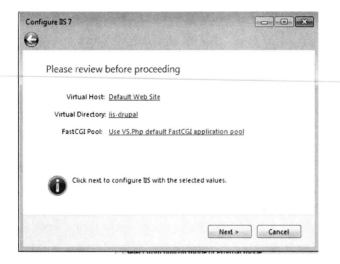

Figure A–31. IIS configuration review screen

This screen shows our choices, so we can fix any mistakes we might have made. Click Next to finish the IIS configuration and display the happy screen shown in Figure A–32.

Figure A–32. IIS configuration happy screen

Now click Finish to return to the project Property Pages, as shown in Figure A–33.

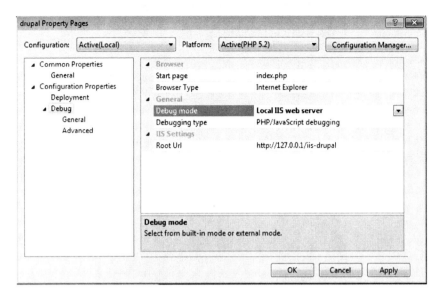

Figure A–33. Project property pages showing IIS configuration

Click OK on the property pages to get back to the development environment.

So far we've installed the Drupal core code, created the database drivers, and set up IIS to be our web server. Now we need to perform the Drupal core installation using these settings. From Visual Studio, press F5 to start debugging.

Visual Studio, working with VS.Php, will open Internet Explorer and start executing the code. You should see a browser open with the Drupal installation program, as shown in Figure A–34.

Figure A–34. Drupal installation screen

At this point, we know that IIS is running and the debugger is being invoked. Select an installation profile and press "Save and continue." This will take you to the screen shown in Figure A–35.

Choose language

English (built-in)

Learn how to install Drupal in other languages

Save and continue

✓ Choose profile

▸ **Choose language**

Verify requirements

Set up database

Install profile

Configure site

Finished

Figure A–35. Choose a language

Your copy of Drupal might have more languages than this, so select the appropriate language and press "Save and continue." The Drupal installation code will check to make sure all of the requirements are met. You might get a screen indicating a problem, as shown in Figure A–36.

Requirements problem

Web server	Microsoft-IIS/7.5
PHP	5.2.14
PHP register globals	Disabled
PHP extensions	Enabled
Database support	Enabled
PHP memory limit	128M

✓ Choose profile

✓ Choose language

▸ **Verify requirements**

Set up database

Install profile

Configure site

Finished

❌   File system

The directory *sites/default/files* does not exist. An automated attempt to create this directory failed, possibly due to a permissions problem. To proceed with the installation, either create the directory and modify its permissions manually or ensure that the installer has the permissions to create it automatically. For more information, see INSTALL.txt or the online handbook.

Figure A–36. A requirements problem

This particular one is easy to rectify by creating the directory and retrying the installation. You might see other requirements problems based on your installation. These must all be resolved before you can get any farther.

Once the requirements are verified, you'll get the database configuration screen shown in Figure A–37.

Figure A–37. Database configuration screen

But we can see a problem here—there's no way to select Microsoft SQL Server. That's because we need to install the drivers where PHP can see them, and then tell PHP where they are.

First, go back into IIS and select the virtual directory you created earlier. (See Figure A–38.)

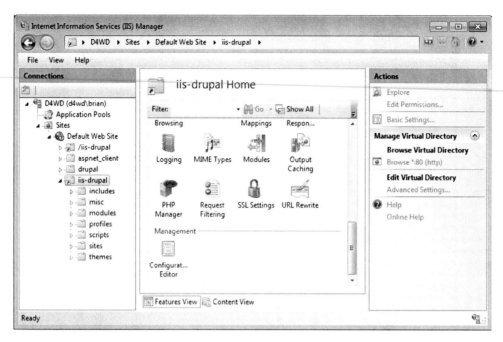

Figure A–38. *Managing the PHP installation*

Double-click on PHP Manager, which will open in the window as shown in Figure A–39.

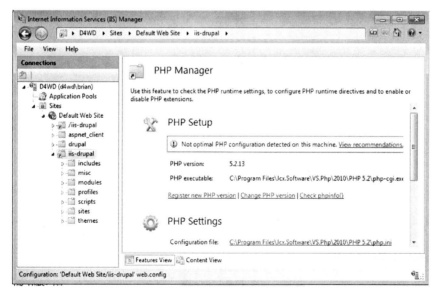

Figure A–39. *PHP Manager in IIS*

Right away, we can see that some settings are not optimal. Clicking on "View recommendations" brings up a window showing the problems and the recommended solutions. (See Figure A–40.)

Figure A–40. Configuration recommendations for PHP

Take all of the recommendations, and click OK. Next, we want to change the PHP version to use the one that the web installer installed. Back on the screen shown in A–39, click "Change PHP version" to get the screen shown in Figure A–41.

Figure A–41. Changing the PHP version

Select the PHP version that's in the PHP directory under Program Files and click OK.

Now we need to add a couple of extensions so PHP knows about our database drivers for SQL Server. Under PHP Extensions, click "Add an extension." (See Figure A–42.)

PHP Extensions

There are 20 extensions enabled.

There are 20 extensions installed.

Enable or disable an extension | Add an extension

Figure A–42. Managing PHP extensions

Now enter the location of the extension, as shown in Figure A–43.

Add an extension	? ✕
Provide a path to extension's binary file:	
C:\Program Files\PHP\ext\php_pdo_sqlsrv.dll	...
Example: C:\Temp\php_wincache.dll	
	OK Cancel

Figure A–43. Adding the SQL Server PHP extension

The installer should have placed the driver files in C:\Program Files\PHP\ext. If they aren't there, you'll need to find them and copy them to this directory. Now repeat the process to add php_sqlsrv.dll. This is the actual driver that talks to the database.

Now we can check the configuration all at once. From the PHP Manager, click on "Check phpinfo()" as shown in Figure A–44.

 PHP Manager

Use this feature to check the PHP runtime settings, to configure PHP runtime directives and to enable or disable PHP extensions.

PHP version: 5.2.14

PHP executable: C:\Program Files\PHP\php-cgi.exe

Register new PHP version | Change PHP version | Check phpinfo()

Figure A–44. PHP Manager

This loads a PHP page and executes the command phpinfo(), which will dump all kinds of configuration information to the window. First, though, it will ask where it should be executed, as shown in Figure A–45.

Figure A–45. Launching phpinfo()

The results of phpinfo() will display. Scroll down the page and look for the section titled "PDO," shown in Figure A–46.

PDO

PDO support	enabled
PDO drivers	mysql, sqlite, sqlsrv

pdo_mysql

PDO Driver for MySQL, client library version	5.0.51a

pdo_sqlite

PDO Driver for SQLite 3.x	enabled
PECL Module version	1.0.1 $Id: pdo_sqlite.c 293036 2010-01-03 09:23:27Z sebastian $
SQLite Library	3.3.7undefined

pdo_sqlsrv

pdo_sqlsrv support	enabled

Directive	Local Value	Master Value
pdo_sqlsrv.log_severity	0	0

Figure A–46. The PDO section of the phpinfo() *report*

As we can see, the SQL Server PDO driver is loaded and PHP recognizes it.

■ **Tip** After making changes to the initialization files, you may need to reset IIS. From any command prompt, issue the command `iisreset`.

Now return to the browser where the installation is taking place and press refresh (F5). SQL Server now shows up as a choice (Figure A–47).

Database type *

○ MySQL, MariaDB, or equivalent

○ SQLite

◉ Microsoft SQL Server

The type of database your Drupal data will be stored in.

Database name *

```
drupal
```

The name of the database your Drupal data will be stored in. It must exist on your server before Drupal can be installed.

Database username *

```
drupal-service
```

Database password

```
••••••••••
```

▼ ADVANCED OPTIONS

These options are only necessary for some sites. If you're not sure what you should enter here, leave the default settings or check with your hosting provider.

Database host *

```
localhost\sqlexpress
```

If your database is located on a different server, change this.

Figure A–47. SQL Server appears as a choice.

We're almost done. Just give the name of the database that the script created, and the name of a user who owns the database.

Tip: If you have a non-default SQL Server instance (such as `sqlexpress`), you'll need to specify it in the Advanced Options area shown in Figure A–47.

If the information is correct, the installer will create and populate all of the tables while showing the progress. (See Figure A–48.)

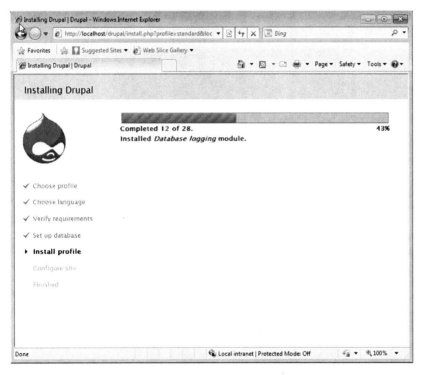

Figure A–48. The installer throbber

Once the tables are created, it's time to provide some information about the site, as shown in Figure A–49.

Configure site

All necessary changes to *./sites/default* and *./sites/default/settings.php* have been made. They have been set to read-only for security.

SITE INFORMATION

Site name *
Drupal SQL/IIS site

Site e-mail address *
brian.travis+d4wd@gmail.com

Automated e-mails, such as registration information, will be sent from this address. Use an address ending in your site's domain to help prevent these e-mails from being flagged as spam.

✓ Choose profile
✓ Choose language
✓ Verify requirements
✓ Set up database
✓ Install profile
▶ **Configure site**

Figure A–49. Basic site information

The installer writes the site information to the database and displays the installation-complete happy screen, shown in Figure A–50.

Drupal installation complete

All necessary changes to *./sites/default* and *./sites/default/settings.php* have been made. They have been set to read-only for security.

Congratulations, you installed Drupal!

Visit your new site.

✓ Choose profile
✓ Choose language
✓ Verify requirements
✓ Set up database
✓ Install profile
✓ Configure site
✓ Finished

Figure A–50. Site installation happy screen

Clicking "Visit your new site" takes you to the top screen where you can start administering the site and creating content.

Summary and Caveat

We've just created a site using IIS and SQL Server instead of Apache and MySQL. This is truly on the cutting edge of Drupal development and it comes with certain risks. You should consider these risks as you start to develop your site using this "WISP" stack.

The most important thing to realize is that not everyone is as enlightened as you when it comes to using the database. The data abstraction layer in Drupal 7 gives the programmer everything she needs to do any operation without direct knowledge of which database engine is currently in use. This is the way it was designed, and all Drupal 7 core modules have been tested to assure that this is the case.

However, you will certainly be using modules contributed by other authors. Many of the modules you'll be considering have been ported from earlier versions of Drupal, and the authors might not be as careful as they should be when writing code that accesses the database. Their programs might not use the abstraction layer but, instead, read or write directly to a database assuming it is MySQL. If they only test on MySQL, they might think their module works. But as soon as you install it on your WISP stack, it probably will break.

Don't despair. As people become more accustomed to working with the database abstraction layer, they'll learn to write in a database-agnostic way. This is good for reasons that don't have anything with databases; it tends to make code more secure and can also make the code more readable to others. I discuss the database abstraction layer in detail in Chapter 9.

In the next section, we will install a tool that has become indispensible to many Drupal developers. That tool is Drush.

Drush

Drush is short for "Drupal shell." It is a PHP script that takes care of a lot of the things you'll find yourself doing often. Drush is designed to handle many administrative tasks from the command line. You could live your life as a Drupal developer without using Drush, but you could also go out back, shoot a squirrel, and then dress it and cook it in a pie for dinner. But why would you do that, when you can just buy ready-made squirrel pies from the frozen foods section of your grocery store?

And that's what Drush is. A tasty treat that is packaged for your convenience. Drush makes otherwise repetitive tasks easy and scriptable.

Many hosting providers that offer Drupal have Drush installed already. Drush calls upon several standard *nix tools, like `wget`, `tar`, and `gzip`. And since most Drupal hosting providers run in a *nix environment, adding Drush is simple for them.

Installing Drush

Unfortunately, the standard Windows machine doesn't have all of those tools, so you'll need to install them on yours. This is sort of a hassle, but I guarantee you, if you spend a few minutes now getting this environment set up, you'll save far more time as you start developing your Drupal applications in a Windows environment.

Here is how to get those tools loaded and running.

First, download the Drush bits at `http://drupal.org/project/drush`. Grab the latest version as shown in Figure A–51.

Downloads

Recommended releases

Version	Downloads	Date	Links
All-versions-4.0	tar.gz (237.84 KB) | zip (277.95 KB)	2011-Jan-07	Notes
All-versions-3.3	tar.gz (170.79 KB)	2010-Aug-10	Notes

Figure A–51. Download the Drush bits.

Use your favorite unzipper to put the files in the appropriate directory. I use c:\drush. We'll add that to our environment path a little later.

Now, we need to get the Drush prerequisites. These are all open source tools, and they each have Windows binaries with an installer. The download page for the first one, libarchive, is shown in Figure A–52. It is located at http://gnuwin32.sourceforge.net/packages/libarchive.htm.

Download

If you download the Setup program of the package, any requirements for running applications, such as dynamic link libraries (DLL's) from the dependencies as listed below under Requirements, are already included. If you download the package as Zip files, then you must download and install the dependencies zip file yourself. Developer files (header files and libraries) from other packages are however not included; so if you wish to develop your own applications, you must separately install the required packages.

Description	Download	Size	Last change	Md5sum
• Complete package, except sources	Setup	1140310	27 June 2008	73e612405a10f690beffa8033a76cd46
• Sources	Setup	856349	27 June 2008	6b22d9e7e503b1bc1da79eccdf004eef
• Binaries	Zip	263534	27 June 2008	f2bd5a4ee39d9fc64b456d516f90afad
• Developer files	Zip	37691	27 June 2008	63f6e778ea3e8ef7fe198c08197d855c
• Documentation	Zip	717837	3 February 2008	f776dae5e66a25e69652be39c9a63bbd
• Sources	Zip	1399362	27 June 2008	63f0bbda21069c456a62f518fb2220d6
• Dependencies	Zip	73020	31 March 2008	737a54c70e4a42923f6707321c6a6aa6
• Original source	http://people.freebsd.org/~kientzle/libarchive/src/libarchive-2.4.12.tar.gz			

Figure A–52. Download page for the open source libarchive tool

Grab whatever flavor you want. I usually just download the setup program for the complete package. Run the setup program and use the defaults. (See Figure A–53.) This will install your program, but won't make changes to the path. We'll deal with that in a moment.

Figure A–53. Setup program for the libarchive *tool*

You'll need a total of four GNU packages to make Drush work:

1. http://gnuwin32.sourceforge.net/packages/libarchive.htm

2. http://gnuwin32.sourceforge.net/packages/gzip.htm

3. http://gnuwin32.sourceforge.net/packages/wget.htm

4. http://gnuwin32.sourceforge.net/packages/gtar.htm

Now we need to set the PATH environment variable to include Drush, PHP, and the binaries installed above. To do this, you need to get to the Environment Variables screen, which varies depending on your OS. Right-click Computer, select Properties. Click Advanced system settings, and then Environment Variables. You will see a screen like the one shown in Figure A–54.

Figure A–54. *Environment variables dialog*

Under User variables, click New… You will see the Edit User Variable window, shown in Figure A–55.

Figure A–55. *User variable dialog*

Enter path as the Variable name and the new directories in the Variable value field. Be sure to include the path to a compatible version of PHP, since Drush will be using that. I used c:\Program Files\Jcx.Software\VS.Php\2010\Php 5.3;C:\drush\;C:\Program Files\GnuWin32\bin\, but your system might be different.

The semicolon separates the paths, which indicate where the following files are located: php.exe, drush.bat, and the tar/gzip/wget binaries.

If you have a command prompt open already, you'll need to close it and open another one for it to read the new path.

Running Drush

Now let's test to see if we were successful in installing Drush and its prerequisites. At a command prompt, change to the directory just above the modules and themes directories. Mine is C:\wamp\www\drupal7\sites\all\.

Type drush at the command prompt. You'll get a nice long list of the wonderful things you can do, as shown in Figure A–56.

```
D:\wamp\www\drupal7\sites\all>drush
Drush has significant limitations on Windows. We seek a co-maintainer  [warning]
to remedy them. See http://drupal.org/project/drush for more
information, and for instructions on disabling this warning.
Execute a drush command. Run `drush help [command]` to view command-specific
help.  Run `drush topic` to read even more documentation.

Global options (see `drush topic` for the full list):
 -r <path>, --root=<path>             Drupal root directory to use
                                      (default: current directory)
 -l http://example.com,               URI of the drupal site to use (only
 --uri=http://example.com             needed in multisite environments)
 -v, --verbose                        Display extra information about the
                                      command.
 -d, --debug                          Display even more information,
                                      including internal messages.
 -y, --yes                            Assume 'yes' as answer to all
                                      prompts
 -n, --no                             Assume 'no' as answer to all prompts
 -s, --simulate                       Simulate all relevant actions (don't
                                      actually change the system)
 -p, --pipe                           Emit a compact representation of the
                                      command for scripting.
 -h, --help                           This help system.
 --version                            Show drush version.
 --php                                The absolute path to your PHP
                                      intepreter, if not 'php' in the
                                      path.


Core drush commands: (core)
 cache-clear (cc)    Clear a specific cache, or all drupal caches.
 core-cli (cli)      Enter a new shell optimized for drush use.
 core-cron (cron)    Run all cron hooks in all active modules for specified
                     site.
```

Figure A–56. The Drush help screen

■ **Note** I have gotten a message on some machines indicating that a particular DLL is missing.

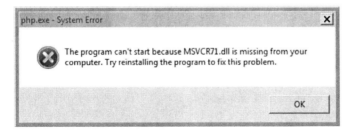

I don't know exactly why this happens, but you can download the DLL at http://www.dll-files.com/dllindex/dll-files.shtml?msvcr71.

If this works for you, you have just made your Drupal experience a lot more productive. Drush helps you do a lot of things that would otherwise require a lot of mousing around.

Drush knows where the Drupal projects are out in the 'tubes. It also knows the database location and login information by reading the settings.php file created by the installer. Because of this, it can perform administrative tasks without requiring the GUI. That means, of course, that anyone who has access to Drush and your directory structure can do the same thing. Standard security precautions are applicable.

The first useful thing you'll probably do in Drush is to use the download command, dl. The download command grabs the most recent version of a project from the directory in the projects area of drupal.org where the project is maintained Dusing wget (one of the tools you installed a few minutes ago). It then unzips and unpacks the package (again, using the tools you installed) and puts the project folder in the appropriate spot. It knows whether a particular project is a module or a theme, for example.

Downloading the Omega theme, for example, requires just a single command:

```
drush dl omega
```

Figure A–57 shows what this looks like:

```
D:\wamp\www\drupal7\sites\all\themes>drush dl omega
Project omega (7.x-1.1) downloaded to                          [success]
D:/wamp/www/drupal7/sites/all/themes/omega.
Project omega contains 4 themes: omega_starterkit, gamma_starterkit, gamma, omega.

D:\wamp\www\drupal7\sites\all\themes>
```

Figure A–57. *Downloading the Omega theme with Drush*

You can also download and enable modules using Drush. Let's add a module that creates a hierarchical administration menu. The project is admin_menu, and it takes just two Drush commands to get it installed (see Figure A–58):

```
drush dl admin_menu
drush en admin_menu
```

```
D:\wamp\www\drupal7\sites\all>drush dl admin_menu
Project admin_menu (7.x-3.0-rc1) downloaded to                 [success]
D:/wamp/www/drupal7/sites/all/modules/admin_menu.
Project admin_menu contains 4 modules: admin_views, admin_menu_toolbar, admin_devel, admin_menu.

D:\wamp\www\drupal7\sites\all>drush en admin_menu
The following extensions will be enabled: admin_menu
Do you really want to continue? (y/n): y
//admin_menu was enabled successfully.                         [ok]
```

Figure A–58. *Downloading and enabling a module*

Loading the site, we can see that it works, as shown in Figure A–59.

Figure A–59. The Administration menu enabled

Drush can take care of a lot of the things you do on the administration pages of your site—enabling and disabling modules, for example, or clearing caches. You can also interrogate system properties, evaluate variables, and interrogate the database. Plus, Drush has its own API, so other module developers can attach their commands to the Drush core. Brilliant!

Appendix C has a list of built-in Drush commands.

Summary

Drupal was originally designed to run under the LAMP stack. Much progress has been made in the standardization of the code to make it possible to move beyond that particular technology stack. With Drupal 7, you can now use different web servers and databases. Here, we did just that, first replacing Linux with Windows, and then replacing Apache with IIS and MySQL with Microsoft SQL Server.

I expect there will be a lot of demand for Drupal running under Windows with the WISP stack, and that a Windows-focused community will appear and champion this platform to make Drupal more popular than ever.

■ ■ ■

From Start to Omega: Using the Omega Starter Kit

The Omega theme is built on the 960 Grid System (960gs), a design platform whose methodology relies on the inherent divisibility of 960 to devise a layout for design elements on a page. The Omega theme, along with the Omega Starter Kit and Omega Tools developer resources, provide a rich set of functions you can use to create a unique theme with minimal development time.

In this appendix, I'll go through the process of starting with a Photoshop mock-up of a site and turning it into a rich CSS-based design that integrates with the Omega Starter Kit.

960 Grid System

The 960 Grid System (http://960.gs) was created as a set of CSS styles that represent a web page in a fixed-width form 960 pixels wide. The number 960 was chosen for the same reason there are 36 dancers in a chorus line: the numbers can be divided evenly into a variety of different configurations. In the case of the 960.gs standard, you can divide the fixed number of pixels into a number of larger columns. Those columns, in turn, provide a vertical guide for laying out the elements of a page. Each layout column has a 10-pixel margin on each side, giving a 20-pixel gutter between columns. Creating a layout becomes the task of creating columns of content that line up with the grid boundaries.

Take, for example, the drupal.org site, shown in Figure B–1.

Notice that the site uses a 12-column grid. Other popular grids are 16 and 24 columns. See how the top banner has two defined regions, the first being 6 columns and the second being 5, with a one-column gap in between. The Omega theme provides tools and a foundation that allow you to theme your site quickly and consistently.

Designers commonly use Photoshop to create a mock-up for a web site. The problem is that the creative people who make wonderful-looking mock-ups in Photoshop sometimes don't understand the details involved in building a content-rich web site that must rebuild every page based on the content desired by the user.

The trick, then, is to come up with an environment where the creative graphics people can design, and the creative programmer people can use that design to build a site.

In this example, we will use the 960 grid system, along with Omega, to achieve those goals.

Figure B–1. *The* drupal.org *site is based on the 960 grid system*

Designing in Photoshop

We've been given the task of creating a site. The client is the Civil Disobedience Evolution Fund, an educational charity devoted to providing information and support for "good people who break bad laws." The designer prefers to build mock-ups in Photoshop, and so I sent her a grid template.

This template is written as a Photoshop plug-in—an action script that must be installed in the Presets/Actions directory of the Photoshop program directory. Once it's installed, the plug-in will create a series of guides corresponding to the columns and gutters of the chosen 960gs scheme. In this case, we chose the 16-column grid.

Figure B–2 shows the Actions window after the plug-in was installed.

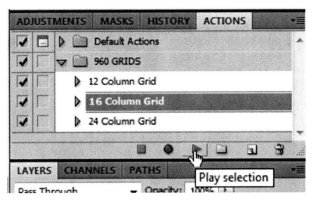

Figure B–2. The Photoshop Actions window showing the guide-producing action scripts

Selecting the 16 Column Grid action and pressing play gives us a new, empty document with guides at the appropriate column points, as shown in Figure B–3.

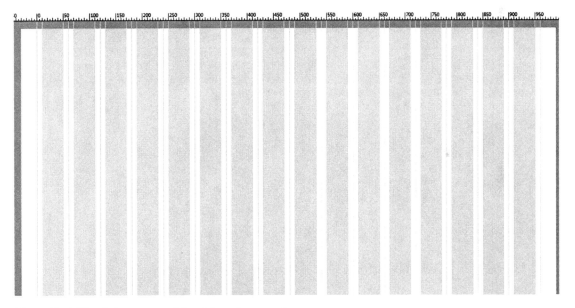

Figure B–3. Blank document with grids and an overlay

Notice that an overlay is also created to show where content goes and where the gutters are. Gutters are the white area. Each of the 16 columns has two gutters, one on each side. The width of these gutters varies with the template. For the 16-column template, each column is 60 pixels wide: 40 pixels for content and 20 pixels for gutters. The gutter space is split between the right and left side of the content column.

The gutter space is germane only when the gutter is at the edge of the region we are defining. This will become more evident as we go through the process, but suffice it to say, for now, that we will have 20 pixels between our elements once we start defining them on the page.

Note: The grid action script opens a new document. If you have an existing design and want to lay the guides over that, you must uncheck the first action in the script.

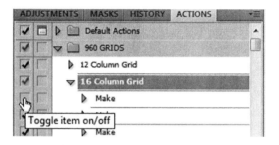

This is the action that opens a new document. To use an existing document, load it, uncheck the first "Make," and then run. The gridlines will show up and the overlay will be added as a new layer.

Once the guides have been established, the designer can create her mock-up, using the columns to guide the design. The final design is shown in Figure B–4.

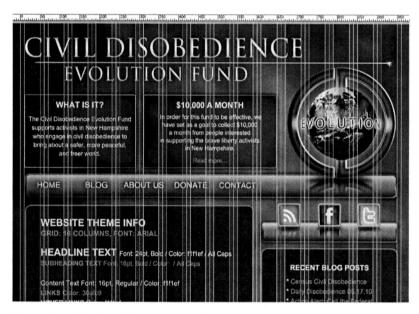

Figure B–4. The final Photoshop mock-up

Notice that all of the content areas line up inside of the guides. The top brand area is 16 columns wide. The block titled "What is it?" is 5 columns and the next, "$10,000 a Month," is 6 columns. The main content area is 10 columns and the sidebar on the right is 6 columns.

There are some other components that we'll deal with later, but for now, let's get started on our Omega theme.

Omega Sub-Theme

The Omega theme, like many "base" themes available in the Drupal world, doesn't really do anything after you install it. That is, such themes don't have pretty backgrounds or hover-over effects or much, if any, UI presentation. They are simply engines you can use to plug in your vision for theming.

The way Drupal enables this vision is through sub-theming. I discussed this in Chapter 7, so we'll do it here with the Omega theme.

Creating your Omega Sub-Theme

Omega ships with a starter kit ready for you to use for your sub-theme. You'll find it in the themes directory as shown in Figure B–5.

Figure B–5. *The Omega starter kit*

To get started with your sub-theme, follow these steps:

1. Copy the `starterkit` folder from the default Omega theme directory and place it in your `sites/all/themes` directory.

2. Rename the folder to the theme name of your choice. I'm calling mine `cdef_omega`.

3. Rename omega_starterkit.info to cdef_omega.info and modify the default information in the .info file as needed. This is shown in Listing B–1.

Listing B–1. Modifying the .info File

```
; $Id:$
;
```

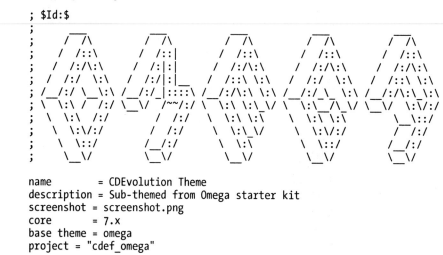

```
name        = CDEvolution Theme
description = Sub-themed from Omega starter kit
screenshot = screenshot.png
core        = 7.x
base theme = omega
project = "cdef_omega"
```

4. Open template.php and search and replace omega_starterkit with cdef_omega. This is shown in Listing B–2.

Listing B–2. Updating template.php for Your Sub-Theme

```php
<?php
// $Id: template.php,v 1.3.2.2.2.1 2010/11/01 16:26:38 himerus Exp $

/**
 * @file
 * Starter template.php file for sub-themes of Omega.
 */

/**
 * Implements hook_theme().
 */
function cdef_omega_theme(&$existing, $type, $theme, $path) {
  $hooks = array();
  //$hooks = omega_theme($existing, $type, $theme, $path);
  return $hooks;
}
```

5. Open theme-settings.php and search and replace omega_starterkit with cdef_omega, as shown in Listing B–3.

Listing B–3. Updating theme-settings.php for Your Sub-Theme

```php
<?php
// $Id: theme-settings.php,v 1.3.2.3 2010/08/03 14:19:52 himerus Exp $
```

```
/**
 * @file
 * Theme settings for the Omega theme.
 */

/**
 * Implements hook_form_system_theme_settings_alter().
 *
 * @param $form
 *   Nested array of form elements that comprise the form.
 * @param $form_state
 *   A keyed array containing the current state of the form.
 */
function cdef_omega_form_system_theme_settings_alter(&$form, &$form_state) {
  // Include any changes to the theme settings here.
}
```

6. Go to Appearance on the administration menu and enable the new sub-theme as shown in Figure B–6

DISABLED THEMES

CDEvolution Theme 7.x-2.0-alpha5

Sub-themed from Omega starter kit

Enable | Enable and set default

Enable CDEvolution Theme as default theme

Figure B–6. Enabling the new sub-theme

7. Click on Settings to start the configuration process (see Figure B–7).

ENABLED THEME

**CDEvolution Theme 7.x-2.0-alpha5
(default theme)**

Sub-themed from Omega starter kit

Settings

Settings for CDEvolution Theme theme

Figure B-7. *Starting the configuration process*

This will display the Omega configuration administration screen, as shown in Figure B–8.

| Global settings | CDEvolution Theme | Seven |

These options control the display settings for the *CDEvolution Theme* theme. When your site is displayed using this theme, these settings will be used.

960gs Omega Settings

960gs Default Config	**Default container width**
User Zone Config	16 column grid (940 usable pixels) ▾
Branding Zone Config	This width is used for regions like $help, $messages and other non-important regions in page.tpl.php
Header Zone Config	
Preface Zone Config	**Fixed / Fluid Layout**
Location Zone Config	⦿ Fixed width (theme default)
Content Zone Config	○ Fluid width
Postscript Zone Config	You may select fluid layout, or the default fixed width layout.
Footer Zone Config	

Figure B-8. *The Omega configuration administration screen*

Omega is a fairly complex theme, but it has an interface that allows you to set things up in a consistent way. For this reason, I feel it's safe to introduce the new Drupal developer to such complexity. I've used many themes in Drupal and found the Omega-based theme the most accessible one that has real power.

The first thing we will do is to set the default number of columns for the page. Our designer used the 16-column Photoshop guides, so we select a 16-column grid as our default.

The Omega 960 theme introduces the concept of zones—horizontal areas that are stacked vertically on top of each other to create a page. Each zone can have a different number of 960gs columns, but we'll stick with 16 columns for each zone in our theme.

Some zones contain "special" items like the breadcrumb, logo/title/slogan, etc. that are normally output separately in `page.tpl.php`.

By default, Omega defines eight zones, each broken into one or more regions.

- **user**. The user zone is a set of two regions at the top of the page primarily used to display things like a horizontal login bar, user account menu, search block, etc. The two regions defined in the user zone are:

  - `user_bar_first`

  - `user_bar_second`

- **branding**. The branding zone contains the default Drupal items for logo/site title/slogan, followed by the primary menu. The branding zone is required and contains "special" content items. The two regions defined in the branding zone are:

  - `branding`

  - `menu`

- **header**. The header zone contains two simple regions for items below the primary menu. The header regions are usually used for callout items on specific pages, or for other items you want above your primary page content. The two regions defined in the header zone are:

  - `header_first`

  - `header_second`

- **preface**. The preface zone works much like the header zone as a place for the themer to put various things. The three regions defined in the preface zone are:

  - `preface_first`

  - `preface_second`

  - `preface_third`

- **location**. The location zone is required and contains the default system breadcrumb on pages where the breadcrumb is specified

- **content**. The content zone is required and contains required content items. The content region should *always* be first for source ordering. Ordering is important because search engines generally assume that the higher something appears on a page, the more important it is. Omega has a feature that allows you to specify the content first and the first sidebar second, but still lets you render the first sidebar to the left of the content. This gives you the search-engine optimization you want, as well as the ability to lay out the page that makes the most sense to your designer. The three regions defined in the content zone are:

  - `content`

  - `sidebar_first`

  - `sidebar_second`

- **postscript**. The postscript zone is another place to put various elements. It is pretty common these days for a site to have a number of blocks at the bottom of the page, below the content but above the final footer. The four regions defined in the postscript zone are:

  - postscript_first

  - postscript_second

  - postscript_third

  - postscript_fourth

- **footer**. The footer zone is the last one on the page. This is usually where the copyrights and any other such information are placed. The two regions defined in the footer zone are:

  - footer_first

  - footer_second

These zones and regions are shipped with the Omega starter kit. As with most things in Drupal, they can be edited or extended. These zones and regions (and a lot more) are defined in the .info file of your sub-theme. As a word of caution, tread lightly here; you should understand how all of the pieces work together before editing this file.

The next step is to map these zones and regions to our Photoshop mock-up.

Mapping Photoshop to Omega

In picking our zones, we need to refer back to the Photoshop mock-up. Figure B–9 shows the mock-up with potential zones displayed as boxes.

Figure B–9. Mapping zones

This map shows the Branding region on top, followed by the Header First and Header Second regions in the Header zone. And there's a Preface zone, which contains our Preface First region. After that are two regions in the Content zone, Content and Sidebar First. But there's a problem.

The problem is that zones are designed to be horizontal boxes that sit on top of each other and don't overlap. The Preface First region is not only not a rectangle, but it overlays the Branding region. This will not work with the theme as it is designed.

But not to despair. We can do some tricks with CSS to make this work. First, we'll go into Photoshop and select the graphic elements in the Preface First region and everything below it. Then, we'll move them all down to create nice rectangle boxes, as shown in Figure B–10.

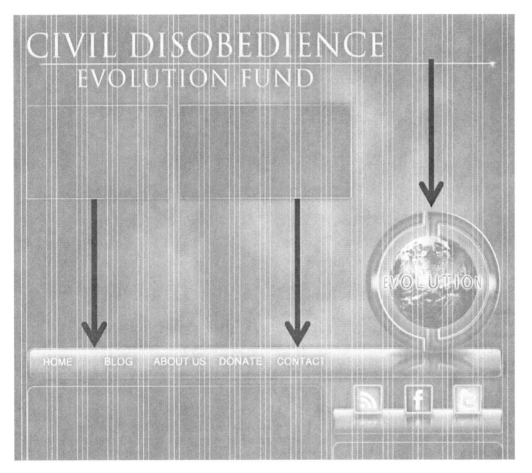

Figure B–10. *Moving elements down to make boxes*

After moving the graphic elements down, we can remap the mock-up, creating nice boxes that sit on top of each other without overlapping. (See Figure B–11.)

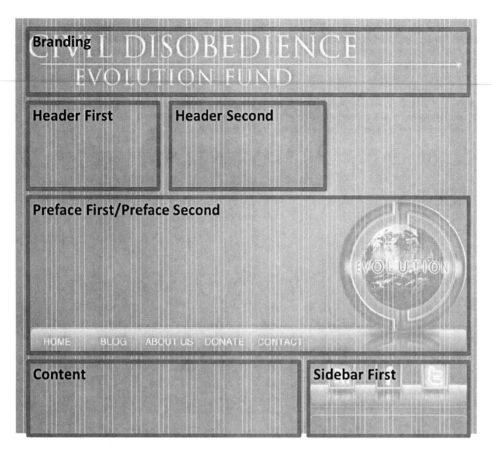

Figure B–11. Nice boxes that follow the rules

When we get to the CSS part of the exercise, we'll move the Preface First region back up to where it should be.

Configuring Zones

Now that we have our regions mapped out, let's continue with the Omega administration pages to declare the information about each zone. This is just a matter of going down the list of zones and setting various parameters. The first zone, User, will not be used in our theme, so we can turn it off. (See Figure B–12.)

Figure B–12. *Disabling a zone*

We will be using the next zone, Branding. This is a simple zone and we'll use just a single region. First, we need to enabled the zone and set the container width to 16 columns as shown in Figure B–13.

Figure B–13. *Configuring the Branding Zone*

We'll set the Zone Type to Static, which is the default. There is a feature in the 960 Grid System that allows zones to stack on the page. If, for example, you have a 16-column grid and you define three 6-column regions inside of it, they won't fit. Omega will put the first two regions next to each other, and then stack the third one underneath the first two. We will be using this feature later.

Setting the Zone Type to Static Zone produces this behavior.

In contrast, choosing Dynamic Zone causes a region to expand and collapse depending on the nature of other regions in the same zone. For example, suppose you had a region that had only a user logon box. Once a user logs on, there's no need to show that box. If the logon box is not present, you might want the content next to it to fill the empty space. A dynamic zone lets this happen.

The Branding zone has two default regions, but we are only using one. The Branding region will hold our logo and will be 16-columns wide. (See Figure B–14.)

Additional Zone Classes

branding-zone

You can quickly add custom CSS classes to your zone here.

Branding (special region)

Prefix   **Width**   **Suffix**

0 ▾   16 ▾   0 ▾

Additional Region Classes

branding-region

You can quickly add custom CSS classes to your regions here.

Menu (special region)

Prefix   **Width**   **Suffix**

0 ▾   0 ▾   0 ▾

Additional Region Classes

menu-region

You can quickly add custom CSS classes to your regions here.

Figure B–14. The Branding Zone regions

The Additional Zone Classes field is displayed on top, giving you a chance to provide CSS class names to the DIV that wraps all of the regions in the zone. You'll also notice the Additional Region Classes field that does the same thing for the DIV that wraps everything placed in the region.

We can see two regions declared for the Branding zone. Each region contains three settings, Prefix, Width, and Suffix. The width is the number of columns that will contain content. The Prefix and Suffix fields indicate the number of columns that will appear blank before and after the content.

It's important that the total of all of the selections on all of the regions add up to no more than the number of columns in the container. In this case, it's pretty easy; the width of the Branding region is the full 16 columns and everything else is set to zero.

Now let's look at the Header Zone, shown in Figure B–15.

Additional Zone Classes

header-zone

You can quickly add custom CSS classes to your zone here.

Header First

Prefix	Width	Suffix
0 ▼	5 ▼	0 ▼

Additional Region Classes

header-first-region

You can quickly add custom CSS classes to your regions here.

Header Second

Prefix	Width	Suffix
0 ▼	6 ▼	0 ▼

Additional Region Classes

header-second-region

You can quickly add custom CSS classes to your regions here.

Figure B–15. The Header Zone configuration

This is also a 16-column static zone, but we must now declare two regions to hold the content. The first region, Header First, is five columns with no prefix and suffix, and the second region, Header Second, is six columns wide with no prefix or suffix. Notice that the total of all fields is less than the 16-column width of our container. That's OK, since it fits with our design. The total columns, 11, will be formatted from the left, leaving five columns on the right empty. We will need that area empty when we use CSS magic to move the logo up the page.

The Preface zone will also be 16 columns and we will use two regions, Preface First and Preface Second. Preface First will hold the logo and background for the menu bar. Preface Second will contain the actual menu, generated by Drupal based on the content of the site. In this case, we'll need to stack to two regions vertically within the same zone. See Figure B–16 to see how we pull this off.

Additional Zone Classes

preface-zone

You can quickly add custom CSS classes to your zone here.

Preface First

Prefix   **Width**   **Suffix**

0 ▼   16 ▼   0 ▼

Additional Region Classes

preface-first-region

You can quickly add custom CSS classes to your regions here.

Preface Second

Prefix   **Width**   **Suffix**

0 ▼   16 ▼   0 ▼

Additional Region Classes

preface-second-region

You can quickly add custom CSS classes to your regions here.

Preface Third

Prefix   **Width**   **Suffix**

0 ▼   0 ▼   0 ▼

Additional Region Classes

preface-third-region

You can quickly add custom CSS classes to your regions here.

Figure B–16. Stacking two regions in one zone

Notice the Width of the Preface First region. It is set to 16, which will completely fill the zone. But the Preface Second region is also set to 16. Because the first region fills up the zone, the second region will appear directly below it, which is exactly what we want.

Notice the third preface as well. We won't be using it in this theme, so we just set all three values to zero. If we wanted to optimize the site for maximum performance, we would go into the .info file and remove the Preface Third region altogether. For now, let's just set it to zero.

We won't be using the next zone, Location, either, so we'll clear the "Enable this Zone" checkbox.

The next zone, Content, is where our main content and sidebars will go. This is shown in Figure B–17.

Additional Zone Classes

content-zone

You can quickly add custom CSS classes to your zone here.

Content (special region)

Prefix   **Width**   **Suffix**

0 ▾   10 ▾   0 ▾

Additional Region Classes

content-region

You can quickly add custom CSS classes to your regions here.

Sidebar First

Prefix   **Width**   **Suffix**

0 ▾   6 ▾   0 ▾

Additional Region Classes

sidebar-first-region

You can quickly add custom CSS classes to your regions here.

Sidebar Second

Prefix   **Width**   **Suffix**

0 ▾   0 ▾   0 ▾

Additional Region Classes

sidebar-second-region

You can quickly add custom CSS classes to your regions here.

Figure B–17. The Content Zone

There's nothing special here. The content has a width of 10 columns, and the sidebar is 6 columns.

We won't be using the Postscript Zone or Footer Zone, so I'll clear the "Enable this Zone" checkbox for each of those. Now that the zones are set up, let's start filling in the regions with content and graphics.

Blocks

We can place content in each region we defined in this exercise using blocks. For three of the regions, we have standard Drupal blocks, as shown in Figure B–18.

BLOCK	REGION	OPERATIONS
Content		
✛ Main page content	Content ▾	configure
User Bar First		
No blocks in this region		
User Bar Second		
No blocks in this region		
Sidebar First		
✛ Recent content	Sidebar First ▾	configure
Sidebar Second		
No blocks in this region		
Location Bar		
No blocks in this region		
Header First		
No blocks in this region		
Header Second		
No blocks in this region		
Preface First		
No blocks in this region		
Preface Second		
✛ Main menu	Preface Second ▾	configure

Figure B–18. Drupal-created blocks are assigned to regions

The main page content goes in our Content region. Recent content is placed in the first sidebar, and our main menu is placed in the Second Preface region. The main menu has a title by default, which we don't want since our menu will be formatted horizontally in the space our designer created. To get rid of the title, we need to click "configure" next to the main menu and set the title to <none>. (See Figure B–19.)

Home » Administration » Structure » Blocks

'Main menu' block ⚙

Block title

<none>

Override the default title for the block. Use *<none>* to display no title, or leave blank to use the default block title.

REGION SETTINGS

Specify in which themes and regions this block is displayed.

CDEvolution Theme (default theme)

Preface Second ▾

Figure B–19. Removing the Main menu title

Now that we have the three Drupal-created blocks, we need to create three more blocks to hold our static information. This includes the two preface blocks above the menu bar and the follow block that will appear above the recent content in the first sidebar.

To create these blocks, we need to add them on the blocks administration page. Clicking "Add block" on that page brings up the new block screen shown in Figure B–20.

Block description *

What Is It?

A brief description of your block. Used on the Blocks administration page.

Block title

What Is It?

The title of the block as shown to the user.

Block body *

The Civil Disobedience Evolution Fund supports activists in New Hampshire who engage in civil disobedience to bring about a safer, more peaceful, and freer world.
<a href="http://cdevolution.org/10000">Read more...</a>

Text format Full HTML

More information about text formats

- Web page addresses and e-mail addresses turn into links automatically.
- Lines and paragraphs break automatically.

The content of the block as shown to the user.

REGION SETTINGS

Specify in which themes and regions this block is displayed.

CDEvolution Theme (default theme)

Header First

Figure B–20. Creating a new block

The Block description field indicates how the block will appear on the blocks administration page, and the Block title is the text that will be placed on the top of the block. If you don't want a title, enter <none>. In the Block body field, we enter the short text of the block and provide a link as an HTML tag. If you put HTML in the block, make sure the appropriate Text format filter is selected.

Finally, we indicate that we want this block to appear in the first header region. We do the same for the other two blocks.

Now it's time to put everything together on the page using CSS.

Content Generation

When you create a new site, it's a blank slate. You don't have any themes except the default. You don't have any modules except the core modules that were installed as part of your profile, and you don't have any content. Creating content takes time, and is really what your site is about. But it might be nice to have some content generated for you, just so you can see how a page will look with, say, 10 blog teasers. Or what a recent-content menu would look like with 20 articles.

If you'd like to be able to do this, you're not alone, and there's a module that can help. The Devel module provides a toolbox of fun for the developer. If you want to create content, download and enable the Devel module and make sure the Devel generate module is enabled (see Figure B–21).

Figure B–21. *The Devel modules*

To create content, go to Configuration...Generate content. You'll see the screen shown in Figure B–22.

Generate content ○

Content types

☑ Blog entry. Comments: Open

☑ Article. Comments: Open

☑ Book page. Comments: Open

☑ Basic page. Comments: Hidden

☐ **Delete all content** in these content types before generating new content.

How many nodes would you like to generate?

90

How far back in time should the nodes be dated?

1 month ago ▾

Node creation dates will be distributed randomly from the current time, back to the selected time.

Maximum number of comments per node.

5

You must also enable comments for the content types you are generating. Note that some nodes will randomly receive zero comments. Some will receive the max.

Max word length of titles

7

☐ Add an url alias for each node.

   Requires path.module

Figure B–22. *Generating content with Devel generate*

The first section on the page has a list of content types that are currently installed and enabled. The other parameters are pretty self-explanatory. You'll see the throbber going (Figure B–23) and then the happy screen showing how much content was generated.

Figure B–23. The throbber showing content generation

Now if we go to the front page of our site, we'll see the not-too-impressive, un-themed (but full of content) site (see Figure B–24).

Figure B–24. Un-themed site with starterkit theme applied

Notice that the title and slogan appear at the top, as do the two blocks we created for the header zone. Also, notice that the second preface region has the main menu with our single link, Home. The content zone has the content region and the first sidebar, which contains a list of recent blog posts. And above that is the block that contains our follow links.

▧ **Tip** The content created by Devel generate is "greeked." That is, Devel generates dummy text, written in pseudo Latin, to bulk up the page. You might also notice geometric graphics placed randomly on various content that was generated.

As you can see, the site is already adhering to the 16-column layout we designed. The Omega theme has a debugging feature that turns on the columns as an overlay so you can see how your theme is adhering to your specified layout. You can turn this on from the Settings page of your theme, as shown in Figure B–25.

General Omega Settings

Optional CSS	☑ Enable grid overlay/toggle for selected roles.
Search Settings	☑ Turn on grid overlay on page load. (otherwise requires clicking to enable)
Page titles	**Roles that may use the grid overlay/debugging tool. (User 1 Automatically has access.)**
Breadcrumb settings	☐ authenticated user
Menu settings	☐ administrator
Grid Overlay / Debugging	

Figure B–25. Enabling the grid overlay feature in Omega

By turning on the feature and going to the front page again, you can see that our columns are as we specified, as shown in Figure B–26.

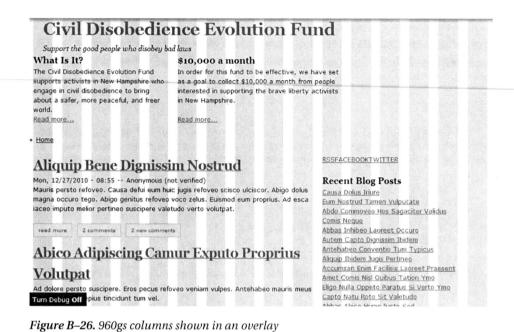

Figure B–26. 960gs columns shown in an overlay

This can be toggled on and off by clicking the "Turn Debug Off" button in the lower left corner of the page. A nice feature of the Devel module and Omega theme is the ability to hover over a block and see the styling characteristics. Figure B–27 shows an example.

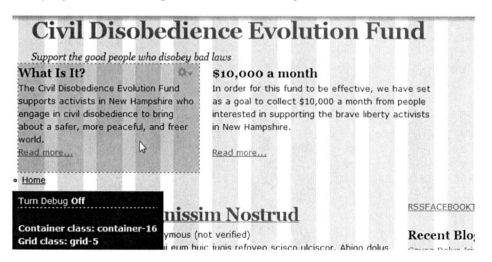

Figure B–27. The Devel module works with Omega to display styling information.

I hope you see that we're really farther along than it looks, and now it's time to start styling.

Theming with CSS

Cascading Style Sheets are used heavily in Drupal's theming layer. The syntax of CSS is beyond the scope of this book, but you'll be seeing a lot of CSS in the next sections. Even if you're not familiar with it, you will probably be able to figure things out. If you want to know more about CSS, you'll find plenty of resources on the Internet where you can get more detailed information.

The Omega theme, like most, has a set of CSS files that perform certain styling tasks. We'll need to enhance those styles to create our own for this site. You should know by now that it's a bad practice to modify the core code or contributed modules unless you are on the project team. Fortunately, you don't need to do that. Drupal's theming engine let's add our own CSS classes to the ones defined by the other parts of Drupal that create our page.

Our first step, then, is to create our own CSS file. The Omega starter kit has a place to put our custom CSS files, and a handy README.txt file that explains what to do. You can call the file anything you want, but it needs to go into the hierarchy of the theme we have been creating.

For my site, I used Visual Studio to create a new CSS file called cdef-custom.css in the directory sites/all/themes/cdef_omega/css, as shown in Figure B–28.

Figure B–28. Creating a new CSS file

Now we need to tell Drupal to be aware of the file when it builds our pages. We do this the same way as when we add any other file that has code Drupal needs to know about, in the .info file. Listing B–4 shows the sample.

Listing B–4. Modifying the .info File to Recognize a Style Sheet File

```
name        = CDEvolution Theme
description = Sub-themed from Omega starter kit
screenshot  = screenshot.png
core        = 7.x
base theme  = omega
project     = "cdef_omega"

stylesheets[all][] = css/cdef-custom.css
```

The stylesheets[] array contains all style sheets we want to add. The path is defined relative to the directory containing the theme's root file. We are defining a style sheet for all media types. Media types are defined by a W3C standard and are as follows:

- all: Suitable for all devices.

- braille: Intended for braille tactile feedback devices.

- embossed: Intended for paged braille printers.

- handheld: Intended for handheld devices (small screen, limited bandwidth).

- print: Intended for paged material and for documents viewed on screen in print preview mode.

- projection: Intended for projected presentations.

- screen: Intended primarily for color computer screens.

- speech: Intended for speech synthesizers.

- tty: Intended for media using a fixed-pitch character grid (such as teletypes, terminals, or portable devices with limited display capabilities). Authors should not use pixel units with the tty media type.

- tv: Intended for television-type devices (low resolution, color, limited scrolling, screens, sound available).

If you select [all], the style sheet will be used as the default for all media output types. By specifying various media types in your theme, you can provide different output for different devices. If you want a particular style sheet to be used by more than one media type, but not all, you can list them in a comma-delimited list in the array: stylesheet[handheld, tv][].

▓ **Note** Be sure to include the empty brackets after the media type. This ensures that your style sheet get loaded as next in the list of style sheets to be included.

Now that we've configured our style sheet, let's start entering our styles. I like to start with the easy big-ticket styles that will show up as noticeable changes on the site. That way, I get a feeling of accomplishment right away, and can build on that with the finer styles. Let's do the background first.

If you're lucky, your designer has extracted all of the graphic pieces as individual files so you can start right in with your theming. But chances are you'll have to do that yourself. Photoshop's capabilities are beyond the scope of this chapter, so I'll assume you've isolated the various parts of your mock-up to image files and placed them on the file system. The images I've isolated are shown in Table B–1.

Table B–1. Graphics Extracted from the Photoshop Mock-Up

	`CDEF-background-960.jpg`
	`CDEF-logo-menu.png`
	`CDEF-name.png`
	`Follow-Buttons-Bar.png`
	`facebook.png`
	`rss.png`
	`twitter.png`

The most convenient place to put these images is in your sub-theme directory. I created a directory named with a single character to make typing easier. The structure is shown in Figure B–29.

```
▲  📁 themes
    ▲  📁 cdef_omega
        ▲  📁 css
                🅰 cdef-custom.css
                📄 README.txt
        ▲  📁 i
                📷 CDEF-background.jpg
                📷 CDEF-logo-menu.png
                📷 CDEF-logo.png
                📷 CDEF-name.png
                📷 facebook.png
                📷 Follow-Buttons-Bar.png
                📷 menu-bar.png
                📷 rss.png
                📷 twitter.png
        ▷  📁 js
```

Figure B–29. Image files ready for inclusion in the CSS stylesheet

Now that the files are in the right place and Drupal knows everything it should, the easy and fun part starts.

Theming with Images

Our first task is to put the background image, CDEF-background.jpg in the CSS file we just created. We'll start with the block shown in Listing B–5.

Listing B–5. CSS Block for Document Body

```
body {
    background: url('../i/CDEF-background-960.jpg') center top black;
    background-repeat:repeat-x;
    background-attachment:fixed;
    color:#f1f1ef;
    font-family:Arial;
    font-size:12pt;
}
```

You can see if everything is set up correctly by saving the CSS file and refreshing the site. You should get something like what's shown in Figure B–30.

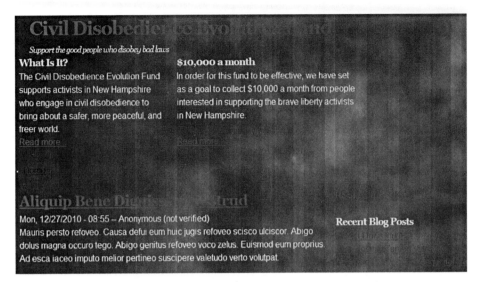

Figure B–30. Background appears indicating everything is working

If you refresh and don't see the background image, either something is not set up right in your chain of configuration settings or your theme information has been cached. You can clear the cache by going to Configuration➤Performance and clicking the "Clear all caches" button.

■ **Tip** You can also use Drush to clear caches. The command is `drush cc theme` to clear just the theme cache, or `drush cc all` to clear all caches. I usually keep a command window open to issue these Drush commands from time to time. Very handy. You can learn more about Drush in Appendix A.

Setting a style for the body is pretty easy. Now we need to start placing the other graphics and setting other parameters to get our site just right.

Next, we'll put the main logo at the top. In our layout specification, we saw that the logo was set in the Branding zone. We need to find out the name of the container DIV and set the background image of that HTML element to our graphic. Here's where the browser-based developer tools come in handy. In Internet Explorer, the tools are accessed using F12. This brings up the tools window, as shown in Figure B–31.

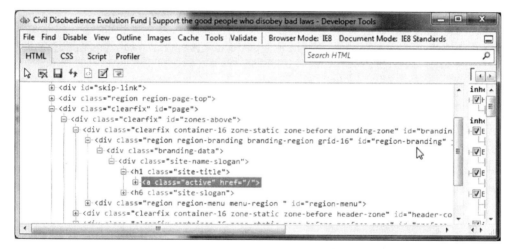

Figure B–31. *The Developer Tools window in Internet Exlplorer*

Clicking on the inspection arrow above the code window (or using Ctrl-B) allows you to select an element and see what it looks like in the source document. If we select the title, we can see that the link is somewhere in the middle of a group of nested DIV containers, as shown in Figure B–32.

Figure B–32. *Inspecting the HTML source*

We can see that there's a DIV with an ID of `region-branding`. That's the one we'll use to attach our graphic. The code in Listing B–6 shows the CSS code for this.

Listing B–6. *CSS Code for Attaching a Graphic to an Identified DIV*

```
#region-branding {
 background: transparent url('../i/CDEF-name.png') no-repeat right top;
 min-height :131px;
 float:right;
}
```

This locates the element with the specified ID and sets the background to the graphic. It also sets a couple of other parameters. Notice the min-height parameter. This is the actual height of the graphic. It's a good idea to specify this so the browser's rendering engine doesn't have to work as hard, and it will render faster for the user.

Saving the CSS file and refreshing the browser provides the desired results as shown in Figure B–33.

Figure B–33. *Attaching a graphic to a DIV*

But there's a problem. The text title that contains the name of the site still prints, and it now displays on top of the graphic. There are a couple ways we can deal with this. On the settings page for the sub-theme, there is a section titled Toggle Display that lets you turn the display of various content items on or off. This is shown in Figure B–34.

> **▾ TOGGLE DISPLAY**
>
> Enable or disable the display of certain page elements.
>
> ☐ Logo
>
> ☑ Site name
>
> ☑ Site slogan
>
> ☑ User pictures in posts
>
> ☑ User pictures in comments

Figure B–34. *Toggling certain content items*

We could uncheck the Site name and Site slogan checkboxes so they don't appear on top of our graphic. While this will solve the problem of text overlays, it causes another problem. Search engines that crawl the web look for certain pieces of information to help optimize their results as they process their search queries. One of the important parts of your page is the title of your site. Even though we humans can see the title of the site because it's in the image, a site-crawling spider relies only on the HTML that is generated. If we remove the title, the search spider doesn't know the name of the site, and so we may miss getting our site to the eyes of potential users.

The trick, then, is to have Drupal generate the name of our site but have CSS hide it from view so it doesn't mess up the layout of the page. The code in Listing B–7 does just that.

Listing B–7. Using a Negative text-indent to Hide Text

```
.site-name-slogan {
  text-indent:-2000px;
}
```

This will take all text in the DIV container with the class site-name-slogan and indent the text 2,000 pixels to the left. The text will be rendered to the browser's canvas, but so far to the left that no human should see it. But search engines should.

So how did I know the name of the container that needed indenting? The same way I did above. In fact, the answer is in Listing B–7. The site-name-slogan is a container for an H1 element that contains the name, site-title, and an H6 that contains site-slogan.

This technique can be used any time you want to ensure search-engine optimization (SEO) but you don't want the text to appear to the user.

CSS Positioning

The next step is to position the main logo and menu bar so that it appears where our designer wanted it. If you recall from earlier in the text, this is the menu bar and globe logo that had to be moved down the page so we could capture it. Now we get to put it back where it belongs.

The CSS code to get started is shown in Listing B–8.

Listing B–8. Adding an Image That Will Be Shifted Up

```
#preface-container {
  background: transparent url('../i/CDEF-logo-menu.png') no-repeat center top;
  min-height:334px;
  width:960px;
}
```

Here we set the background image and specify its height and width. The resulting effect is shown in Figure B–35.

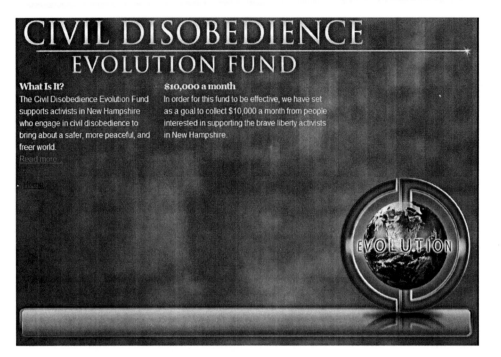

Figure B–35. Placing a graphic inline

This is probably what we should have expected from that code, but not really what we want. But adding three lines of code will give us exactly what we want (see Listing B–9).

Listing B–9. Shifting the Image Out and Up

```
#preface-container {
  background: transparent url('../i/CDEF-logo-menu.png') no-repeat center top;
  min-height:334px;
  width:960px;
  position:relative;
  top:-240px;
  z-index:100;
}
```

First, we need to establish that the image is relative to the container in which it's located. This will give us an anchor on which to establish the top of the image. The top is specified as having a negative value, which will move it up on the page by 240 pixels. Finally, by moving the graphic up the page, it will be sitting on top of the artifacts above, so we need to move the image back a bit using the z-index parameter. The results of our efforts are shown in Figure B–36.

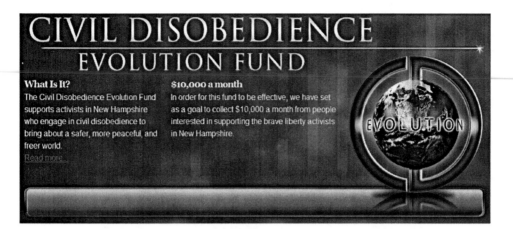

Figure B–36. *The image is positioned correctly*

Now for the menu. Remember that we placed the main menu in the Preface Second region. We need to put that in the horizontal bar under the globe logo. The CSS in Listing B–10 will do the trick.

Listing B–10. *Placing the Main Menu Where It Belongs*

```
#region-preface_second {
  position:relative;
  top:276px;
  left:10px;
}

#block-system-main-menu ul.menu {
  font-weight:bold;
  font-size:16pt;
  margin: 0;
  padding: 0;
  list-style-type:none;
  text-transform:uppercase;
}

#block-system-main-menu ul.menu li {
  padding: .2em;
  display:inline;
}

#block-system-main-menu ul.menu li a {
  text-decoration: none;
  color:#f1f1ef;
}
```

The identifier for the container is `region-preface_second`. That container is inside of the container that we hiked up the page, `preface-container`. Therefore, we need to move the menu back down a bit so it appears where we want it. That's the positive value in the `top` parameter, and the `position` parameter assures that there's something to move against.

The main menu is generated as an HTML unordered list. Setting list-style-type to none and display to inline will flatten the list so we can render it on a single line. The text-decoration parameter will get rid of the bullet. The rest of the settings are there to get the text to look just right. The menu appears as we would expect, as shown in Figure B–37.

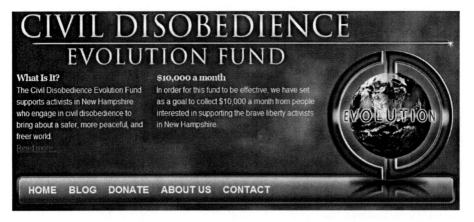

Figure B–37. Rendering the main menu in the proper location and format

The two header boxes are next. The code to format them is shown in Listing B–11.

Listing B–11. Header Box Formatting

```
#region-header_first,
#region-header_second {
  border:3pt solid #3399cc;
  background-color:#336666;
  border-radius: 15px;
  -webkit-border-radius: 15px;
  -moz-border-radius: 15px;
}

#region-header_first,
#region-header_second {
  height: 180px;
  margin:6px;
  color:#f1f1ef;
  text-align:center;
  z-index:200;
}

#region-header_first a:link,
#region-header_second a:link {
  color:#a1f1ef;
}

#region-header_first h2.block-title,
#region-header_second h2.block-title {
  color:#f1f1ef;
```

```
    font-size:16pt;
    font-family:Arial;
    text-transform:uppercase;
}
```

The parameters are pretty straightforward except for the radius parameters in `region-header_first` and `region-header_second`. Our designer specified rounded rectangles on those two regions. In older browsers, rounded borders were quite a chore. To create the effect, the designer had to create the four different rounded corners and stitch them together in the HTML.

Fortunately, with CSS 3, there is a new parameter, `border-radius`, that effortlessly creates rounded borders. The problem is that hardly anyone supports it yet. Figure B–38 shows the page rendered in Internet Explorer.

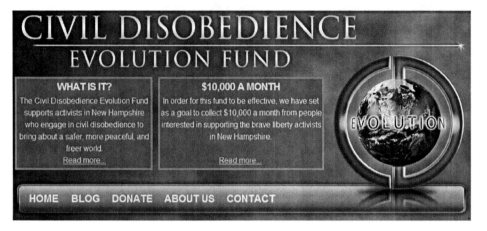

Figure B–38. *Rounded borders don't round in Internet Explorer 8*

Firefox and Google Chrome both support rounded corners, but they require their own extensions. That's why you see the three different parameters that do the same thing (`border-radius`, `-webkit-border-radius`, and `-moz-border-radius`). The `-moz` prefix is read by Firefox, and the `-webkit` prefix is read by Chrome. Some day, I imagine, all browsers will support the standard syntax, so I'll keep the standard `border-radius` parameter in the style sheet for now.

Figure B–39 shows our page rendered in Google Chrome.

The next item to style is the block that contains the social network links under the globe logo. Our designer gave us four graphics, one for the background bar and one for each of the links, RSS, Facebook, and Twitter.

The easiest way to get started is to create a new block with the HTML code we need to insert the links and images. We can create the block from Structure➤Blocks➤Add block as shown in Figure B–40.

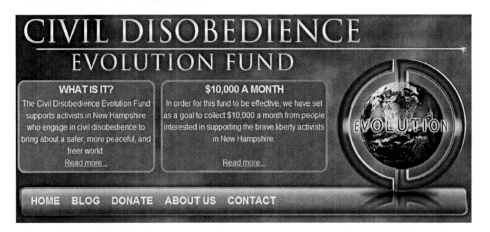

Figure B–39. Chrome supports rounded borders

Block description *

Follow Block

A brief description of your block. Used on the Blocks administration page.

Block title

<none>

The title of the block as shown to the user.

Block body *

```
<a href="rss.xml" class="rss-image">RSS</a><a href="http://facebook.com/cdevolution" class="facebook-
image">FACEBOOK</a><a href="http://twitter.com/cdevolve" class="twitter-image">TWITTER</a>
```

Text format Full HTML ▾   More information about text formats ?

- Web page addresses and e-mail addresses turn into links automatically.
- Lines and paragraphs break automatically.

The content of the block as shown to the user.

REGION SETTINGS

Specify in which themes and regions this block is displayed.

CDEvolution Theme (default theme)

Sidebar First ▾

Figure B–40. Creating a block with images and links

Notice that the HTML is placed directly into the body of the block and each of the links is given a class so we can hook into them to set our background images. The CSS code to style this is shown in Listing B–12.

Listing B–12. Styling Images and Links

```
#follow-block {
  text-align:center;
  background: url('../i/Follow-Buttons-Bar.png') no-repeat bottom center;
  min-height:120px;
  overflow:visible;
}

a.rss-image,
a.facebook-image,
a.twitter-image {
  text-indent:-2000px;
  height:96px;
  width:90px;
  display:inline-block;
}

a.rss-image {
  background: url('../i/rss.png') no-repeat bottom center;
}

a.facebook-image {
  background: url('../i/facebook.png') no-repeat bottom center;
}

a.twitter-image {
  background: url('../i/twitter.png') no-repeat bottom center;
}

#region-sidebar_first {
  position:relative;
  top:-240px;
}
```

The four images are set to be the background of each object, and some other parameters are set to make everything look just right. Notice the region-sidebar_first block. Just as we moved the logo up the page, we need to move the follow block.

The result of this styling is shown in Figure B–41.

Figure B–41. *The follow block is moved into position*

Rounding out this part of the style process requires some minor styling of the text in the main content region. This requires a simple CSS block, as shown in Listing B–13.

Listing B–13. *Tweaking the Position and Layout of the Content Block*

```
#region-content {
  color:#f1f1ef;
  position:relative;
  top:-240px;
}
```

The block is shown in Figure B–42.

Figure B–42. *The content region is moved up to meet the other objects*

Now that most of the content has been formatted, another problem becomes apparent. Look at the contents of the first sidebar, the one to the right of the main content. It is formatted as a table, which is not what our designer envisioned. In order to change it, we'll need to go deeper into the theming layer and create a new template file.

Template File

If you've done everything according to best practices, all theming done by Drupal's theming layer is performed by the theme() function. It is the job of that function to create a list of candidates that it can invoke at a particular time, and then select the most appropriate candidate.

By default, the list of recent blog posts is formatted as a table. I'd rather just have a list of titles with a link that goes directly to each page.

In Chapter 7, I covered the topic of custom theme functions. We'll be creating one here, and then creating a template file to render the content in the block.

First, we need to declare the theme function and let Drupal know what arguments are to be passed to it. Since this theme will be specific to the theme we are using, it should be placed in a program file that's known to our theme. The file, template.php, is a standard part of most themes, and is available to us as part of our starter kit.

In that file, there is a placeholder function, cdef_omega_theme() that we will expand to declare our function. The code in Listing B–14 shows what we need.

Listing B–14. *Declaring a Theme Function in the Theme Hook*

```
/**
 * Implements hook_theme().
 */
function cdef_omega_theme(&$existing, $type, $theme, $path) {
  $hooks = array(
    'recent_list' => array(
      'arguments' => array(
        'node-title' => NULL,
        'node-id' => NULL,
      )
    )
  );
  return $hooks;
}
```

The theme hook returns an array with the names of all of the themes we wish to register, just one in this case: recent_list. The structure also declares the names and default values of the two arguments that will be passed.

In keeping with the PHP requirement for unique function names, we will craft a function that Drupal's theme engine will find. The function, prefixed with the theme name, is shown in Listing B–15.

Listing B–15. *The Theme Function*

```
function cdef_omega_recent_list($variables) {
  $title = $variables['node_title'];
  $id = $variables['node_id'];
  $content = '<div class="recent-title">' . l($title, 'node/' . $id) . '</div>';
  return $content;
}
```

The function builds a single DIV element with a class we can style and a link with the article title. We can now call this particular function through the theme() function. The call passes the name of the function, along with the arguments it is looking for: theme('recent_list', array(node_title => 'Some Title', node_id => 123);.

▓ **Tip** Notice the function used to create a link, l(). This handy function provides little gifts to us. First, it takes care of formatting a link, the HTML <a> tag. It also outputs whatever attributes are necessary to create the link we need. Plus, it takes care of escaping text in the link's URL. You should always use the l() function to create a link.

The last step is to figure out the name of the function that currently formats the table that we want to change. By setting some breakpoints and watching what was executing, I discovered that the name of the theme function is node_recent_block. We can work off of that name to build everything we need.

First, we need to create a function to process the data before it gets to the theming function. To do this, we will invoke the preprocess hook. The name of this function takes the form {theme name}_preprocess_{theme function} and is shown in Listing B–16.

Listing B–16. The Preprocess Hook

```
function cdef_omega_preprocess_node_recent_block(&$vars) {
  $content = '';
  foreach ($vars['nodes'] as $recent_node) {
    $variables['node_title'] = $recent_node->title;
    $variables['node_id'] = $recent_node->nid;
    $content .= theme('recent_list', $variables);
  }
  $vars['content'] = $content;
}
```

This function is called with a reference to an array that contains the pertinent information. In this case, &$vars contains all of the nodes in the recent block. Creating the structure can be accomplished by simply iterating over this list, isolating the two variables we need, and then calling the theme function with the appropriate call. This calls the cdef_omega_recent_list() function we created above.

Now that we've created the content, we need to do something with it. There are several things we can do, but I've chosen to use a template. The name of the template is important, as it will be used by Drupal's theme() function to determine whether to load the template or execute a function to do the theming.

The name of the file is the name of the theme function with the underscores turned into hyphens. The extension of the file is tpl.php. In this case, the theme function is node_recent_block(), so our file name will be node-recent-block.tpl.php. Notice that the underscores have been converted to hyphens. The best place to put this file is in the templates folder of our sub-theme.

The structure of the file is straightforward, as you can see in Listing B–17.

Listing B–17. The Theme Template Program

```
<div id="recent-block">
  <?php print $content; ?>
</div>
```

The variable $content is the value of the member of the &$vars array that has the same name. That's why we set $vars['content'] to the HTML that was returned from the recent_list theme call. If we want other variables to be available in the template, all we need to do is create members of that &$vars array with the name of the variable as the name of the array key. This is described a bit more in Chapter 7.

Judging from the result shown in Figure B–43, it looks like the theming was a success.

Figure B–43. Results of the theme template

That's about all I wanted to cover for this particular theme, though there are plenty of little tweaks we could do to make the site look just like our designer intended.

Summary

In this appendix, we went from a designer's mock-up of a site to an actual site using the Omega theme. Omega is an advanced theming environment but it need not be intimidating if you just understand a couple of fundamental concepts. As we've seen, Omega allows designers to design, and still let the developer make the content fit into the design's constraints. Other themes that are available for Drupal are not always as flexible as this. For this reason, I think the Omega theme and starter kit should get a lot of attention as Drupal 7 is implemented for more and more sites.

There are simpler themes and starter kits out there, but you'll be able to get comfortable with any of them once you learn how Drupal's page rendering engine works, and how the theming layer provides industrial-strength tools to enable rendering of just about any kind of site you can come up with.

Selected Reference Material

This appendix is for all the things I promised in the rest of the book. It is a helper for commonly used reference materials, such as Drupal's API section, http://api.drupal.org—the best place to learn about the functions and classes available in Drupal. Remember, the Drupal core is always evolving and the calls might change from version to version. The Drupal API site will also show you the most recent version of all interfaces.

Core Template Variables

In Chapter 7, I talked about using Drupal's theme template engine to get control over the look of various parts of the content created by the Drupal database engine. The Drupal core ships with a number of templates. Each of these templates makes available certain variables, depending on the template.

Each of the variables ($styles, $site_name, $content, $search_box, etc.) must be generated in a module and made available as global variables so the Drupal's page-creation logic can render them. Table C-1 provides a list of variables for each template that ships with the Drupal 7 core.

Table C–1. Drupal 7 Core Templates

Template	Available Variables	
block.tpl.php	$block->subject	Block title.
	$content	Block content.
Default theme implementation to display a block.	$block->module	Module that generated the block.
	$block->delta	An ID for the block, unique within each module.
	$block->region	The block region embedding the current block.
	$classes	String of classes that can be used to style contextually through CSS. The string can be manipulated through the variable $classes_array from preprocess functions. The default values can be one or more of the following:
		block — The current template type, i.e., the "theming hook."
		block-[module] — The module generating the block. For example, the user module is responsible for handling the default user navigation block. In that case, the class would be "block-user."

Template	Available Variables	
	$title_prefix	An array containing additional output populated by modules, intended to be displayed in front of the main title tag that appears in the template.
	$title_suffix	An array containing additional output populated by modules, intended to be displayed after the main title tag that appears in the template.
	$classes_array	Array of HTML class attribute values. It is flattened into a string within the variable $classes.
	$block_zebra	Outputs 'odd' and 'even' dependent on each block region.
	$zebra	Same output as $block_zebra but independent of any block region.
	$block_id	Counter dependent on each block region.
	$id	Same output as $block_id but independent of any block region.
	$is_front	Flags true when presented in the front page.
	$logged_in	Flags true when the current user is a logged-in member.
	$is_admin	Flags true when the current user is an administrator.
	$block_html_id	A valid HTML ID and guaranteed unique.
comment-wrapper.tpl.php Default theme implementation to provide an HTML container for comments.	$content	The array of content-related elements for the node. Use render($content) to print them all, or print a subset such as render($content['comment_form']).
	$classes	String of classes that can be used to style contextually through CSS. The string can be manipulated through the variable $classes_array from preprocess functions. The default value has the following: comment-wrapper: The current template type, i.e., the "theming hook."
	$title_prefix	An array containing additional output populated by modules, intended to be displayed in front of the main title tag that appears in the template.
	$title_suffix	An array containing additional output populated by modules, intended to be displayed after the main title tag that appears in the template.
	$node	Node object the comments are attached to.
	$classes_array	Array of HTML class attribute values. It is flattened into a string within the variable $classes.
comment.tpl.php Default theme implementation for comments.	$author	Comment author. Can be a link or plain text.
	$content	An array of comment items. Use render($content) to print them all, or print a subset such as render($content['field_example']). Use hide($content['field_example']) to temporarily suppress the printing of a given element.

Template	Available Variables	
		Formatted date and time when the comment was created. Preprocess functions can reformat it by calling `format_date()` with the desired parameters on the `$comment->created` variable.
	`$changed`	Formatted date and time when the comment was last changed. Preprocess functions can reformat it by calling `format_date()` with the desired parameters on the `$comment->changed` variable.
	`$new`	New comment marker.
	`$permalink`	Comment permalink.
	`$picture`	The author's picture.
	`$created`	The author's signature.
	`$status`	Comment status. Possible values are: comment-unpublished comment-published, comment-preview.
	`$title`	Linked title.
	`$classes`	String of classes that can be used to style contextually through CSS. The string can be manipulated through the variable `$classes_array` from preprocess functions. The default values can be one or more of the following:
		`comment` — The current template type, i.e., the "theming hook."
		`comment-by-anonymous` — Comment by an unregistered user.
		`comment-by-node-author` — Comment by the author of the parent node.
		`comment-preview` — Preview of a new or edited comment.
		`comment-unpublished` — An unpublished comment visible only to administrators.
		`comment-by-viewer` — Comment by the user currently viewing the page.
		`comment-new` — New comment since last the visit.
	`$title_prefix`	An array containing additional output populated by modules, intended to be displayed in front of the main title tag that appears in the template.
	`$title_suffix`	An array containing additional output populated by modules, intended to be displayed after the main title tag that appears in the template.
	`$comment`	Full comment object.
	`$node`	Node object the comments are attached to.
	`$classes_array`	Array of HTML class attribute values. It is flattened into a string within the variable `$classes`.

391

Template	Available Variables
`field.tpl.php` Default template implementation to display the value of a field. This file is not used and is here as a starting point for customization only.	• `$items`: An array of field values. Use `render()` to output them. • `$label`: The item label. • `$label_hidden`: Whether the label display is set to `'hidden'`. • `$classes`: String of classes that can be used to style contextually through CSS. The string can be manipulated through the variable `$classes_array` from preprocess functions. The default values can be one or more of the following: • `field`: The current template type, i.e., the "theming hook." • `field-name-[field_name]`: The current field name. For example, if the field name is "field_description," the result would be "field-name-field-description." • `field-type-[field_type]`: The current field type. For example, if the field type is "text," the result would be "field-type-text." • `field-label-[label_display]`: The current label position. For example, if the label position is "above," the result would be "field-label-above." Other variables: • `$element['#object']`: The entity to which the field is attached. • `$element['#view_mode']`: View mode, e.g., `'full'`, `'teaser'`... • `$element['#field_name']`: The field name. • `$element['#field_type']`: The field type. • `$element['#field_language']`: The field language. • `$element['#field_translatable']`: Whether the field is translatable or not. • `$element['#label_display']`: Position of label display, inline, above, or hidden. • `$field_name_css`: The css-compatible field name. • `$field_type_css`: The css-compatible field type. • `$classes_array`: Array of HTML class attribute values. It is flattened into a string within the variable `$classes`.
`html.tpl.php` Default theme implementation to display the basic HTML structure of a single Drupal page.	• `$css`: An array of CSS files for the current page. • `$language`: (object) The language the site is being displayed in. • `$language->language`: Contains its textual representation. • `$language->dir`: Contains the language direction, either be `'ltr'` or `'rtl'`. • `$rdf_namespaces`: All the RDF namespace prefixes used in the HTML document. • `$grddl_profile`: A GRDDL profile allowing agents to extract the RDF data. • `$head_title`: A modified version of the page title, for use in the TITLE tag. • `$head`: Markup for the HEAD section (including meta tags, keyword tags, and so on). • `$styles`: Style tags for importing all CSS files for the page. • `$scripts`: Script tags for loading the JavaScript files and settings for the page.

Template	Available Variables
	• $page_top: Initial markup from any modules that have altered the page. This variable should always be output first, before all other dynamic content. • $page: The rendered page content. • $page_bottom: Final closing markup from any modules that have altered the page. This variable should always be output last, after all other dynamic content. $classes: String of classes that can be used to style contextually through CSS.

node.tpl.php
 	
Default theme implementation to display a node
	• $title: the (sanitized) title of the node.
	
	• $content: An array of node items. Use render($content) to print them all, or print a subset such as render($content['field_example']). Use hide($content['field_example']) to temporarily suppress the printing of a given element.
	
	• $user_picture: The node author's picture from user-picture.tpl.php.
	
	• $date: Formatted creation date. Preprocess functions can reformat it by calling format_date() with the desired parameters on the $created variable.
	
	• $name: Themed username of node author output from theme_username().
	
	• $node_url: Direct URL of the current node.
	
	• $display_submitted: whether submission information should be displayed.
	
	• $classes: String of classes that can be used to style contextually through CSS. The string can be manipulated through the variable $classes_array from preprocess functions. The default values can be one or more of the following:
	
	  • node: The current template type, i.e., the "theming hook."
	
	  • node-[type]: The current node type. For example, if the node is a "Blog entry" the result would be "node-blog." Note that the machine name will often be in a short form of the human readable label.
	
	  • node-teaser: Nodes in teaser form.
	
	  • node-preview: Nodes in preview mode.
	
	  • node-promoted: Nodes promoted to the front page.
	
	  • node-sticky: Nodes ordered above other non-sticky nodes in teaser listings.
	
	  • node-unpublished: Unpublished nodes visible only to administrators.
	
	• $title_prefix: An array containing additional output populated by modules, intended to be displayed in front of the main title tag that appears in the template.
	
	• $title_suffix: An array containing additional output populated by modules, intended to be displayed after the main title tag that appears in the template.
	
	Other variables:
	
	• $node: Full node object. Contains data that may not be safe.
	
	• $type: Node type, i.e., story, page, blog, etc.
	
	• $comment_count: Number of comments attached to the node.
	
	• $uid: User ID of the node author.

Template	Available Variables
	• $created: Time the node was published, formatted in Unix timestamp.
	• $classes_array: Array of html class attribute values. It is flattened into a string within the variable $classes.
	• $zebra: Outputs either "even" or "odd." Useful for zebra striping in teaser listings.
	• $id: Position of the node. Increments each time its output.
	Node status variables:
	• $view_mode: View mode, e.g., 'full', 'teaser'...
	• $teaser: Flag for the teaser state (shortcut for $view_mode == 'teaser').
	• $page: Flag for the full page state.
	• $promote: Flag for front page promotion state.
	• $sticky: Flags for sticky post setting.
	• $status: Flag for published status.
	• $comment: State of comment settings for the node.
	• $readmore: Flags true if the teaser content of the node can't hold the main body content.
	• $is_front: Flags true when presented on the front page.
	• $logged_in: Flags true when the current user is a logged-in member.
	• $is_admin: Flags true when the current user is an administrator.
	Field variables: for each field instance attached to the node a corresponding variable is defined, e.g., $node->body becomes $body. When it's necessary to access a field's raw values, developers/themers are strongly encouraged to use these variables. Otherwise, you'll have to explicitly specify the desired field language, such as $node->body['en'], thus overriding any language negotiation rule that was previously applied.
page.tpl.php Default theme implementation to display a single Drupal page.	• $base_path: The base URL path of the Drupal installation. At the very least, this will always default to /.
	• $directory: The directory the template is located in, such as modules/system or themes/garland.
	• $is_front: TRUE if the current page is the front page.
	• $logged_in: TRUE if the user is registered and signed in.
	• $is_admin: TRUE if the user has permission to access administration pages.
	Site identity:
	• $front_page: The URL of the front page. Use this instead of $base_path, when linking to the front page. It includes the language domain or prefix.
	• $logo: The path to the logo image, as defined in theme configuration.
	• $site_name: The name of the site, empty when display has been disabled in theme settings.
	• $site_slogan: The slogan of the site, empty when display has been disabled in theme settings.

Template	Available Variables
	Navigation:
	• $main_menu: An array containing the Main menu links for the site, if they have been configured.
	• $secondary_menu: An array containing the Secondary menu links for the site, if they have been configured.
	• $breadcrumb: The breadcrumb trail for the current page.
	Page content (in order of occurrence in the default page.tpl.php):
	• $title_prefix: An array containing additional output populated by modules, intended to be displayed in front of the main title tag that appears in the template.
	• $title: The page title, for use in the actual HTML content.
	• $title_suffix: An array containing additional output populated by modules, intended to be displayed after the main title tag that appears in the template.
	• $messages: HTML for status and error messages. Should be displayed prominently.
	• $tabs: Tabs linking to any sub-pages beneath the current page (e.g., the view and edit tabs when displaying a node).
	• $action_links: Actions local to the page, such as 'Add menu' on the menu administration interface.
	• $feed_icons: A string of all feed icons for the current page.
	• $node: The node object, if there is an automatically-loaded node associated with the page; the node ID is the second argument in the page's path (e.g., node/12345 and node/12345/revisions, but not comment/reply/12345).
	Regions:
	• $page['help']: Dynamic help text, mostly for admin pages.
	• $page['highlight']: Items for the highlighted content region.
	• $page['content']: The main content of the current page.
	• $page['sidebar_first']: Items for the first sidebar.
	• $page['sidebar_second']: Items for the second sidebar.
	• $page['header']: Items for the header region.
	• $page['footer']: Items for the footer region.
region.tpl.php Default theme implementation to display a region.	• $content: The content for this region, typically blocks.
	• $classes: String of classes that can be used to style contextually through CSS. The string can be manipulated through the variable $classes_array from preprocess functions. The default values can be one or more of the following:
	• region: The current template type i.e., the "theming hook."
	• region-[name]: The name of the region with underscores replaced by dashes. For example, the page_top region would have a region-page-top class.
	• $region: The name of the region variable as defined in the theme's .info file.

Template	Available Variables
	Helper variables: • `$classes_array`: Array of HTML class attribute values. It is flattened into a string within the variable $classes. • `$is_admin`: Flags true when the current user is an administrator. • `$is_front`: Flags true when presented on the front page. • `$logged_in`: Flags true when the current user is a logged-in member.

SimpleTest Reference

SimpleTest is the testing framework that is built into Drupal 7. Table C-2 shows some binary assertions. Table C-3 lists content assertions. Table C-4 shows SimpleTest navigation functions. Table C-5 shows request modifiers.

Table C–2. SimpleTest Binary Assertions

Assertion	Description
`assertTrue($x)`	Fail if $x is false.
`assertFalse($x)`	Fail if $x is true.
`assertNull($x)`	Fail if $x is set.
`assertNotNull($x)`	Fail if $x not set.
`assertIsA($x, $t)`	Fail if $x is not the class or type $t.
`assertNotA($x, $t)`	Fail if $x is of the class or type $t.
`assertEqual($x, $y)`	Fail if $x == $y is false.
`assertNotEqual($x, $y)`	Fail if $x == $y is true.
`assertWithinMargin($x, $y, $m)`	Fail if abs($x - $y) < $m is false.
`assertOutsideMargin($x, $y, $m)`	Fail if abs($x - $y) < $m is true.
`assertIdentical($x, $y)`	Fail if $x == $y is false or a type mismatch.
`assertNotIdentical($x, $y)`	Fail if $x == $y is true and types match.
`assertReference($x, $y)`	Fail unless $x and $y are the same variable.
`assertClone($x, $y)`	Fail unless $x and $y are identical copies.
`assertPattern($p, $x)`	Fail unless the regex $p matches $x.
`assertNoPattern($p, $x)`	Fail if the regex $p matches $x.
`expectError($x)`	Swallow any upcoming matching error.
`assert($e)`	Fail on failed expectation object $e.

Table C–3. SimpleText Content Assertions

Assertion	Description
assertTitle($title)	Pass if title is an exact match.
assertText($text)	Pass if matches visible and "alt" text.
assertNoText($text)	Pass if doesn't match visible and "alt" text.
assertPattern($pattern)	A Perl pattern match against the page content.
assertNoPattern($pattern)	A Perl pattern match to not find content.
assertLink($label)	Pass if a link with this text is present.
assertNoLink($label)	Pass if no link with this text is present.
assertLinkById($id)	Pass if a link with this id attribute is present.
assertNoLinkById($id)	Pass if no link with this id attribute is present.
assertField($name, $value)	Pass if an input tag with this name has this value.
assertFieldById($id, $value)	Pass if an input tag with this id has this value.
assertResponse($codes)	Pass if HTTP response matches this list.
assertMime($types)	Pass if MIME type is in this list.
assertAuthentication($protocol)	Pass if the current challenge is this protocol.
assertNoAuthentication()	Pass if there is no current challenge.
assertRealm($name)	Pass if the current challenge realm matches.
assertHeader($header, $content)	Pass if a header was fetched matching this value.
assertNoHeader($header)	Pass if a header was not fetched.
assertCookie($name, $value)	Pass if there is currently a matching cookie.
assertNoCookie($name)	Pass if there is currently no cookie of this name.

Table C–4. SimpleTest Navigation Methods

Method	Description
getUrl()	Get the current location.
get($url, $parameters)	Send a GET request with these parameters.
post($url, $parameters)	Send a POST request with these parameters.
head($url, $parameters)	Send a HEAD request without replacing the page content.
retry()	Reload the last request.
back()	Like the browser back button.
forward()	Like the browser forward button.
authenticate($name, $password)	Retry after a challenge.
restart()	Restart the browser as if a new session.
getCookie($name)	Get the cookie value for the current context.
ageCookies($interval)	Age current cookies prior to a restart.
clearFrameFocus()	Go back to treating all frames as one page.
clickSubmit($label)	Click the first button with this label.
clickSubmitByName($name)	Click the button with this name attribute.
clickSubmitById($id)	Click the button with this ID attribute.
clickImage($label, $x, $y)	Click an input tag of type image by title or alt text.
clickImageByName($name, $x, $y)	Click an input tag of type image by name.
clickImageById($id, $x, $y)	Click an input tag of type image by ID attribute.
submitFormById($id)	Submit a form without the submit value.
clickLink($label, $index)	Click an anchor by the visible label text.
clickLinkById($id)	Click an anchor by the ID attribute.
getFrameFocus()	Get the name of the currently selected frame.
setFrameFocusByIndex($choice)	Focus on a frame counting from 1.
setFrameFocus($name)	Focus on a frame by name.

Table C–5. SimpleTest Request Modifiers

Request modifier	Description
getTransportError()	Get the last socket error.
showRequest()	Dump the outgoing request.
showHeaders()	Dump the incoming headers.
showSource()	Dump the raw HTML page content.
ignoreFrames()	Do not load framesets.
setCookie($name, $value)	Set a cookie from now on.
addHeader($header)	Always add this header to the request.
setMaximumRedirects($max)	Stop after this many redirects.
setConnectionTimeout($timeout)	Kill the connection after this time between bytes.
useProxy($proxy, $name, $password)	Make requests via this proxy URL.

Install Hooks

In Chapter 10, I covered the Drupal installation process. Table C-6 lists hooks that are specific to the .install file.

Table C–6. Install Hooks

Hook	Description
hook_install()	Perform setup tasks when the module is installed.
hook_uninstall()	Remove any information that the module sets.
hook_update_N()	Perform a single update. For each patch that requires a database change, add a new hook_update_N()that will be called by update.php. The database updates are numbered sequentially according to the version of Drupal you are compatible with.
hook_schema()	Define the current version of the database schema.
hook_modules_installed()	Perform necessary actions after modules are installed.

Hook	Description
hook_modules_uninstalled()	Perform necessary actions after modules are uninstalled.
hook_install_tasks()	Return an array of tasks to be performed by an installation profile.
hook_install_tasks_alter()	Alter the full list of installation tasks.
hook_requirements()	Check installation requirements and do status reporting.
hook_enable()	Perform necessary actions after module is enabled. The hook is called every time the module is enabled.
hook_disable()	Perform necessary actions before module is disabled. The hook is called every time the module is disabled.

Schema API

A Drupal schema definition is an array structure representing one or more tables and their related keys and indexes. A schema is defined by hook_schema(), which usually lives in a modulename.install file.

By implementing hook_schema() and specifying the tables your module declares, you can easily create and drop these tables on all supported database engines. You don't have to deal with the different SQL dialects for table creation and alteration of the supported database engines.

Drupal defines a number of structures for content management. The most ubiquitous is the node, which is the core container for content types. All Drupal-managed content extends from the node.

The field framework allows the user to create custom content types that extend the Drupal content even farther for specialized needs.

But there are other managed objects, such as users, blocks, and taxonomy terms, for which there are many functions to query, modify, and delete these objects.

These Drupal-managed objects are handy and create a powerful, extensible platform, but might be too cumbersome if you merely want to store away a small piece of data, or even a large set that would not necessarily be considered traditional Drupal content.

In other words, you might want to add tables to the Drupal database that you will manage in your modules and that the Drupal core doesn't really need to know or care about.

Creating database tables in a database-agnostic way is a bit tricky, but fortunately, Drupal's Schema API makes it possible. Instead of passing CREATE TABLE or ALTER TABLE queries directly to the database, we use a syntax that's consistent with other Drupal structures.

Schema API Classes

Drupal has a number of classes that can be used to access your schema information in a database-agnostic way. The classes are listed in Table C-7.

Table C–7. Schema API Classes

Name	Description
DatabaseSchema	Implements QueryPlaceholderInterface to provide a generic means of accessing the Schema API.
DatabaseSchemaObjectDoesNotExistException	Throws exception if an object being modified doesn't exist yet.
DatabaseSchemaObjectExistsException	Throws exception if an object being created already exists.
DatabaseSchema_mysql DatabaseSchema_pgsql DatabaseSchema_sqlite DatabaseSchema_sqlsvr	Implements features specific to a particular database engine.

Schema API Functions and Methods

If you will be creating custom schemas for your module, you'll probably create schemas using the schema hook in the .install file. In addition, there are a number of functions and methods that allow you to manipulate the schema in your code. These are listed in Table C-8.

Table C–8. Schema API Functions and Methods

Name	Description
db_add_field	Adds a new field to a table.
db_add_index	Adds an index.
db_add_primary_key	Adds a primary key to a database table.
db_add_unique_key	Adds a unique key.
db_change_field	Changes a field definition.
db_create_table	Creates a new table from a Drupal table definition.
db_drop_field	Drops a field.
db_drop_index	Drops an index.
db_drop_primary_key	Drops the primary key of a database table.

`db_drop_table`	Drops a table.
`db_drop_unique_key`	Drops a unique key.
`db_field_exists`	Checks if a column exists in the given table.
`db_field_names`	Returns an array of field names from an array of key/index column specifiers.
`db_field_set_default`	Sets the default value for a field.
`db_field_set_no_default`	Sets a field to have no default value.
`db_find_tables`	Finds all tables that are like the specified base table name.
`db_index_exists`	Checks if an index exists in the given table.
`db_rename_table`	Renames a table.
`db_table_exists`	Checks if a table exists.
`drupal_get_schema`	Gets the schema definition of a table, or the whole database schema.
`drupal_get_schema_unprocessed`	Returns the unprocessed and unaltered version of a module's schema.
`drupal_install_schema`	Creates all tables in a module's hook_schema() implementation.
`drupal_schema_fields_sql`	Retrieves a list of fields from a table schema. The list is suitable for use in a SQL query.
`drupal_uninstall_schema`	Removes all tables that a module defines in its hook_schema().
`drupal_write_record`	Saves a record to the database based upon the schema.
`hook_schema`	Defines the current version of the database schema. See next section.

Schema Hook

The best way to create schemas for your module is to create an array that defines all aspects of your data structures and use the schema hook in your `.install` file. I discuss this topic in Chapter 10.

The schema hook should return an array with a key for each table the module defines. The following keys are defined:

- `'description'`: A string in non-markup plain text describing this table and its purpose. References to other tables should be enclosed in curly-brackets. For example, the node_revisions table description field might contain "Stores per-revision title and body data for each {node}."

- `'fields'`: An associative array (`'fieldname'` => `specification`) that describes the table's database columns. The specification is also an array. The following specification parameters are defined:

    - `'description'`: A string in non-markup plain text describing this field and its purpose. References to other tables should be enclosed in curly-brackets.

    - `'type'`: The generic data type: `'char'`, `'varchar'`, `'text'`, `'blob'`, `'int'`, `'float'`, `'numeric'`, `'serial'`, `'date'`, `'datetime'` or `'time'`. Most types just map to the corresponding database engine-specific data types. Use `'serial'` for auto-incrementing fields. This will expand to `'INT auto_increment'` on MySQL.

    - `'serialize'`: A Boolean indicating whether the field will be stored as a serialized string.

    - `'size'`: The data size: `'tiny'`, `'small'`, `'medium'`, `'normal'`, `'big'`. This is a hint about the largest value the field will store and determines which of the database engine-specific data types will be used (e.g., on MySQL, TINYINT vs. INT vs. BIGINT). `'normal'`, the default, selects the base type (e.g., on MySQL, INT, VARCHAR, BLOB, etc.). Not all sizes are available for all data types. See DatabaseSchema::getFieldTypeMap() for possible combinations.

    - `'not null'`: If true, no NULL values will be allowed in this database column. Defaults to false.

    - `'default'`: The field's default value. The PHP type of the value matters: `' '`, `'0'`, and 0 are all different. If you specify `'0'` as the default value for a type `'int'` field it will not work because `'0'` is a string containing the character "zero", not an integer.

    - `'length'`: The maximal length of a type `'char'`, `'varchar'` or `'text'` field. Ignored for other field types.

    - `'unsigned'`: A Boolean indicating whether a type (`'int'`, `'float'`, and `'numeric'` only) is signed or unsigned. Defaults to FALSE. Ignored for other field types.

    - `'precision'`, `'scale'`: For type `'numeric'` fields, indicates the precision (total number of significant digits) and scale (decimal digits right of the decimal point). Both values are mandatory. Ignored for other field types.

    All parameters apart from `'type'` are optional except that type `'numeric'` columns must specify `'precision'` and `'scale'`.

- `'primary key'`: An array of one or more key column specifiers (see below) that form the primary key.

- `'unique keys'`: An associative array of unique keys (`'keyname'` => `specification`). Each specification is an array of one or more key column specifiers (see below) that form a unique key on the table.

- `'foreign keys'`: An associative array of relations (`'my_relation'` => `specification`). Each specification is an array containing the name of the referenced table (`'table'`), and an array of column mappings (`'columns'`). Column mappings are defined by key pairs (`'source_column'` => `'referenced_column'`).

- `'indexes'`: An associative array of indexes (`'indexname'` => `specification`). Each specification is an array of one or more key column specifiers (see below) that form an index on the table.

A key column specifier is either a string naming a column or an array of two elements: column name and length, specifying a prefix of the named column.

Globals

The Drupal core uses certain global variables in the construction of a page. Global variables are discussed in Chapter 3. The globals used in the core are listed in Table C-9.

Table C–9. Drupal Core Global Variables

Name	Location	Description
`$base_path`	`includes/bootstrap.inc`	The base path of the Drupal installation. This will at least default to '/'.
`$base_root`	`includes/bootstrap.inc`	The root URL of the host, excluding the path.
`$base_theme_info`	`includes/theme.inc`	An array of objects that represent the base theme.
`$base_url`	`includes/bootstrap.inc`	The base URL of the Drupal installation.
`$channel`	`modules/aggregator/ aggregator.parser.inc`	An associative array containing title, link, description, and other keys. Links should be an absolute URL.
`$conf`	`./settings.php`	Site configuration values defined in the global settings file.
`$conf`	`includes/bootstrap.inc`	Array of persistent variables stored in 'variable' table.
`$cookie_domain`	`includes/bootstrap.inc`	The domain to be used for session cookies. For hosts such as 'localhost' or those that expos only an IP address, the cookie domain will not be set.

Name	Location	Description
$databases	./settings.php	Array of database connections.
$drupal_test_info	modules/simpletest/ drupal_web_test_case.php	Global variable that holds information about the tests being run.
$element	modules/aggregator/ aggregator.parser.inc	Structured array describing the data to be rendered.
$forum_topic_list_header	modules/forum/forum.module	An array of forum topic header information.
$image	modules/aggregator/ aggregator.parser.inc	Current image tag used by aggregator parsing.
$installed_profile	includes/bootstrap.inc	The name of the profile that has just been installed.
$item	modules/aggregator/ aggregator.parser.inc	General string or array.
$items	modules/aggregator/ aggregator.parser.inc	Array of items used by aggregator.
$language	includes/bootstrap.inc	An object containing the information for the active interface language. It represents the language the user interface textual elements such as titles, labels or messages, are to be displayed in.
$language_content	modules/field/ field.multilingual.inc	An object containing the information for the active content language. It is used by the Field API as a default value when no language is specified to select the field translation to be displayed.
$language_url	includes/locale.inc	An object containing the information for the active URL language. It is used as a default value by URL-related functions such as l() when no language is explicitly specified.
$menu_admin	includes/path.inc	Boolean indicating that a menu administrator is running a menu access check.

Name	Location	Description
$multibyte	includes/unicode.inc	The current multibyte mode. Possible values: UNICODE_ERROR, UNICODE_SINGLEBYTE, UNICODE_MULTIBYTE.
$pager_limits	includes/pager.inc	Array of the number of items per page for each pager. The array index is the pager element index (0 by default).
$pager_page_array	includes/pager.inc	Array of current page numbers for each pager.
$pager_total	includes/pager.inc	Array of the total number of pages for each pager. The array index is the pager element index (0 by default).
$pager_total_items	includes/pager.inc	Array of the total number of items for each pager. The array index is the pager element index (0 by default).
$tag	modules/aggregator/ aggregator.parser.inc	Active tag name.
$theme	includes/theme.inc	Active theme name.
$theme_engine	includes/theme.inc	The theme engine related to the active theme.
$theme_info	includes/theme.inc	Active theme object.
$theme_key	includes/theme.inc	Name of the active theme.
$theme_path	includes/theme.inc	The path to the active theme.
$timers	includes/bootstrap.inc	Timers that have been created by timer_start().
$update_free_access	sites/default/ settings.php	Allows the update.php script to be run when not logged in as administrator. Be sure to set to FALSE for production systems!
$user	includes/bootstrap.inc	An object representing the currently logged-in user. Contains preferences and other user information.

Field CRUD API

The Field CRUD API is for creating fields, bundles, and instances. Fields are covered in Chapter 9. Functions and methods are shown in Table C-10.

Table C–10. Field CRUD API Functions and Methods

Name	Description
field_create_field	Creates a field.
field_create_instance	Creates an instance of a field, binding it to a bundle.
field_delete_field	Marks a field and its instances and data for deletion.
field_delete_instance	Marks a field instance and its data for deletion.
field_read_field	Reads a single field record directly from the database.
field_read_fields	Reads in fields that match an array of conditions.
field_read_instance	Reads a single instance record directly from the database.
field_read_instances	Reads in field instances that match an array of conditions.
field_update_field	Updates a field.
field_update_instance	Updates an instance of a field.
hook_field_create_field	Acts on a field being created.
hook_field_create_instance	Acts on a field instance being created.
hook_field_delete_field	Acts on a field being deleted.
hook_field_delete_instance	Acts on a field instance being deleted.
hook_field_purge_field	Acts when a field record is being purged.
hook_field_purge_field_instance	Acts when a field instance is being purged.
hook_field_read_field	Acts on field records being read from the database.
hook_field_read_instance	Acts on a field record being read from the database.

Name	Description
hook_field_storage_purge	Removes field storage information when field data is purged.
hook_field_storage_purge_field	Removes field storage information when a field record is purged.
hook_field_storage_purge_field_instance	Removes field storage information when a field instance is purged.
hook_field_update_field	Acts on a field being updated.
hook_field_update_forbid	Forbids a field update.
hook_field_update_instance	Acts on a field instance being updated.
_field_write_instance	Stores an instance record in the field configuration database.

Field Attach API

The Field Attach API allows you to operate on Field API data that has been attached to Drupal entities. Fields are covered in Chapter 9. Functions and methods are listed in Table C-11.

Table C–11. Field Attach API Functions and Methods

Name	Description
field_attach_create_bundle	Notifies field.module that a new bundle was created.
field_attach_delete	Deletes field data for an existing entity. This deletes all revisions of field data for the entity.
field_attach_delete_bundle	Notifies field.module that a bundle was deleted.
field_attach_delete_revision	Deletes field data for a single revision of an existing entity. The passed entity must have a revision id attribute.
field_attach_form	Adds form elements for all fields for an entity to a form structure.
field_attach_form_validate	Performs field validation against form-submitted field values.

Name	Description
field_attach_insert	Saves field data for a new entity.
field_attach_load	Loads fields for the current revisions of a group of entities.
field_attach_load_revision	Loads all fields for previous versions of a group of entities.
field_attach_prepare_translation	Prepares an entity for translation.
field_attach_prepare_view	Prepares field data prior to display.
field_attach_preprocess	Populates the template variables with the field values available for rendering.
field_attach_presave	Performs necessary operations just before field data gets saved.
field_attach_rename_bundle	Notifies field.module that a bundle was renamed.
field_attach_submit	Performs necessary operations on field data submitted by a form.
field_attach_update	Saves field data for an existing entity.
field_attach_validate	Performs field validation against the field data in an entity.
field_attach_view	Returns a renderable array for the fields on an entity.
hook_field_attach_create_bundle	Acts on field_attach_create_bundle().
hook_field_attach_delete	Acts on field_attach_delete().
hook_field_attach_delete_bundle	Acts on field_attach_delete_bundle().
hook_field_attach_delete_revision	Acts on field_attach_delete_revision().
hook_field_attach_form	Acts on field_attach_form().
hook_field_attach_insert	Acts on field_attach_insert().
hook_field_attach_load	Acts on field_attach_load().

Name	Description
`hook_field_attach_prepare_translation_alter`	Performs alterations on `field_attach_prepare_translation()`.
`hook_field_attach_preprocess_alter`	Alters `field_attach_preprocess()` variables.
`hook_field_attach_presave`	Acts on `field_attach_presave()`.
`hook_field_attach_purge`	Acts on `field_purge_data()`.
`hook_field_attach_rename_bundle`	Acts on `field_attach_rename_bundle()`.
`hook_field_attach_submit`	Acts on `field_attach_submit()`.
`hook_field_attach_update`	Acts on `field_attach_update()`.
`hook_field_attach_validate`	Acts on `field_attach_validate()`.
`hook_field_attach_view_alter`	Performs alterations on `field_attach_view()` or `field_view_field()`.
`hook_field_available_languages_alter`	Alters `field_available_languages()` values.
`hook_field_language_alter`	Performs alterations on `field_language()` values.
`_field_invoke`	Invokes a field hook.
`_field_invoke_default`	Invokes `field.module`'s version of a field hook.
`_field_invoke_get_instances`	Helpers for `_field_invoke()`: retrieves a list of instances to operate on.
`_field_invoke_multiple`	Invokes a field hook across fields on multiple entities.
`_field_invoke_multiple_default`	Invokes `field.module`'s version of a field hook on multiple entities.

Drush Reference

Drush, the Drupal shell, is a handy tool for performing certain tasks in Drupal from the command line. Installing and running Drush is covered in Appendix A. Table C-12 shows a list of core Drush commands.

Note that Drush is an extensible tool, so other modules and themes can add functionality to an installed version of Drush.

Table C–12. Drush Commands

Command	Description
batch-process	Processes operations in the specified batch set.
cache-clear	Clears a specific cache, or all drupal caches.
cc	Clears a specific cache, or all drupal caches.
cli	Enters a new shell optimized for drush use. All .bashrc customizations are still available.
core-readme	Displays README.txt.
core-rsync	Rsyncs the Drupal tree to or from another server using ssh. Relative paths start from the Drupal root folder if a site alias is used; otherwise they start from the current working directory.
cron	Runs all cron hooks.
dd	Returns the file system path for projects and themes and other key folders. Used by the cli command for handy commands cdd and lsd.
dis	Disables one or more modules or themes.
dl	Downloads core Drupal and contributed modules and themes. It will automatically figure out which project version you want based on its latest release, or you may specify a particular version.
en	Enables one or more modules or themes.
eval	Evaluates arbitrary php code after bootstrapping Drupal.
field-clone	Clones a field and all its instances.
field-create	Creates fields and instances. Returns URLs for field editing.
field-delete	Deletes a field and its instances.
field-info	Views information about fields, field_types, and widgets.
field-update	Returns URL for field editing web page.
help	Prints this help message. See drush help help for more options.
php-eval	Evaluates arbitrary php code after bootstrapping Drupal.

Command	Description
php-script	Runs the given php script(s) after a full Drupal bootstrap. A useful alternative to eval command when your php is lengthy or you can't be bothered to figure out bash quoting.
pm-info	Shows info for one or more projects.
pm-releases	Views all releases for a given project (modules, themes, profiles, translations). Useful for deciding which version to install or update.
pm-uninstall	Uninstalls one or more modules. Modules must be disabled first.
pm-updatecode-notify-pending-db-updates	Notifies of pending db updates.
rf	Refreshes update status information.
sa	Prints site alias records for all known site aliases and local sites.
search-index	Indexes the remaining search items without wiping the index.
search-reindex	Forces the search index to be rebuilt.
search-status	Shows how many items remain to be indexed out of the total.
si	Installs Drupal along with modules, themes, and configuration using the specified install profile. Be careful with this command; it will drop your database and create a fresh one.
sm	Shows a list of available modules and themes.
sql-conf	Prints database connection details using print_r().
sql-connect	A string for connecting to the DB.
sql-drop	Drop all tables in a given database.
sql-dump	Prints the whole database to STDOUT or saves to a file.
sql-sync	Copies source database to target database using rsync.
sqlc	Opens a SQL command-line interface using Drupal's credentials.
sqlq	Execute a query against the site database.
st	Provides a birds-eye view of the current Drupal installation, if any.

Command	Description
status	Provides a birds-eye view of the current Drupal installation, if any.
sm	Shows a list of available modules and themes.
sup	Executes a major version upgrade for Drupal core and enabled contributed modules. Command will download next version of Drupal and all available contributed modules that have releases (if not already downloaded).
sync	Rsyncs the Drupal tree to/from another server using ssh. Relative paths start from the Drupal root folder if a site alias is used; otherwise they start from the current working directory.
topic	Reads detailed documentation on a given topic.
ublk	Blocks the specified user(s).
ucan	Cancels a user account with the specified name.
ucrt	Creates a user account with the specified name.
uinf	Displays information about a user identified by username, uid or e-mail address.
uli	Displays a one-time login link for the given user account (defaults to uid 1).
uninstall	Uninstalls one or more modules.
up	Displays available update information and allow updating of all installed projects to the specified version (or latest by default), followed by applying any database updates required (as with running update.php).
upc	Displays available update information and allow updating of all installed project code to the specified version (or latest by default).
updatedb-batch-process	Performs update functions.
updb	Executes the update.php process from the command line.
upwd	Sets or resets the password for the user account with the specified name.
urol	Adds a role to the specified user accounts.
urrol	Removes a role from the specified user accounts.

Command	Description
uublk	Unblocks the specified user(s).
vdel	Deletes a variable.
vget	Gets a list of some or all site variables and values.
vset	Sets a variable.
wd	Deletes watchdog messages.
wd-list	Shows available message types and severity levels. A prompt will ask for a choice to show watchdog messages.
ws	Shows watchdog messages.

Drush has a set of global options that work on most commands. See Table C-13.

Table C–13. *Drush Global Options*

Option	Description
-r , --root=	Drupal root directory to use (default: current directory).
-l , --uri=http://example.com	URI of the Drupal site to use (only needed in multisite environments).
-v, --verbose	Displays extra information about the command.
-d, --debug	Displays even more information, including internal messages.
-q, --quiet	Hides all output.
-y, --yes	Assumes "yes" as answer to all prompts.
-n, --no	Assumes "no" as answer to all prompts.
-s, --simulate	Simulates all relevant actions (doesn't actually change the system).
-i, --include	A list of paths to search for drush commands.
-c, --config	Specifies a config file to use. See example.drushrc.php.
-u, --user	Specifies a user to login; may be a name or a number.

Option	Description
-b, --backend	Hides all output and returns structured data (internal use only).
-p, --pipe	Emits a compact representation of the command for scripting.
--nocolor	Suppresses color highlighting on log messages.
--show-passwords	Shows database passwords in commands that display connection information.
-h, --help	This help system.
--php	The absolute path to your PHP interpreter, if not 'php' in the path.

Summary

The Drupal core is a powerful framework for managing content and displaying it for visitors to your web site. The power derives from the rich set of functions and classes that comprise the Drupal API.

In this appendix, I have listed tables of common API functions that I use a lot. Still, the best place to find information about any part of the Drupal API is http://api.drupal.org.

Index

Special Characters and Numbers

■ X, Y

■ Z

Breinigsville, PA USA
08 February 2011
255071BV00004B/10/P

9 781430 231530